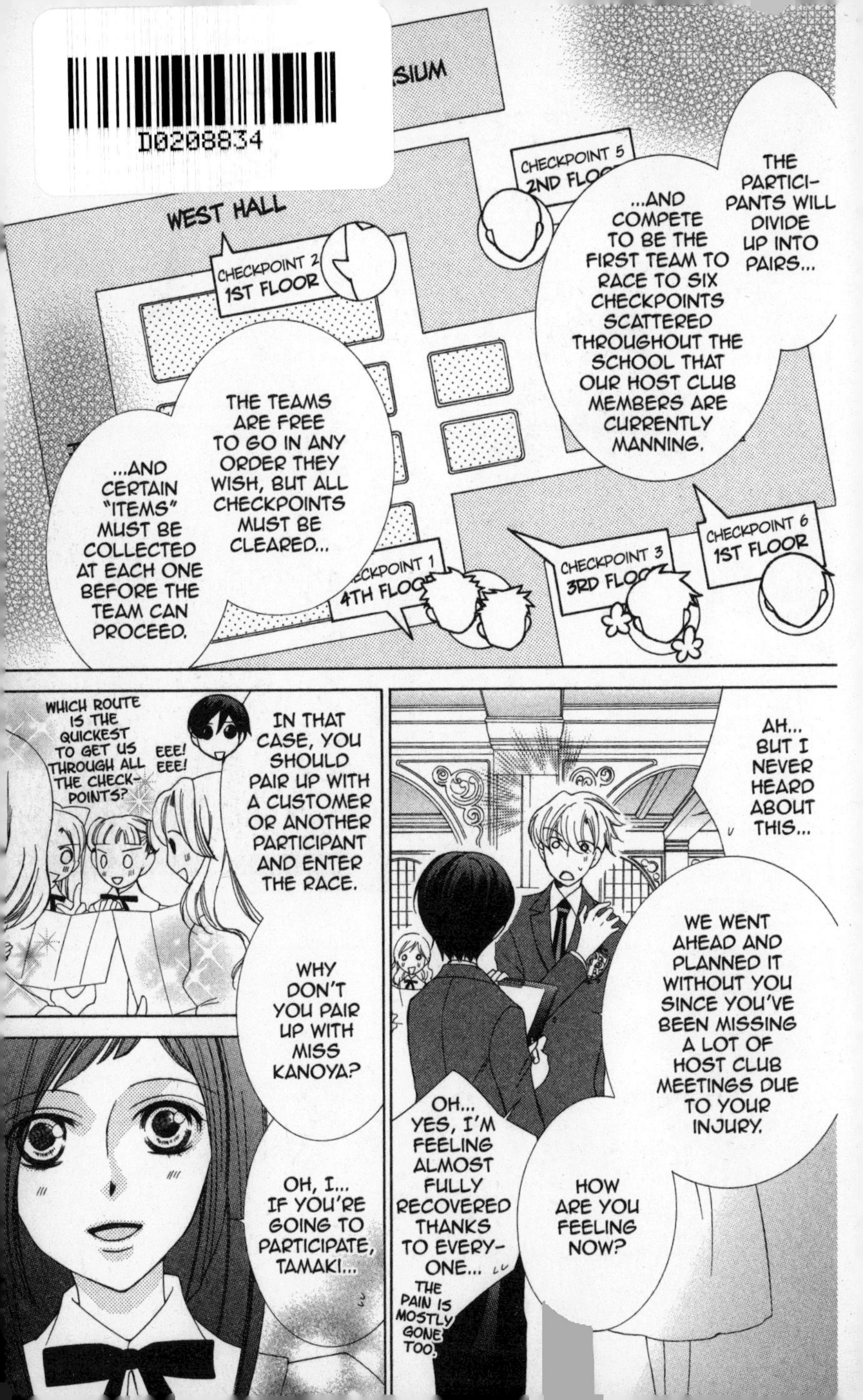

SIUM
WEST HALL
CHECKPOINT 5 2ND FLO
CHECKPOINT 2 1ST FLOOR
CHECKPOINT 1 4TH FLO
CHECKPOINT 3 3RD FLO
CHECKPOINT 6 1ST FLOOR
THE PARTICIPANTS WILL DIVIDE UP INTO PAIRS...
...AND COMPETE TO BE THE FIRST TEAM TO RACE TO SIX CHECKPOINTS SCATTERED THROUGHOUT THE SCHOOL THAT OUR HOST CLUB MEMBERS ARE CURRENTLY MANNING.
THE TEAMS ARE FREE TO GO IN ANY ORDER THEY WISH, BUT ALL CHECKPOINTS MUST BE CLEARED...
...AND CERTAIN "ITEMS" MUST BE COLLECTED AT EACH ONE BEFORE THE TEAM CAN PROCEED.
AH... BUT I NEVER HEARD ABOUT THIS...
WE WENT AHEAD AND PLANNED IT WITHOUT YOU SINCE YOU'VE BEEN MISSING A LOT OF HOST CLUB MEETINGS DUE TO YOUR INJURY.
HOW ARE YOU FEELING NOW?
OH... YES, I'M FEELING ALMOST FULLY RECOVERED THANKS TO EVERYONE...
THE PAIN IS MOSTLY GONE TOO.
IN THAT CASE, YOU SHOULD PAIR UP WITH A CUSTOMER OR ANOTHER PARTICIPANT AND ENTER THE RACE.
EEE! EEE!
WHICH ROUTE IS THE QUICKEST TO GET US THROUGH ALL THE CHECKPOINTS?
WHY DON'T YOU PAIR UP WITH MISS KANOYA?
OH, I... IF YOU'RE GOING TO PARTICIPATE, TAMAKI...

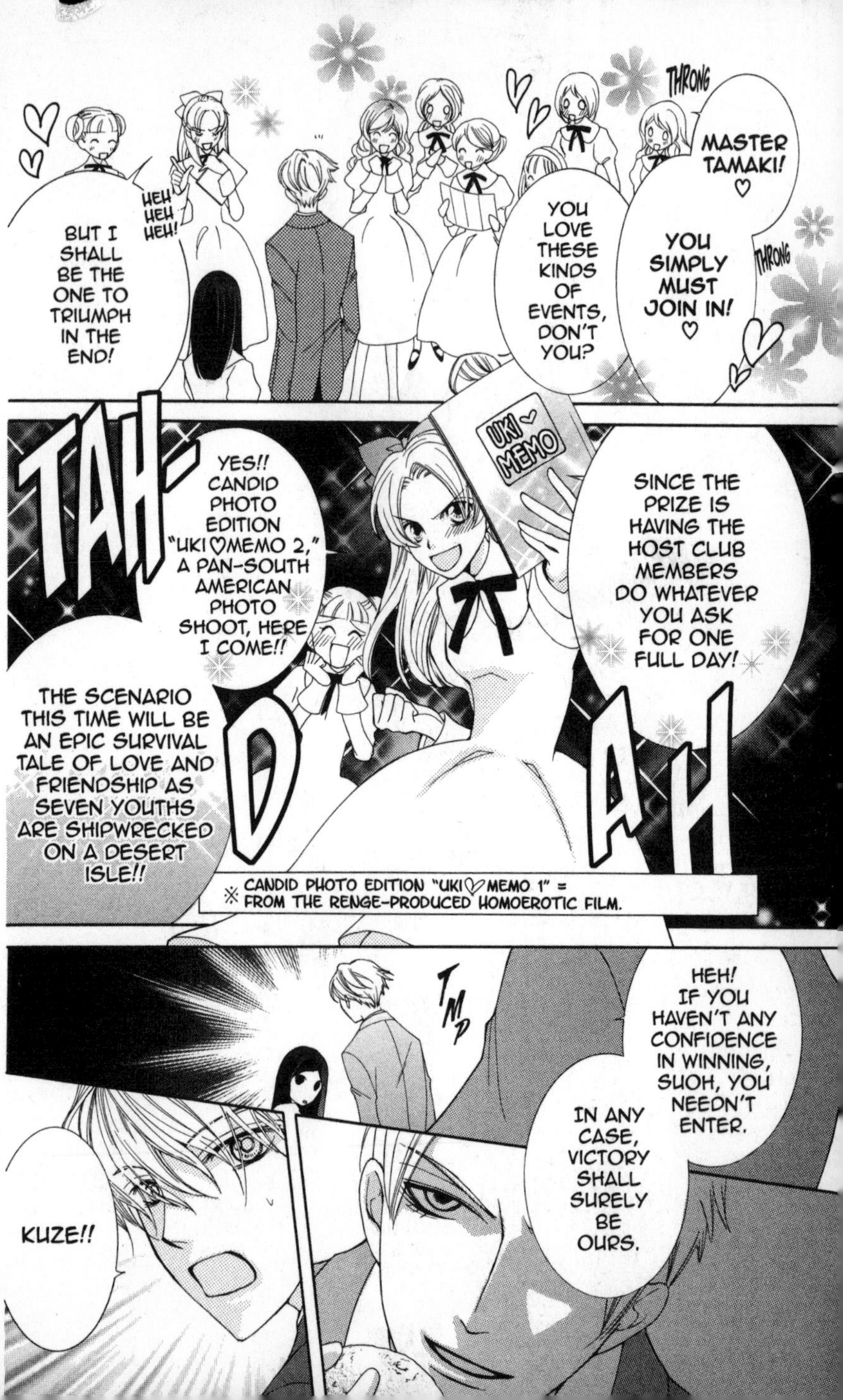
THRONG
MASTER TAMAKI! ♡
YOU SIMPLY MUST JOIN IN! ♡
THRONG
YOU LOVE THESE KINDS OF EVENTS, DON'T YOU?
HEH HEH HEH!
BUT I SHALL BE THE ONE TO TRIUMPH IN THE END!
UKI♡ MEMO
SINCE THE PRIZE IS HAVING THE HOST CLUB MEMBERS DO WHATEVER YOU ASK FOR ONE FULL DAY!
YES!! CANDID PHOTO EDITION "UKI♡MEMO 2," A PAN-SOUTH AMERICAN PHOTO SHOOT, HERE I COME!!
TAH-
THE SCENARIO THIS TIME WILL BE AN EPIC SURVIVAL TALE OF LOVE AND FRIENDSHIP AS SEVEN YOUTHS ARE SHIPWRECKED ON A DESERT ISLE!!
D
AH
※ CANDID PHOTO EDITION "UKI♡MEMO 1" = FROM THE RENGE-PRODUCED HOMOEROTIC FILM.
TMP
HEH! IF YOU HAVEN'T ANY CONFIDENCE IN WINNING, SUOH, YOU NEEDN'T ENTER.
IN ANY CASE, VICTORY SHALL SURELY BE OURS.
KUZE!!

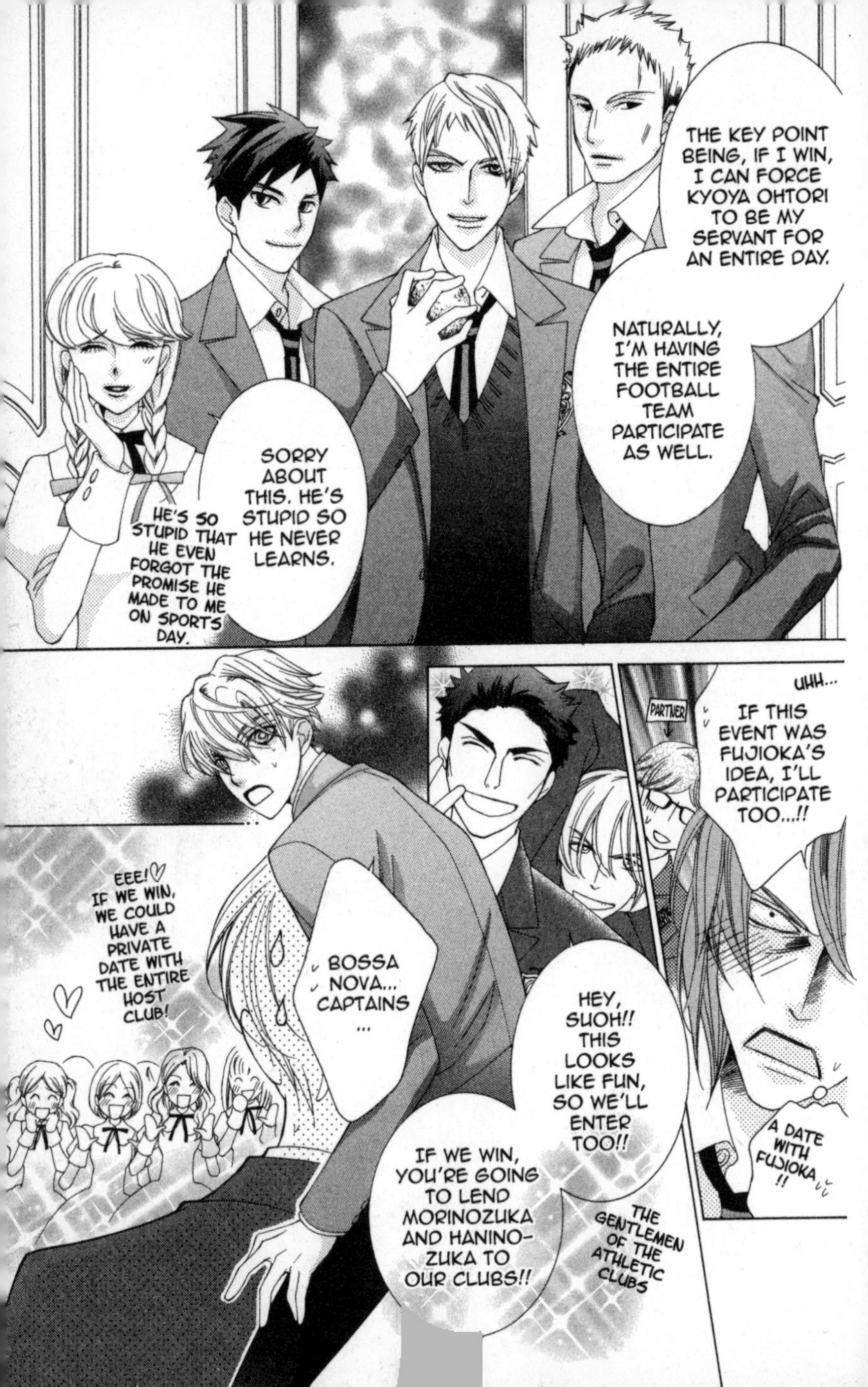
THE KEY POINT BEING, IF I WIN, I CAN FORCE KYOYA OHTORI TO BE MY SERVANT FOR AN ENTIRE DAY.
NATURALLY, I'M HAVING THE ENTIRE FOOTBALL TEAM PARTICIPATE AS WELL.
SORRY ABOUT THIS. HE'S STUPID SO HE NEVER LEARNS.
HE'S SO STUPID THAT HE EVEN FORGOT THE PROMISE HE MADE TO ME ON SPORTS DAY.
UHH...
PARTNER
IF THIS EVENT WAS FUJIOKA'S IDEA, I'LL PARTICIPATE TOO...!!
A DATE WITH FUJIOKA!!
HEY, SUOH!! THIS LOOKS LIKE FUN, SO WE'LL ENTER TOO!!
IF WE WIN, YOU'RE GOING TO LEND MORINOZUKA AND HANINOZUKA TO OUR CLUBS!!
THE GENTLEMEN OF THE ATHLETIC CLUBS
BOSSA NOVA... CAPTAINS ...
EEE! IF WE WIN, WE COULD HAVE A PRIVATE DATE WITH THE ENTIRE HOST CLUB!

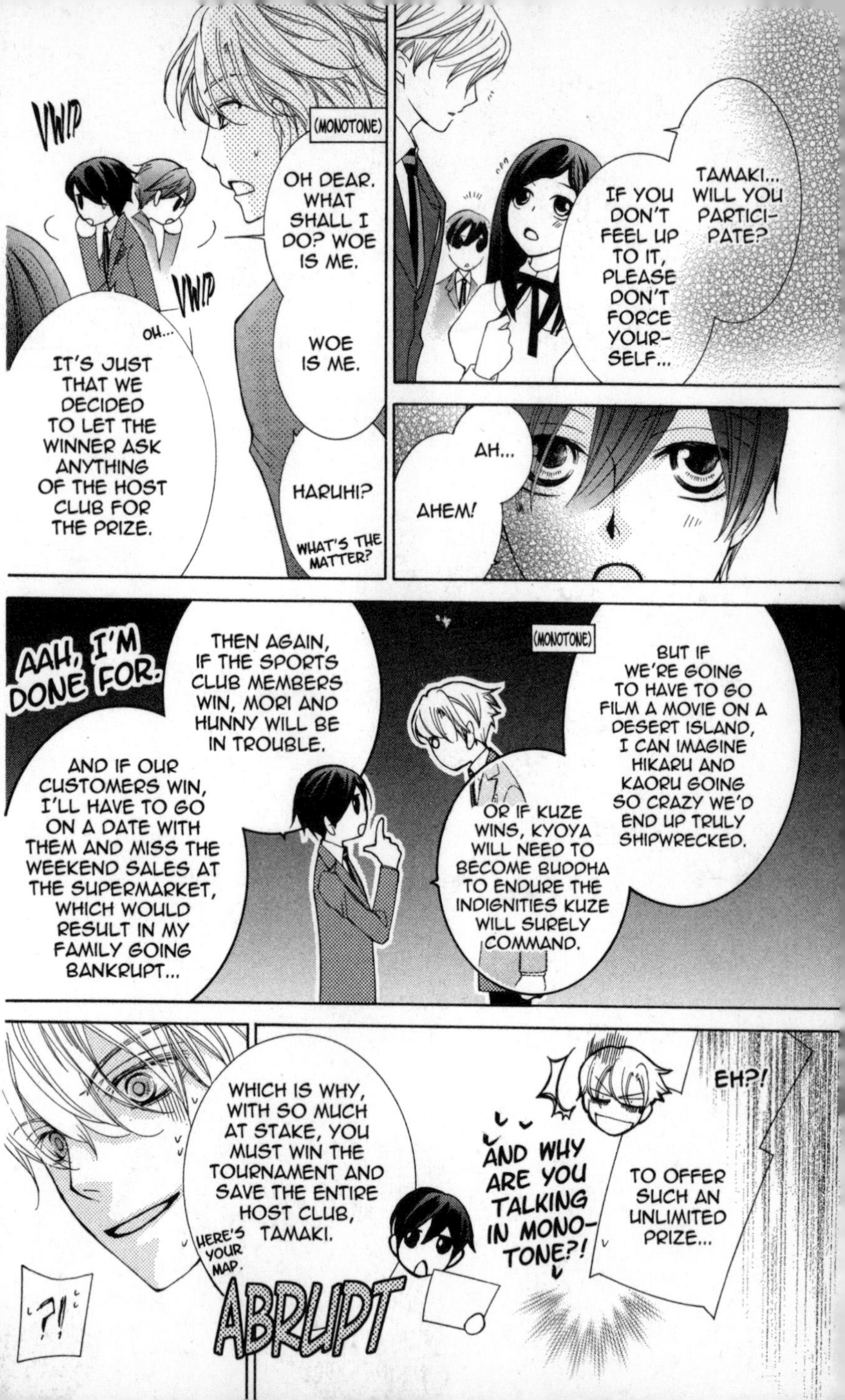
TAMAKI... WILL YOU PARTICIPATE?
IF YOU DON'T FEEL UP TO IT, PLEASE DON'T FORCE YOURSELF...
AH...
AHEM!
(MONOTONE)
OH DEAR. WHAT SHALL I DO? WOE IS ME.
WOE IS ME.
VWIP
VWIP
HARUHI?
WHAT'S THE MATTER?
OH...
IT'S JUST THAT WE DECIDED TO LET THE WINNER ASK ANYTHING OF THE HOST CLUB FOR THE PRIZE.
(MONOTONE)
BUT IF WE'RE GOING TO HAVE TO GO FILM A MOVIE ON A DESERT ISLAND, I CAN IMAGINE HIKARU AND KAORU GOING SO CRAZY WE'D END UP TRULY SHIPWRECKED.
THEN AGAIN, IF THE SPORTS CLUB MEMBERS WIN, MORI AND HUNNY WILL BE IN TROUBLE.
AAH, I'M DONE FOR.
OR IF KUZE WINS, KYOYA WILL NEED TO BECOME BUDDHA TO ENDURE THE INDIGNITIES KUZE WILL SURELY COMMAND.
AND IF OUR CUSTOMERS WIN, I'LL HAVE TO GO ON A DATE WITH THEM AND MISS THE WEEKEND SALES AT THE SUPERMARKET, WHICH WOULD RESULT IN MY FAMILY GOING BANKRUPT...
EH?!
TO OFFER SUCH AN UNLIMITED PRIZE...
AND WHY ARE YOU TALKING IN MONOTONE?!
WHICH IS WHY, WITH SO MUCH AT STAKE, YOU MUST WIN THE TOURNAMENT AND SAVE THE ENTIRE HOST CLUB, TAMAKI.
HERE'S YOUR MAP.
ABRUPT
?!

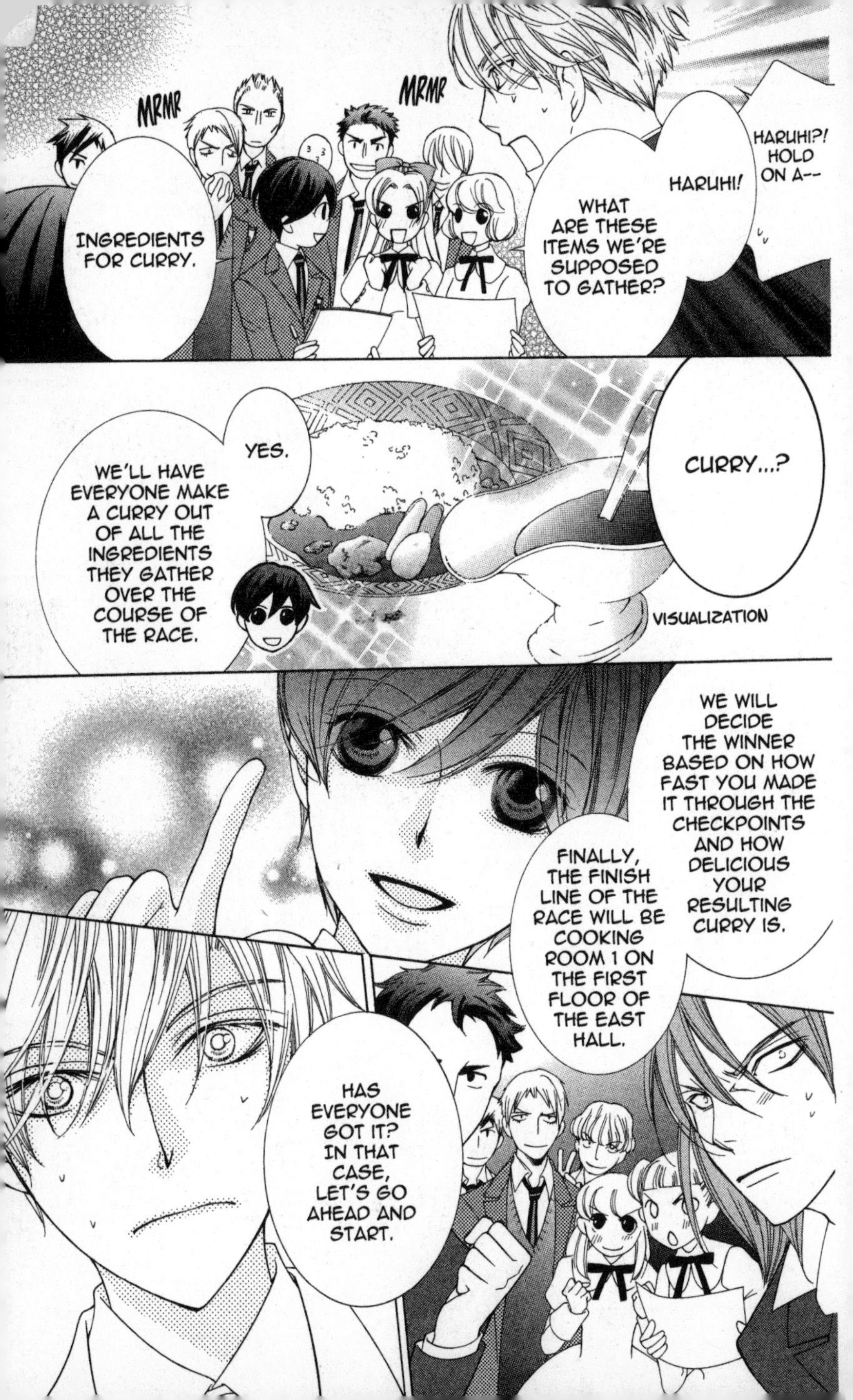
HARUHI?! HOLD ON A--
HARUHI!
WHAT ARE THESE ITEMS WE'RE SUPPOSED TO GATHER?
MRMR
MRMR
INGREDIENTS FOR CURRY.
CURRY...?
VISUALIZATION
YES.
WE'LL HAVE EVERYONE MAKE A CURRY OUT OF ALL THE INGREDIENTS THEY GATHER OVER THE COURSE OF THE RACE.
WE WILL DECIDE THE WINNER BASED ON HOW FAST YOU MADE IT THROUGH THE CHECKPOINTS AND HOW DELICIOUS YOUR RESULTING CURRY IS.
FINALLY, THE FINISH LINE OF THE RACE WILL BE COOKING ROOM 1 ON THE FIRST FLOOR OF THE EAST HALL.
HAS EVERYONE GOT IT? IN THAT CASE, LET'S GO AHEAD AND START.

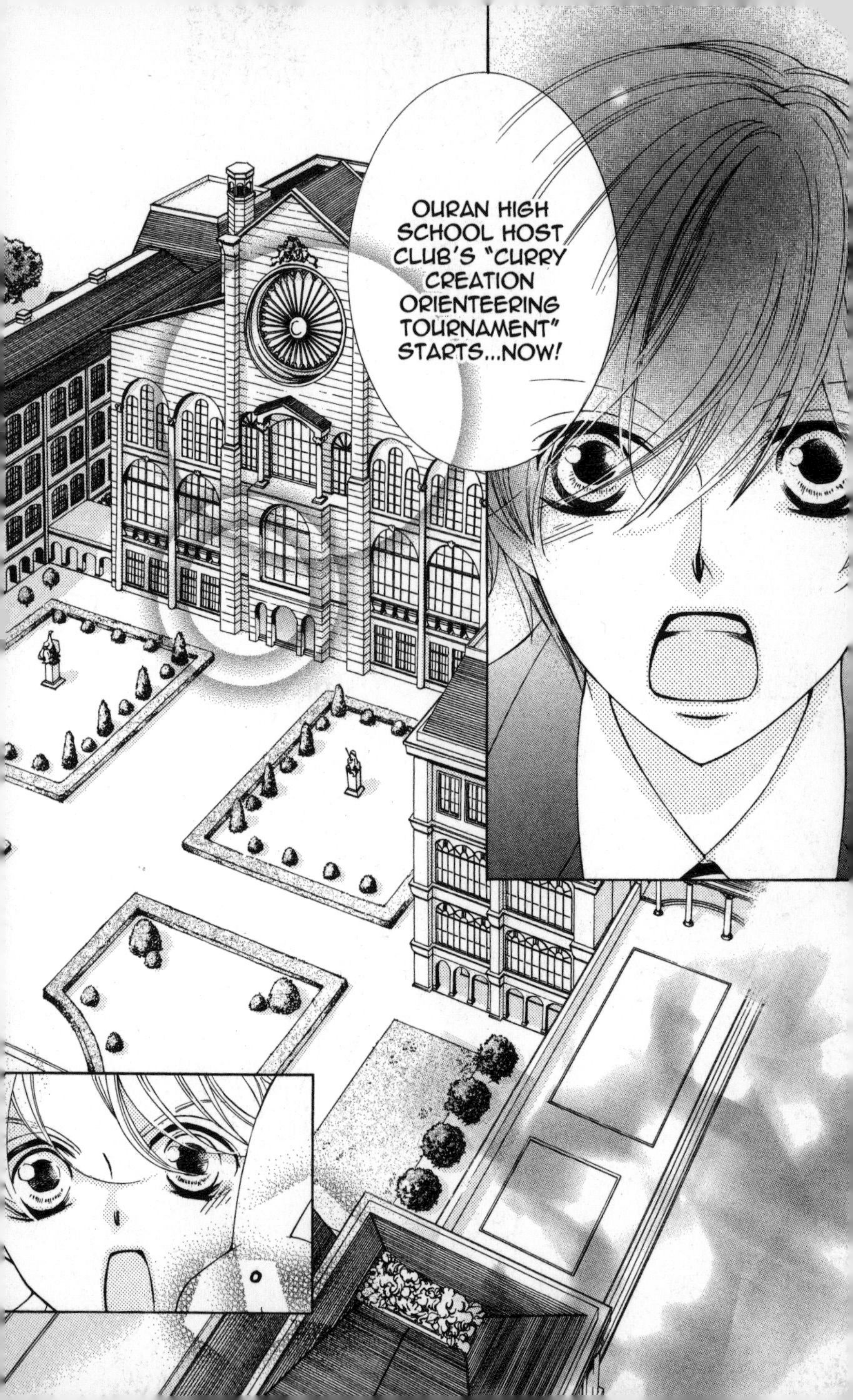
OURAN HIGH SCHOOL HOST CLUB'S "CURRY CREATION ORIENTEERING TOURNAMENT" STARTS...NOW!

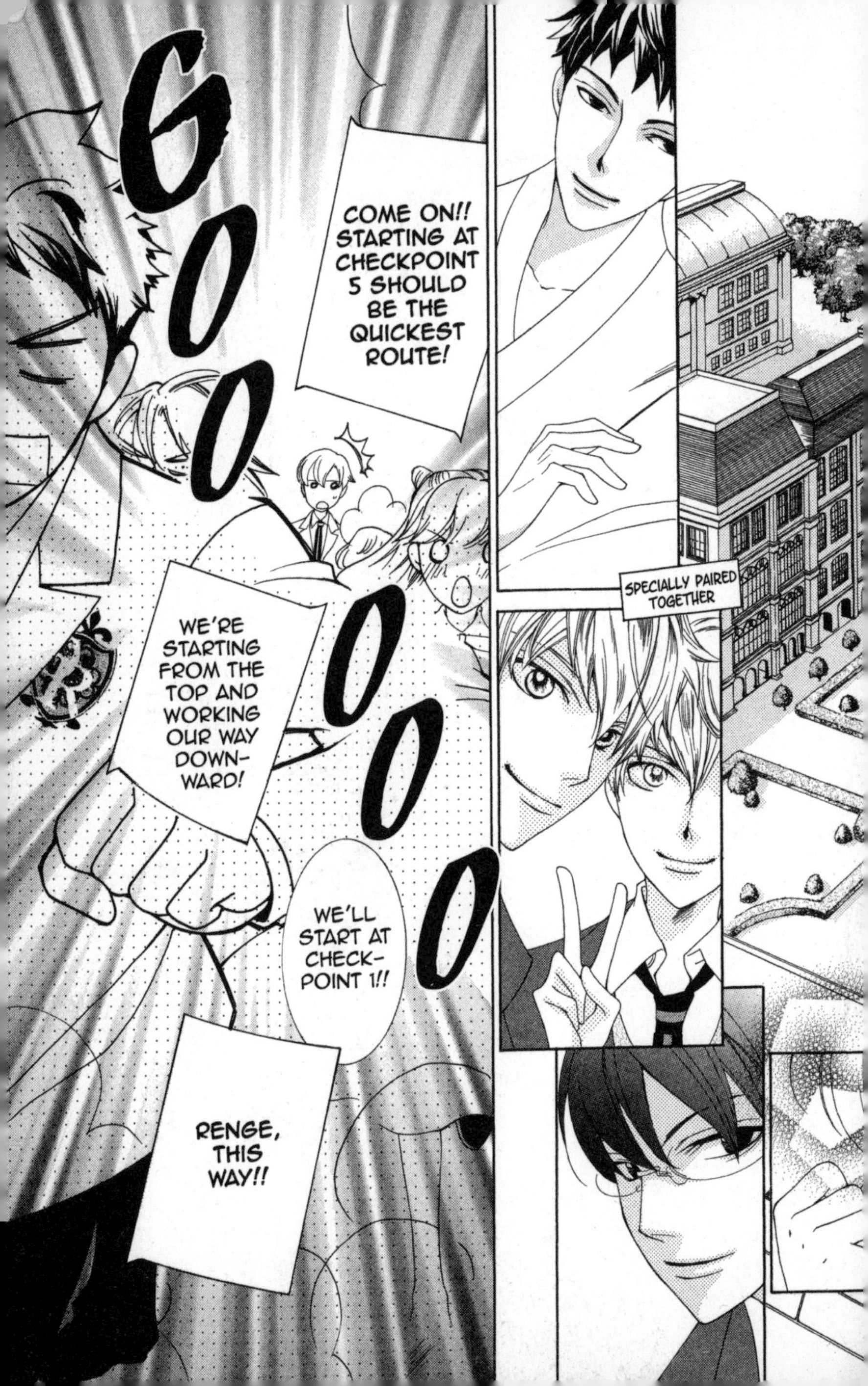
SPECIALLY PAIRED TOGETHER
COME ON!! STARTING AT CHECKPOINT 5 SHOULD BE THE QUICKEST ROUTE!
GOOOOOOO
WE'RE STARTING FROM THE TOP AND WORKING OUR WAY DOWNWARD!
WE'LL START AT CHECKPOINT 1!!
RENGE, THIS WAY!!

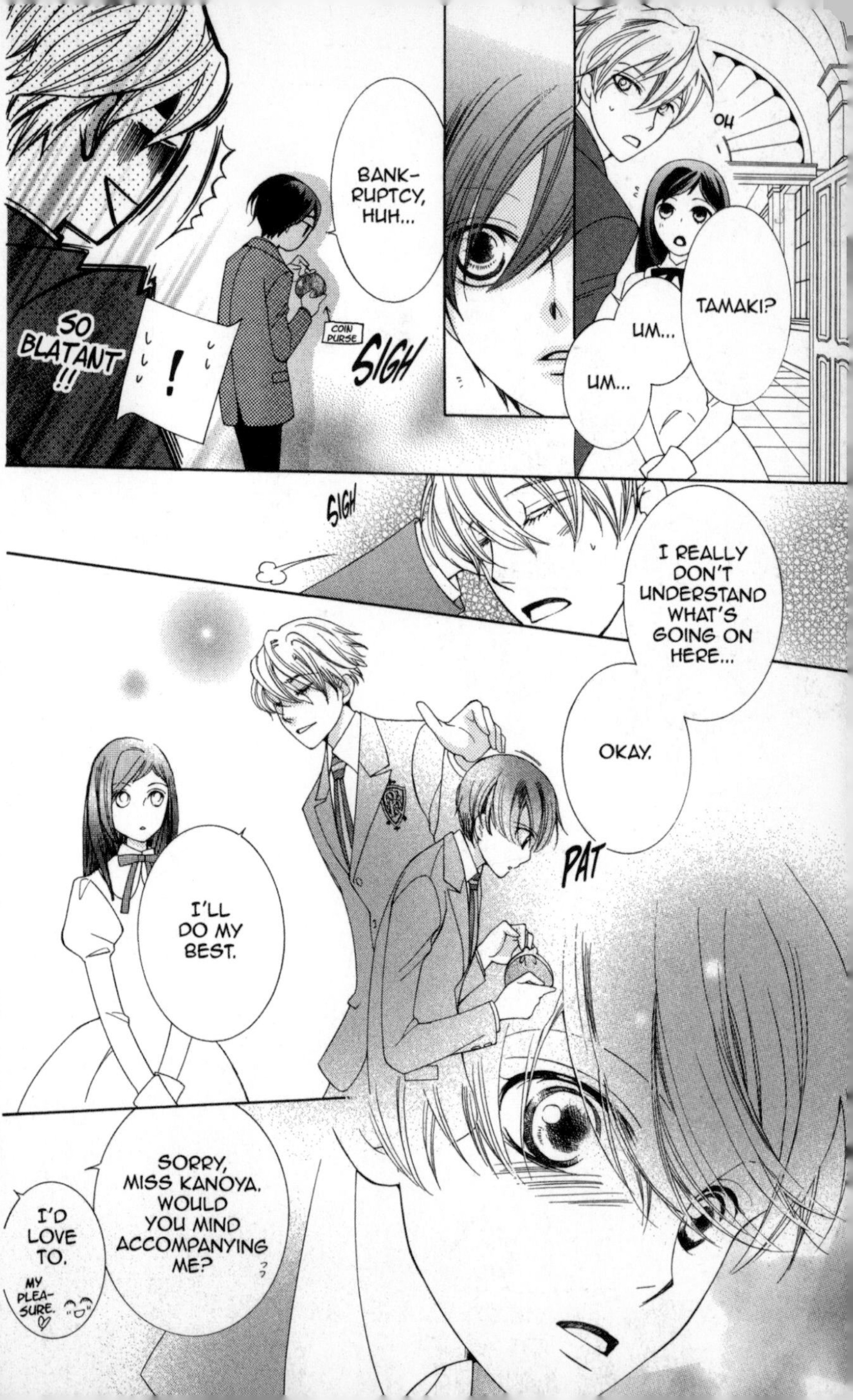
OH
TAMAKI?
UM...
UM...
BANK-RUPTCY, HUH...
COIN PURSE
SIGH
!
SO BLATANT!!
SIGH
I REALLY DON'T UNDERSTAND WHAT'S GOING ON HERE...
OKAY.
PAT
I'LL DO MY BEST.
SORRY, MISS KANOYA. WOULD YOU MIND ACCOMPANYING ME?
I'D LOVE TO.
MY PLEA-SURE.

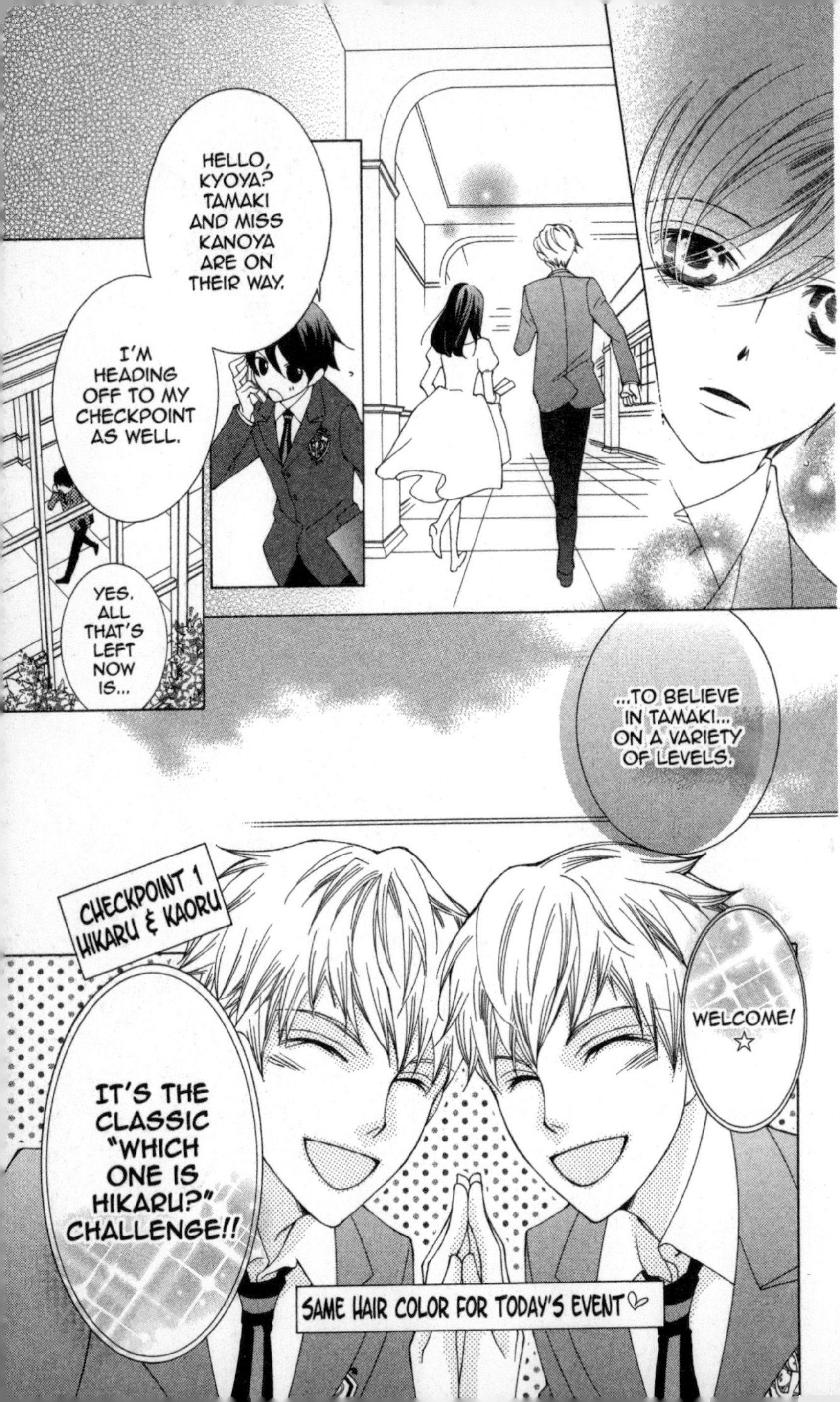
HELLO, KYOYA? TAMAKI AND MISS KANOYA ARE ON THEIR WAY.
I'M HEADING OFF TO MY CHECKPOINT AS WELL.
YES. ALL THAT'S LEFT NOW IS...
...TO BELIEVE IN TAMAKI... ON A VARIETY OF LEVELS.
WELCOME! ☆
CHECKPOINT 1 HIKARU & KAORU
IT'S THE CLASSIC "WHICH ONE IS HIKARU?" CHALLENGE!!
SAME HAIR COLOR FOR TODAY'S EVENT ♡

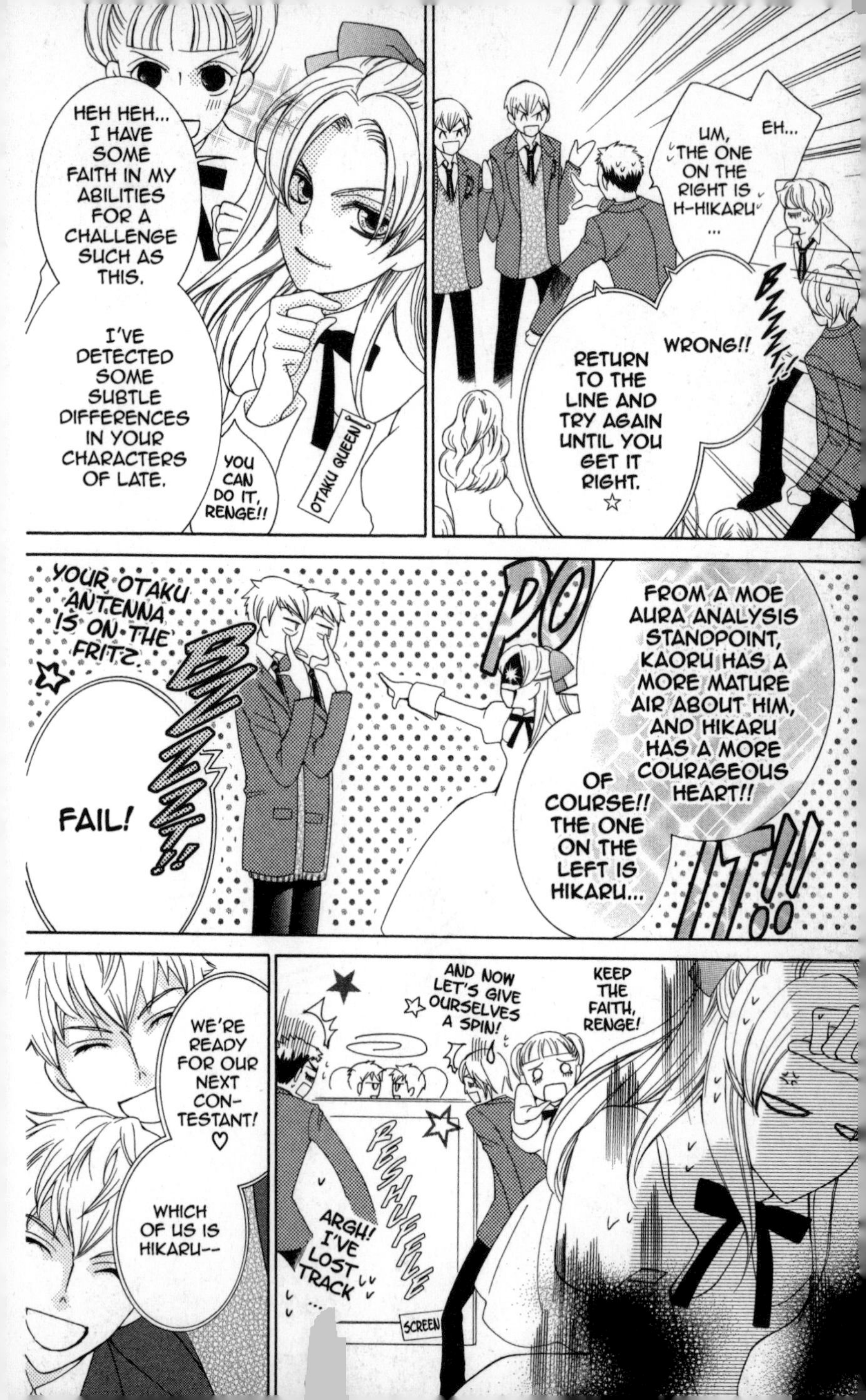

UM, THE ONE ON THE RIGHT IS H-HIKARU...
EH...
WRONG!!
RETURN TO THE LINE AND TRY AGAIN UNTIL YOU GET IT RIGHT. ☆
HEH HEH... I HAVE SOME FAITH IN MY ABILITIES FOR A CHALLENGE SUCH AS THIS.
I'VE DETECTED SOME SUBTLE DIFFERENCES IN YOUR CHARACTERS OF LATE.
OTAKU QUEEN
YOU CAN DO IT, RENGE!!
FROM A MOE AURA ANALYSIS STANDPOINT, KAORU HAS A MORE MATURE AIR ABOUT HIM, AND HIKARU HAS A MORE COURAGEOUS HEART!!
PO
OF COURSE!! THE ONE ON THE LEFT IS HIKARU...
IT!!
FAIL!
YOUR OTAKU ANTENNA IS ON THE FRITZ.
KEEP THE FAITH, RENGE!
AND NOW LET'S GIVE OURSELVES A SPIN!
ARGH! I'VE LOST TRACK ...
SCREEN
WE'RE READY FOR OUR NEXT CON-TESTANT! ♡
WHICH OF US IS HIKARU--

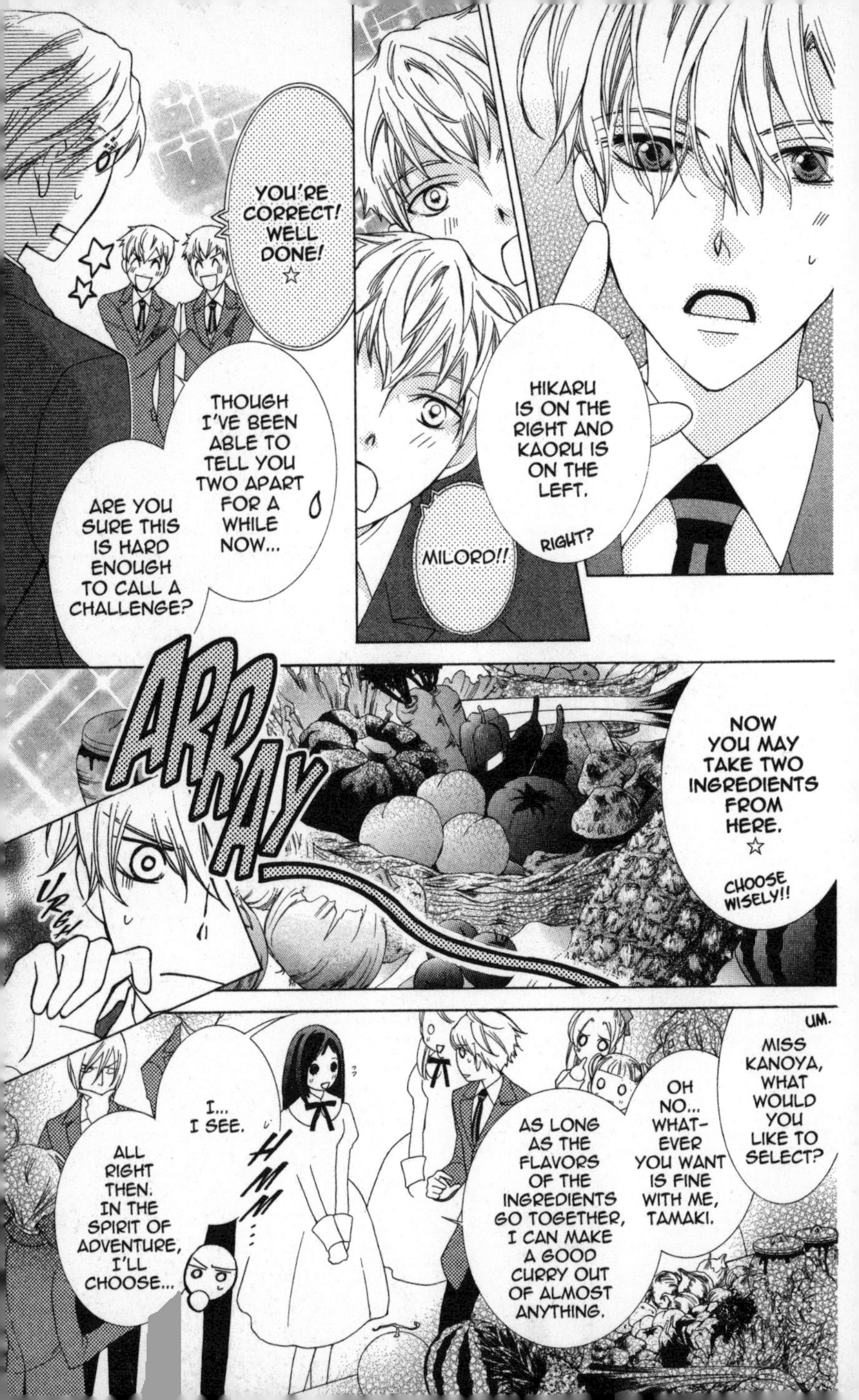
HIKARU IS ON THE RIGHT AND KAORU IS ON THE LEFT.
RIGHT?
MILORD!!
YOU'RE CORRECT! WELL DONE! ☆
THOUGH I'VE BEEN ABLE TO TELL YOU TWO APART FOR A WHILE NOW...
ARE YOU SURE THIS IS HARD ENOUGH TO CALL A CHALLENGE?
NOW YOU MAY TAKE TWO INGREDIENTS FROM HERE. ☆
CHOOSE WISELY!!
ARRAY!
URGH
UM.
MISS KANOYA, WHAT WOULD YOU LIKE TO SELECT?
OH NO... WHAT-EVER YOU WANT IS FINE WITH ME, TAMAKI.
AS LONG AS THE FLAVORS OF THE INGREDIENTS GO TOGETHER, I CAN MAKE A GOOD CURRY OUT OF ALMOST ANYTHING.
I... I SEE.
HMM...
ALL RIGHT THEN. IN THE SPIRIT OF ADVENTURE, I'LL CHOOSE...

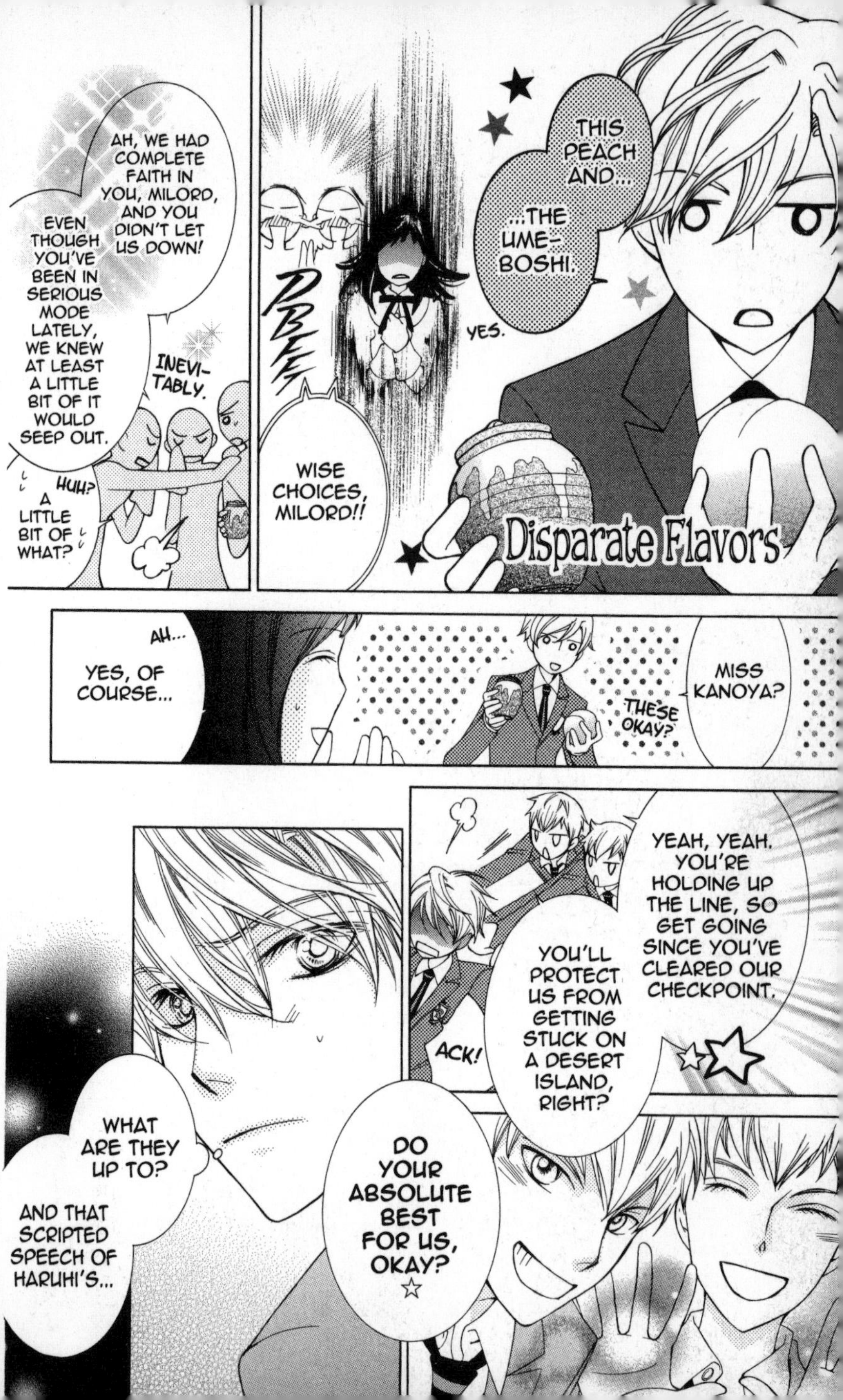
THIS PEACH AND...
...THE UME-BOSHI.
Disparate Flavors
YES.
WISE CHOICES, MILORD!!
AH, WE HAD COMPLETE FAITH IN YOU, MILORD, AND YOU DIDN'T LET US DOWN!
EVEN THOUGH YOU'VE BEEN IN SERIOUS MODE LATELY, WE KNEW AT LEAST A LITTLE BIT OF IT WOULD SEEP OUT.
INEVI-TABLY.
HUH? A LITTLE BIT OF WHAT?
MISS KANOYA?
THESE OKAY?
AH...
YES, OF COURSE...
YEAH, YEAH. YOU'RE HOLDING UP THE LINE, SO GET GOING SINCE YOU'VE CLEARED OUR CHECKPOINT.
ACK!
YOU'LL PROTECT US FROM GETTING STUCK ON A DESERT ISLAND, RIGHT?
DO YOUR ABSOLUTE BEST FOR US, OKAY? ☆
WHAT ARE THEY UP TO?
AND THAT SCRIPTED SPEECH OF HARUHI'S...

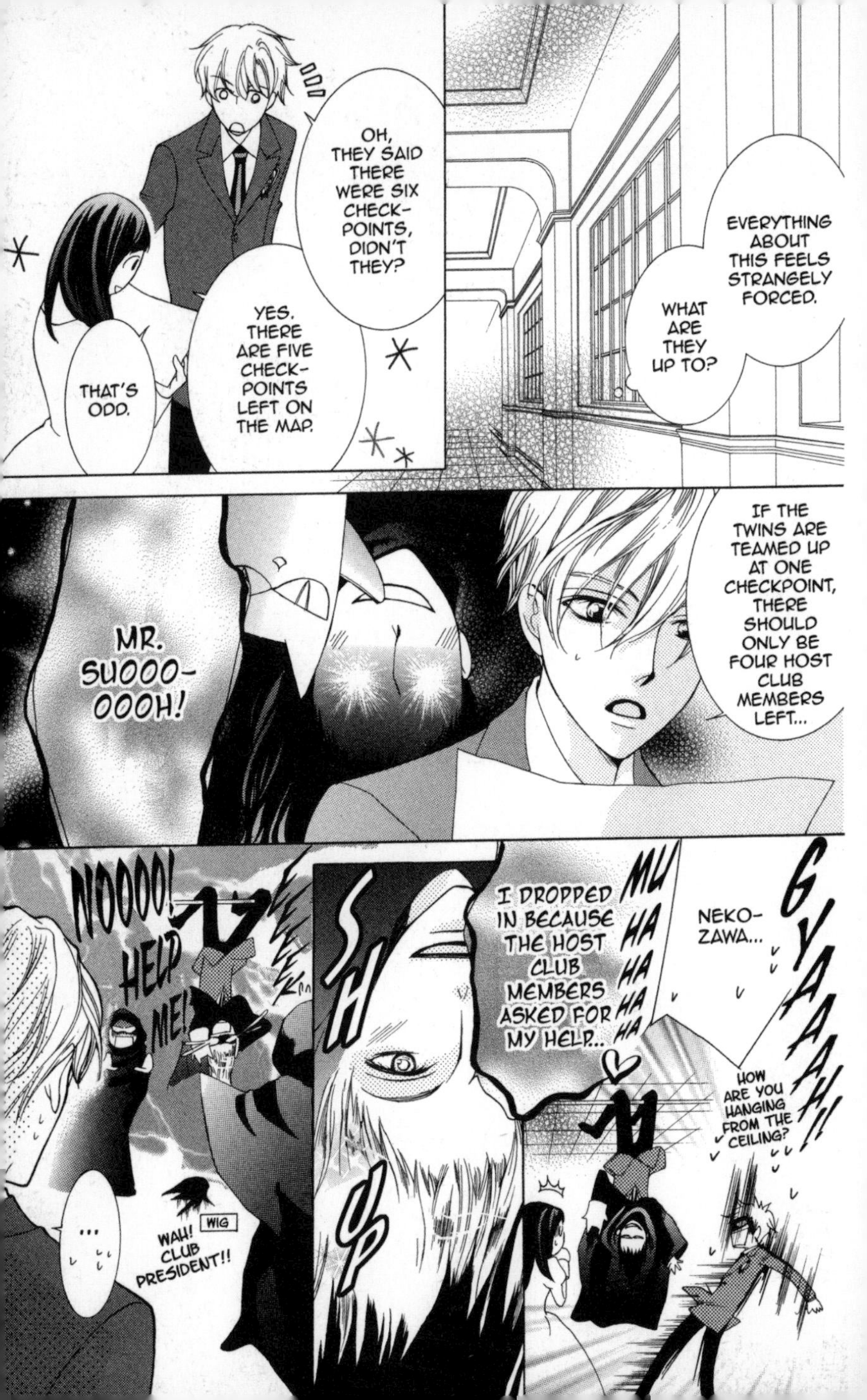
EVERYTHING ABOUT THIS FEELS STRANGELY FORCED.
WHAT ARE THEY UP TO?
OH, THEY SAID THERE WERE SIX CHECK-POINTS, DIDN'T THEY?
YES. THERE ARE FIVE CHECK-POINTS LEFT ON THE MAP.
THAT'S ODD.
IF THE TWINS ARE TEAMED UP AT ONE CHECKPOINT, THERE SHOULD ONLY BE FOUR HOST CLUB MEMBERS LEFT...
MR. SUOOOO-OOOH!
GYAAAAH!!
NEKO-ZAWA...
HOW ARE YOU HANGING FROM THE CEILING?
MUHAHAHAHAHA
I DROPPED IN BECAUSE THE HOST CLUB MEMBERS ASKED FOR MY HELP...
SH
UP
NOOOO! HELP ME!
...
WIG
WAH! CLUB PRESIDENT!!

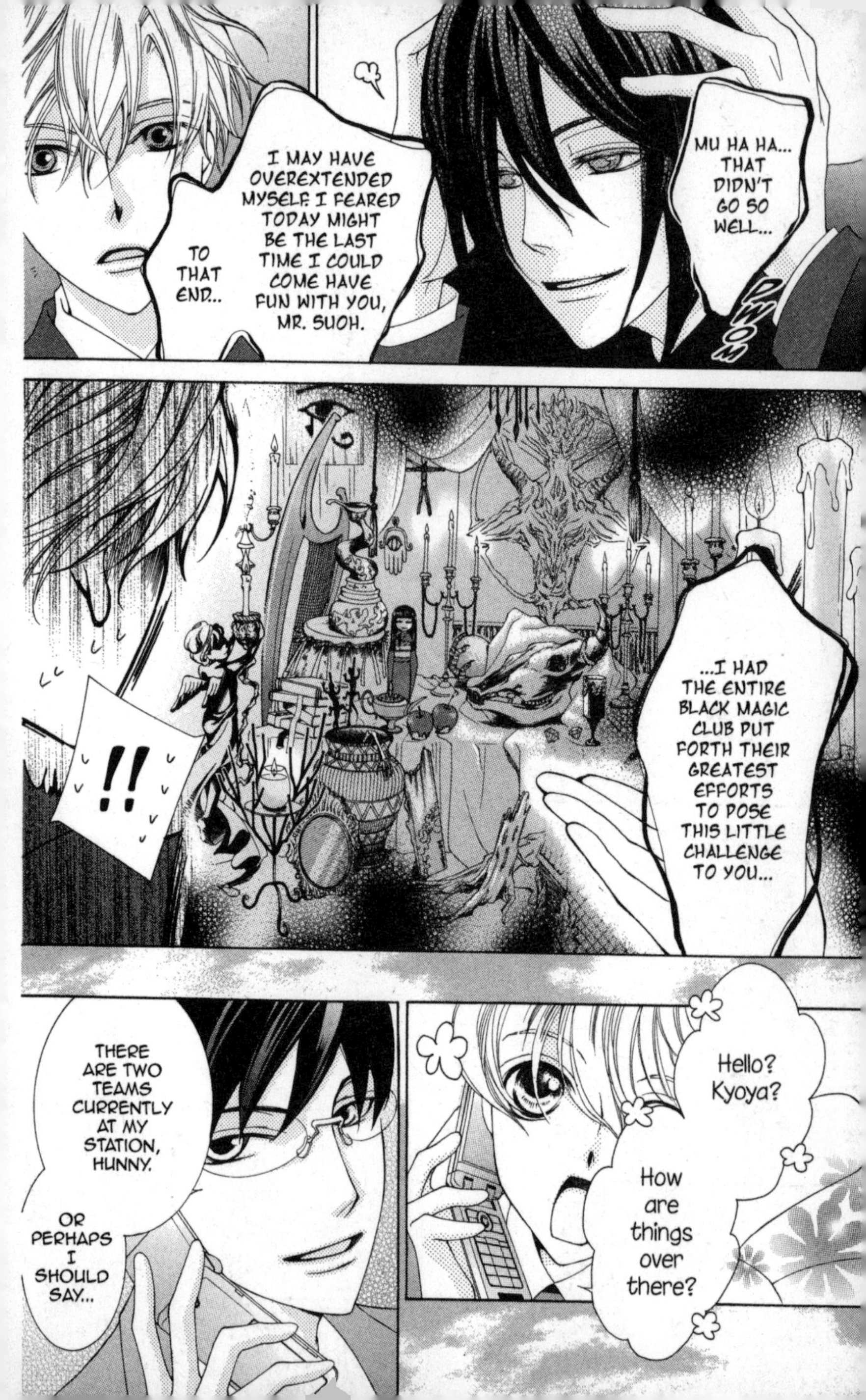
MU HA HA... THAT DIDN'T GO SO WELL...
DWOM
I MAY HAVE OVEREXTENDED MYSELF. I FEARED TODAY MIGHT BE THE LAST TIME I COULD COME HAVE FUN WITH YOU, MR. SUOH.
TO THAT END...
...I HAD THE ENTIRE BLACK MAGIC CLUB PUT FORTH THEIR GREATEST EFFORTS TO POSE THIS LITTLE CHALLENGE TO YOU...
!!
Hello? Kyoya?
How are things over there?
THERE ARE TWO TEAMS CURRENTLY AT MY STATION, HUNNY.
OR PERHAPS I SHOULD SAY...

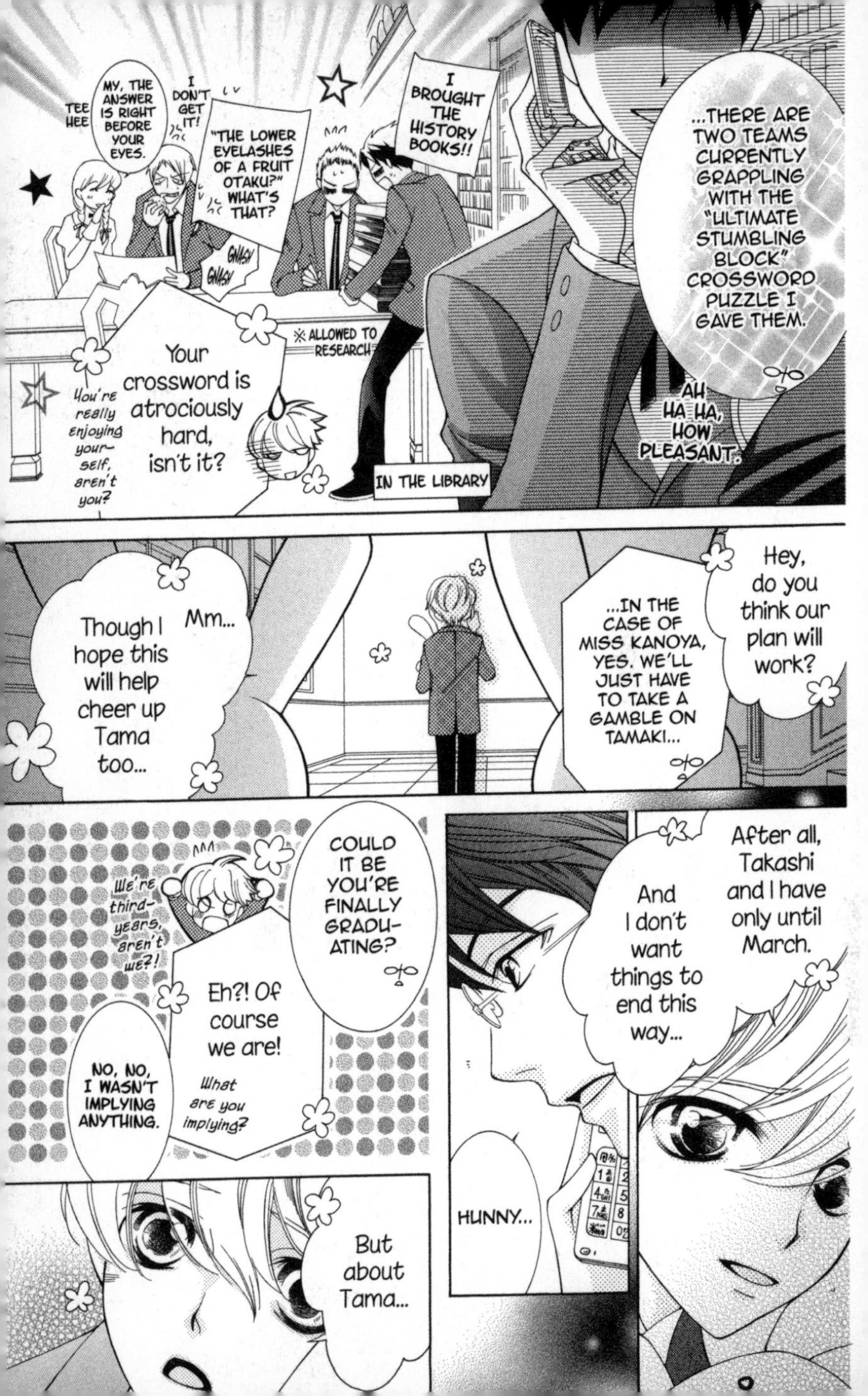
...THERE ARE TWO TEAMS CURRENTLY GRAPPLING WITH THE "ULTIMATE STUMBLING BLOCK" CROSSWORD PUZZLE I GAVE THEM.
AH HA HA, HOW PLEASANT.
I BROUGHT THE HISTORY BOOKS!!
"THE LOWER EYELASHES OF A FRUIT OTAKU?" WHAT'S THAT?
I DON'T GET IT!
MY, THE ANSWER IS RIGHT BEFORE YOUR EYES.
TEE HEE
GNASH GNASH
※ALLOWED TO RESEARCH
Your crossword is atrociously hard, isn't it?
You're really enjoying yourself, aren't you?
IN THE LIBRARY
Hey, do you think our plan will work?
...IN THE CASE OF MISS KANOYA, YES. WE'LL JUST HAVE TO TAKE A GAMBLE ON TAMAKI...
Mm...
Though I hope this will help cheer up Tama too...
After all, Takashi and I have only until March.
And I don't want things to end this way...
HUNNY...
COULD IT BE YOU'RE FINALLY GRADUATING?
We're third-years, aren't we?!
Eh?! Of course we are!
What are you implying?
NO, NO, I WASN'T IMPLYING ANYTHING.
But about Tama...

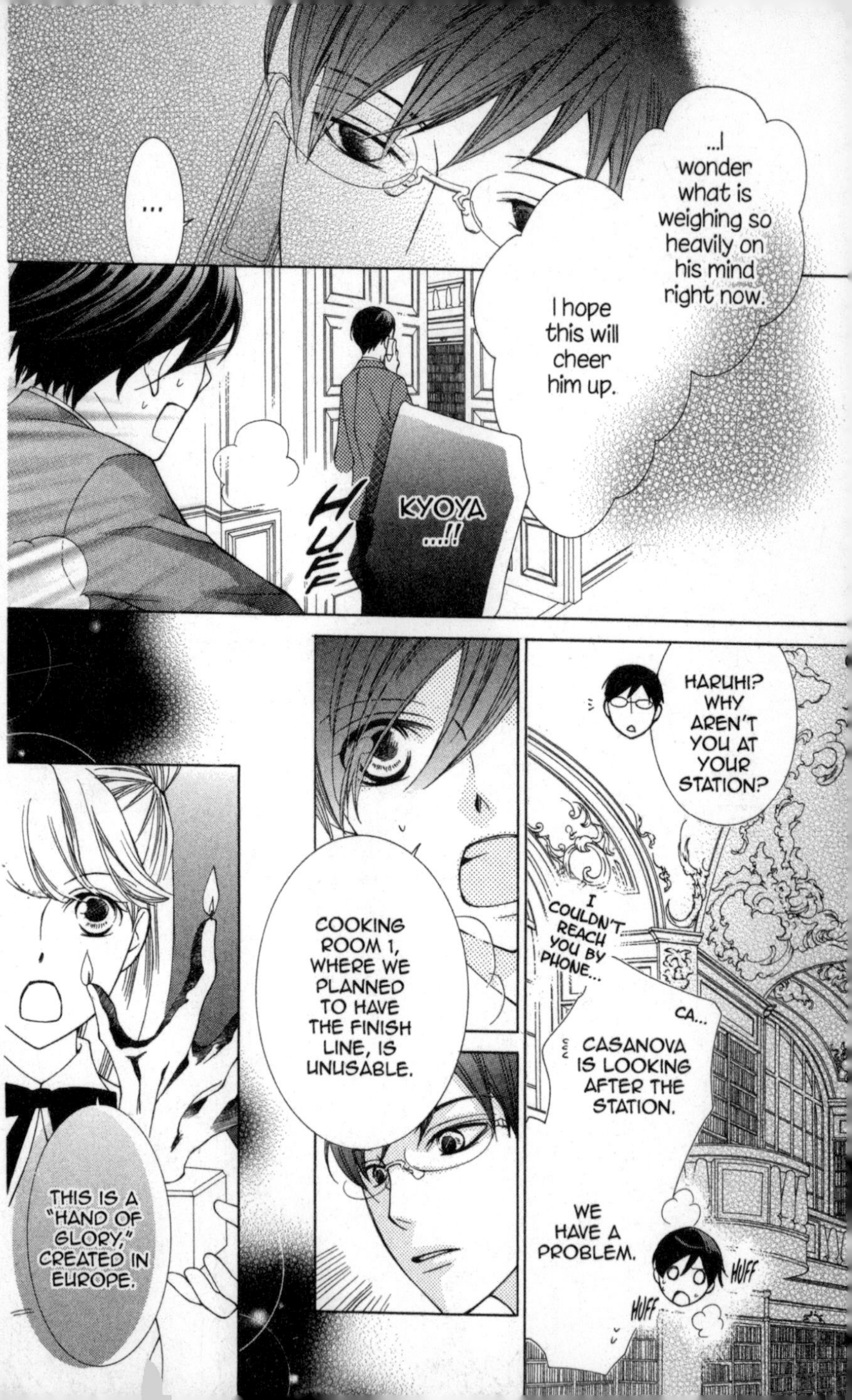
...I wonder what is weighing so heavily on his mind right now.
I hope this will cheer him up.
...
KYOYA ...!!
HUFF
HARUHI? WHY AREN'T YOU AT YOUR STATION?
I COULDN'T REACH YOU BY PHONE...
CA...
CASANOVA IS LOOKING AFTER THE STATION.
WE HAVE A PROBLEM.
HUFF
HUFF
COOKING ROOM 1, WHERE WE PLANNED TO HAVE THE FINISH LINE, IS UNUSABLE.
THIS IS A "HAND OF GLORY," CREATED IN EUROPE.

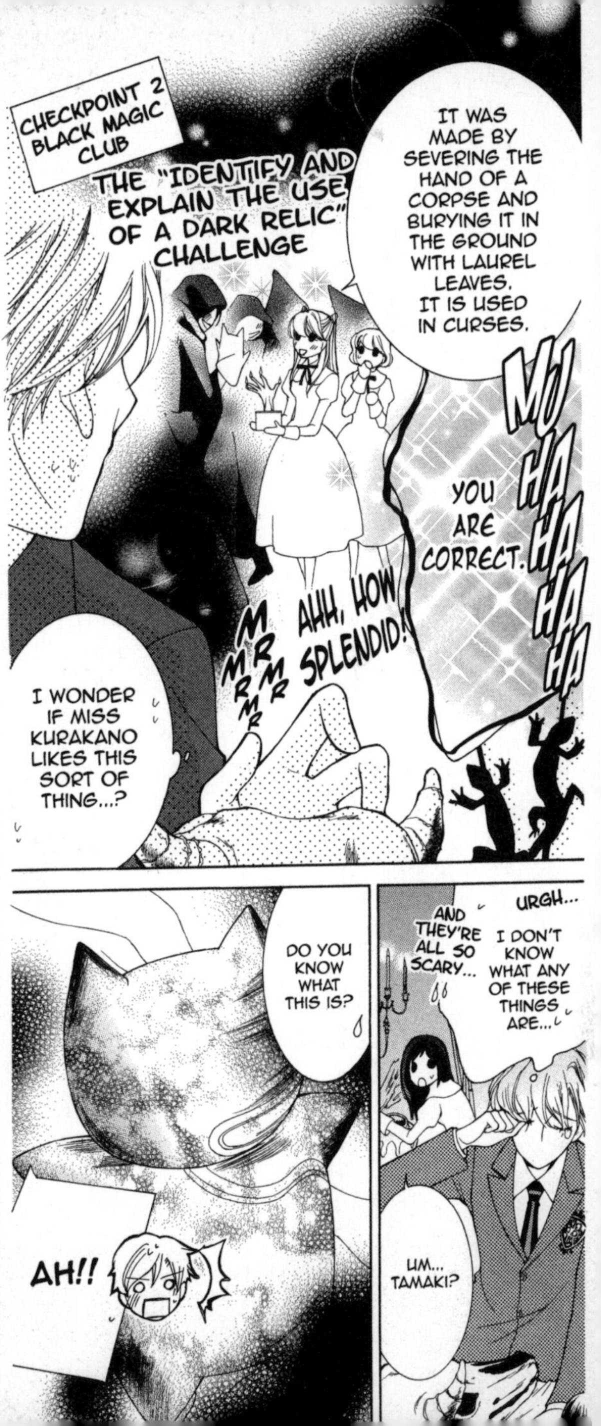
CHECKPOINT 2 BLACK MAGIC CLUB
THE "IDENTIFY AND EXPLAIN THE USE OF A DARK RELIC" CHALLENGE
IT WAS MADE BY SEVERING THE HAND OF A CORPSE AND BURYING IT IN THE GROUND WITH LAUREL LEAVES. IT IS USED IN CURSES.
MU HAHAHAHAHAHA
YOU ARE CORRECT.
AHH, HOW SPLENDID!
MRMRMRMR
I WONDER IF MISS KURAKANO LIKES THIS SORT OF THING...?
URGH... I DON'T KNOW WHAT ANY OF THESE THINGS ARE...
AND THEY'RE ALL SO SCARY...
UM... TAMAKI?
DO YOU KNOW WHAT THIS IS?
AH!!

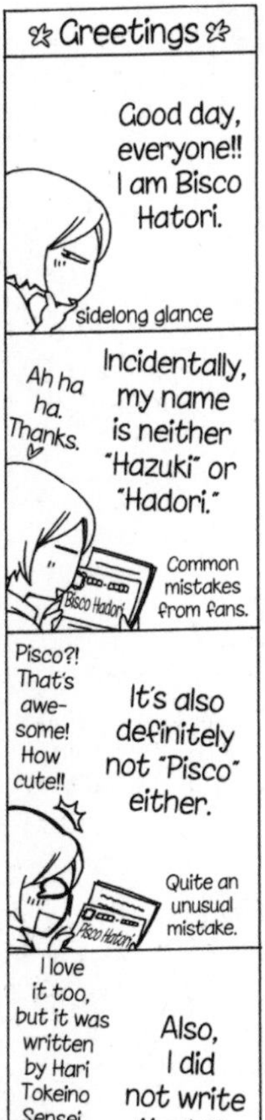
Greetings
Good day, everyone!! I am Bisco Hatori.
sidelong glance
Incidentally, my name is neither "Hazuki" or "Hadori."
Ah ha ha. Thanks.
Bisco Hadori
Common mistakes from fans.
It's also definitely not "Pisco" either.
Pisco?! That's awe-some! How cute!!
Pisco Hatori
Quite an unusual mistake.
Also, I did not write Me & My Brothers.
I love it too, but it was written by Hari Tokeino Sensei, not me.
Dear Bisco Hatori-sama, Me & My Brothers is so funny!!
An extremely unusual mistake.
I really do enjoy every letter I get! Here's hoping you enjoy volume 15 too.

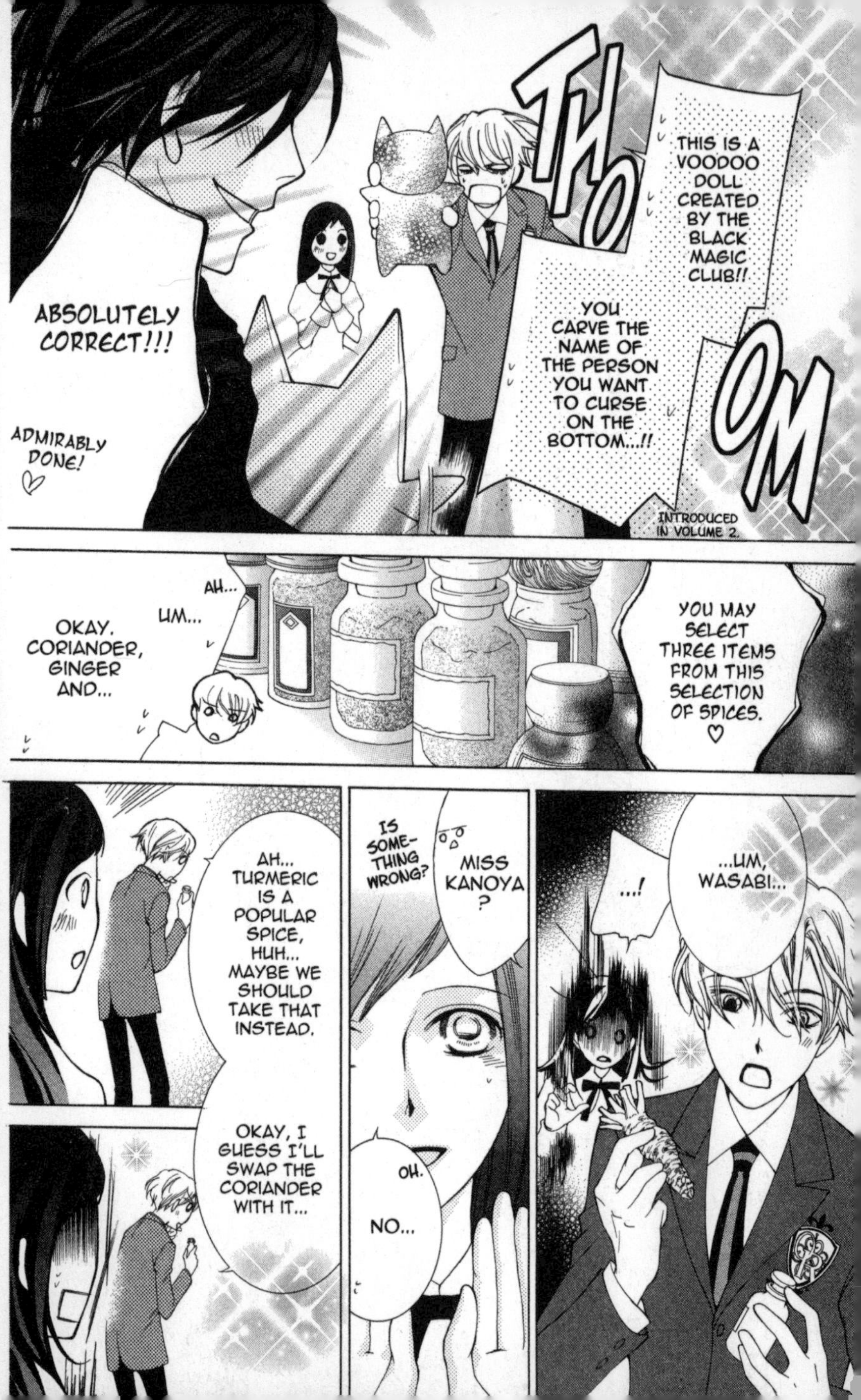
THIS IS A VOODOO DOLL CREATED BY THE BLACK MAGIC CLUB!!
YOU CARVE THE NAME OF THE PERSON YOU WANT TO CURSE ON THE BOTTOM...!!
THOOM
INTRODUCED IN VOLUME 2.
ABSOLUTELY CORRECT!!!
ADMIRABLY DONE! ♡
YOU MAY SELECT THREE ITEMS FROM THIS SELECTION OF SPICES. ♡
AH...
UM...
OKAY. CORIANDER, GINGER AND...
...UM, WASABI...
...!
MISS KANOYA?
IS SOMETHING WRONG?
OH.
NO...
AH... TURMERIC IS A POPULAR SPICE, HUH... MAYBE WE SHOULD TAKE THAT INSTEAD.
OKAY, I GUESS I'LL SWAP THE CORIANDER WITH IT...

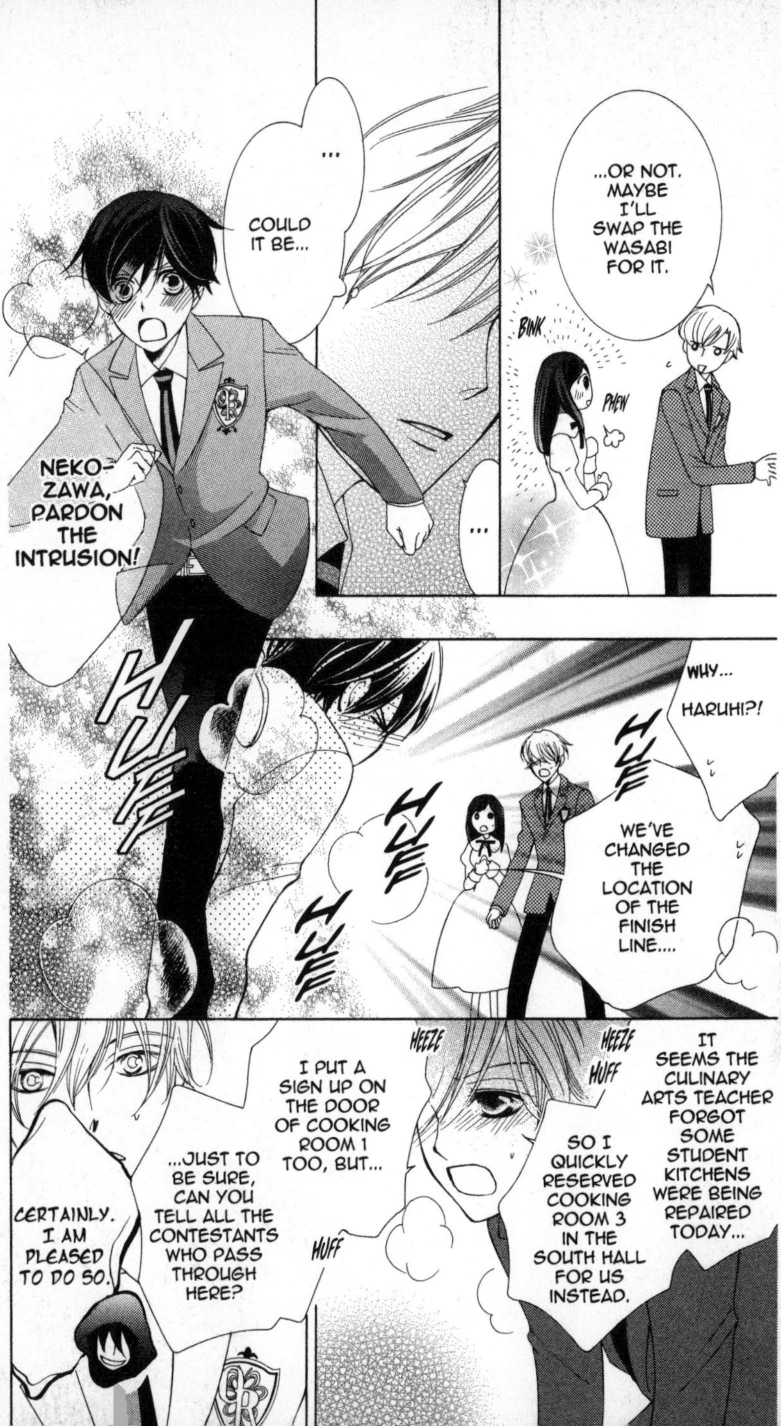
...OR NOT. MAYBE I'LL SWAP THE WASABI FOR IT.
BINK
PHEW
...
COULD IT BE...
...
WHY... HARUHI?!
HUFF
HUFF
HUFF
WE'VE CHANGED THE LOCATION OF THE FINISH LINE....
NEKO-ZAWA, PARDON THE INTRUSION!
HUFF
IT SEEMS THE CULINARY ARTS TEACHER FORGOT SOME STUDENT KITCHENS WERE BEING REPAIRED TODAY...
HEEZE
HUFF
HEEZE
SO I QUICKLY RESERVED COOKING ROOM 3 IN THE SOUTH HALL FOR US INSTEAD.
I PUT A SIGN UP ON THE DOOR OF COOKING ROOM 1 TOO, BUT...
HUFF
...JUST TO BE SURE, CAN YOU TELL ALL THE CONTESTANTS WHO PASS THROUGH HERE?
CERTAINLY. I AM PLEASED TO DO SO.

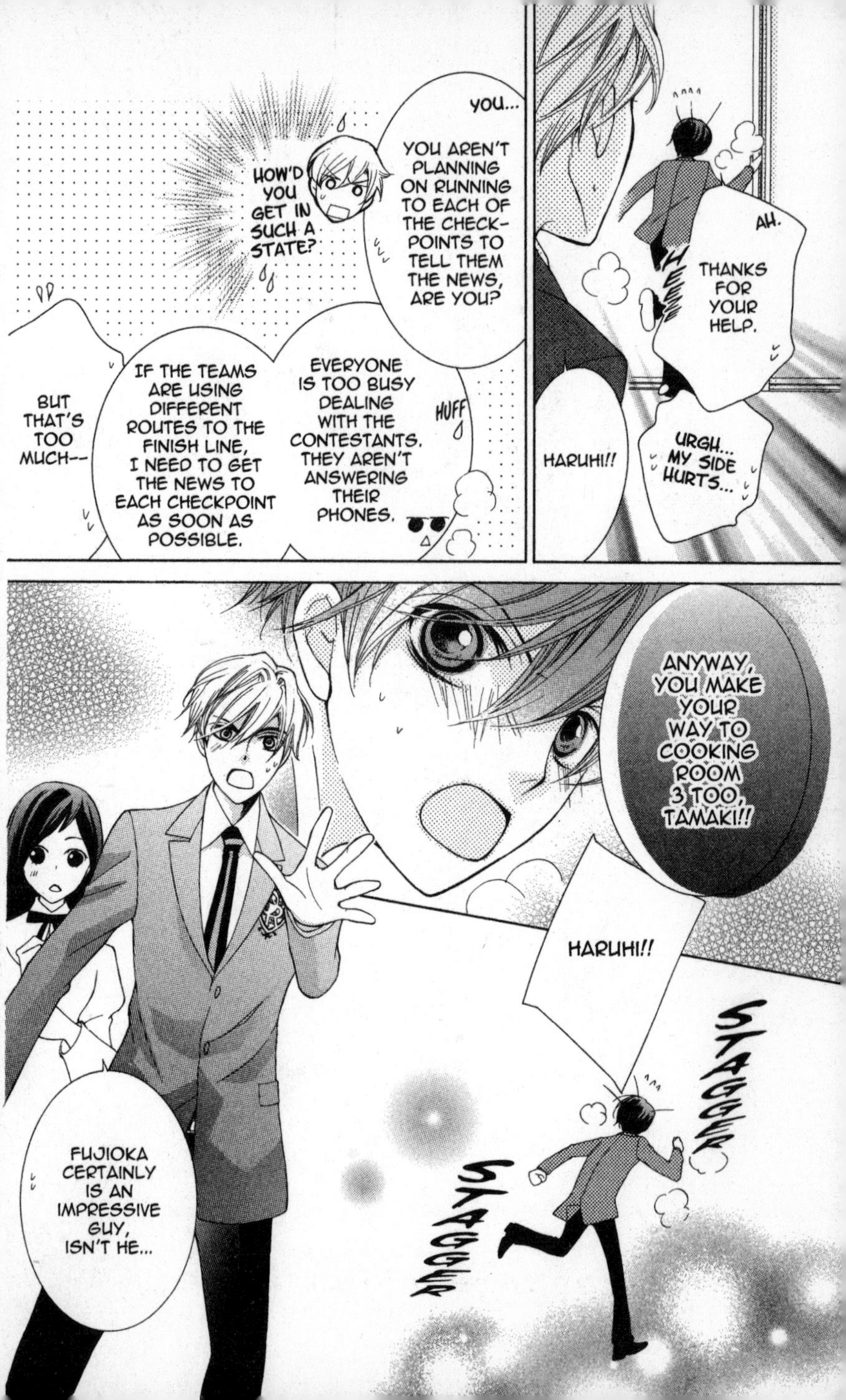

AH.
THANKS FOR YOUR HELP.
URGH... MY SIDE HURTS...
HARUHI!!
YOU...
YOU AREN'T PLANNING ON RUNNING TO EACH OF THE CHECK-POINTS TO TELL THEM THE NEWS, ARE YOU?
HOW'D YOU GET IN SUCH A STATE?
EVERYONE IS TOO BUSY DEALING WITH THE CONTESTANTS. THEY AREN'T ANSWERING THEIR PHONES.
HUFF
IF THE TEAMS ARE USING DIFFERENT ROUTES TO THE FINISH LINE, I NEED TO GET THE NEWS TO EACH CHECKPOINT AS SOON AS POSSIBLE.
BUT THAT'S TOO MUCH--
ANYWAY, YOU MAKE YOUR WAY TO COOKING ROOM 3 TOO, TAMAKI!!
HARUHI!!
STAGGER
STAGGER
FUJIOKA CERTAINLY IS AN IMPRESSIVE GUY, ISN'T HE...

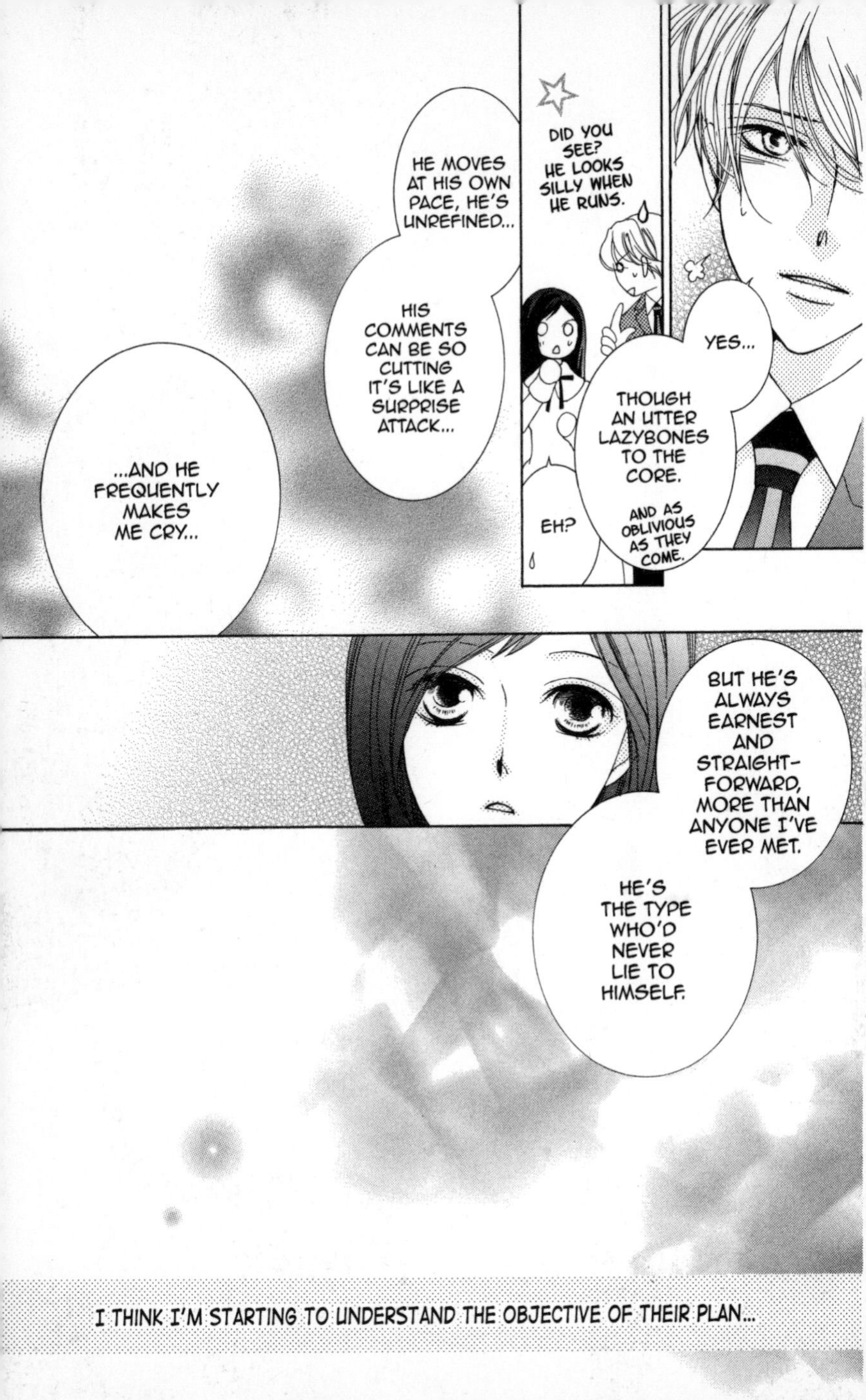
YES...
THOUGH AN UTTER LAZYBONES TO THE CORE.
AND AS OBLIVIOUS AS THEY COME.
DID YOU SEE? HE LOOKS SILLY WHEN HE RUNS.
EH?
HE MOVES AT HIS OWN PACE, HE'S UNREFINED...
HIS COMMENTS CAN BE SO CUTTING IT'S LIKE A SURPRISE ATTACK...
...AND HE FREQUENTLY MAKES ME CRY...
BUT HE'S ALWAYS EARNEST AND STRAIGHT-FORWARD, MORE THAN ANYONE I'VE EVER MET.
HE'S THE TYPE WHO'D NEVER LIE TO HIMSELF.
I THINK I'M STARTING TO UNDERSTAND THE OBJECTIVE OF THEIR PLAN...

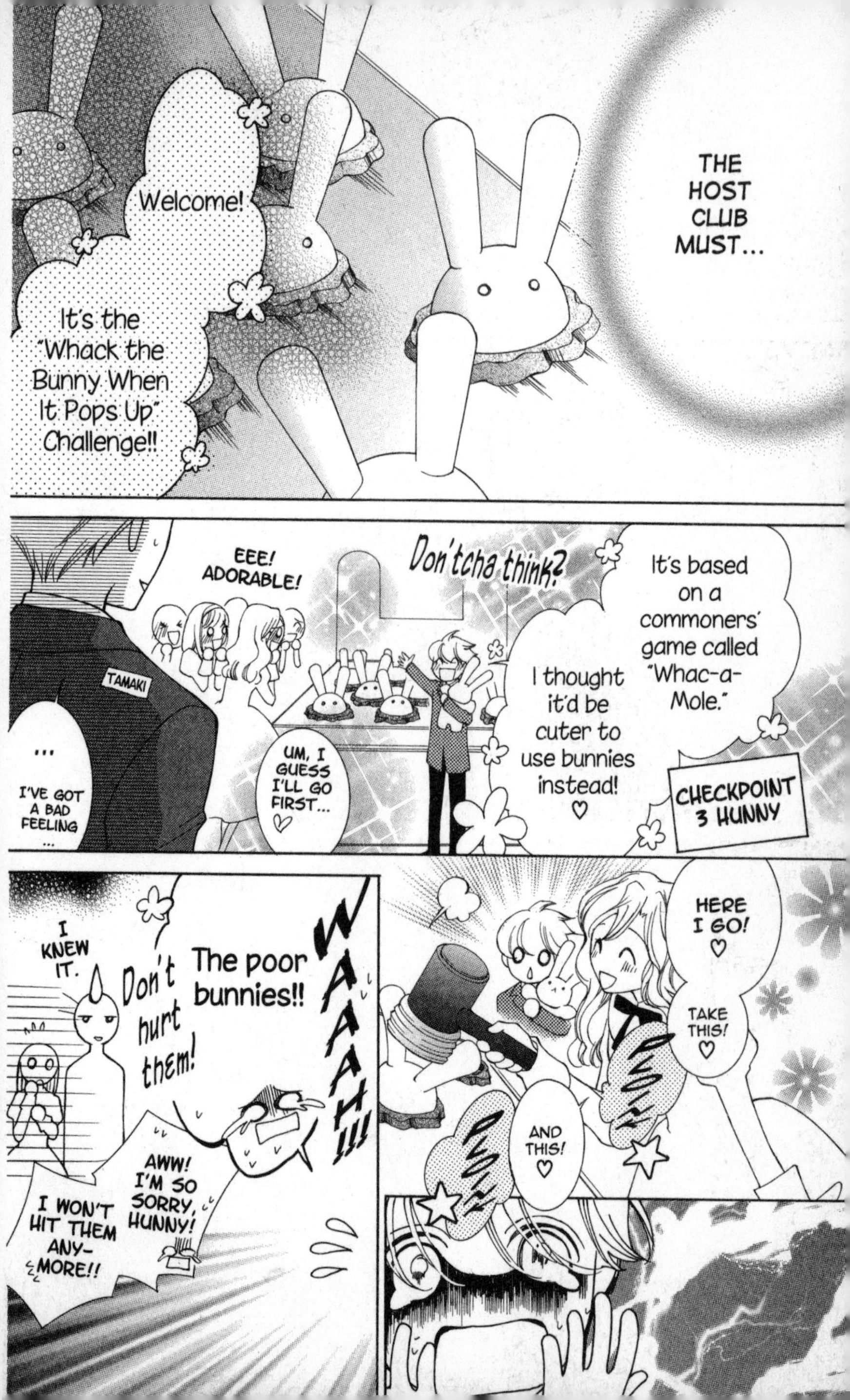
THE HOST CLUB MUST...
Welcome!
It's the "Whack the Bunny When It Pops Up" Challenge!!
It's based on a commoners' game called "Whac-a-Mole."
CHECKPOINT 3 HUNNY
Don'tcha think?
I thought it'd be cuter to use bunnies instead! ♡
EEE! ADORABLE!
UM, I GUESS I'LL GO FIRST... ♡
... I'VE GOT A BAD FEELING ...
HERE I GO! ♡
TAKE THIS! ♡
AND THIS! ♡
WAAAH!!!
The poor bunnies!!
Don't hurt them!
I KNEW IT.
AWW! I'M SO SORRY, HUNNY!
I WON'T HIT THEM ANY-MORE!!

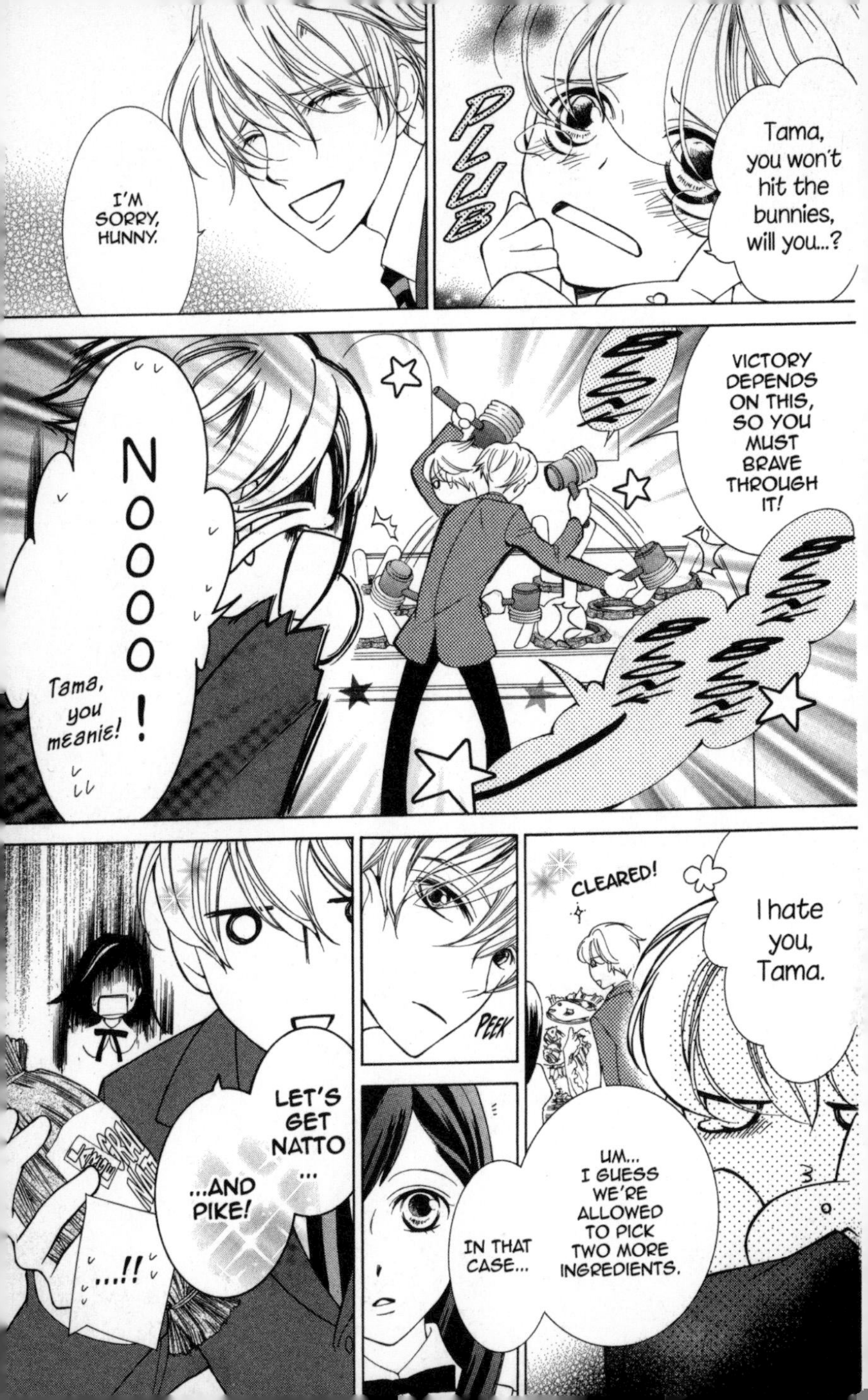
PLUB
Tama, you won't hit the bunnies, will you...?
I'M SORRY, HUNNY.
VICTORY DEPENDS ON THIS, SO YOU MUST BRAVE THROUGH IT!
NOOOO!
Tama, you meanie!
CLEARED!
I hate you, Tama.
PEEK
UM... I GUESS WE'RE ALLOWED TO PICK TWO MORE INGREDIENTS.
IN THAT CASE...
LET'S GET NATTO...
...AND PIKE!
...!!

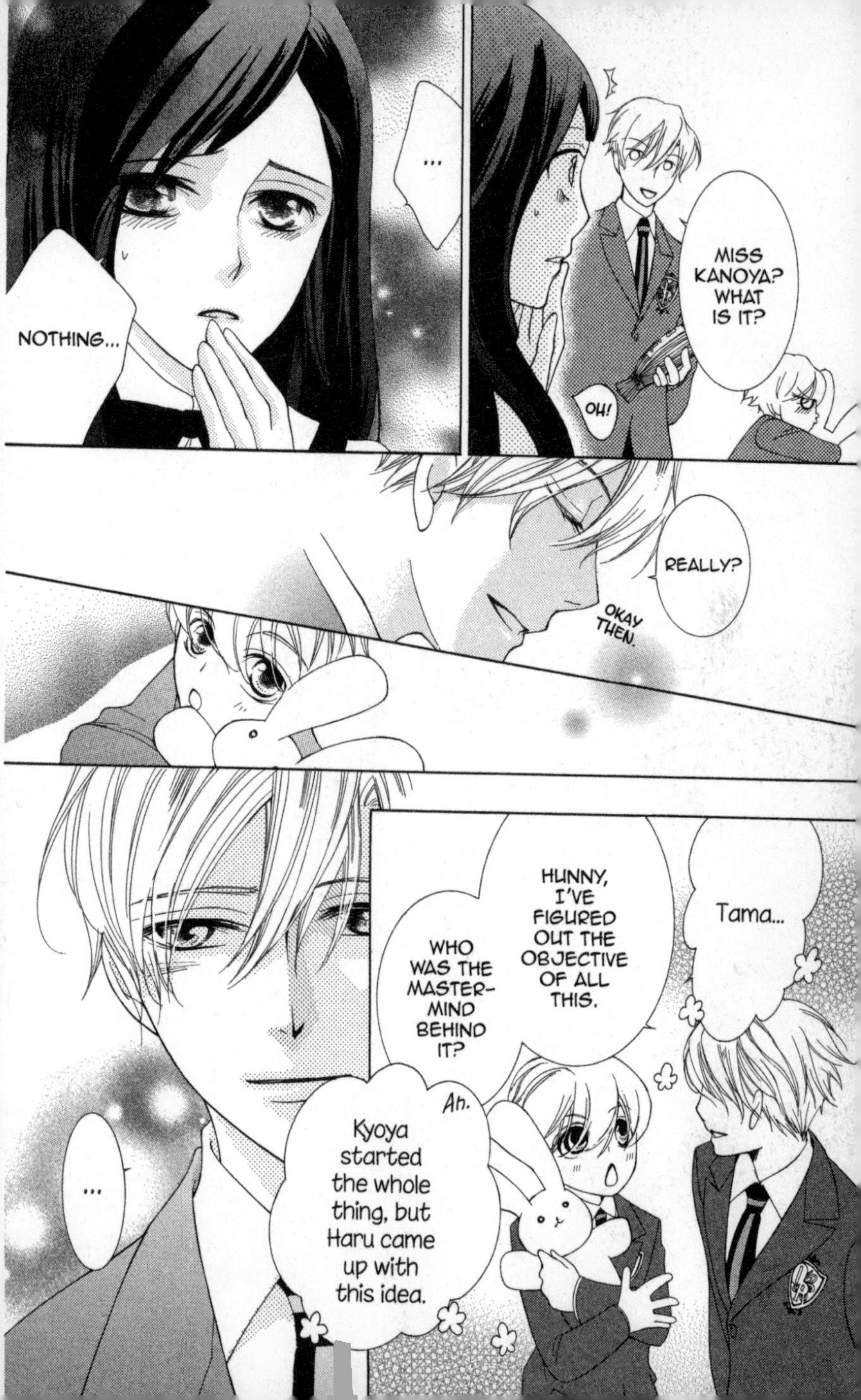

MISS KANOYA? WHAT IS IT?
OH!
...
NOTHING...
REALLY?
OKAY THEN.
Tama...
HUNNY, I'VE FIGURED OUT THE OBJECTIVE OF ALL THIS.
WHO WAS THE MASTER-MIND BEHIND IT?
Ah.
Kyoya started the whole thing, but Haru came up with this idea.
...

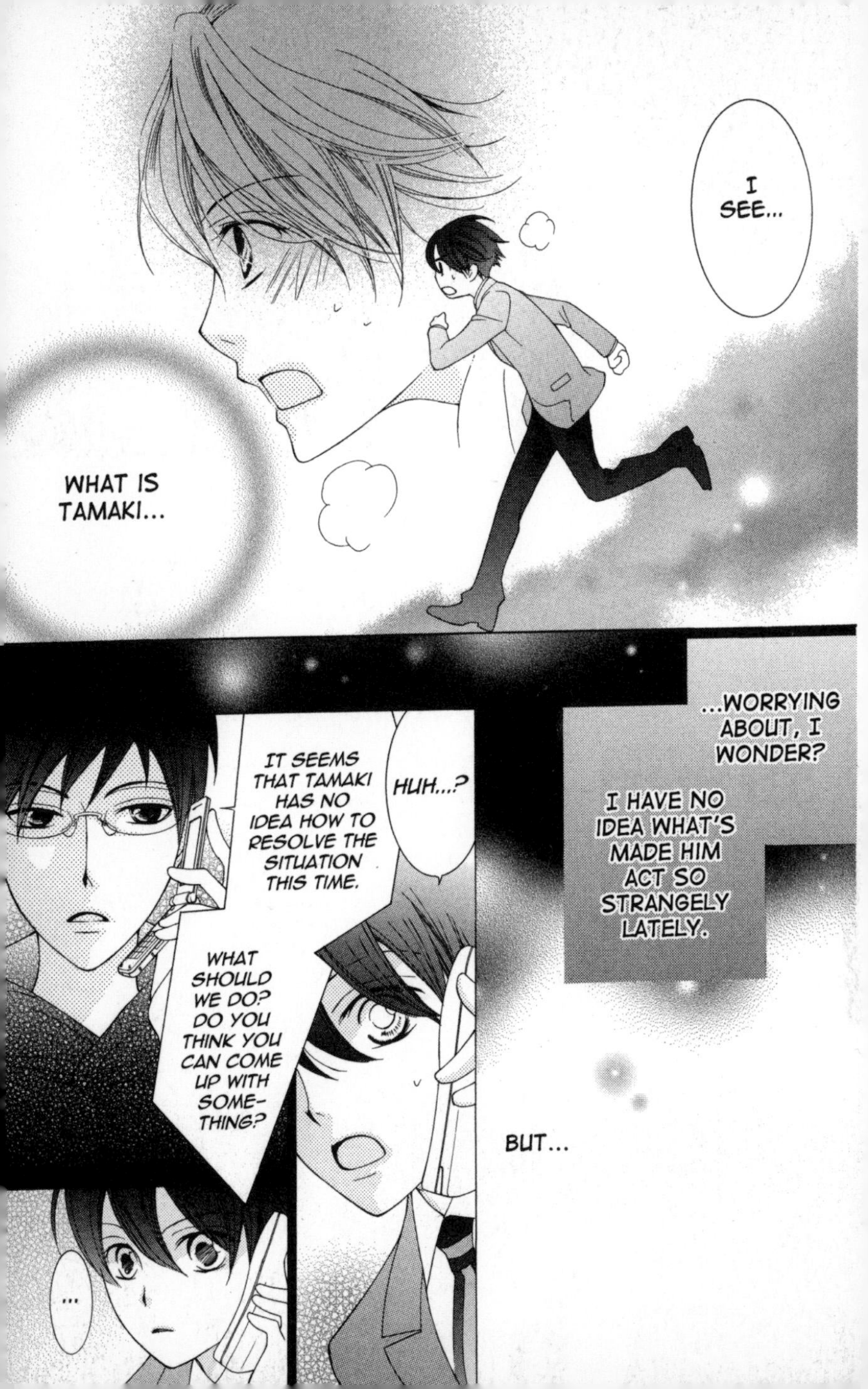
I SEE...
WHAT IS TAMAKI...
...WORRYING ABOUT, I WONDER?
I HAVE NO IDEA WHAT'S MADE HIM ACT SO STRANGELY LATELY.
BUT...
IT SEEMS THAT TAMAKI HAS NO IDEA HOW TO RESOLVE THE SITUATION THIS TIME.
HUH...?
WHAT SHOULD WE DO? DO YOU THINK YOU CAN COME UP WITH SOMETHING?
...

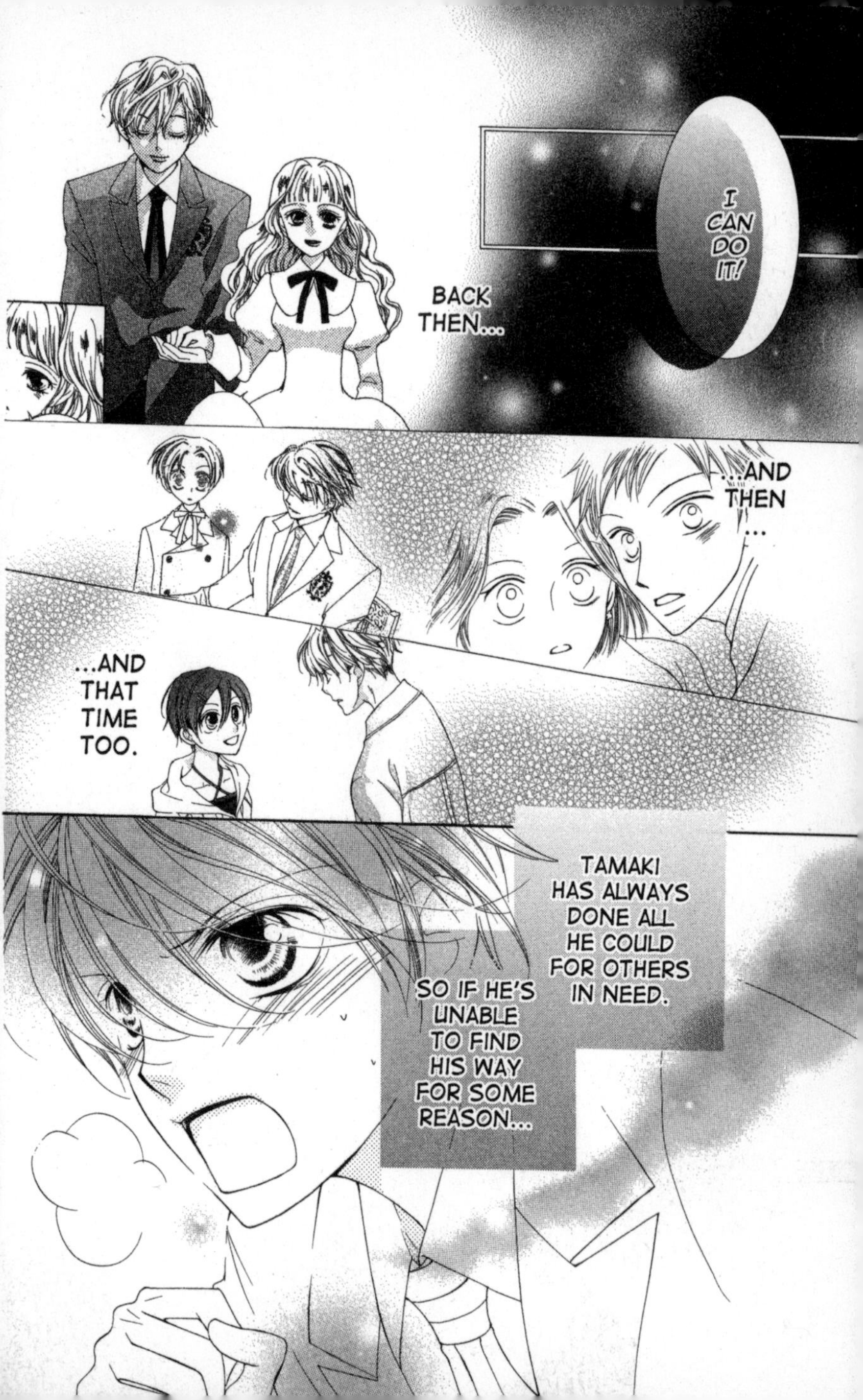
I CAN DO IT!
BACK THEN...
...AND THEN ...
...AND THAT TIME TOO.
TAMAKI HAS ALWAYS DONE ALL HE COULD FOR OTHERS IN NEED.
SO IF HE'S UNABLE TO FIND HIS WAY FOR SOME REASON...

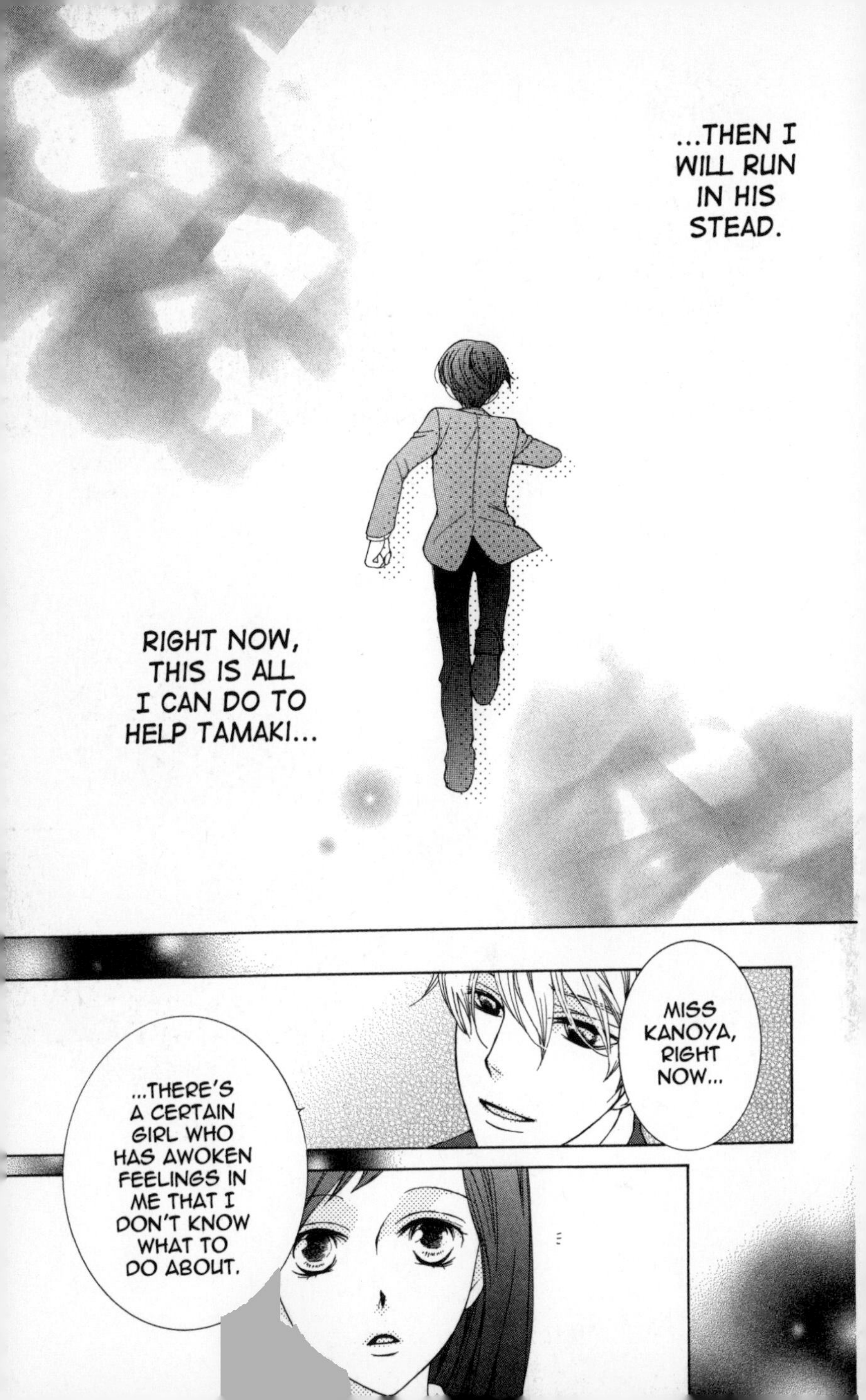
...THEN I WILL RUN IN HIS STEAD.
RIGHT NOW, THIS IS ALL I CAN DO TO HELP TAMAKI...
MISS KANOYA, RIGHT NOW...
...THERE'S A CERTAIN GIRL WHO HAS AWOKEN FEELINGS IN ME THAT I DON'T KNOW WHAT TO DO ABOUT.

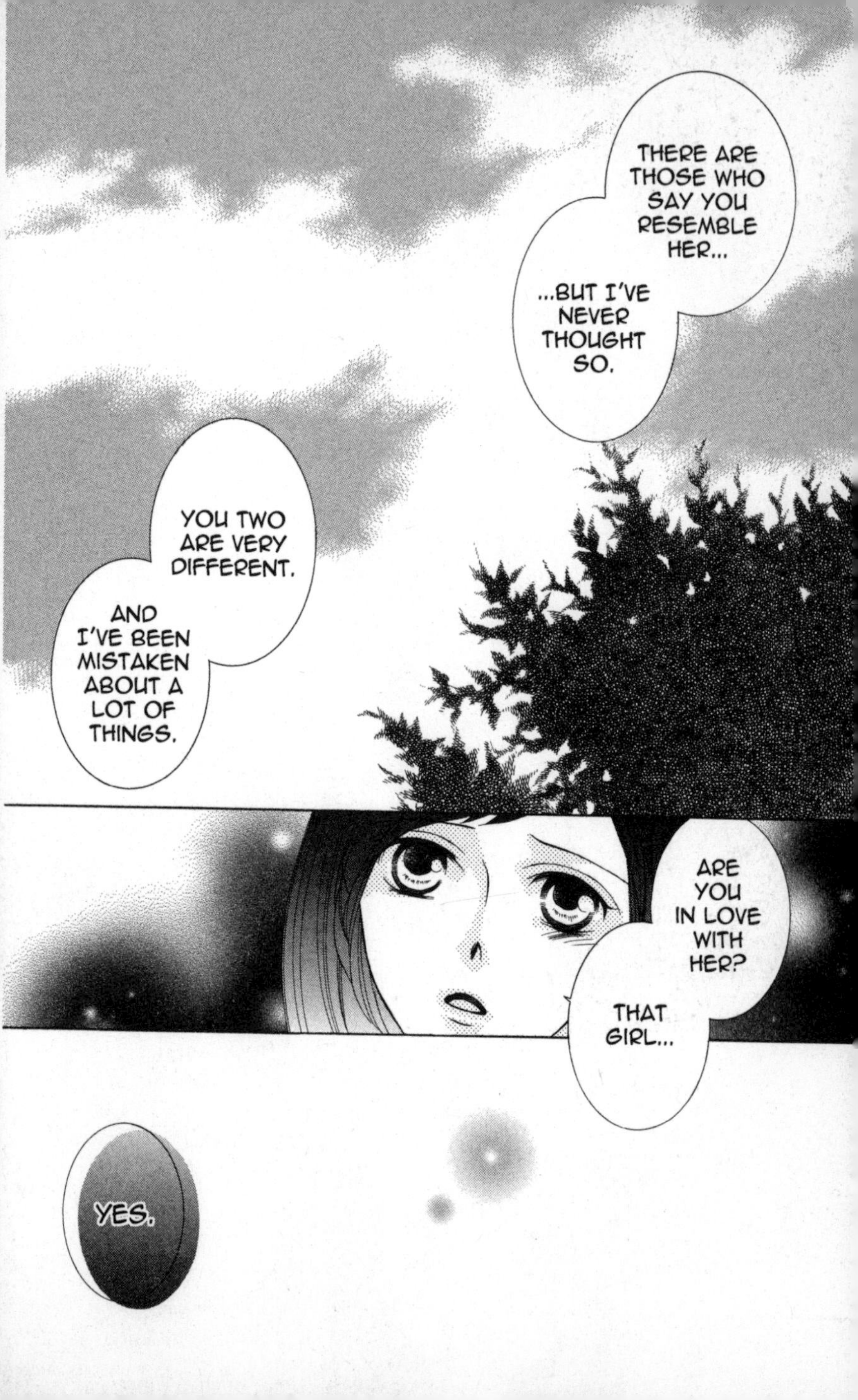
THERE ARE THOSE WHO SAY YOU RESEMBLE HER...
...BUT I'VE NEVER THOUGHT SO.
YOU TWO ARE VERY DIFFERENT.
AND I'VE BEEN MISTAKEN ABOUT A LOT OF THINGS.
ARE YOU IN LOVE WITH HER?
THAT GIRL...
YES.

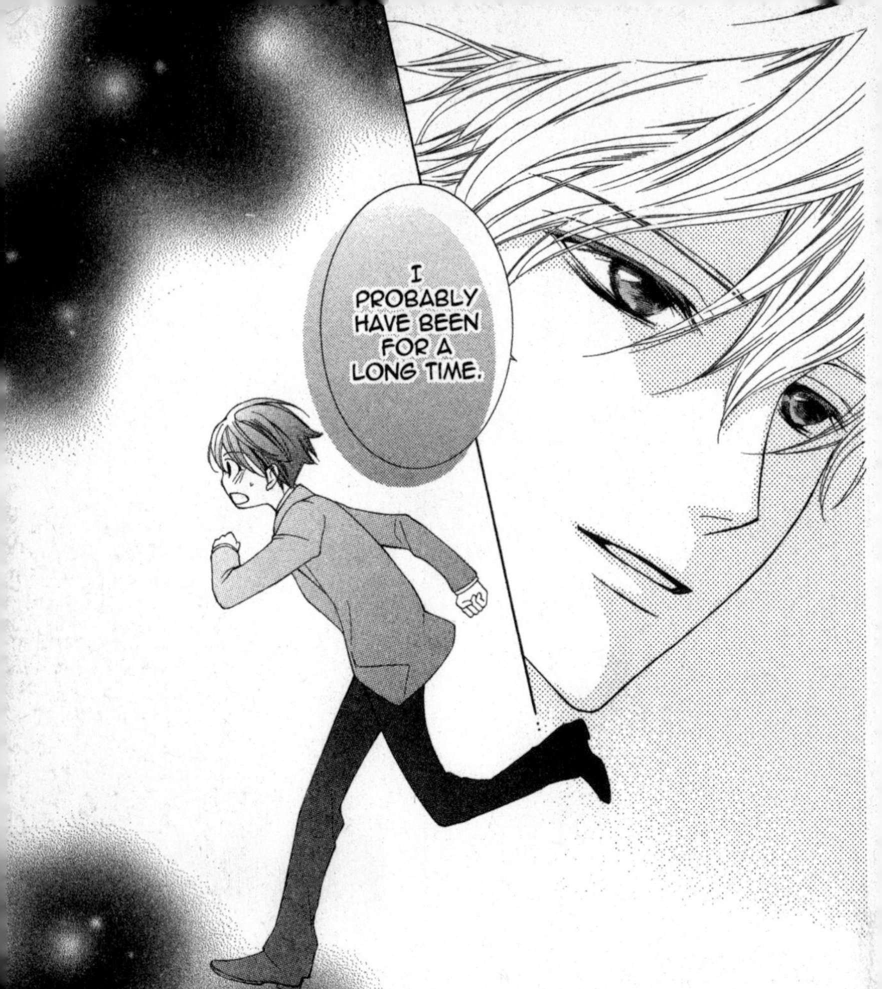
I PROBABLY HAVE BEEN FOR A LONG TIME.

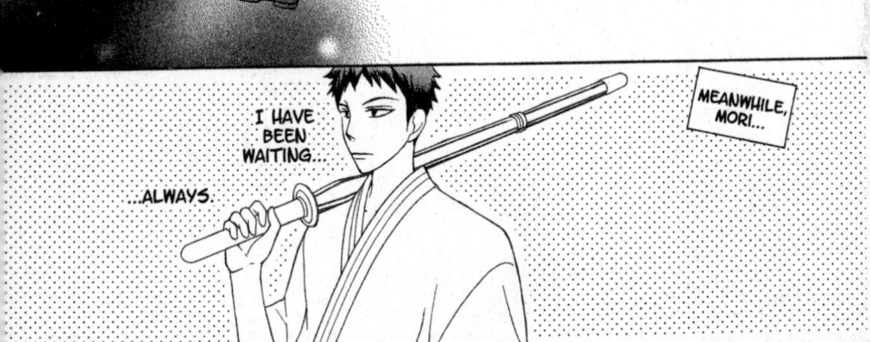
MEANWHILE, MORI...
I HAVE BEEN WAITING...
...ALWAYS.

TEAM ☆ HATORI'S ROOM
YUI NATSUKI

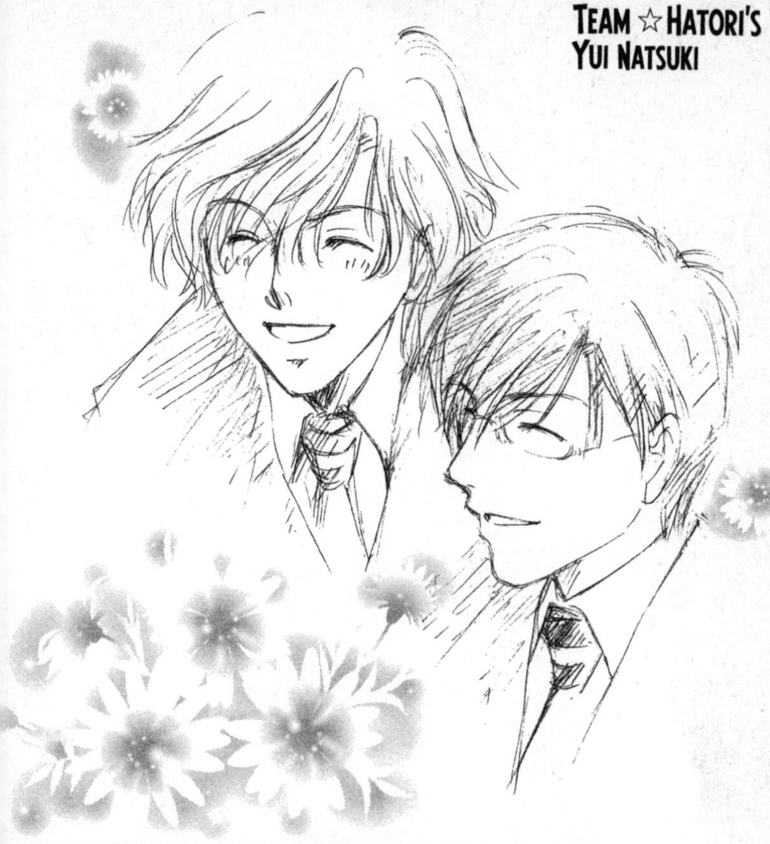

TEAM ☆ HATORI'S MOST POWERFUL STAFF MEMBER, YUI-SAN (WHO KNOWS EVEN MORE ABOUT THE HOST CLUB'S ENVIRONS THAN I DO) HAS DRAWN THIS REFRESHING KYOYA AND TAMAKI PICTURE FOR US!! IT'S SO LOVELY...!! THANK YOU SO MUCH!!

ON TOP OF WORKING ON *HOST CLUB*, YUI-SAN ALSO WORKS ON THE STAFF OF THE THEATRICAL GROUP "PETEKAN."

PETEKAN HTTP://PETEKAN.COM
A THEATER TROUPE THAT OPERATES MAINLY IN CENTRAL TOKYO. SCRIPTWRITER AND DIRECTOR MAKOTO HONDA-SAN HAS PLAYED VARIOUS CHARACTERS IN THE TELEVISION DRAMAS *TRAIN MAN* AND *KAMEN RIDER TEN'OU* AND APPEARS TO BE QUITE THE LOCAL CELEBRITY IN HER HOMETOWN OF MIYAZAKI!!

HONDA-SAN'S TRADEMARK IS HER RED *TRAIN MAN* TRACK JACKET.

I'VE BEEN TO SEE PETEKAN PERFORM NUMEROUS TIMES, AND I'VE JUST GOT TO SAY... **THEY ARE SO HILARIOUS!!!!** SERIOUSLY. DEFINITELY TRY TO GO OUT AND SEE THEIR SHOW. YOU'LL LAUGH SO HARD, YOU'LL CRY.★☆

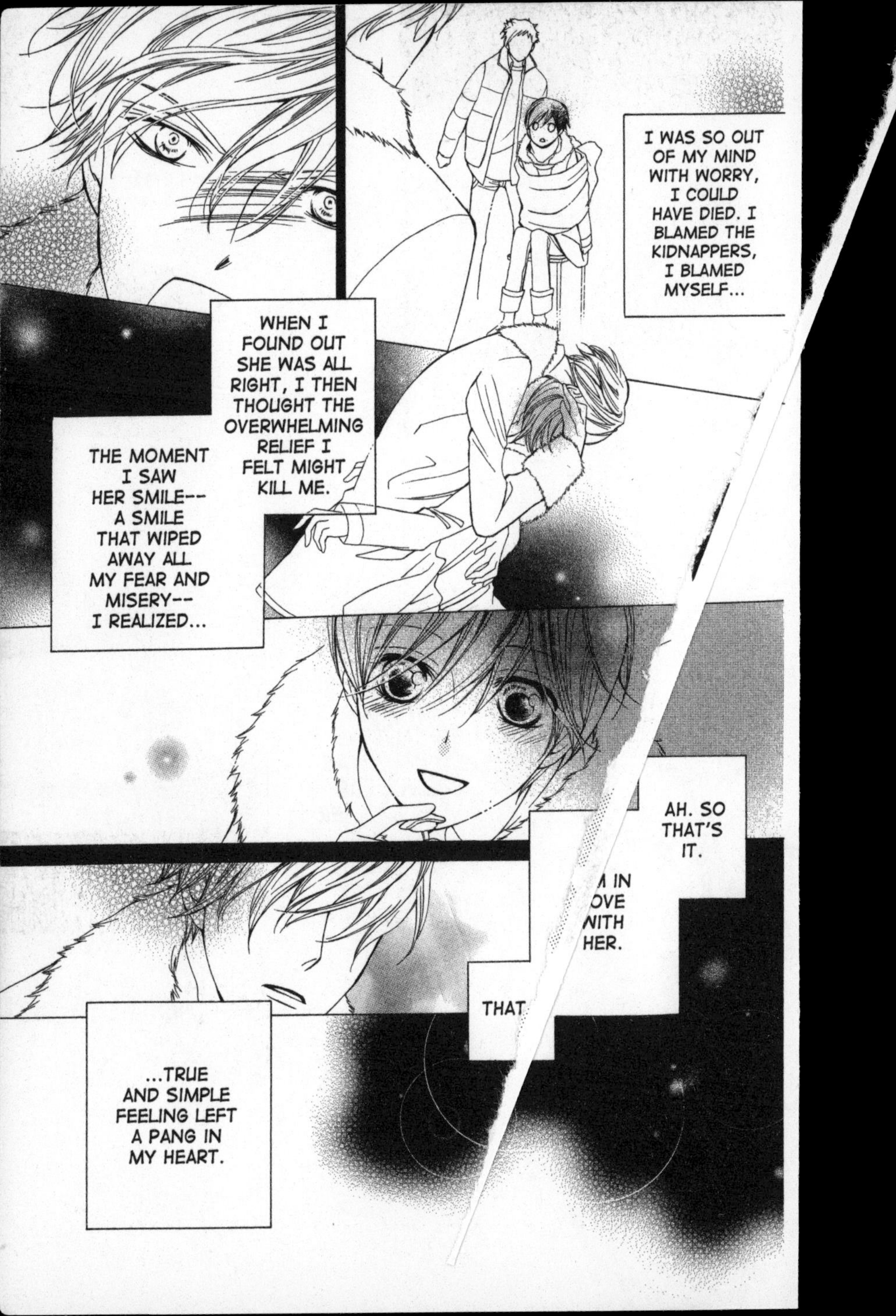
I WAS SO OUT OF MY MIND WITH WORRY, I COULD HAVE DIED. I BLAMED THE KIDNAPPERS, I BLAMED MYSELF...
WHEN I FOUND OUT SHE WAS ALL RIGHT, I THEN THOUGHT THE OVERWHELMING RELIEF I FELT MIGHT KILL ME.
THE MOMENT I SAW HER SMILE-- A SMILE THAT WIPED AWAY ALL MY FEAR AND MISERY-- I REALIZED...
AH. SO THAT'S IT.
M IN OVE WITH HER.
THAT
...TRUE AND SIMPLE FEELING LEFT A PANG IN MY HEART.

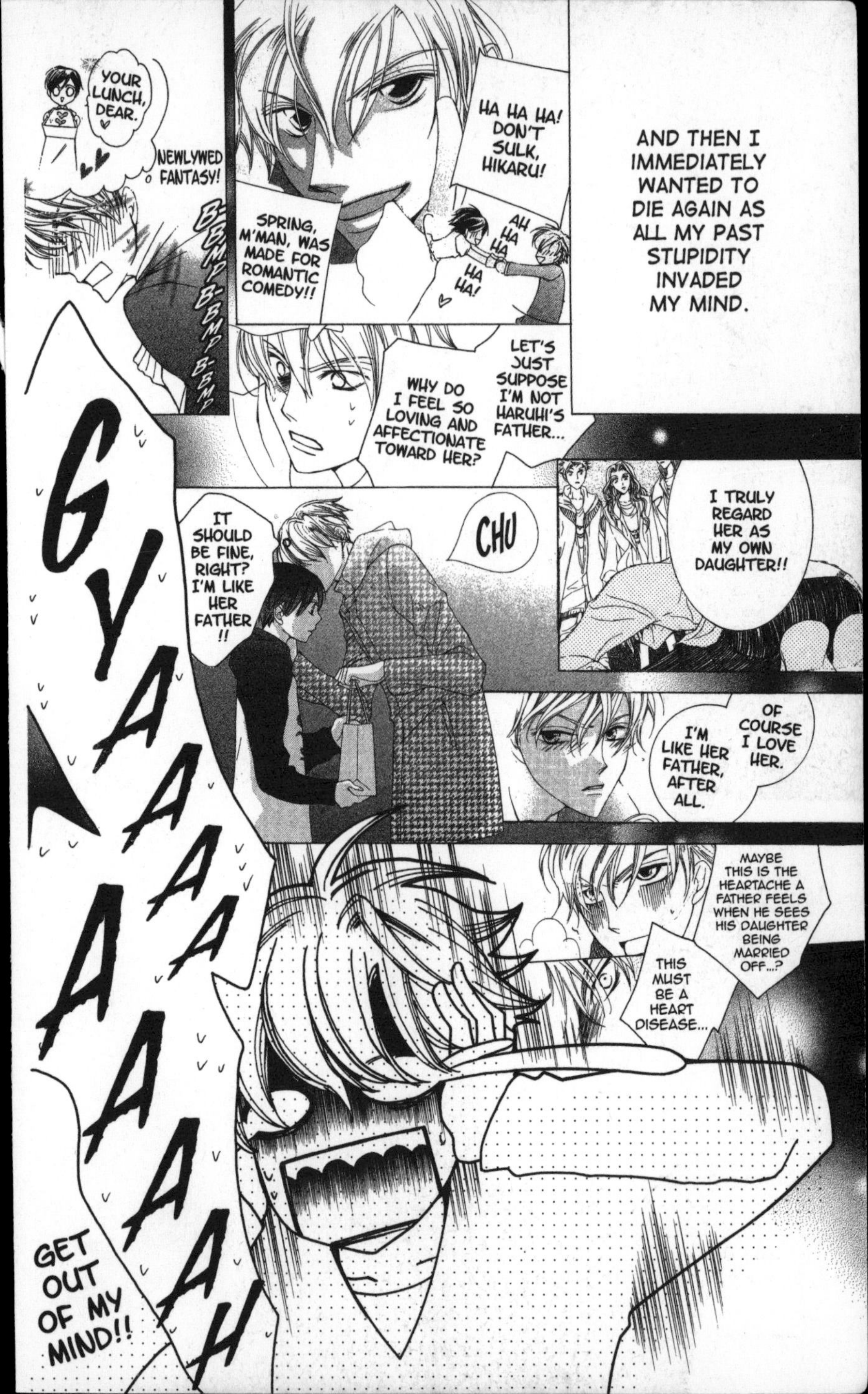
AND THEN I IMMEDIATELY WANTED TO DIE AGAIN AS ALL MY PAST STUPIDITY INVADED MY MIND.
HA HA HA! DON'T SULK, HIKARU!
AH HA HA
HA HA!
SPRING, M'MAN, WAS MADE FOR ROMANTIC COMEDY!!
YOUR LUNCH, DEAR.
NEWLYWED FANTASY!
B-BMP B-BMP B-BMP
LET'S JUST SUPPOSE I'M NOT HARUHI'S FATHER...
WHY DO I FEEL SO LOVING AND AFFECTIONATE TOWARD HER?
I TRULY REGARD HER AS MY OWN DAUGHTER!!
CHU
IT SHOULD BE FINE, RIGHT? I'M LIKE HER FATHER!!
OF COURSE I LOVE HER.
I'M LIKE HER FATHER, AFTER ALL.
MAYBE THIS IS THE HEARTACHE A FATHER FEELS WHEN HIS DAUGHTER BEING MARRIED OFF...?
THIS MUST BE A HEART DISEASE...
GYAAAAAAAAAH
GET OUT OF MY MIND!!

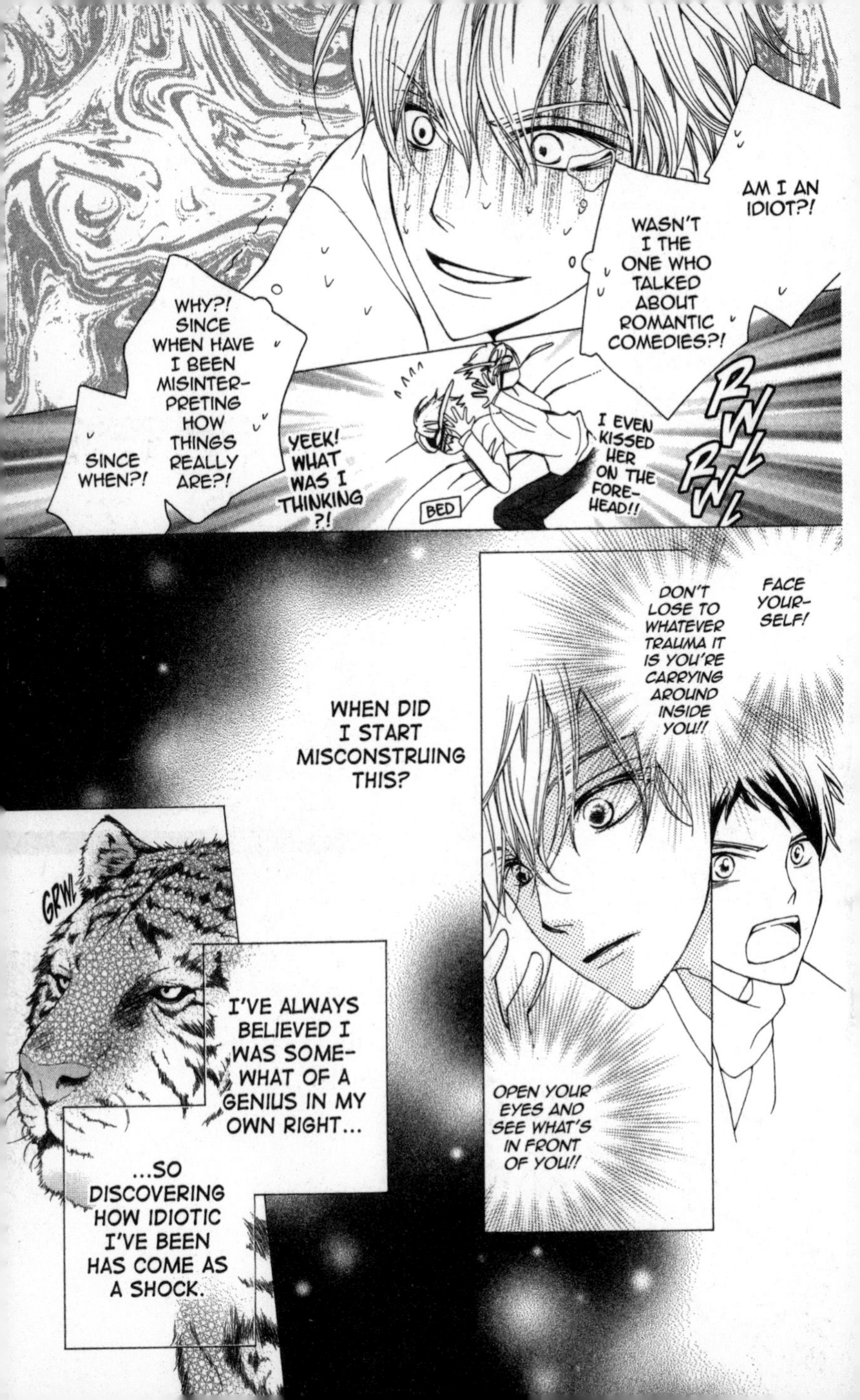
AM I AN IDIOT?!
WASN'T I THE ONE WHO TALKED ABOUT ROMANTIC COMEDIES?!
RWL RWL
I EVEN KISSED HER ON THE FORE-HEAD!!
BED
YEEK! WHAT WAS I THINKING?!
WHY?! SINCE WHEN HAVE I BEEN MISINTER-PRETING HOW THINGS REALLY ARE?!
SINCE WHEN?!
FACE YOUR-SELF!
DON'T LOSE TO WHATEVER TRAUMA IT IS YOU'RE CARRYING AROUND INSIDE YOU!!
OPEN YOUR EYES AND SEE WHAT'S IN FRONT OF YOU!!
WHEN DID I START MISCONSTRUING THIS?
GRWL
I'VE ALWAYS BELIEVED I WAS SOME-WHAT OF A GENIUS IN MY OWN RIGHT...
...SO DISCOVERING HOW IDIOTIC I'VE BEEN HAS COME AS A SHOCK.

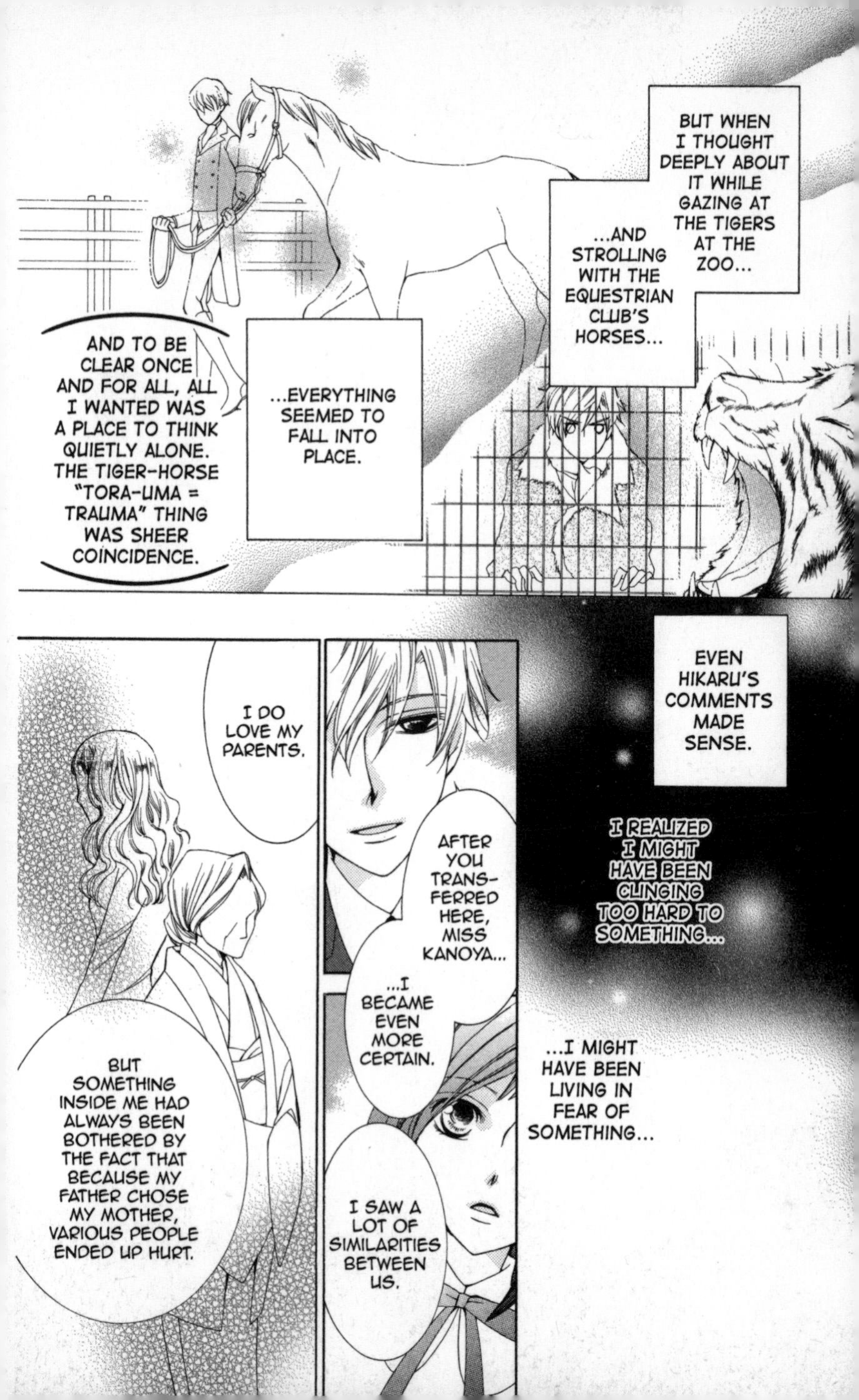
BUT WHEN I THOUGHT DEEPLY ABOUT IT WHILE GAZING AT THE TIGERS AT THE ZOO...
...AND STROLLING WITH THE EQUESTRIAN CLUB'S HORSES...
...EVERYTHING SEEMED TO FALL INTO PLACE.
AND TO BE CLEAR ONCE AND FOR ALL, ALL I WANTED WAS A PLACE TO THINK QUIETLY ALONE. THE TIGER-HORSE "TORA-UMA = TRAUMA" THING WAS SHEER COINCIDENCE.
EVEN HIKARU'S COMMENTS MADE SENSE.
I REALIZED I MIGHT HAVE BEEN CLINGING TOO HARD TO SOMETHING...
...I MIGHT HAVE BEEN LIVING IN FEAR OF SOMETHING...
AFTER YOU TRANSFERRED HERE, MISS KANOYA...
...I BECAME EVEN MORE CERTAIN.
I SAW A LOT OF SIMILARITIES BETWEEN US.
I DO LOVE MY PARENTS.
BUT SOMETHING INSIDE ME HAD ALWAYS BEEN BOTHERED BY THE FACT THAT BECAUSE MY FATHER CHOSE MY MOTHER, VARIOUS PEOPLE ENDED UP HURT.

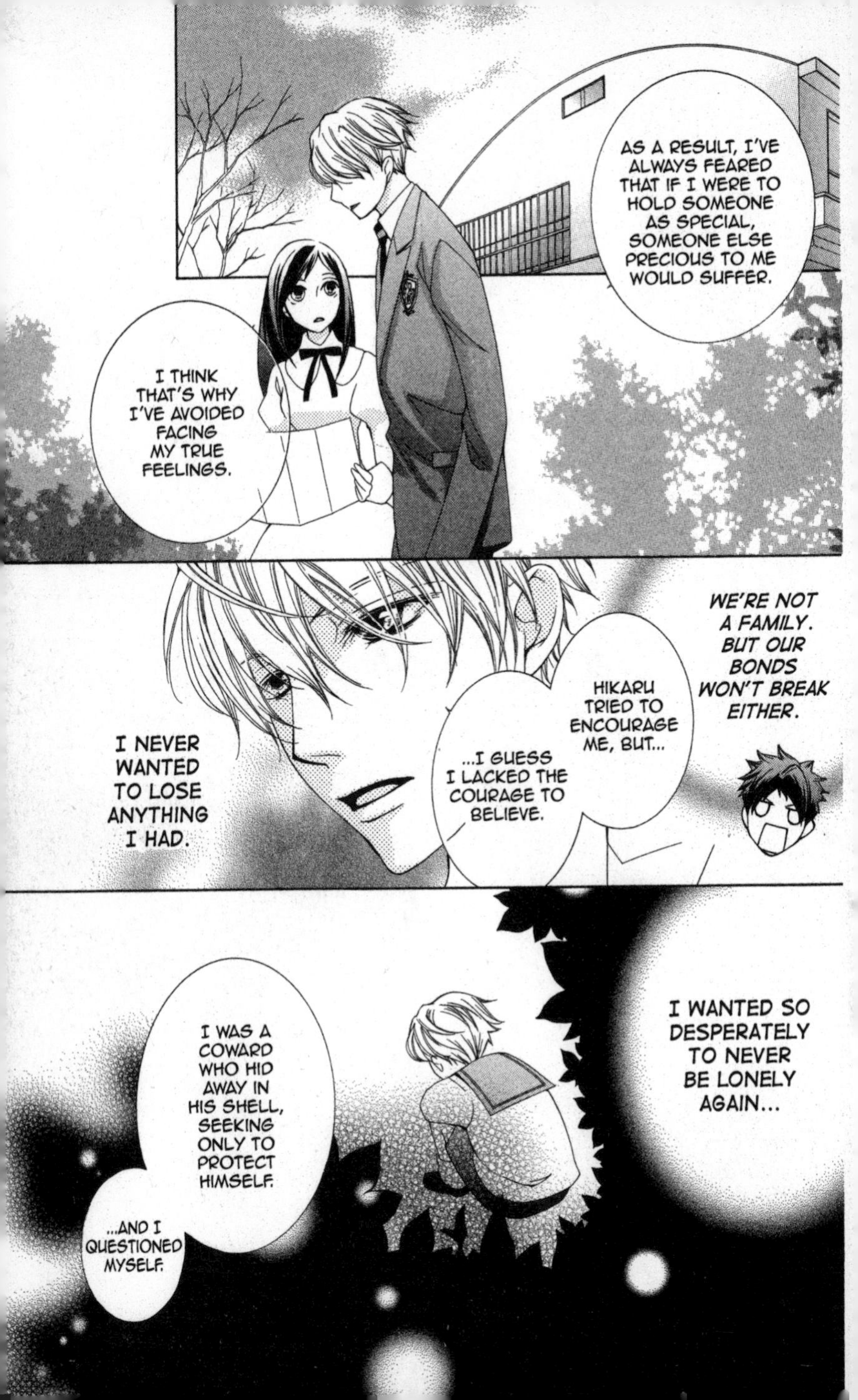
AS A RESULT, I'VE ALWAYS FEARED THAT IF I WERE TO HOLD SOMEONE AS SPECIAL, SOMEONE ELSE PRECIOUS TO ME WOULD SUFFER.
I THINK THAT'S WHY I'VE AVOIDED FACING MY TRUE FEELINGS.
WE'RE NOT A FAMILY. BUT OUR BONDS WON'T BREAK EITHER.
HIKARU TRIED TO ENCOURAGE ME, BUT...
...I GUESS I LACKED THE COURAGE TO BELIEVE.
I NEVER WANTED TO LOSE ANYTHING I HAD.
I WANTED SO DESPERATELY TO NEVER BE LONELY AGAIN...
I WAS A COWARD WHO HID AWAY IN HIS SHELL, SEEKING ONLY TO PROTECT HIMSELF.
...AND I QUESTIONED MYSELF.

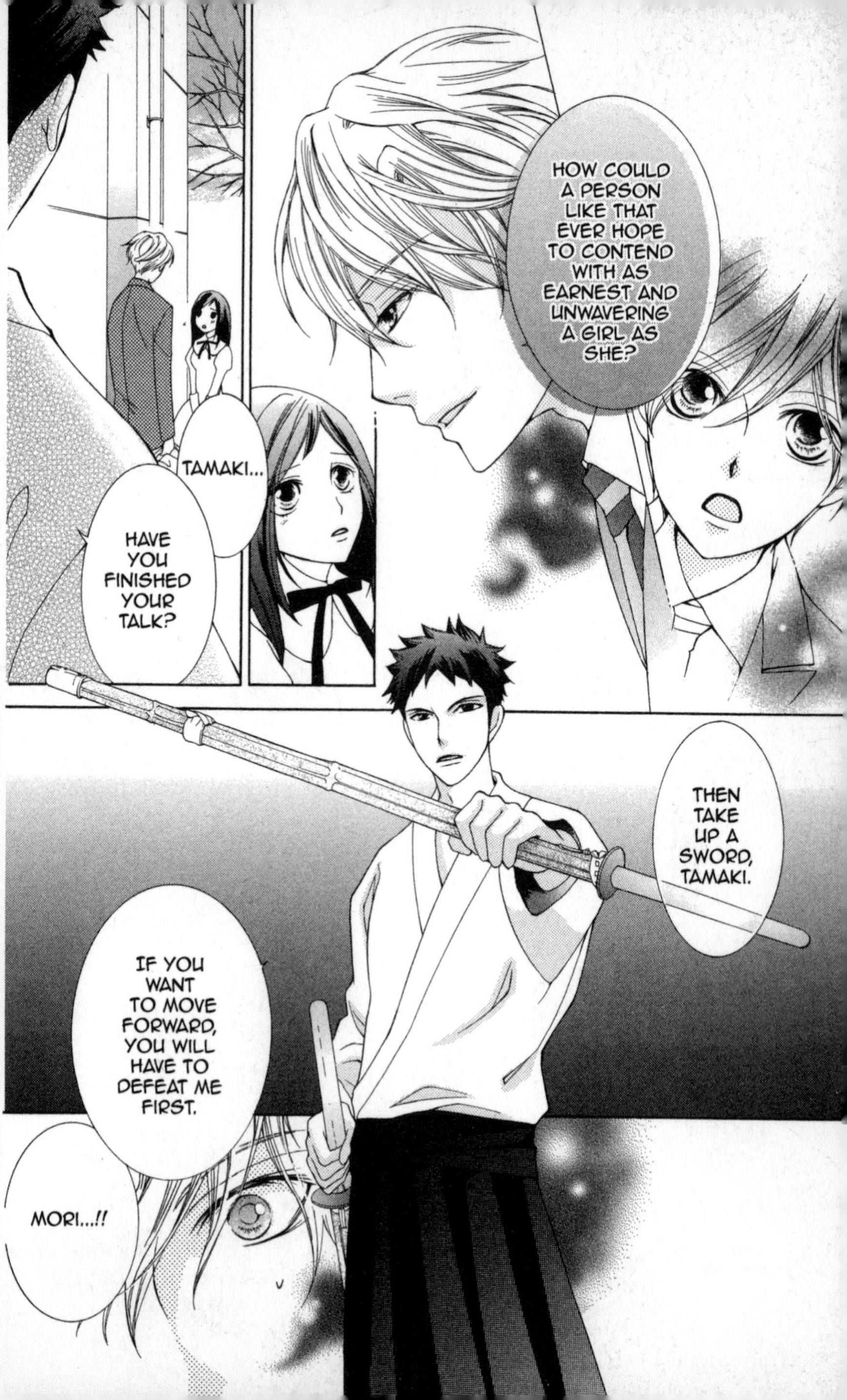
HOW COULD A PERSON LIKE THAT EVER HOPE TO CONTEND WITH AS EARNEST AND UNWAVERING A GIRL AS SHE?
TAMAKI...
HAVE YOU FINISHED YOUR TALK?
THEN TAKE UP A SWORD, TAMAKI.
IF YOU WANT TO MOVE FORWARD, YOU WILL HAVE TO DEFEAT ME FIRST.
MORI...!!

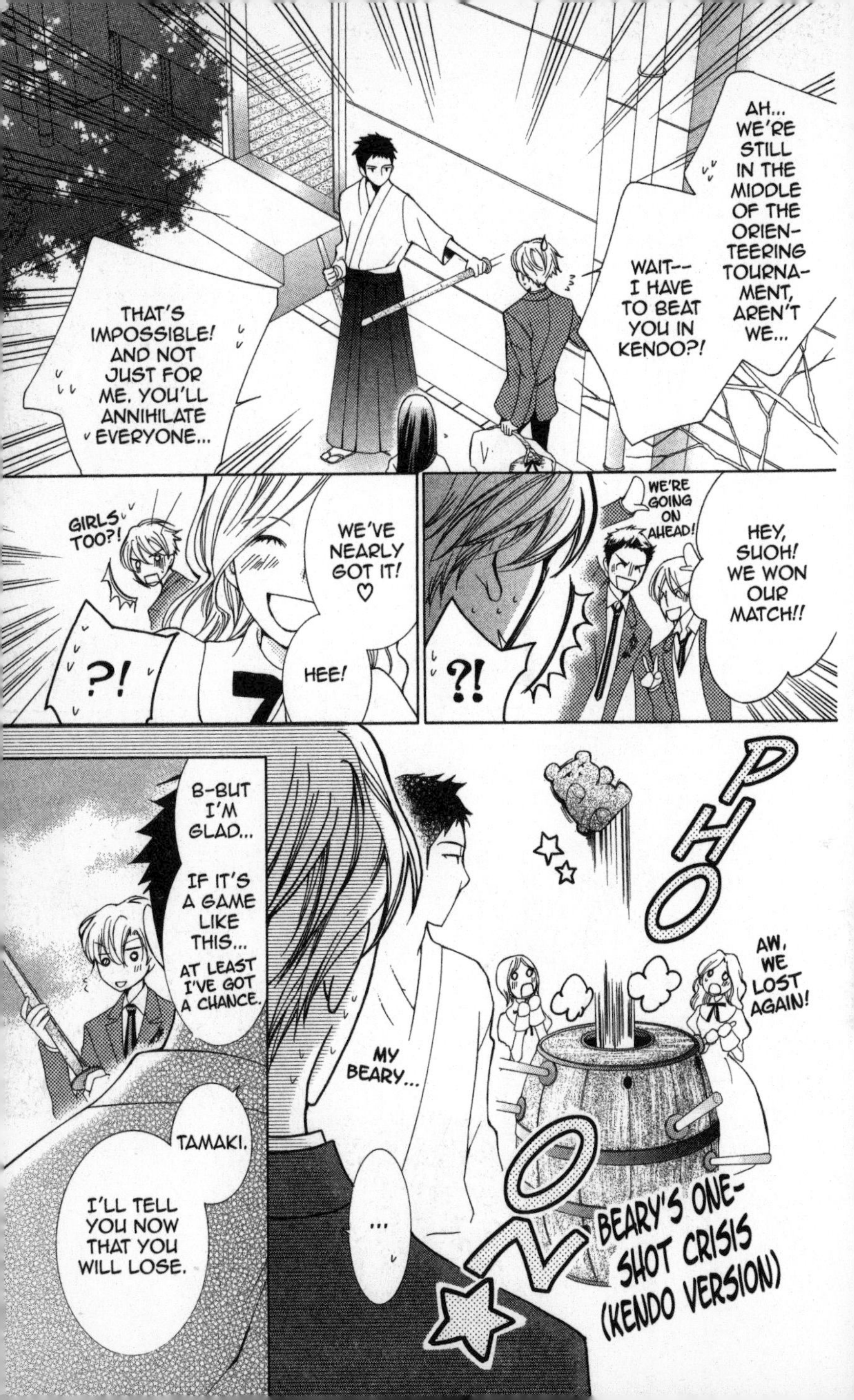

AH... WE'RE STILL IN THE MIDDLE OF THE ORIENTEERING TOURNAMENT, AREN'T WE...
WAIT-- I HAVE TO BEAT YOU IN KENDO?!
THAT'S IMPOSSIBLE! AND NOT JUST FOR ME. YOU'LL ANNIHILATE EVERYONE...
HEY, SUOH! WE WON OUR MATCH!!
WE'RE GOING ON AHEAD!
?!
WE'VE NEARLY GOT IT! ♡
HEE!
GIRLS TOO?!
?!
PHOOON
AW, WE LOST AGAIN!
MY BEARY...
BEARY'S ONE-SHOT CRISIS (KENDO VERSION)
...
B-BUT I'M GLAD...
IF IT'S A GAME LIKE THIS...
AT LEAST I'VE GOT A CHANCE.
TAMAKI.
I'LL TELL YOU NOW THAT YOU WILL LOSE.

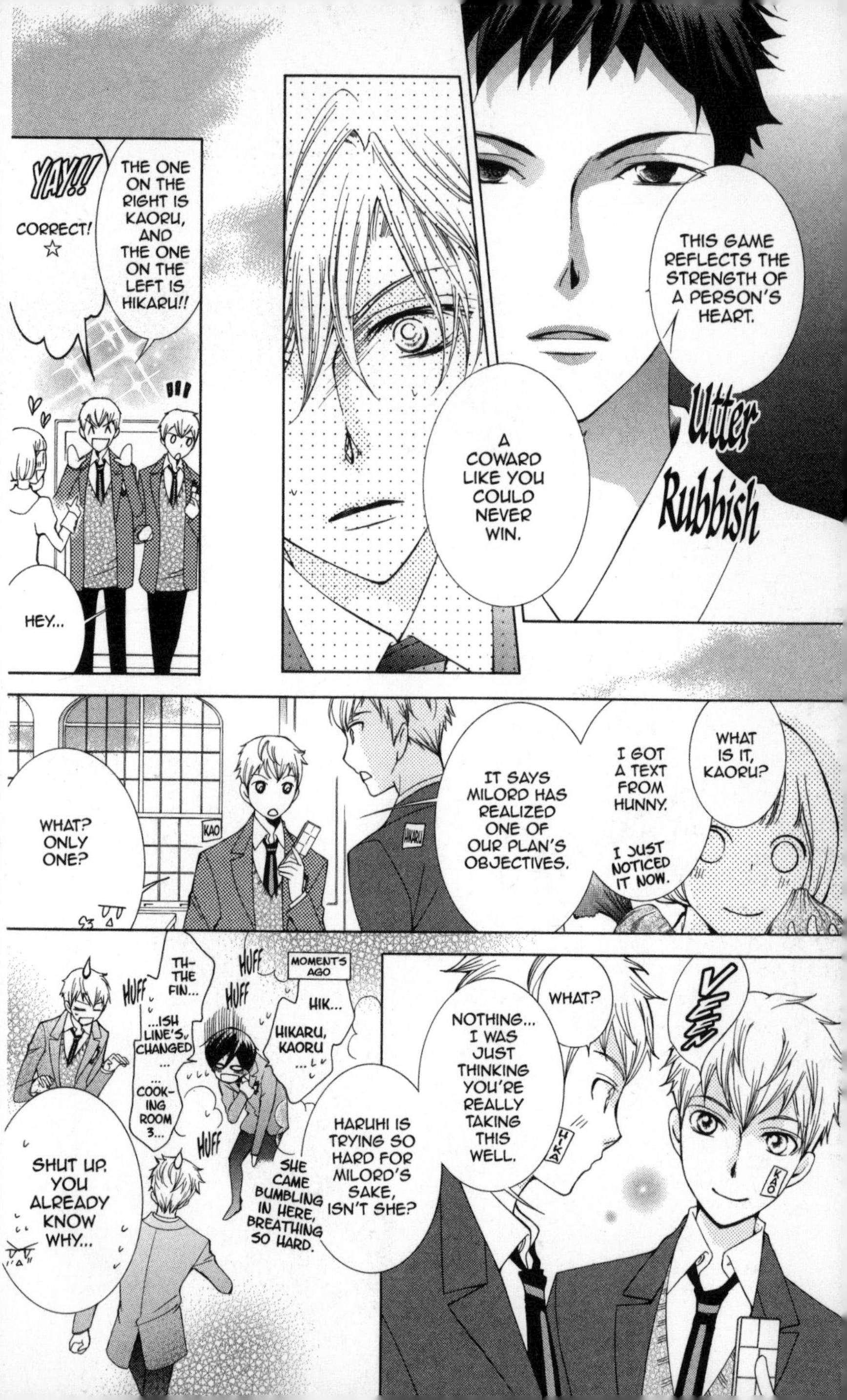
THIS GAME REFLECTS THE STRENGTH OF A PERSON'S HEART.
Utter Rubbish
A COWARD LIKE YOU COULD NEVER WIN.
THE ONE ON THE RIGHT IS KAORU, AND THE ONE ON THE LEFT IS HIKARU!!
YAY!!
CORRECT! ☆
HEY...
WHAT IS IT, KAORU?
I GOT A TEXT FROM HUNNY.
I JUST NOTICED IT NOW.
IT SAYS MILORD HAS REALIZED ONE OF OUR PLAN'S OBJECTIVES.
HIKARU
KAO
WHAT? ONLY ONE?
WHAT?
NOTHING... I WAS JUST THINKING YOU'RE REALLY TAKING THIS WELL.
HIKA
KAO
HARUHI IS TRYING SO HARD FOR MILORD'S SAKE, ISN'T SHE?
MOMENTS AGO
HIK...
HIKARU, KAORU...
HUFF
HUFF
TH-THE FIN...
HUFF
...ISH LINE'S CHANGED...
...COOKING ROOM 3...
HUFF
SHE CAME BUMBLING IN HERE, BREATHING SO HARD.
SHUT UP. YOU ALREADY KNOW WHY...

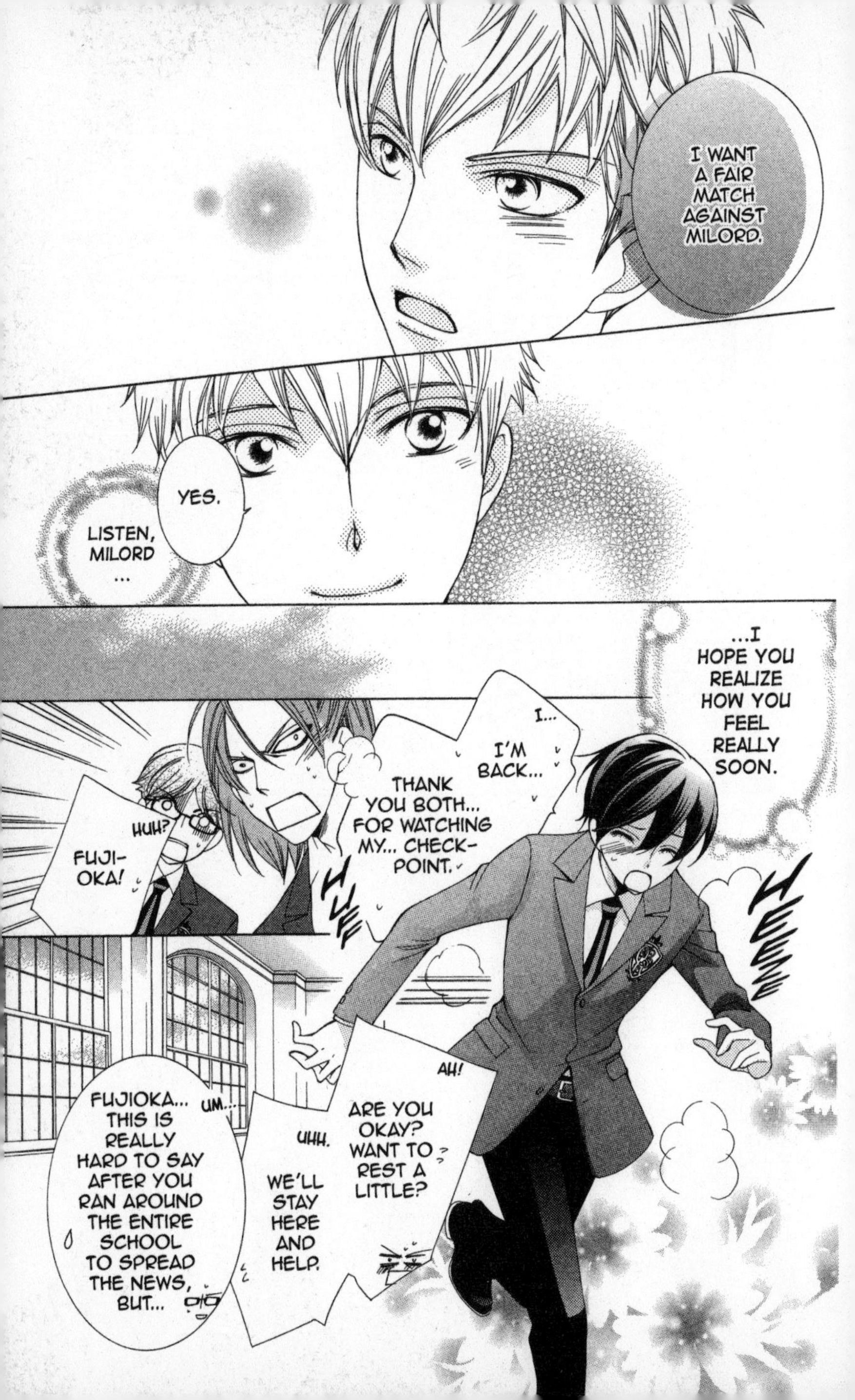
I WANT A FAIR MATCH AGAINST MILORD.
YES.
LISTEN, MILORD ...
...I HOPE YOU REALIZE HOW YOU FEEL REALLY SOON.
I...
I'M BACK...
THANK YOU BOTH... FOR WATCHING MY... CHECK-POINT.
HUFF
HUH?
FUJI-OKA!
AH!
ARE YOU OKAY? WANT TO REST A LITTLE?
UHH.
WE'LL STAY HERE AND HELP.
UM...
FUJIOKA... THIS IS REALLY HARD TO SAY AFTER YOU RAN AROUND THE ENTIRE SCHOOL TO SPREAD THE NEWS, BUT...

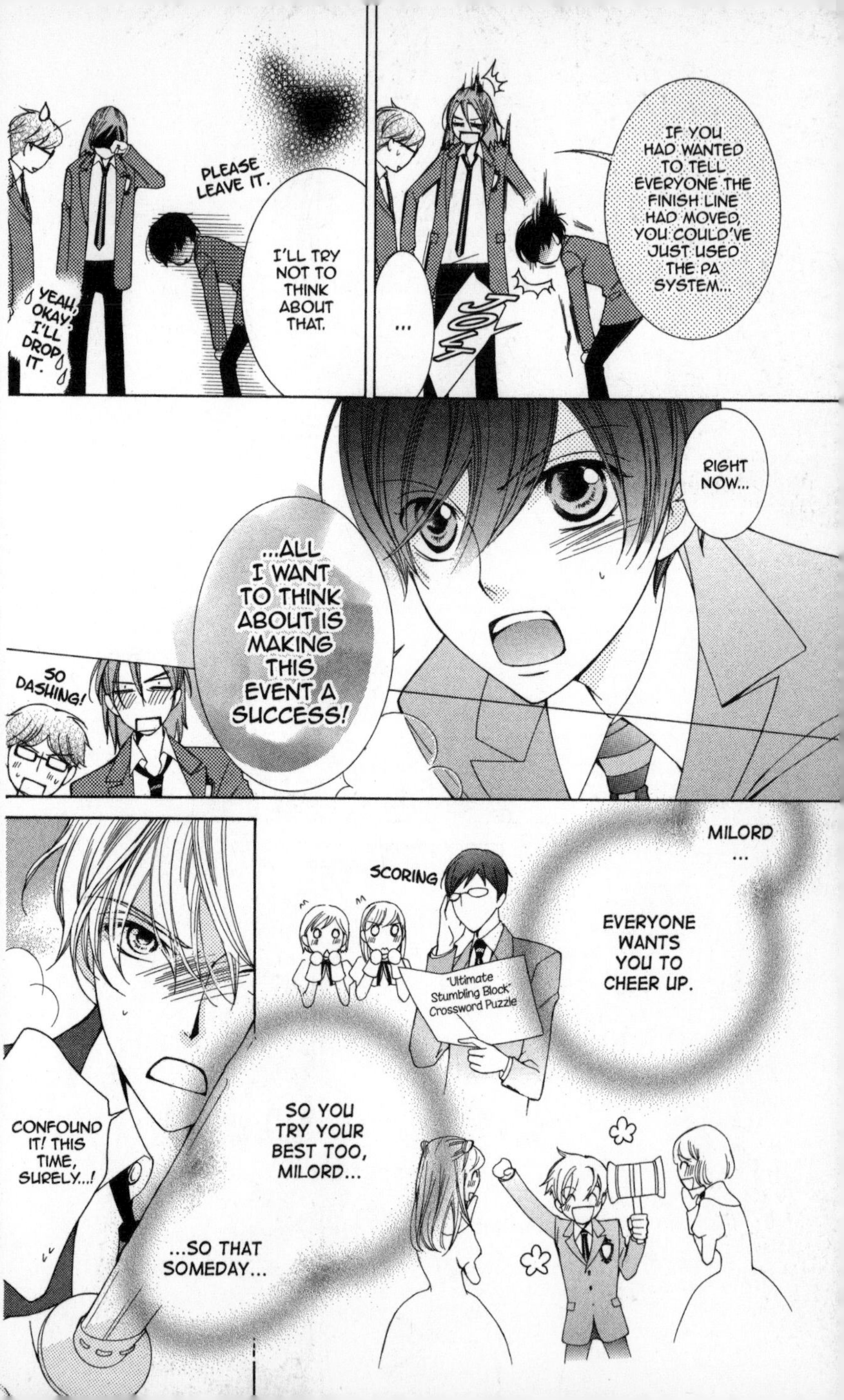
IF YOU HAD WANTED TO TELL EVERYONE THE FINISH LINE HAD MOVED, YOU COULD'VE JUST USED THE PA SYSTEM...
JOLT
...
I'LL TRY NOT TO THINK ABOUT THAT.
PLEASE LEAVE IT.
YEAH, OKAY. I'LL DROP IT.
RIGHT NOW...
...ALL I WANT TO THINK ABOUT IS MAKING THIS EVENT A SUCCESS!
SO DASHING!
MILORD...
EVERYONE WANTS YOU TO CHEER UP.
SCORING
"Ultimate Stumbling Block" Crossword Puzzle
SO YOU TRY YOUR BEST TOO, MILORD...
...SO THAT SOMEDAY...
CONFOUND IT! THIS TIME, SURELY...!

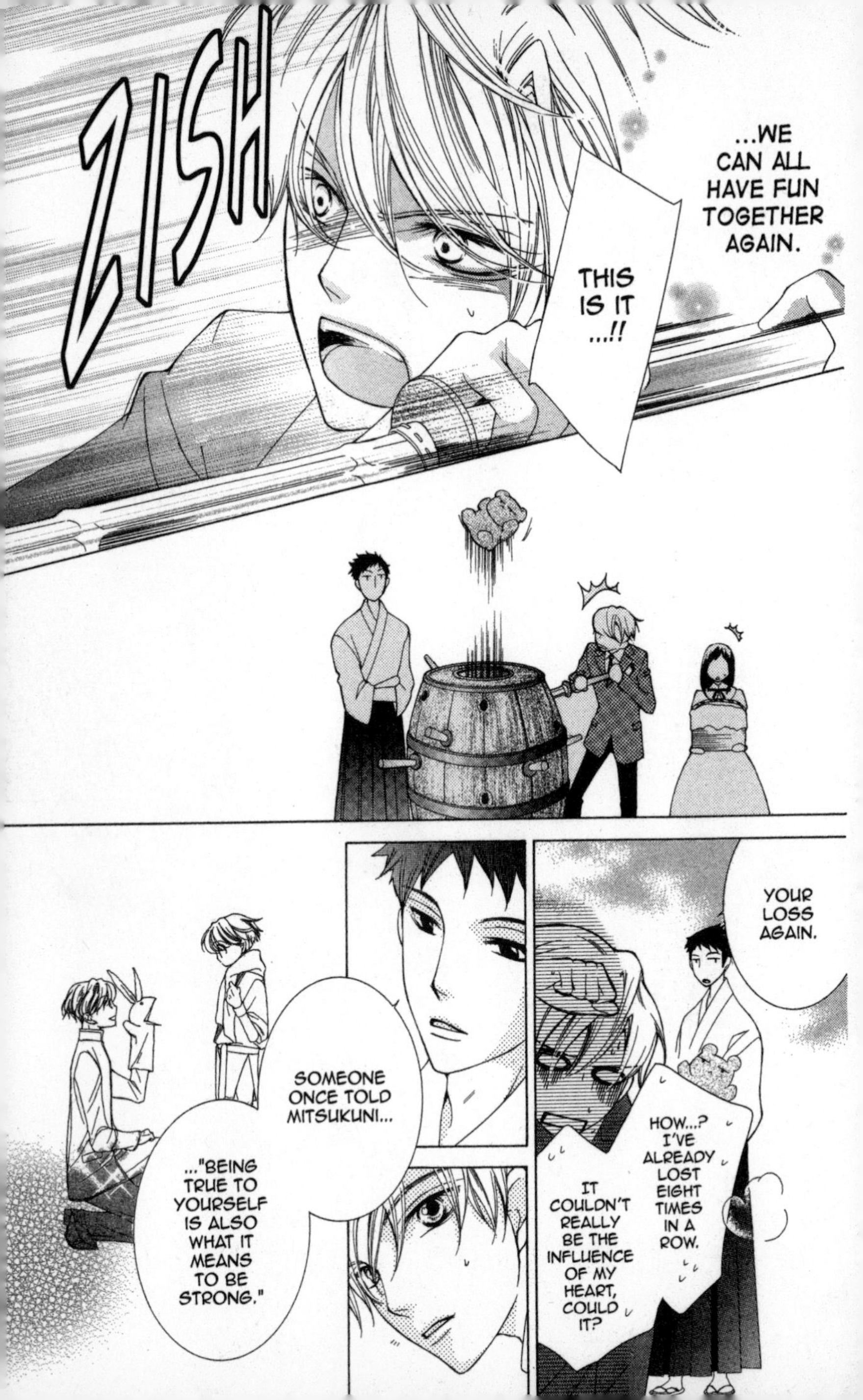

...WE CAN ALL HAVE FUN TOGETHER AGAIN.
THIS IS IT ...!!
ZISH
YOUR LOSS AGAIN.
HOW...? I'VE ALREADY LOST EIGHT TIMES IN A ROW.
IT COULDN'T REALLY BE THE INFLUENCE OF MY HEART, COULD IT?
SOMEONE ONCE TOLD MITSUKUNI...
..."BEING TRUE TO YOURSELF IS ALSO WHAT IT MEANS TO BE STRONG."

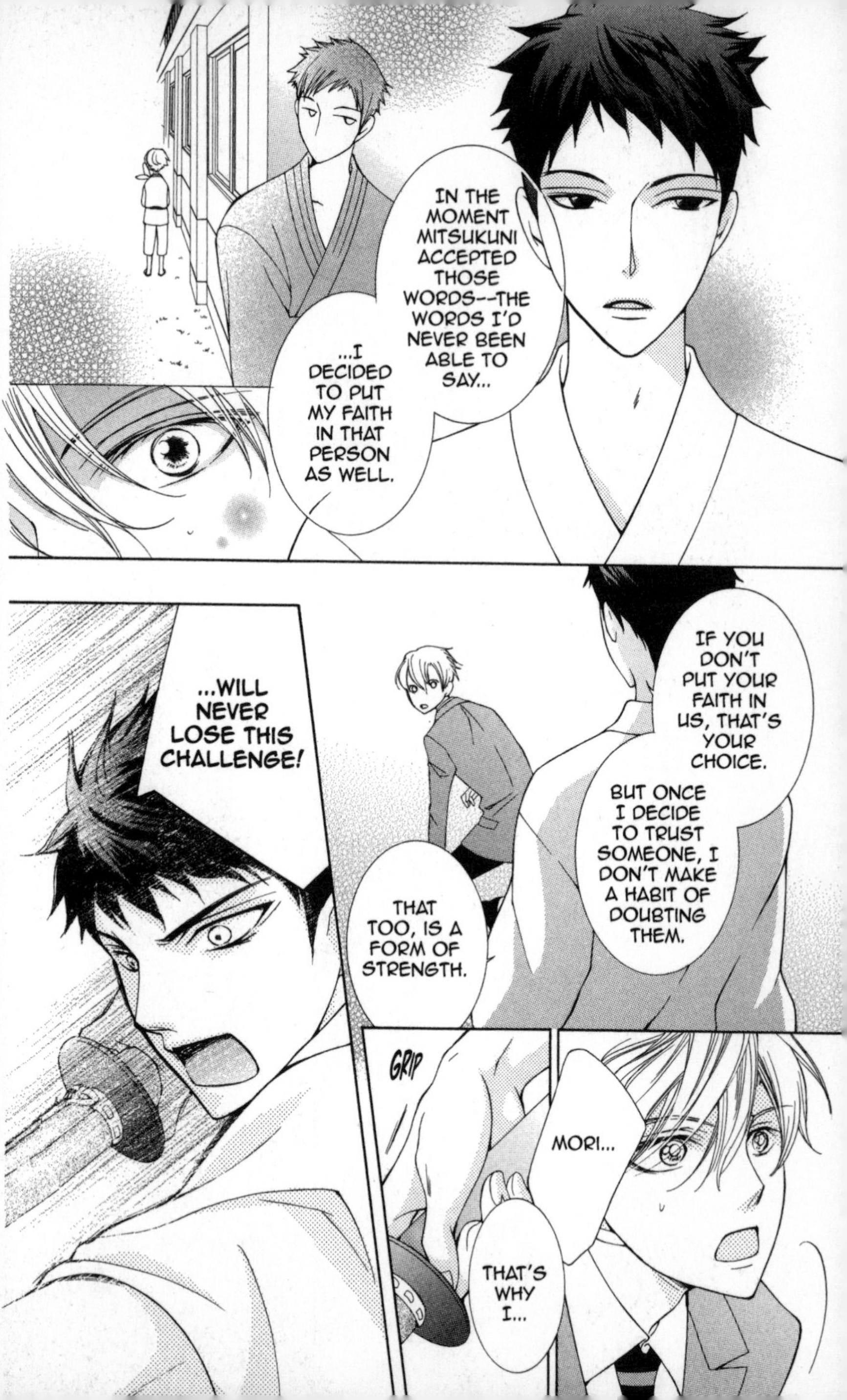
IN THE MOMENT MITSUKUNI ACCEPTED THOSE WORDS--THE WORDS I'D NEVER BEEN ABLE TO SAY...
...I DECIDED TO PUT MY FAITH IN THAT PERSON AS WELL.
IF YOU DON'T PUT YOUR FAITH IN US, THAT'S YOUR CHOICE.
BUT ONCE I DECIDE TO TRUST SOMEONE, I DON'T MAKE A HABIT OF DOUBTING THEM.
THAT TOO, IS A FORM OF STRENGTH.
MORI...
GRIP
THAT'S WHY I...
...WILL NEVER LOSE THIS CHALLENGE!

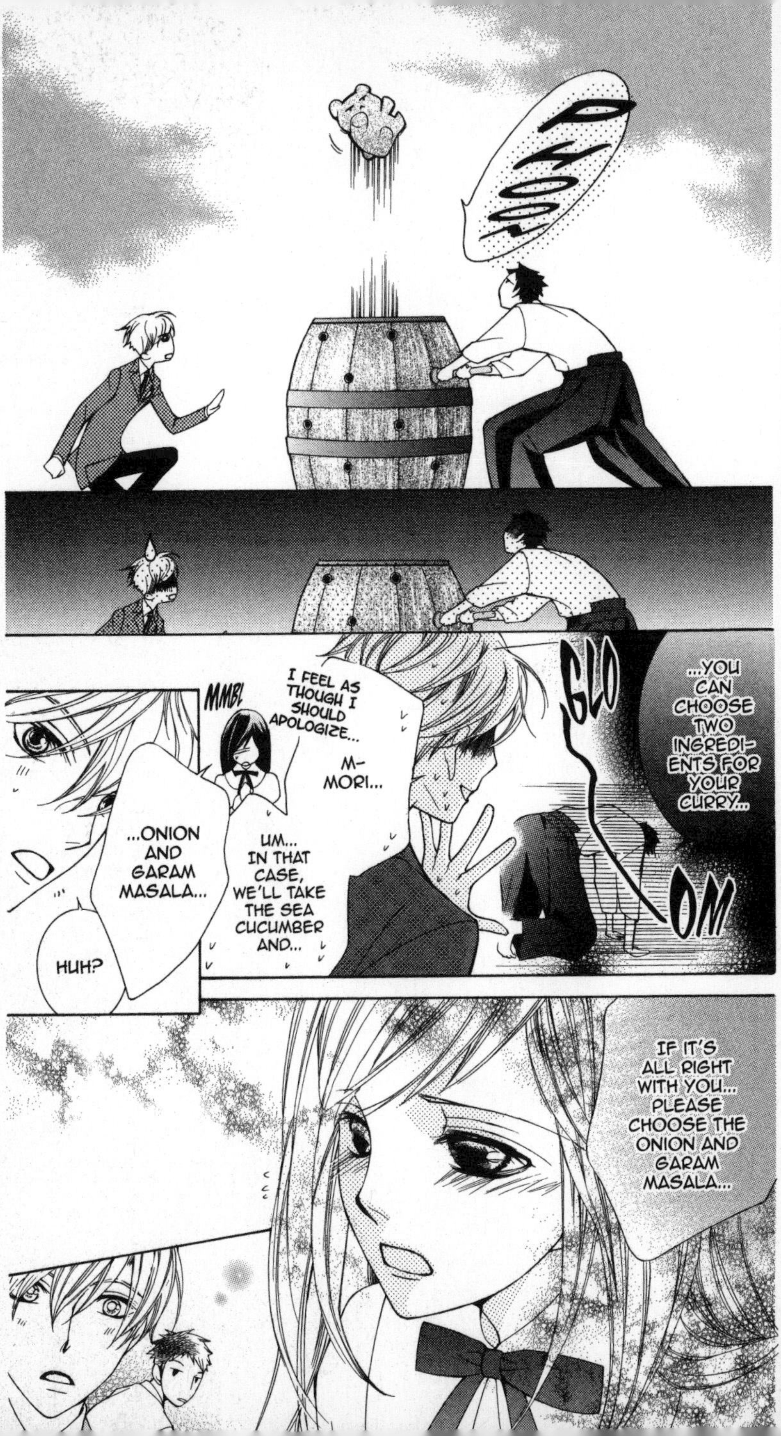
PHOOF
...YOU CAN CHOOSE TWO INGREDI-ENTS FOR YOUR CURRY...
GLOOM
M-MORI...
MMBL
I FEEL AS THOUGH I SHOULD APOLOGIZE...
UM... IN THAT CASE, WE'LL TAKE THE SEA CUCUMBER AND...
...ONION AND GARAM MASALA...
HUH?
IF IT'S ALL RIGHT WITH YOU... PLEASE CHOOSE THE ONION AND GARAM MASALA...

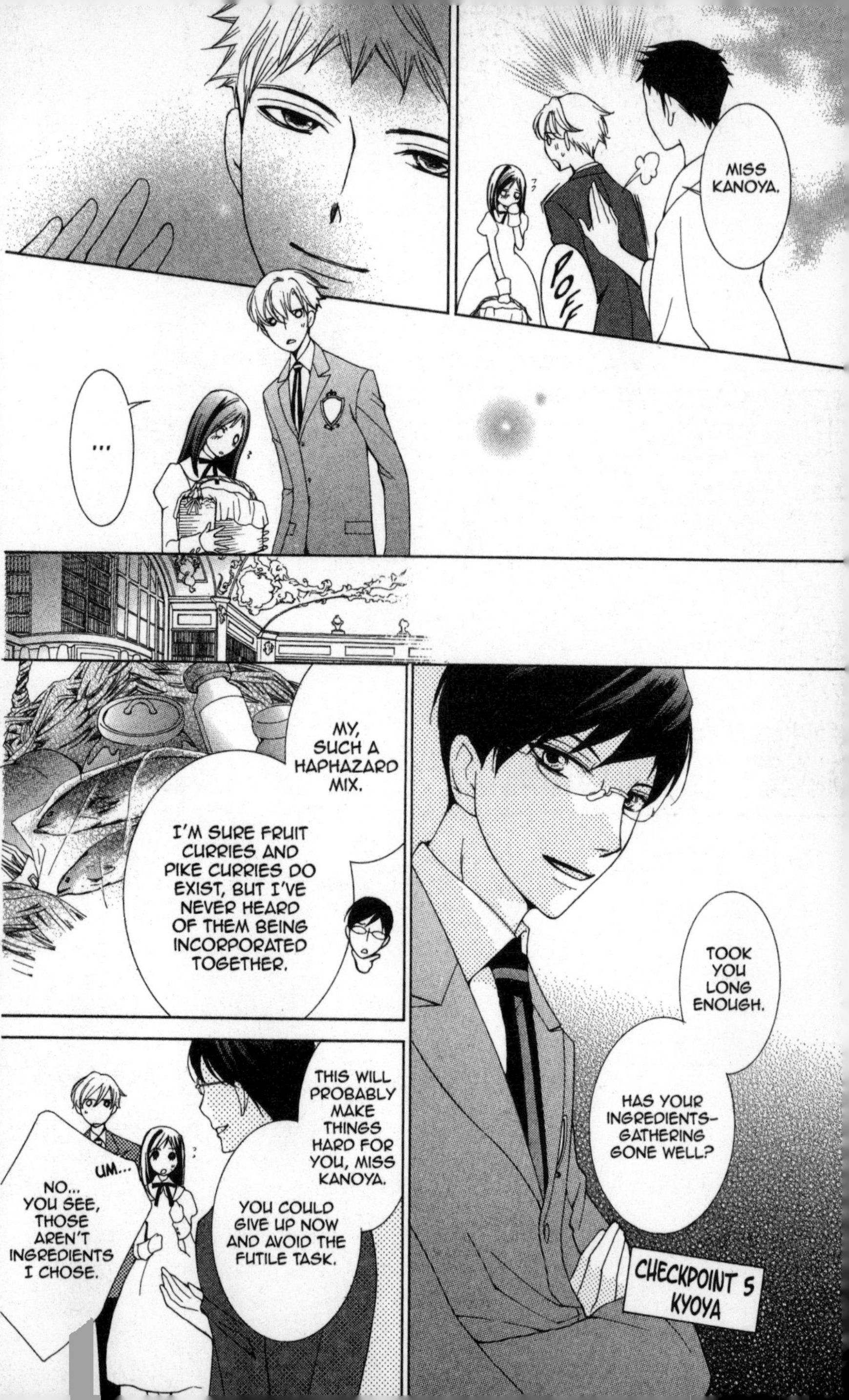
MISS KANOYA.
POFF
...
TOOK YOU LONG ENOUGH.
HAS YOUR INGREDIENTS-GATHERING GONE WELL?
CHECKPOINT 5 KYOYA
MY, SUCH A HAPHAZARD MIX.
I'M SURE FRUIT CURRIES AND PIKE CURRIES DO EXIST, BUT I'VE NEVER HEARD OF THEM BEING INCORPORATED TOGETHER.
THIS WILL PROBABLY MAKE THINGS HARD FOR YOU, MISS KANOYA.
YOU COULD GIVE UP NOW AND AVOID THE FUTILE TASK.
UM...
NO... YOU SEE, THOSE AREN'T INGREDIENTS I CHOSE.

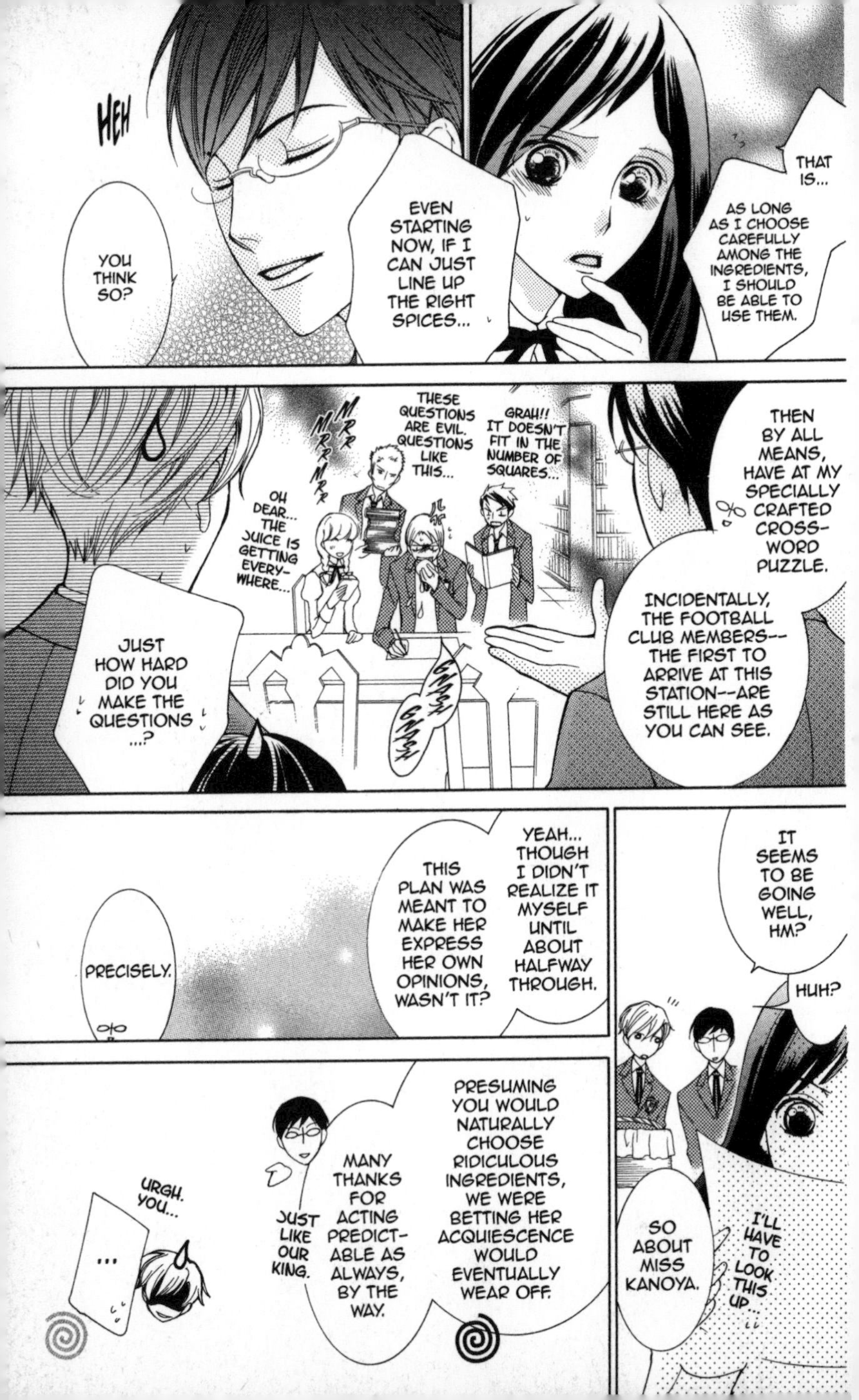
THAT IS...
AS LONG AS I CHOOSE CAREFULLY AMONG THE INGREDIENTS, I SHOULD BE ABLE TO USE THEM.
EVEN STARTING NOW, IF I CAN JUST LINE UP THE RIGHT SPICES...
HEH
YOU THINK SO?
THEN BY ALL MEANS, HAVE AT MY SPECIALLY CRAFTED CROSSWORD PUZZLE.
INCIDENTALLY, THE FOOTBALL CLUB MEMBERS--THE FIRST TO ARRIVE AT THIS STATION--ARE STILL HERE AS YOU CAN SEE.
GRAH!! IT DOESN'T FIT IN THE NUMBER OF SQUARES...
THESE QUESTIONS ARE EVIL. QUESTIONS LIKE THIS...
MRR MRR MRR
OH DEAR... THE JUICE IS GETTING EVERYWHERE...
GNASH GNASH
JUST HOW HARD DID YOU MAKE THE QUESTIONS ...?
IT SEEMS TO BE GOING WELL, HM?
HUH?
I'LL HAVE TO LOOK THIS UP...
SO ABOUT MISS KANOYA.
YEAH... THOUGH I DIDN'T REALIZE IT MYSELF UNTIL ABOUT HALFWAY THROUGH.
THIS PLAN WAS MEANT TO MAKE HER EXPRESS HER OWN OPINIONS, WASN'T IT?
PRECISELY.
PRESUMING YOU WOULD NATURALLY CHOOSE RIDICULOUS INGREDIENTS, WE WERE BETTING HER ACQUIESCENCE WOULD EVENTUALLY WEAR OFF.
MANY THANKS FOR ACTING PREDICTABLE AS ALWAYS, BY THE WAY.
JUST LIKE OUR KING.
URGH. YOU...
...

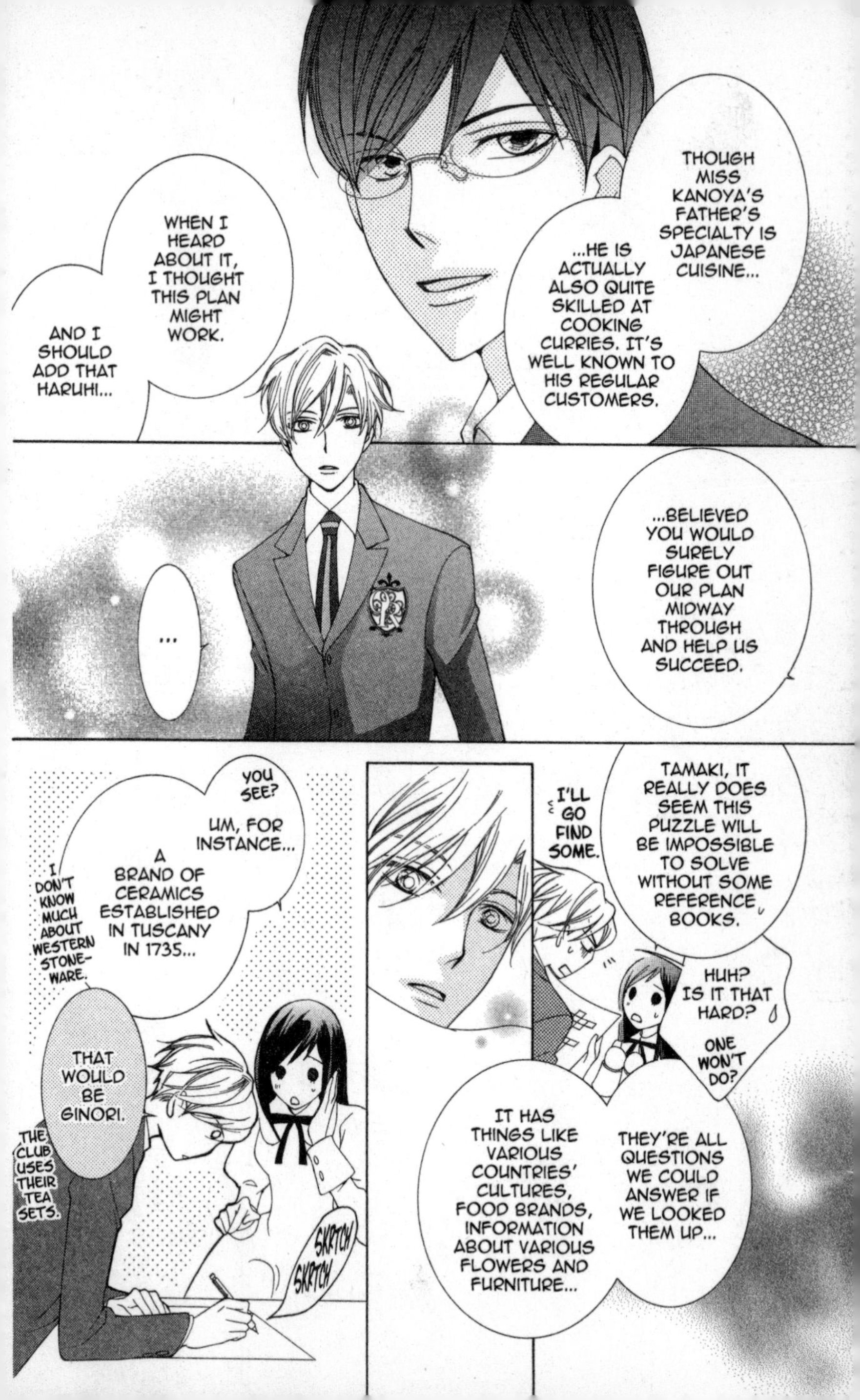
THOUGH MISS KANOYA'S FATHER'S SPECIALTY IS JAPANESE CUISINE...
...HE IS ACTUALLY ALSO QUITE SKILLED AT COOKING CURRIES. IT'S WELL KNOWN TO HIS REGULAR CUSTOMERS.
WHEN I HEARD ABOUT IT, I THOUGHT THIS PLAN MIGHT WORK.
AND I SHOULD ADD THAT HARUHI...
...BELIEVED YOU WOULD SURELY FIGURE OUT OUR PLAN MIDWAY THROUGH AND HELP US SUCCEED.
...
TAMAKI, IT REALLY DOES SEEM THIS PUZZLE WILL BE IMPOSSIBLE TO SOLVE WITHOUT SOME REFERENCE BOOKS.
I'LL GO FIND SOME.
HUH? IS IT THAT HARD?
ONE WON'T DO?
THEY'RE ALL QUESTIONS WE COULD ANSWER IF WE LOOKED THEM UP...
IT HAS THINGS LIKE VARIOUS COUNTRIES' CULTURES, FOOD BRANDS, INFORMATION ABOUT VARIOUS FLOWERS AND FURNITURE...
YOU SEE?
UM, FOR INSTANCE...
A BRAND OF CERAMICS ESTABLISHED IN TUSCANY IN 1735...
I DON'T KNOW MUCH ABOUT WESTERN STONE-WARE.
THAT WOULD BE GINORI.
THE CLUB USES THEIR TEA SETS.
SKRTCH SKRTCH

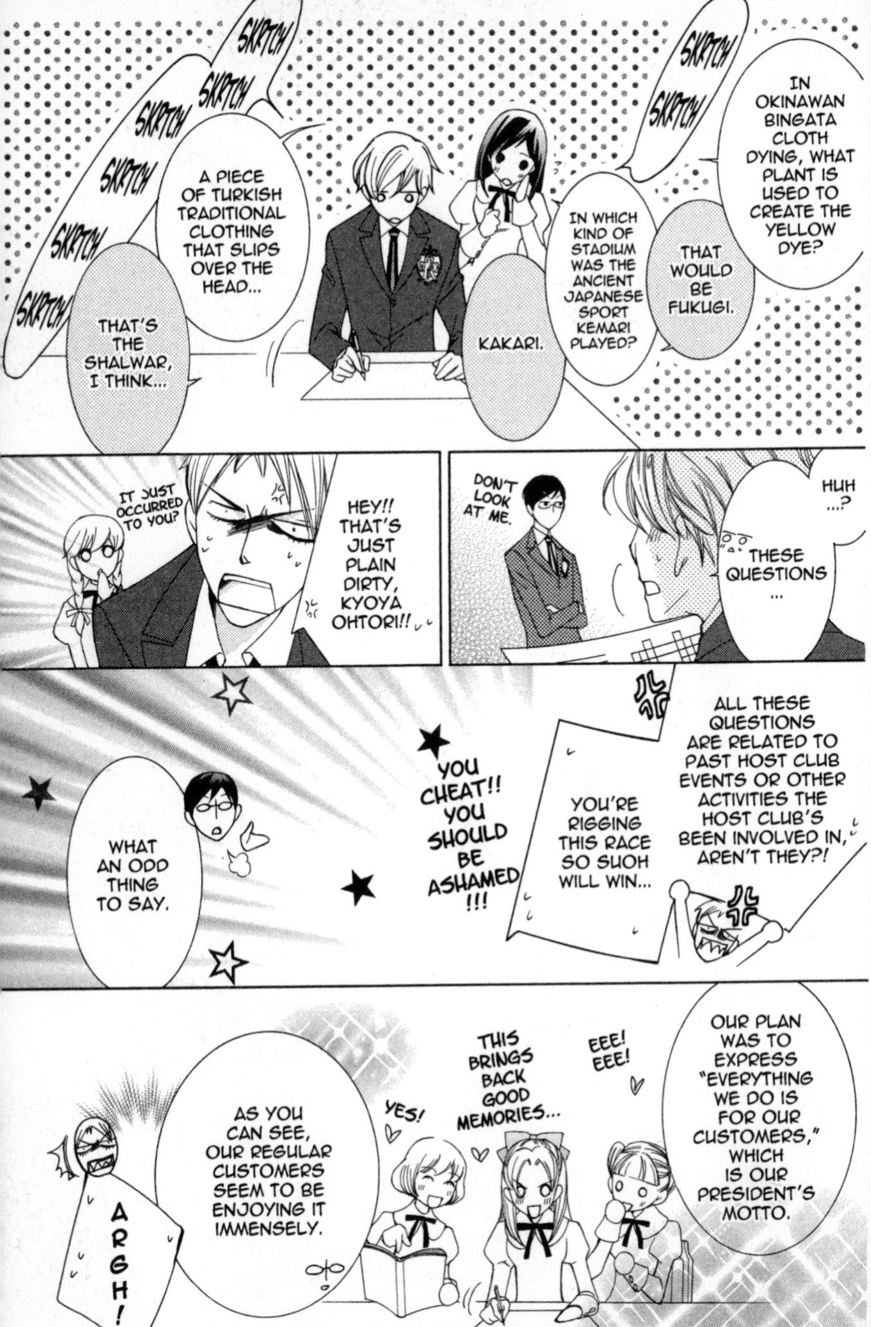
SKRTCH
SKRTCH
IN OKINAWAN BINGATA CLOTH DYING, WHAT PLANT IS USED TO CREATE THE YELLOW DYE?
THAT WOULD BE FUKUGI.
IN WHICH KIND OF STADIUM WAS THE ANCIENT JAPANESE SPORT KEMARI PLAYED?
KAKARI.
SKRTCH
SKRTCH
SKRTCH
SKRTCH
SKRTCH
SKRTCH
A PIECE OF TURKISH TRADITIONAL CLOTHING THAT SLIPS OVER THE HEAD...
THAT'S THE SHALWAR, I THINK...
HUH ...?
THESE QUESTIONS ...
DON'T LOOK AT ME.
HEY!! THAT'S JUST PLAIN DIRTY, KYOYA OHTORI!!
IT JUST OCCURRED TO YOU?
ALL THESE QUESTIONS ARE RELATED TO PAST HOST CLUB EVENTS OR OTHER ACTIVITIES THE HOST CLUB'S BEEN INVOLVED IN, AREN'T THEY?!
YOU'RE RIGGING THIS RACE SO SUOH WILL WIN...
YOU CHEAT!! YOU SHOULD BE ASHAMED!!!
WHAT AN ODD THING TO SAY.
OUR PLAN WAS TO EXPRESS "EVERYTHING WE DO IS FOR OUR CUSTOMERS," WHICH IS OUR PRESIDENT'S MOTTO.
EEE! EEE!
THIS BRINGS BACK GOOD MEMORIES...
YES!
AS YOU CAN SEE, OUR REGULAR CUSTOMERS SEEM TO BE ENJOYING IT IMMENSELY.
ARGH!

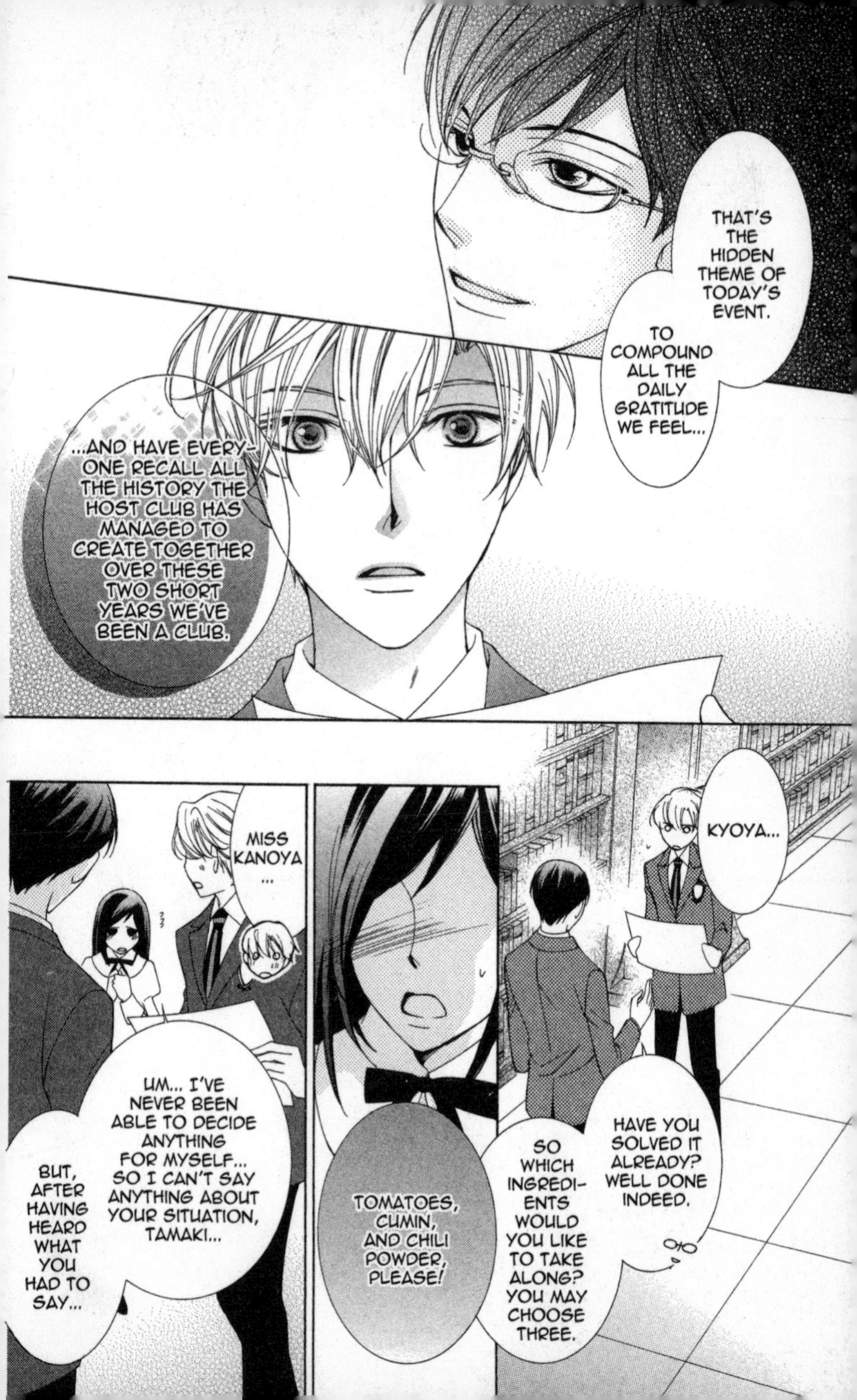
THAT'S THE HIDDEN THEME OF TODAY'S EVENT.
TO COMPOUND ALL THE DAILY GRATITUDE WE FEEL...
...AND HAVE EVERY-ONE RECALL ALL THE HISTORY THE HOST CLUB HAS MANAGED TO CREATE TOGETHER OVER THESE TWO SHORT YEARS WE'VE BEEN A CLUB.
KYOYA...
HAVE YOU SOLVED IT ALREADY? WELL DONE INDEED.
SO WHICH INGREDI-ENTS WOULD YOU LIKE TO TAKE ALONG? YOU MAY CHOOSE THREE.
TOMATOES, CUMIN, AND CHILI POWDER, PLEASE!
MISS KANOYA ...
UM... I'VE NEVER BEEN ABLE TO DECIDE ANYTHING FOR MYSELF... SO I CAN'T SAY ANYTHING ABOUT YOUR SITUATION, TAMAKI...
BUT, AFTER HAVING HEARD WHAT YOU HAD TO SAY...

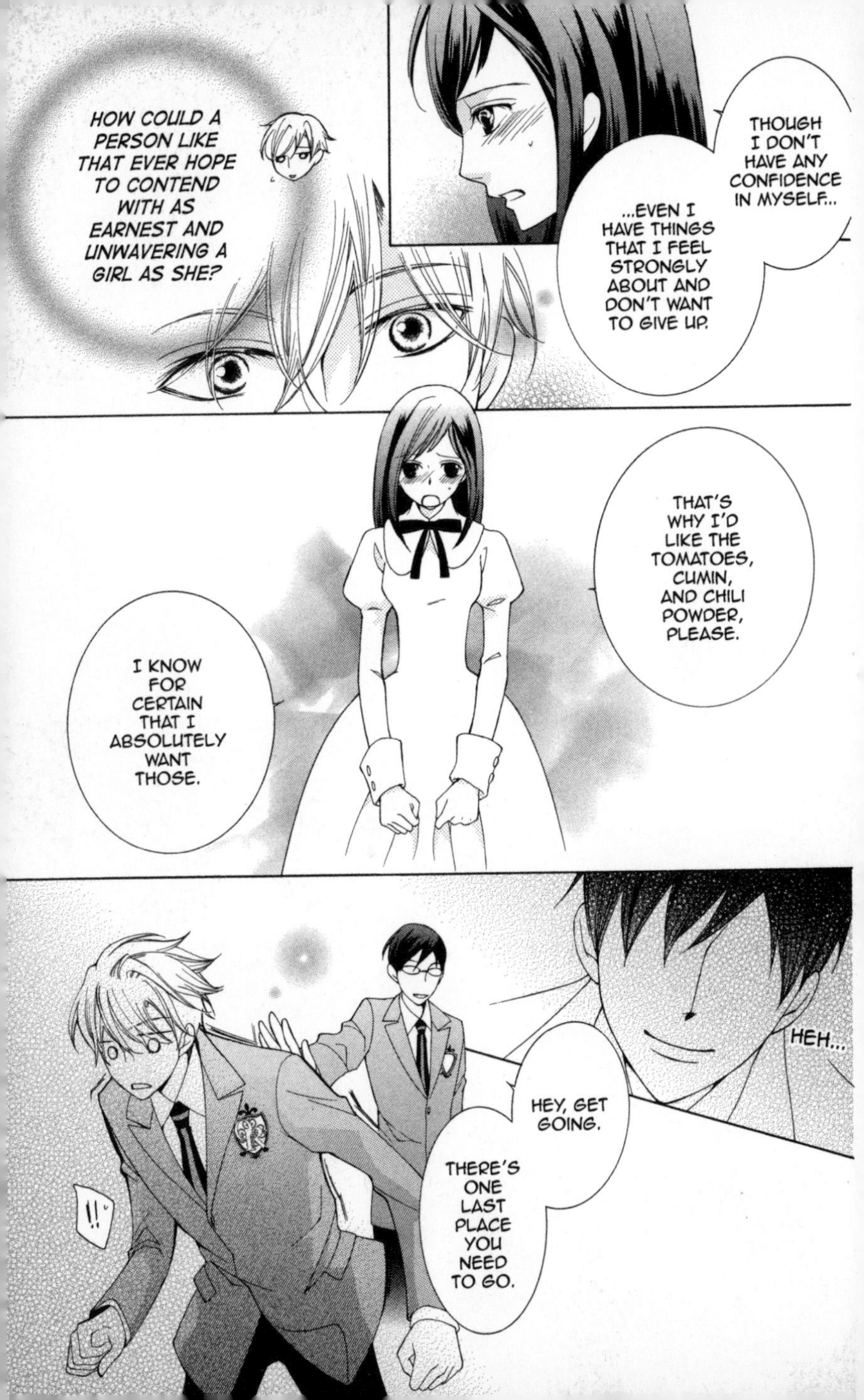
THOUGH I DON'T HAVE ANY CONFIDENCE IN MYSELF...
...EVEN I HAVE THINGS THAT I FEEL STRONGLY ABOUT AND DON'T WANT TO GIVE UP.
HOW COULD A PERSON LIKE THAT EVER HOPE TO CONTEND WITH AS EARNEST AND UNWAVERING A GIRL AS SHE?
THAT'S WHY I'D LIKE THE TOMATOES, CUMIN, AND CHILI POWDER, PLEASE.
I KNOW FOR CERTAIN THAT I ABSOLUTELY WANT THOSE.
HEH...
HEY, GET GOING.
THERE'S ONE LAST PLACE YOU NEED TO GO.
!!

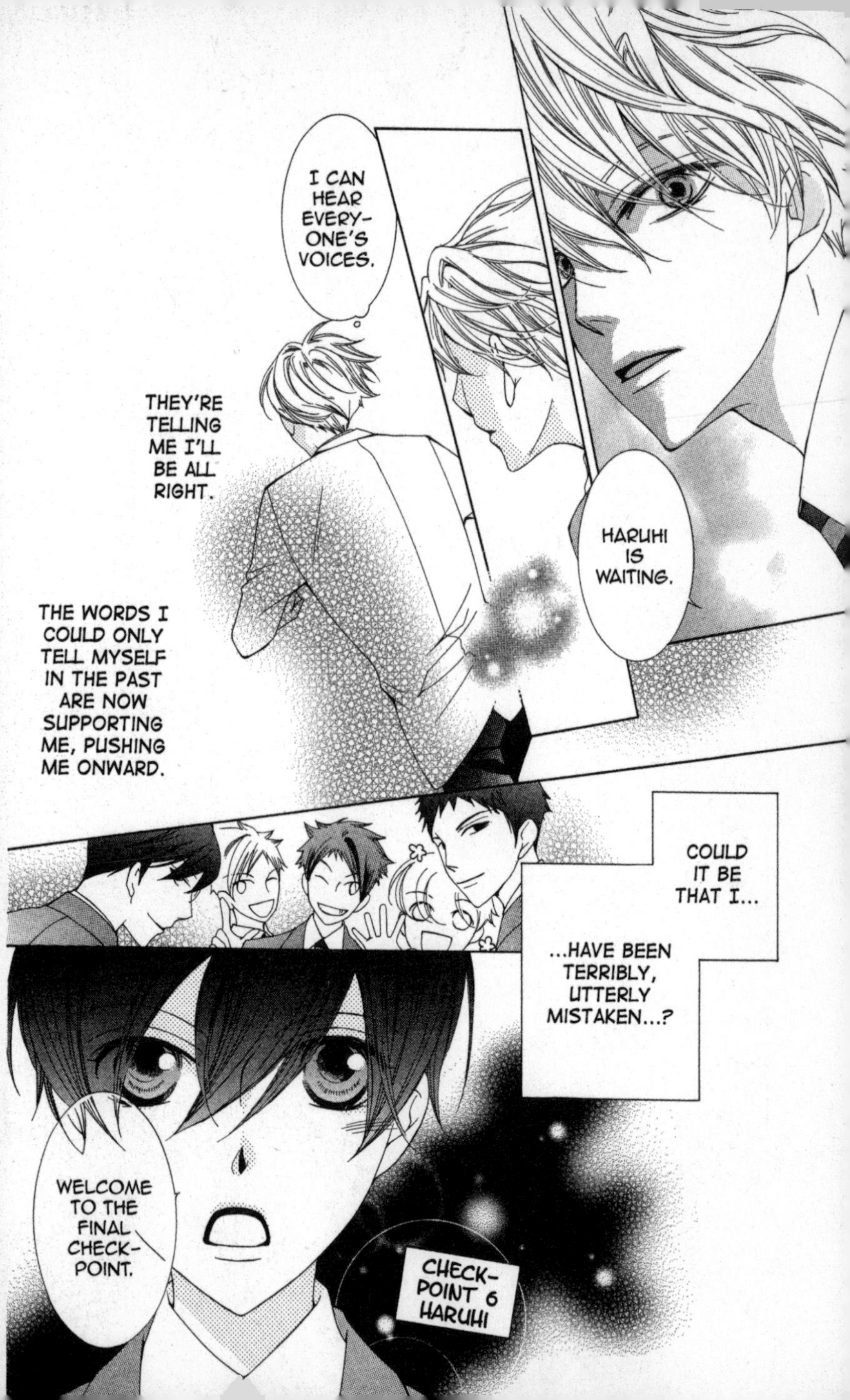
HARUHI IS WAITING.
I CAN HEAR EVERYONE'S VOICES.
THEY'RE TELLING ME I'LL BE ALL RIGHT.
THE WORDS I COULD ONLY TELL MYSELF IN THE PAST ARE NOW SUPPORTING ME, PUSHING ME ONWARD.
COULD IT BE THAT I...
...HAVE BEEN TERRIBLY, UTTERLY MISTAKEN...?
WELCOME TO THE FINAL CHECK-POINT.
CHECK-POINT 6 HARUHI

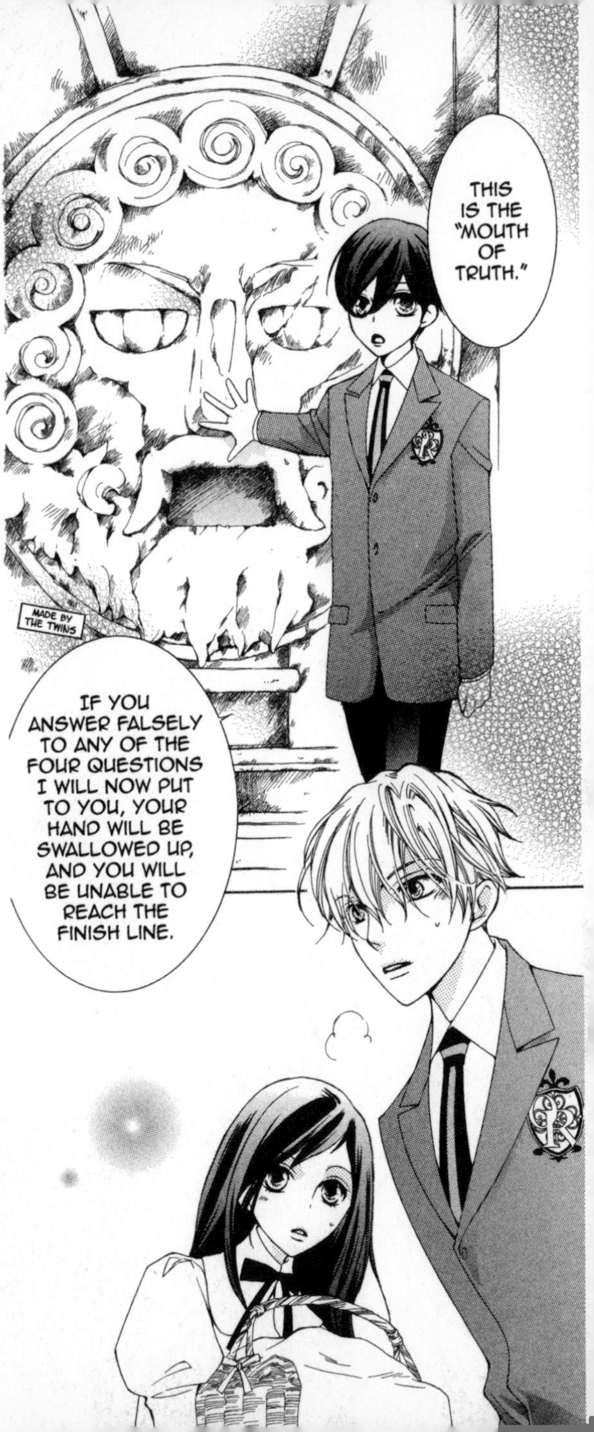
THIS IS THE "MOUTH OF TRUTH."
MADE BY THE TWINS
IF YOU ANSWER FALSELY TO ANY OF THE FOUR QUESTIONS I WILL NOW PUT TO YOU, YOUR HAND WILL BE SWALLOWED UP, AND YOU WILL BE UNABLE TO REACH THE FINISH LINE.

Speaking of Names ①

Recently there was this incident. On a certain day this past August, I went to see a play adaptation of *Glass Mask* and the following happened when I went with everyone to have dinner afterwards.

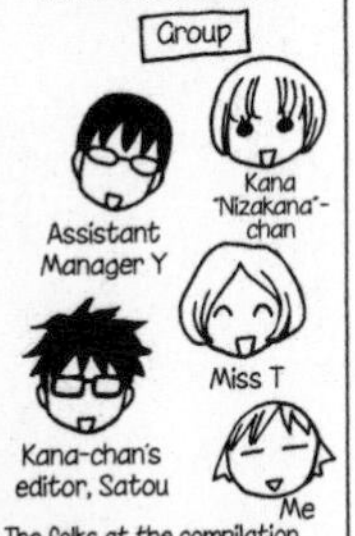
Group
Assistant Manager Y
Kana "Nizakana"-chan
Miss T
Kana-chan's editor, Satou
Me

The folks at the compilation office brought me along. ❤

It was a very nice Italian restaurant. We were at a table on the terrace where we could take in the lovely nighttime scenery. Our discussion of the play continued passionately all through the meal until we were waiting for dessert. Then...

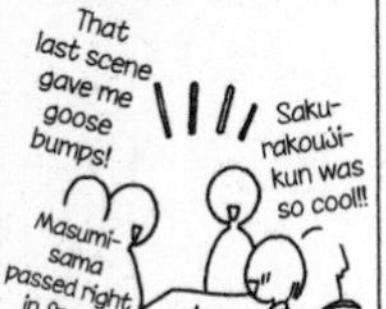
That last scene gave me goose bumps!
Sakurakouji-kun was so cool!!
Masumi-sama passed right in front of me!!

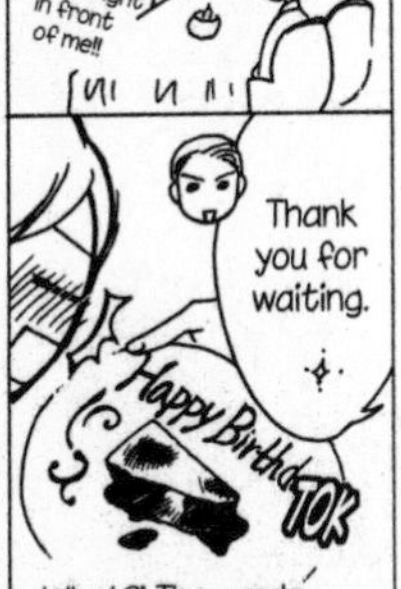
Thank you for waiting.
Happy Birthd
TOK

What?! The words "Happy Birthday" had been written in chocolate on my plate!!

Hatori's birthday is in August.

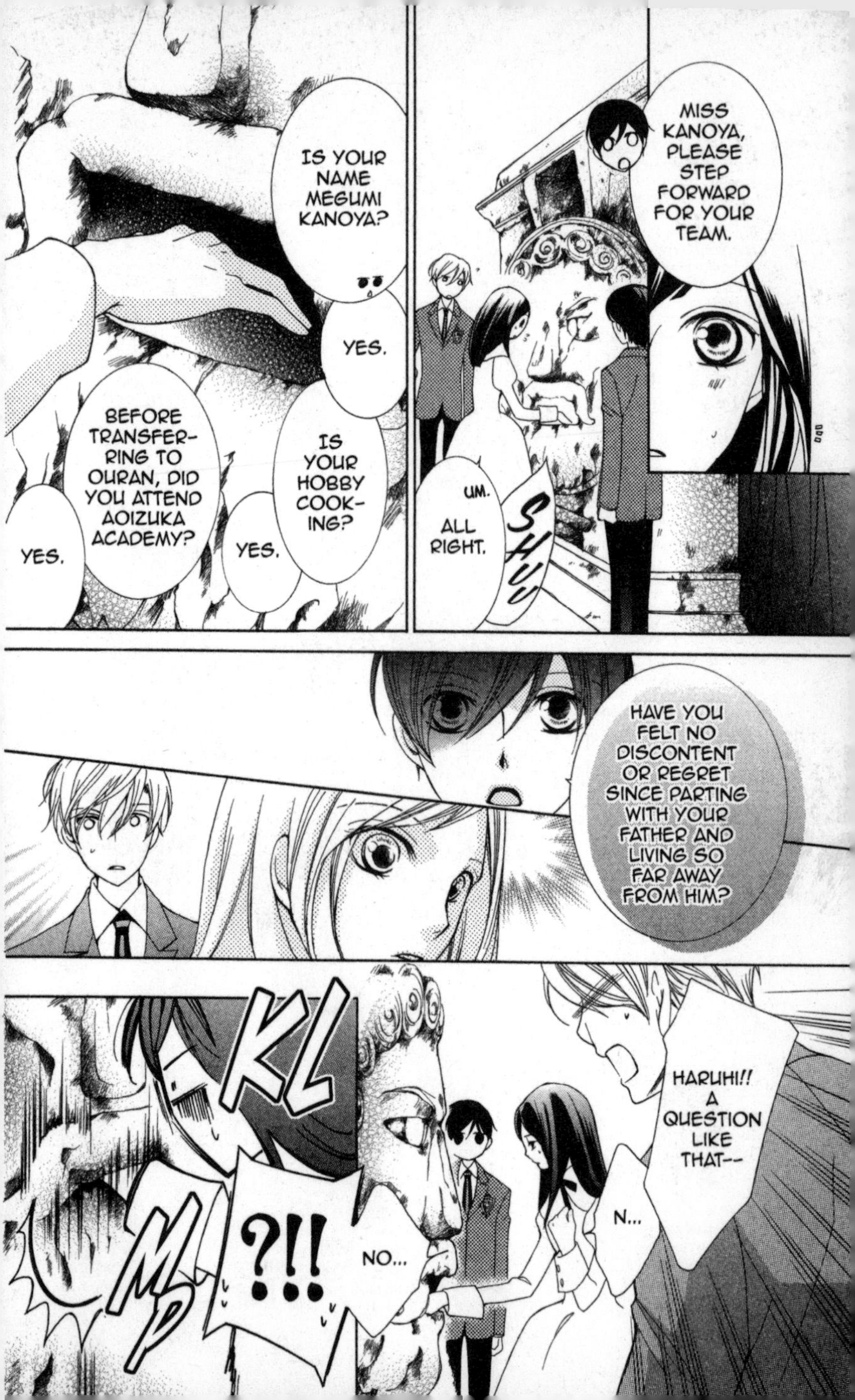
MISS KANOYA, PLEASE STEP FORWARD FOR YOUR TEAM.
UM.
ALL RIGHT.
SHUU
IS YOUR NAME MEGUMI KANOYA?
YES.
IS YOUR HOBBY COOK-ING?
YES.
BEFORE TRANSFER-RING TO OURAN, DID YOU ATTEND AOIZUKA ACADEMY?
YES.
HAVE YOU FELT NO DISCONTENT OR REGRET SINCE PARTING WITH YOUR FATHER AND LIVING SO FAR AWAY FROM HIM?
HARUHI!! A QUESTION LIKE THAT--
N...
NO...
?!!
KL
MP

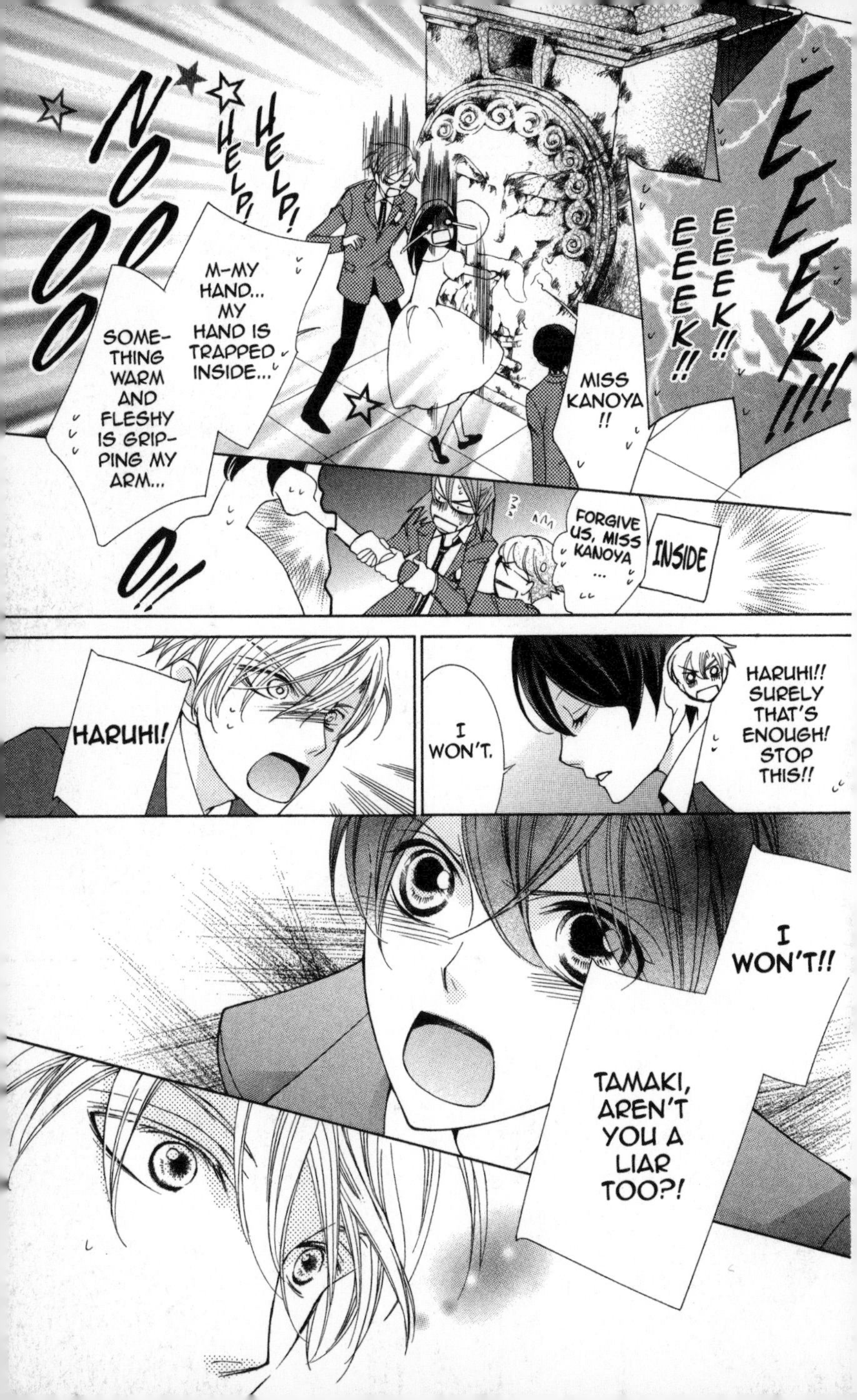
EEEEK!!!
EEEK!!
EEEK!!
MISS KANOYA!!
HELP! HELP!
M-MY HAND... MY HAND IS TRAPPED INSIDE...
NOOOOOO!!
SOME-THING WARM AND FLESHY IS GRIP-PING MY ARM...
INSIDE
FORGIVE US, MISS KANOYA...
HARUHI!! SURELY THAT'S ENOUGH! STOP THIS!!
I WON'T.
HARUHI!
I WON'T!!
TAMAKI, AREN'T YOU A LIAR TOO?!

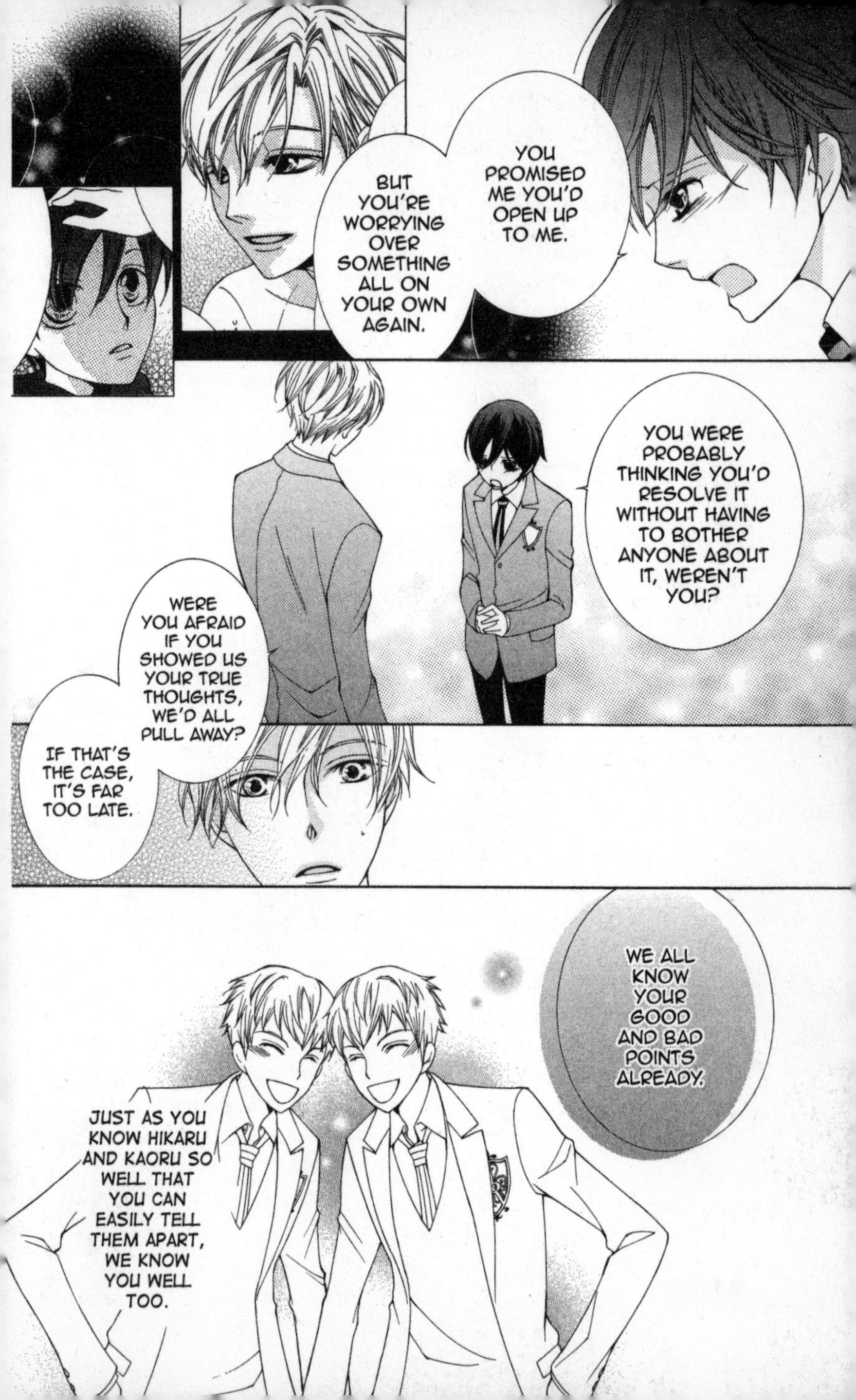
YOU PROMISED ME YOU'D OPEN UP TO ME.
BUT YOU'RE WORRYING OVER SOMETHING ALL ON YOUR OWN AGAIN.
YOU WERE PROBABLY THINKING YOU'D RESOLVE IT WITHOUT HAVING TO BOTHER ANYONE ABOUT IT, WEREN'T YOU?
WERE YOU AFRAID IF YOU SHOWED US YOUR TRUE THOUGHTS, WE'D ALL PULL AWAY?
IF THAT'S THE CASE, IT'S FAR TOO LATE.
WE ALL KNOW YOUR GOOD AND BAD POINTS ALREADY.
JUST AS YOU KNOW HIKARU AND KAORU SO WELL THAT YOU CAN EASILY TELL THEM APART, WE KNOW YOU WELL TOO.

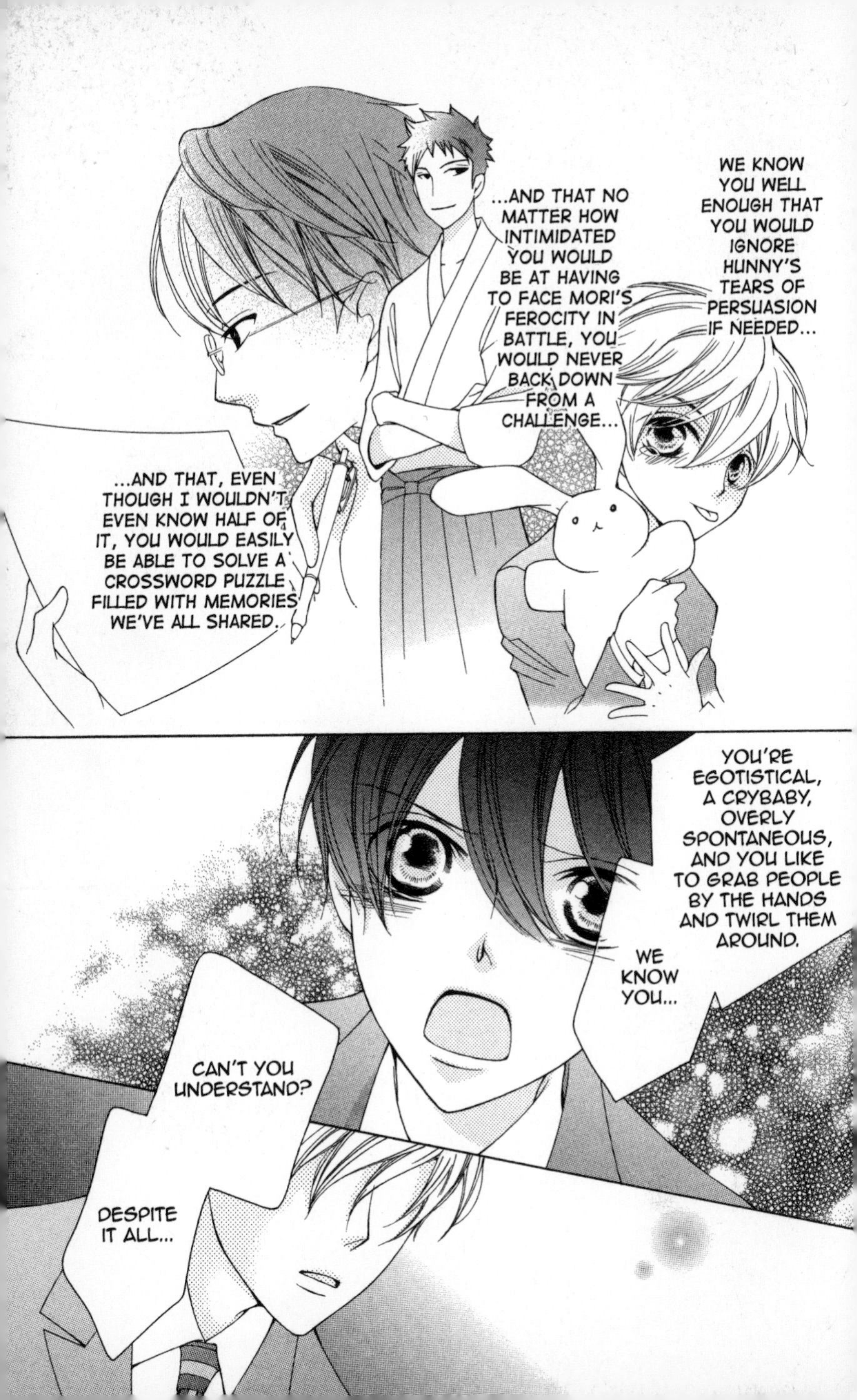
WE KNOW YOU WELL ENOUGH THAT YOU WOULD IGNORE HUNNY'S TEARS OF PERSUASION IF NEEDED...
...AND THAT NO MATTER HOW INTIMIDATED YOU WOULD BE AT HAVING TO FACE MORI'S FEROCITY IN BATTLE, YOU WOULD NEVER BACK DOWN FROM A CHALLENGE...
...AND THAT, EVEN THOUGH I WOULDN'T EVEN KNOW HALF OF IT, YOU WOULD EASILY BE ABLE TO SOLVE A CROSSWORD PUZZLE FILLED WITH MEMORIES WE'VE ALL SHARED.
YOU'RE EGOTISTICAL, A CRYBABY, OVERLY SPONTANEOUS, AND YOU LIKE TO GRAB PEOPLE BY THE HANDS AND TWIRL THEM AROUND.
WE KNOW YOU...
CAN'T YOU UNDERSTAND?
DESPITE IT ALL...

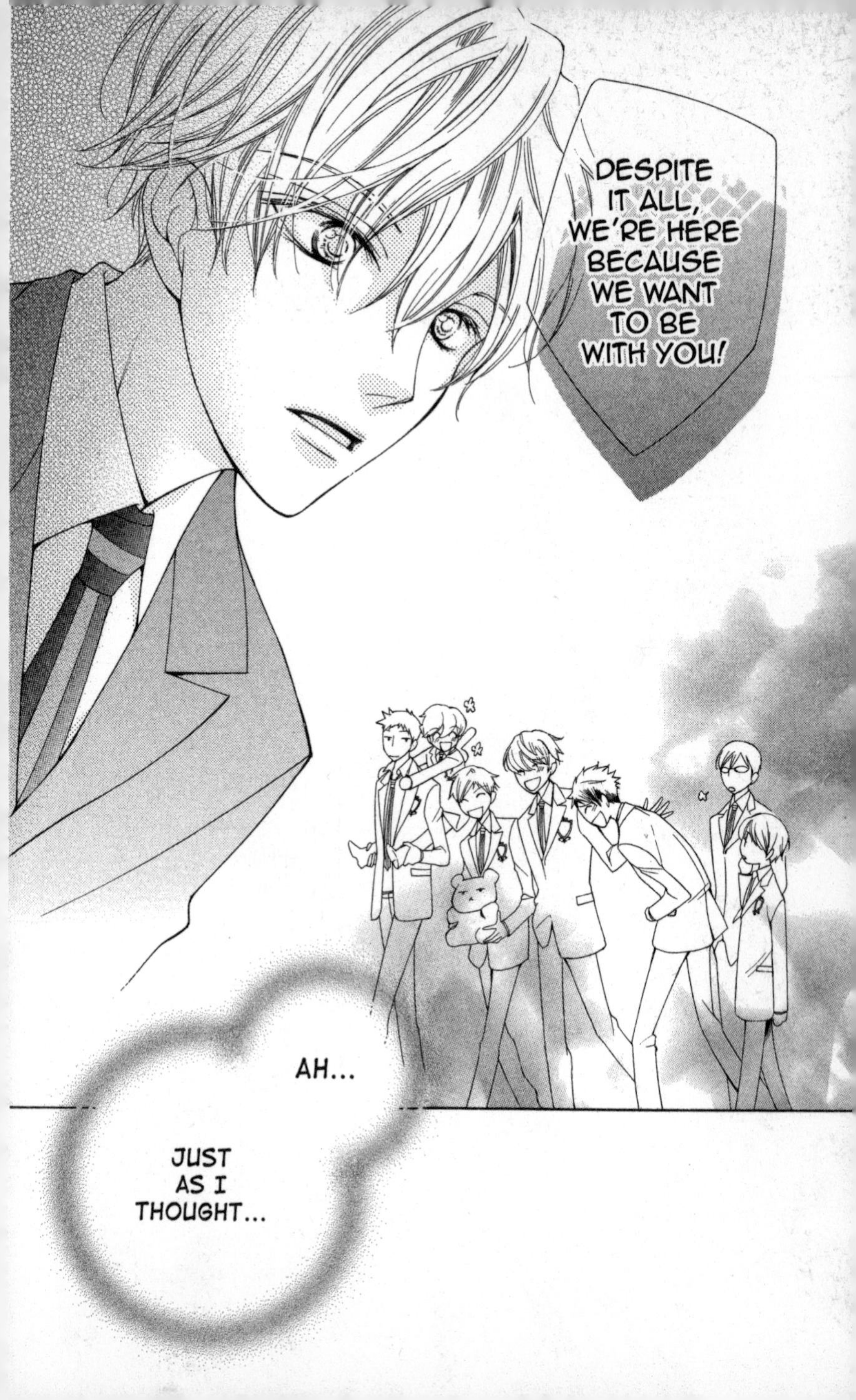
DESPITE IT ALL, WE'RE HERE BECAUSE WE WANT TO BE WITH YOU!
AH...
JUST AS I THOUGHT...

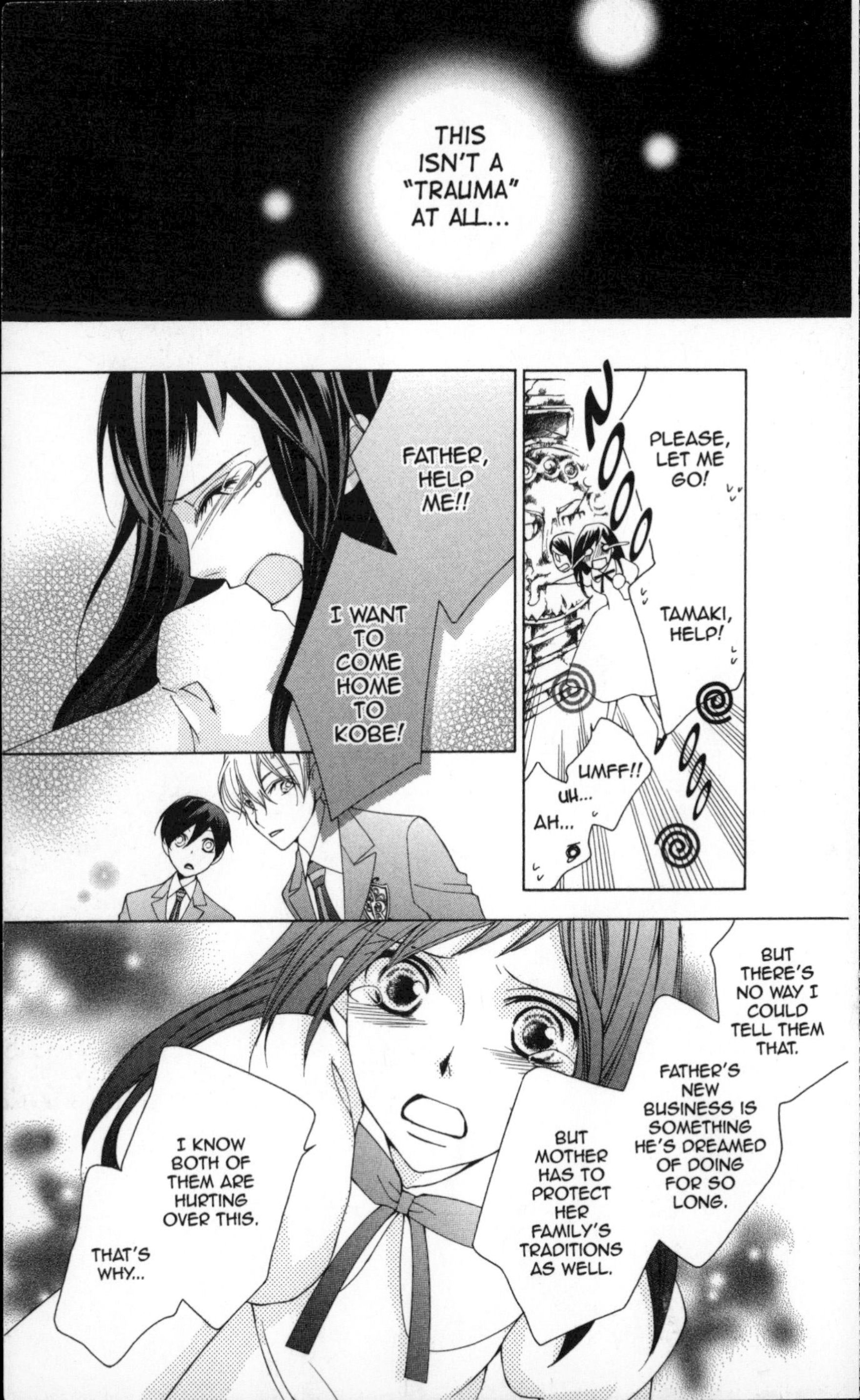
THIS ISN'T A "TRAUMA" AT ALL...
NOOOO
PLEASE, LET ME GO!
TAMAKI, HELP!
UMFF!!
UH...
AH...
FATHER, HELP ME!!
I WANT TO COME HOME TO KOBE!
BUT THERE'S NO WAY I COULD TELL THEM THAT.
FATHER'S NEW BUSINESS IS SOMETHING HE'S DREAMED OF DOING FOR SO LONG.
BUT MOTHER HAS TO PROTECT HER FAMILY'S TRADITIONS AS WELL.
I KNOW BOTH OF THEM ARE HURTING OVER THIS.
THAT'S WHY...

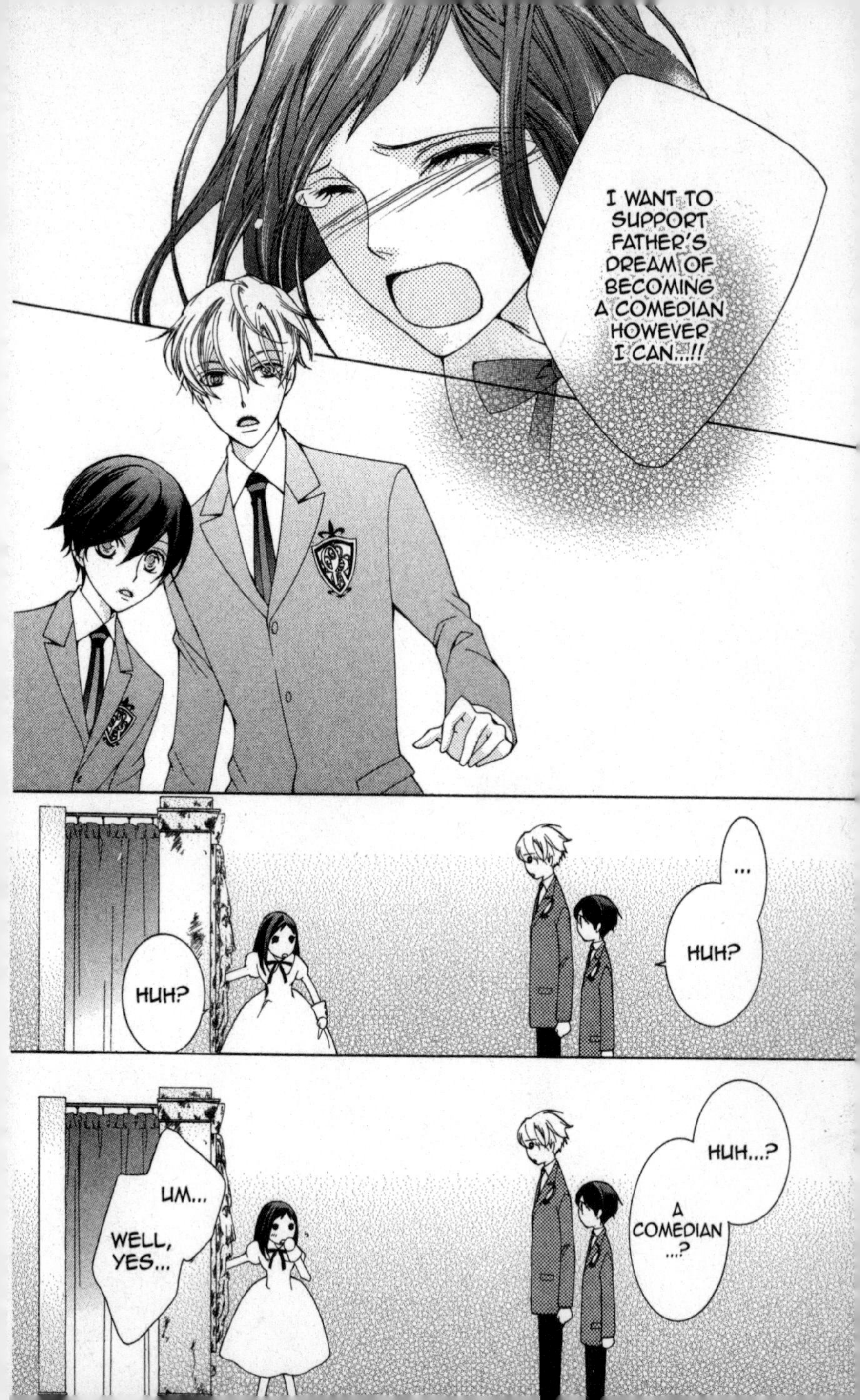
I WANT TO SUPPORT FATHER'S DREAM OF BECOMING A COMEDIAN HOWEVER I CAN...!!
... HUH?
HUH?
HUH...? A COMEDIAN ...?
UM... WELL, YES...

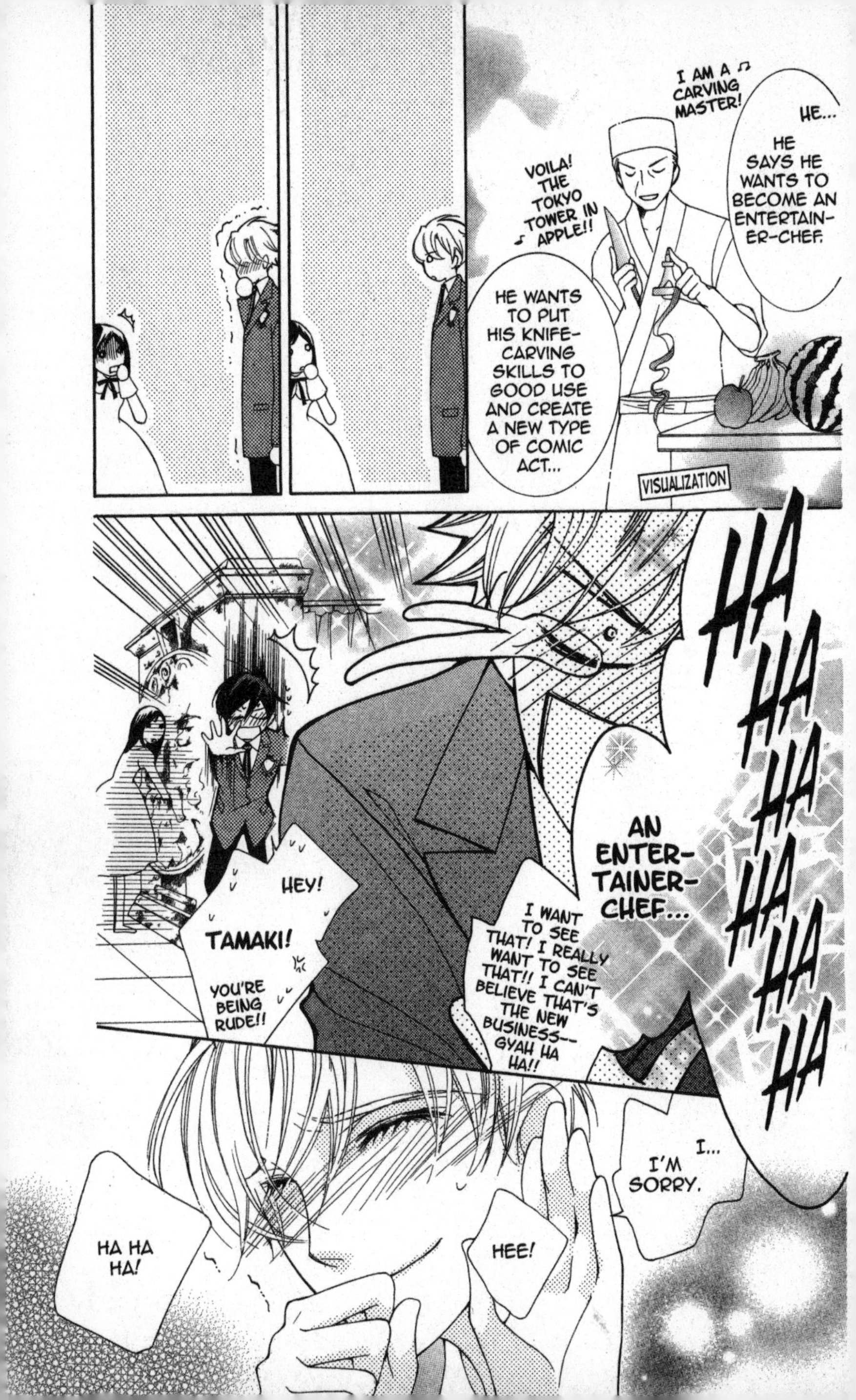
HE...
HE SAYS HE WANTS TO BECOME AN ENTERTAINER-CHEF.
I AM A CARVING MASTER! ♫
VOILA! THE TOKYO TOWER IN APPLE!! ♪
HE WANTS TO PUT HIS KNIFE-CARVING SKILLS TO GOOD USE AND CREATE A NEW TYPE OF COMIC ACT...
VISUALIZATION
HA HA HA HA HA HA HA
AN ENTER-TAINER-CHEF...
I WANT TO SEE THAT! I REALLY WANT TO SEE THAT!! I CAN'T BELIEVE THAT'S THE NEW BUSINESS-- GYAH HA HA!!
HEY!
TAMAKI!
YOU'RE BEING RUDE!!
I...
I'M SORRY.
HEE!
HA HA HA!

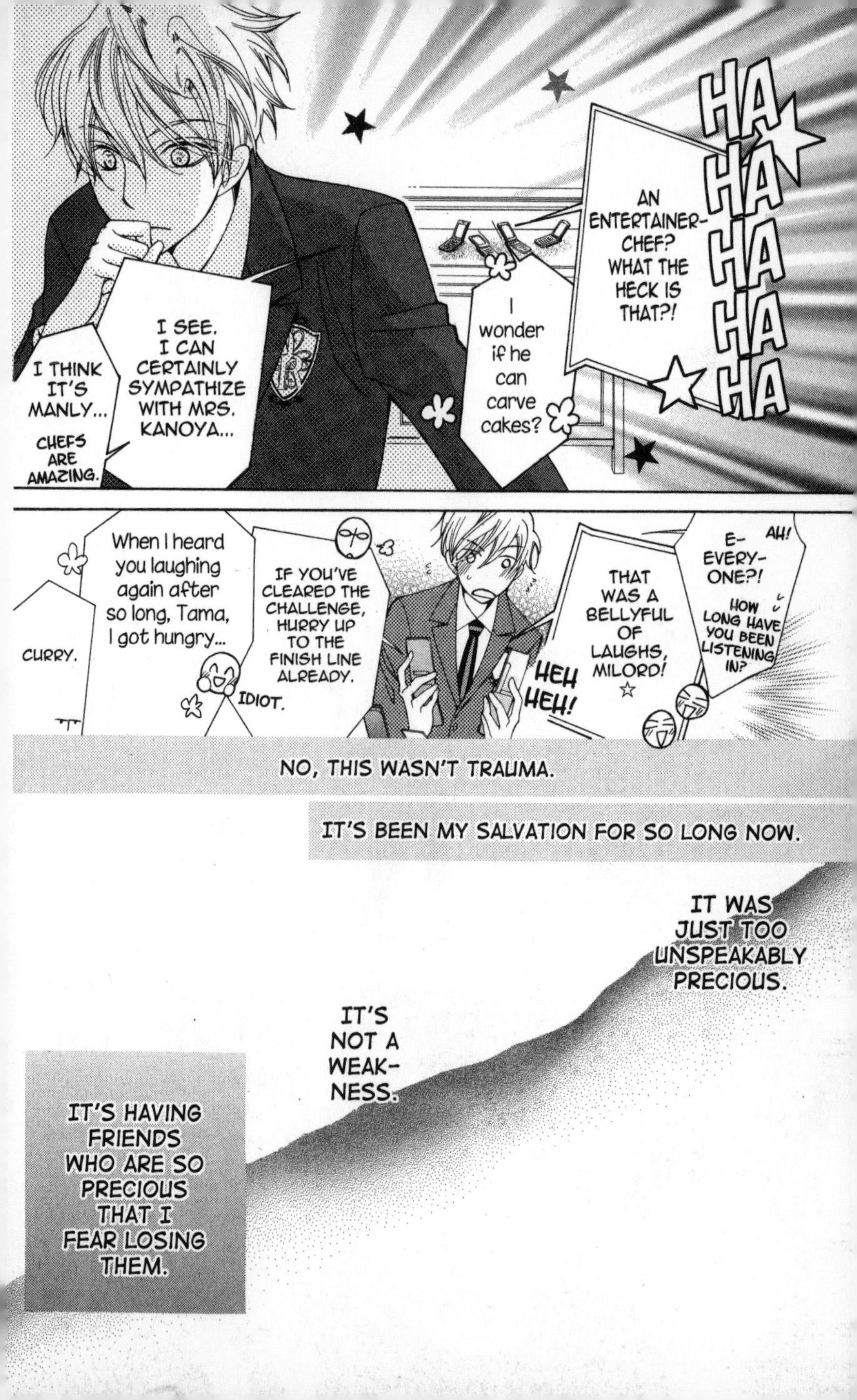
HA HA HA HA HA HA
AN ENTERTAINER-CHEF? WHAT THE HECK IS THAT?!
I wonder if he can carve cakes?
I SEE. I CAN CERTAINLY SYMPATHIZE WITH MRS. KANOYA...
I THINK IT'S MANLY...
CHEFS ARE AMAZING.
AH!
E-EVERYONE?!
HOW LONG HAVE YOU BEEN LISTENING IN?
THAT WAS A BELLYFUL OF LAUGHS, MILORD! ☆
HEH HEH!
IF YOU'VE CLEARED THE CHALLENGE, HURRY UP TO THE FINISH LINE ALREADY.
IDIOT.
When I heard you laughing again after so long, Tama, I got hungry...
CURRY.
NO, THIS WASN'T TRAUMA.
IT'S BEEN MY SALVATION FOR SO LONG NOW.
IT WAS JUST TOO UNSPEAKABLY PRECIOUS.
IT'S NOT A WEAKNESS.
IT'S HAVING FRIENDS WHO ARE SO PRECIOUS THAT I FEAR LOSING THEM.

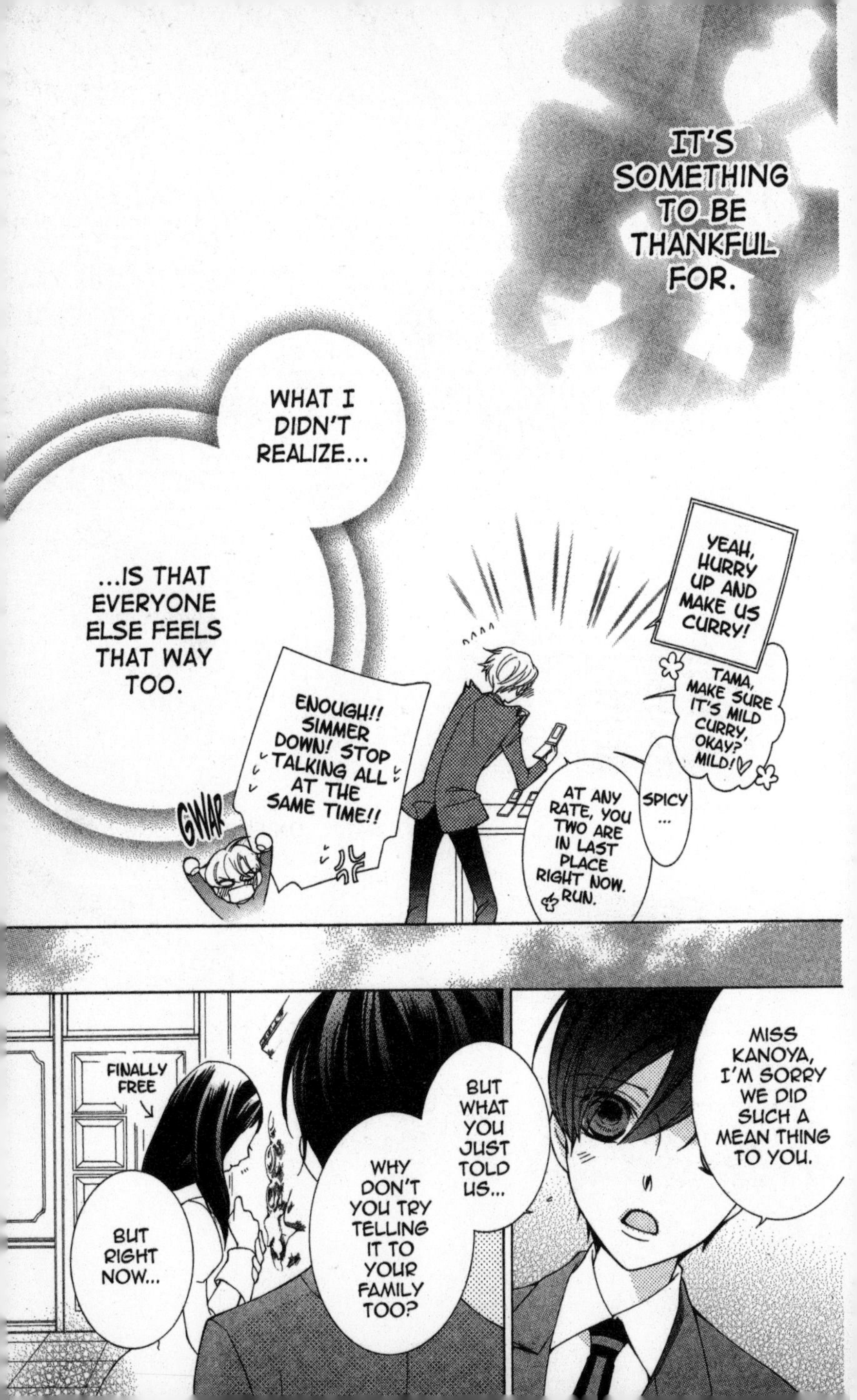
IT'S SOMETHING TO BE THANKFUL FOR.
WHAT I DIDN'T REALIZE...
...IS THAT EVERYONE ELSE FEELS THAT WAY TOO.
YEAH, HURRY UP AND MAKE US CURRY!
TAMA, MAKE SURE IT'S MILD CURRY, OKAY? MILD!
SPICY...
AT ANY RATE, YOU TWO ARE IN LAST PLACE RIGHT NOW. RUN.
ENOUGH!! SIMMER DOWN! STOP TALKING ALL AT THE SAME TIME!!
GWAR
MISS KANOYA, I'M SORRY WE DID SUCH A MEAN THING TO YOU.
BUT WHAT YOU JUST TOLD US...
WHY DON'T YOU TRY TELLING IT TO YOUR FAMILY TOO?
FINALLY FREE
BUT RIGHT NOW...

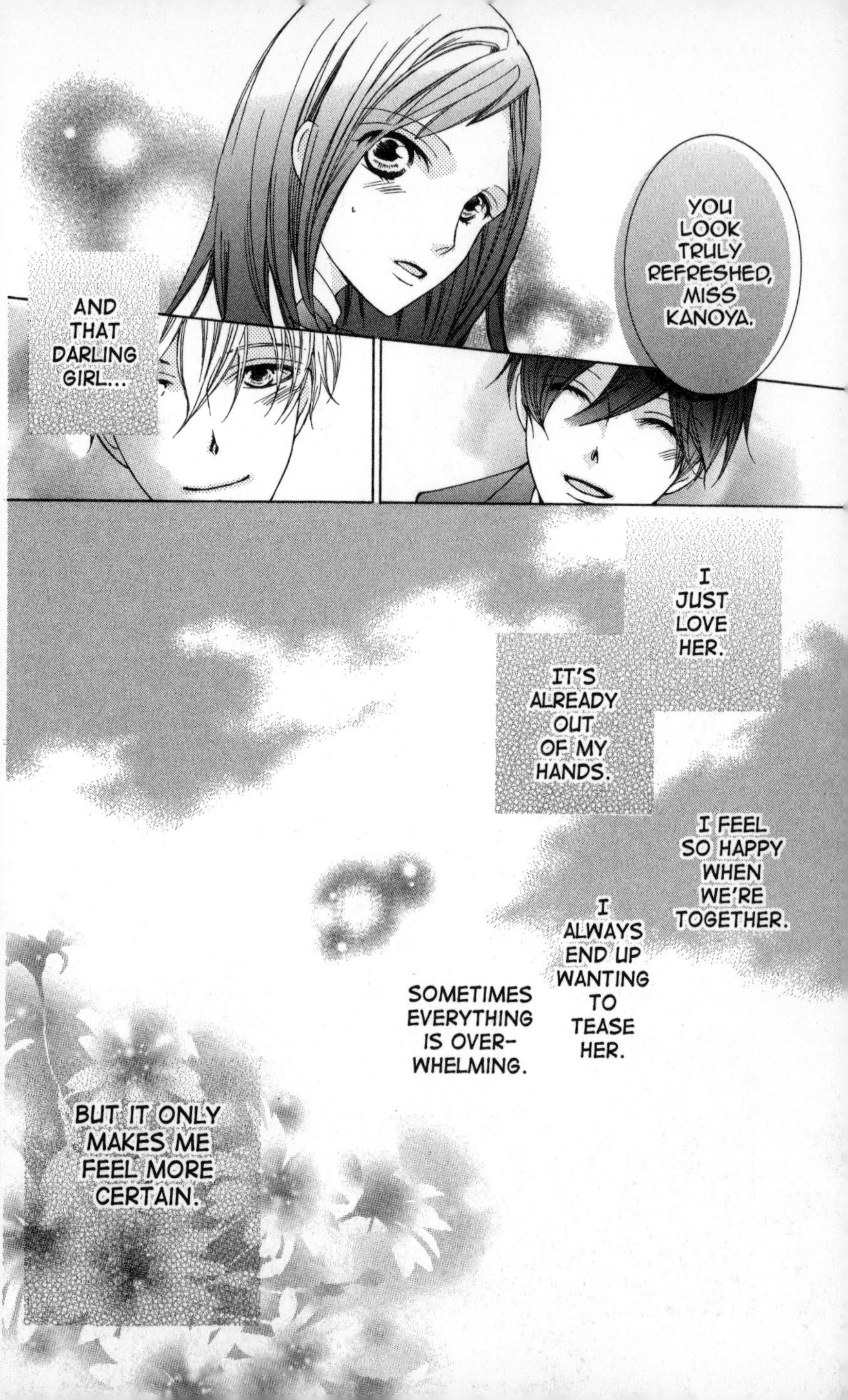
YOU LOOK TRULY REFRESHED, MISS KANOYA.
AND THAT DARLING GIRL...
I JUST LOVE HER.
IT'S ALREADY OUT OF MY HANDS.
I FEEL SO HAPPY WHEN WE'RE TOGETHER.
I ALWAYS END UP WANTING TO TEASE HER.
SOMETIMES EVERYTHING IS OVER-WHELMING.
BUT IT ONLY MAKES ME FEEL MORE CERTAIN.

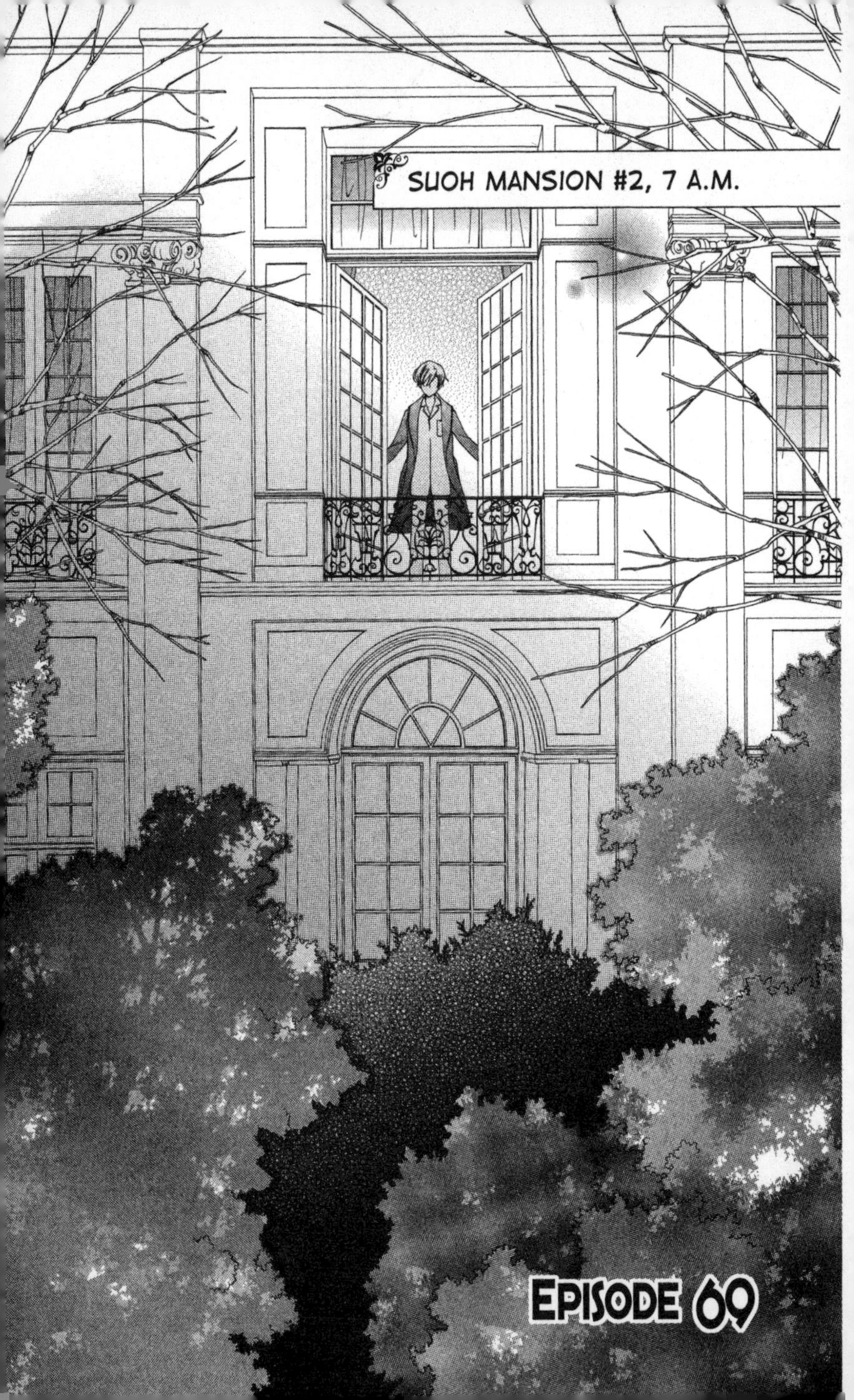
SUOH MANSION #2, 7 A.M.
EPISODE 69

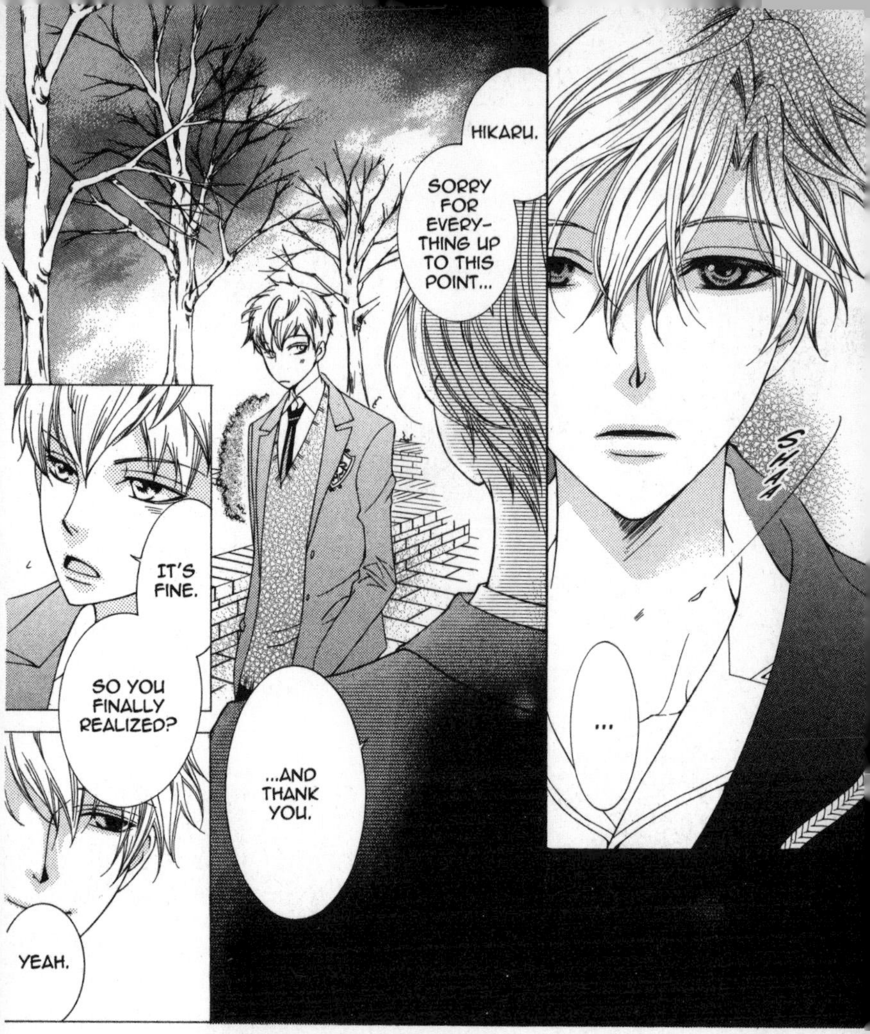
HIKARU.
SORRY FOR EVERY-THING UP TO THIS POINT...
SHAA
...
...AND THANK YOU.
IT'S FINE.
SO YOU FINALLY REALIZED?
YEAH.

✿ SUPPORTING CHARACTERS INTRODUCTION ✿

Kimiko Sakurazuka. Blood Type O.

FIRST-YEAR, CLASS A.

- SHE CAN TALK TO ANYONE, NO MATTER WHO, WITHOUT DISCRIMINATING AT ALL IN ANY WAY. A VERY GOOD-NATURED YOUNG MISS.
- I'VE ALWAYS WANTED TO FEATURE HER OR KURAKANO IN ONE OF THE STORIES, BUT WAS NEVER ABLE TO. TOO BAD.

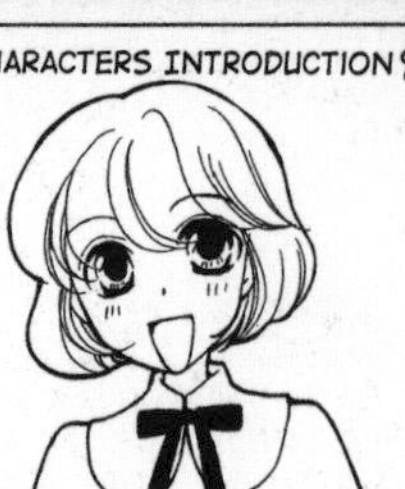

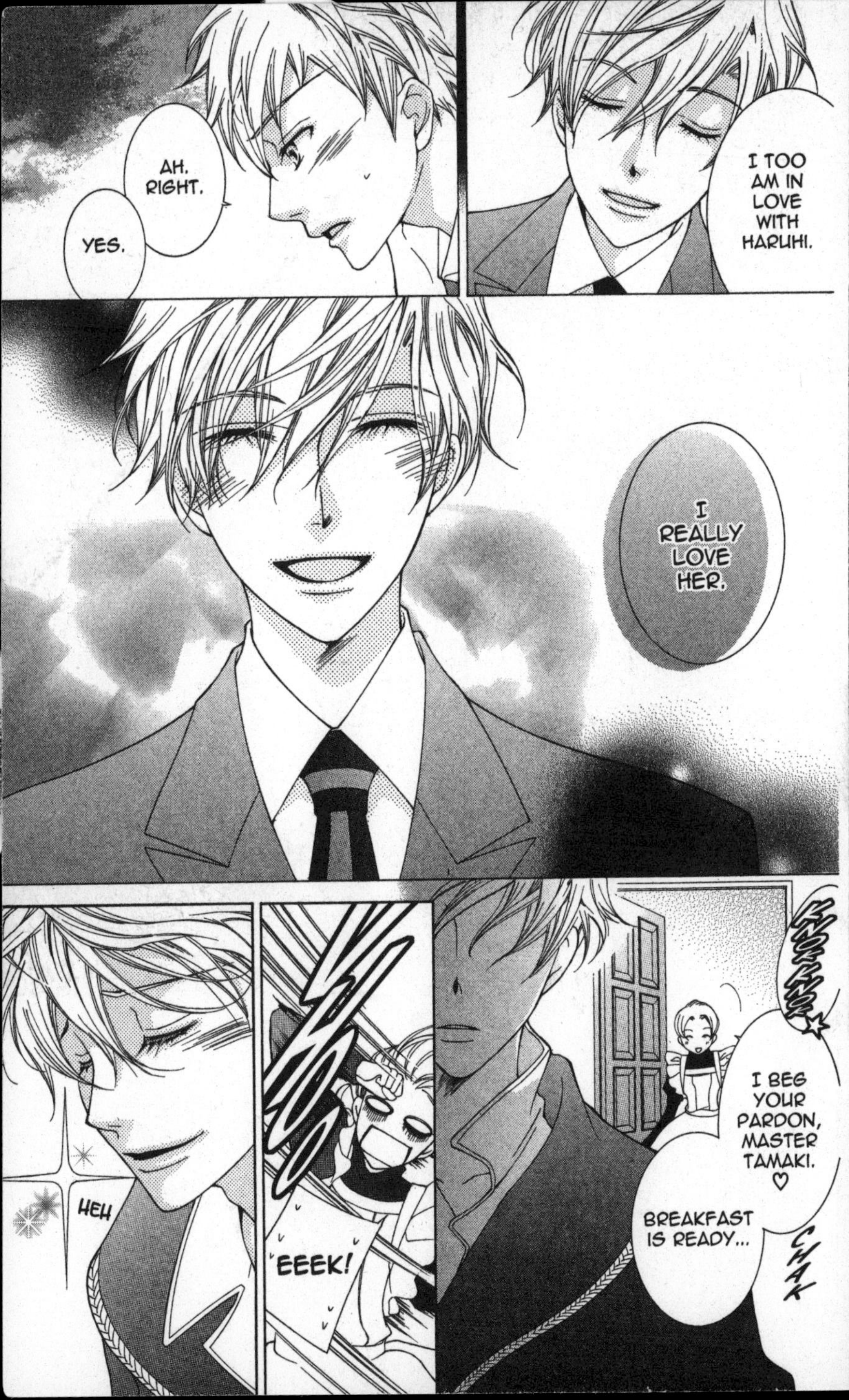
I TOO AM IN LOVE WITH HARUHI.
AH. RIGHT.
YES.
I REALLY LOVE HER.
I BEG YOUR PARDON, MASTER TAMAKI. ♡
BREAKFAST IS READY...
CHAK
EEEK!
HEH

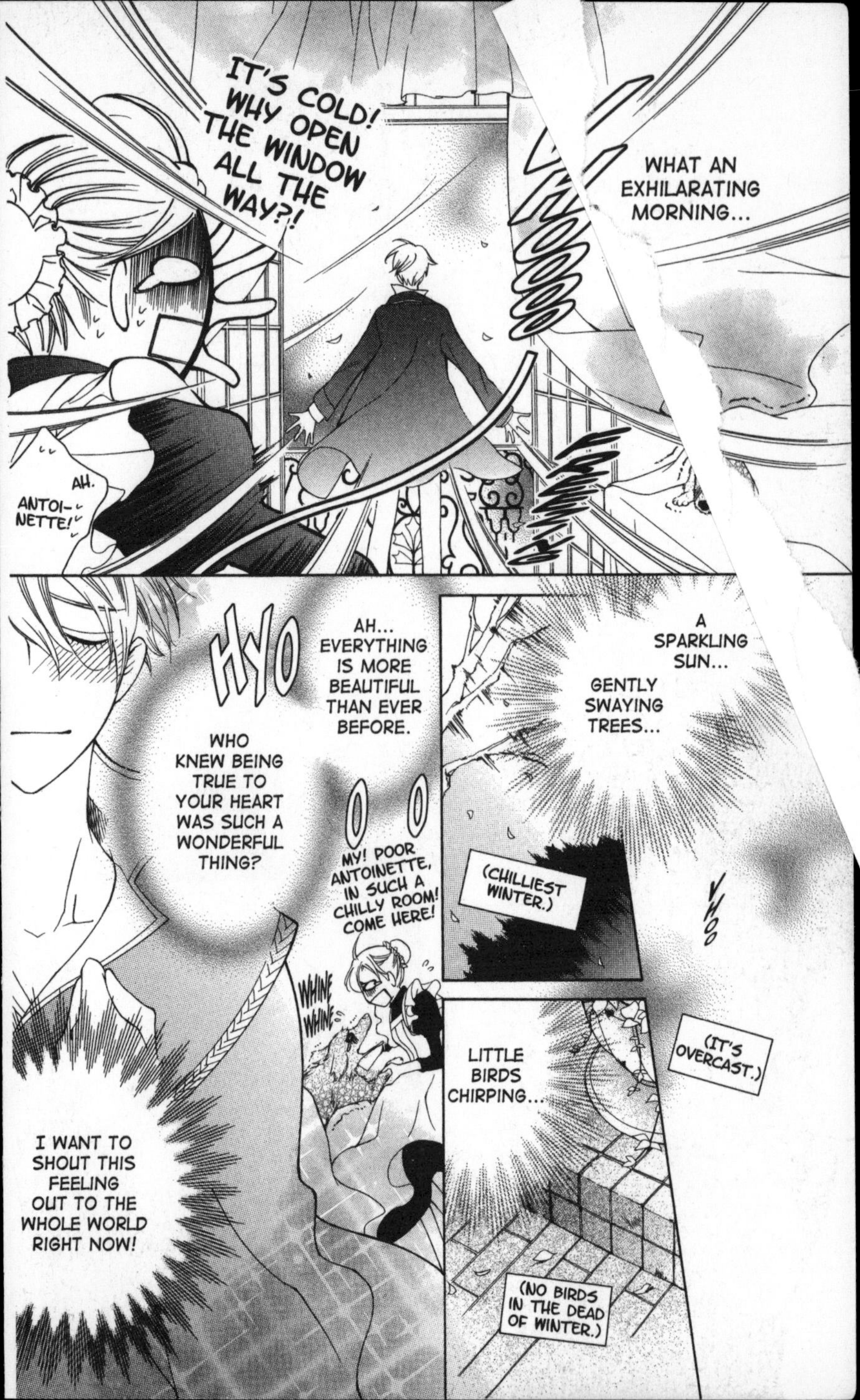

WHAT AN EXHILARATING MORNING...
VWOOOOOOO
IT'S COLD! WHY OPEN THE WINDOW ALL THE WAY?!
AH. ANTOINETTE!
A SPARKLING SUN...
GENTLY SWAYING TREES...
(CHILLIEST WINTER.)
VWOO
(IT'S OVERCAST.)
LITTLE BIRDS CHIRPING...
(NO BIRDS IN THE DEAD OF WINTER.)
AH... EVERYTHING IS MORE BEAUTIFUL THAN EVER BEFORE.
HYO
WHO KNEW BEING TRUE TO YOUR HEART WAS SUCH A WONDERFUL THING?
OO
MY! POOR ANTOINETTE, IN SUCH A CHILLY ROOM! COME HERE!
WHINE WHINE
I WANT TO SHOUT THIS FEELING OUT TO THE WHOLE WORLD RIGHT NOW!

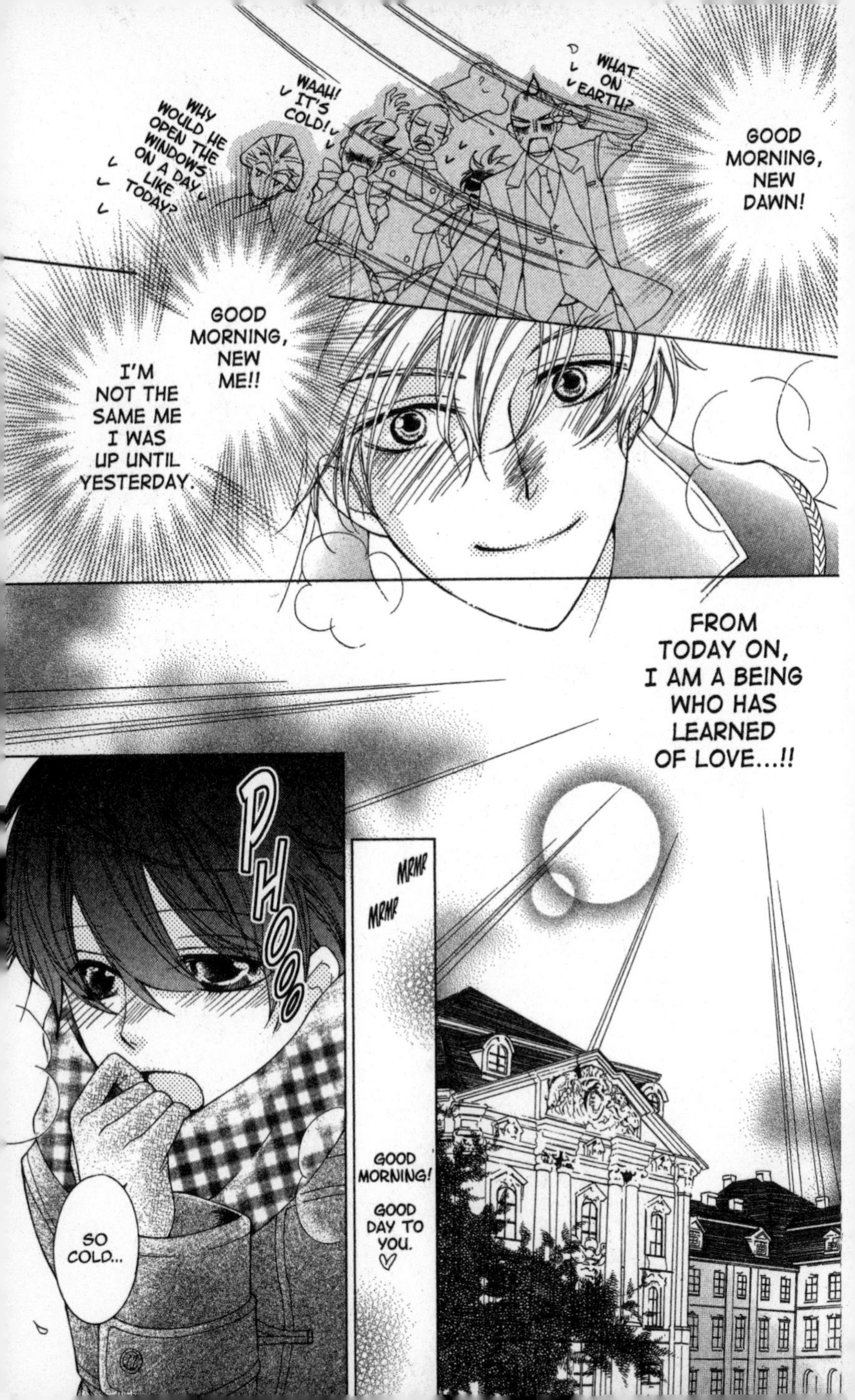
GOOD MORNING, NEW DAWN!
WHAT ON EARTH?
WAAH! IT'S COLD!
WHY WOULD HE OPEN THE WINDOWS ON A DAY LIKE TODAY?
GOOD MORNING, NEW ME!!
I'M NOT THE SAME ME I WAS UP UNTIL YESTERDAY.
FROM TODAY ON, I AM A BEING WHO HAS LEARNED OF LOVE...!!
MRMR
MRMR
GOOD MORNING!
GOOD DAY TO YOU. ♡
PHOOO
SO COLD...

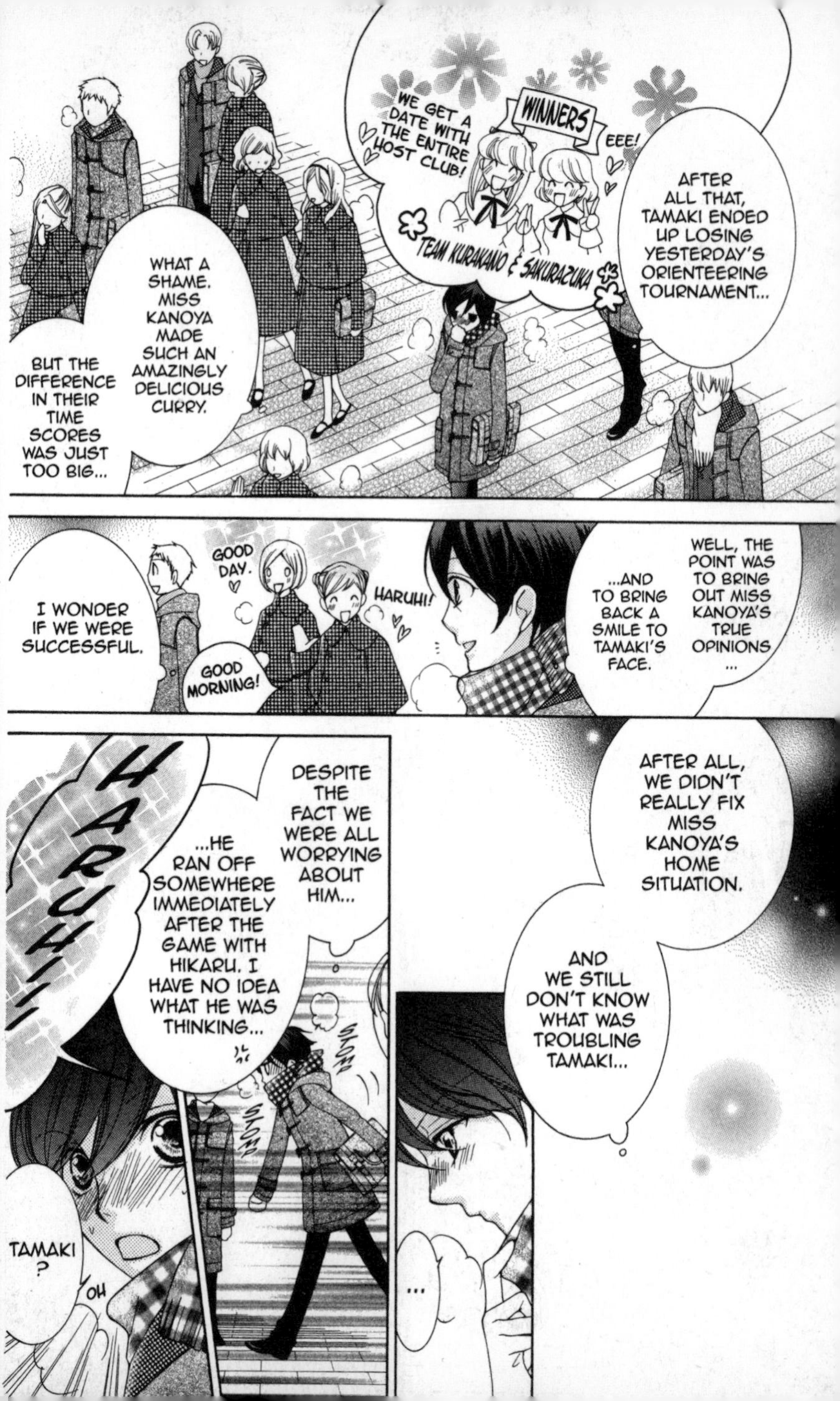
AFTER ALL THAT, TAMAKI ENDED UP LOSING YESTERDAY'S ORIENTEERING TOURNAMENT...
WE GET A DATE WITH THE ENTIRE HOST CLUB!
WINNERS
EEE!
TEAM KURAKANO & SAKURAZUKA
WHAT A SHAME. MISS KANOYA MADE SUCH AN AMAZINGLY DELICIOUS CURRY.
BUT THE DIFFERENCE IN THEIR TIME SCORES WAS JUST TOO BIG...
WELL, THE POINT WAS TO BRING OUT MISS KANOYA'S TRUE OPINIONS ...
...AND TO BRING BACK A SMILE TO TAMAKI'S FACE.
HARUHI!
GOOD DAY.
GOOD MORNING!
I WONDER IF WE WERE SUCCESSFUL.
AFTER ALL, WE DIDN'T REALLY FIX MISS KANOYA'S HOME SITUATION.
AND WE STILL DON'T KNOW WHAT WAS TROUBLING TAMAKI...
...
DESPITE THE FACT WE WERE ALL WORRYING ABOUT HIM...
...HE RAN OFF SOMEWHERE IMMEDIATELY AFTER THE GAME WITH HIKARU. I HAVE NO IDEA WHAT HE WAS THINKING...
STOMP
STOMP
HARUHI!!!
OH
TAMAKI ?

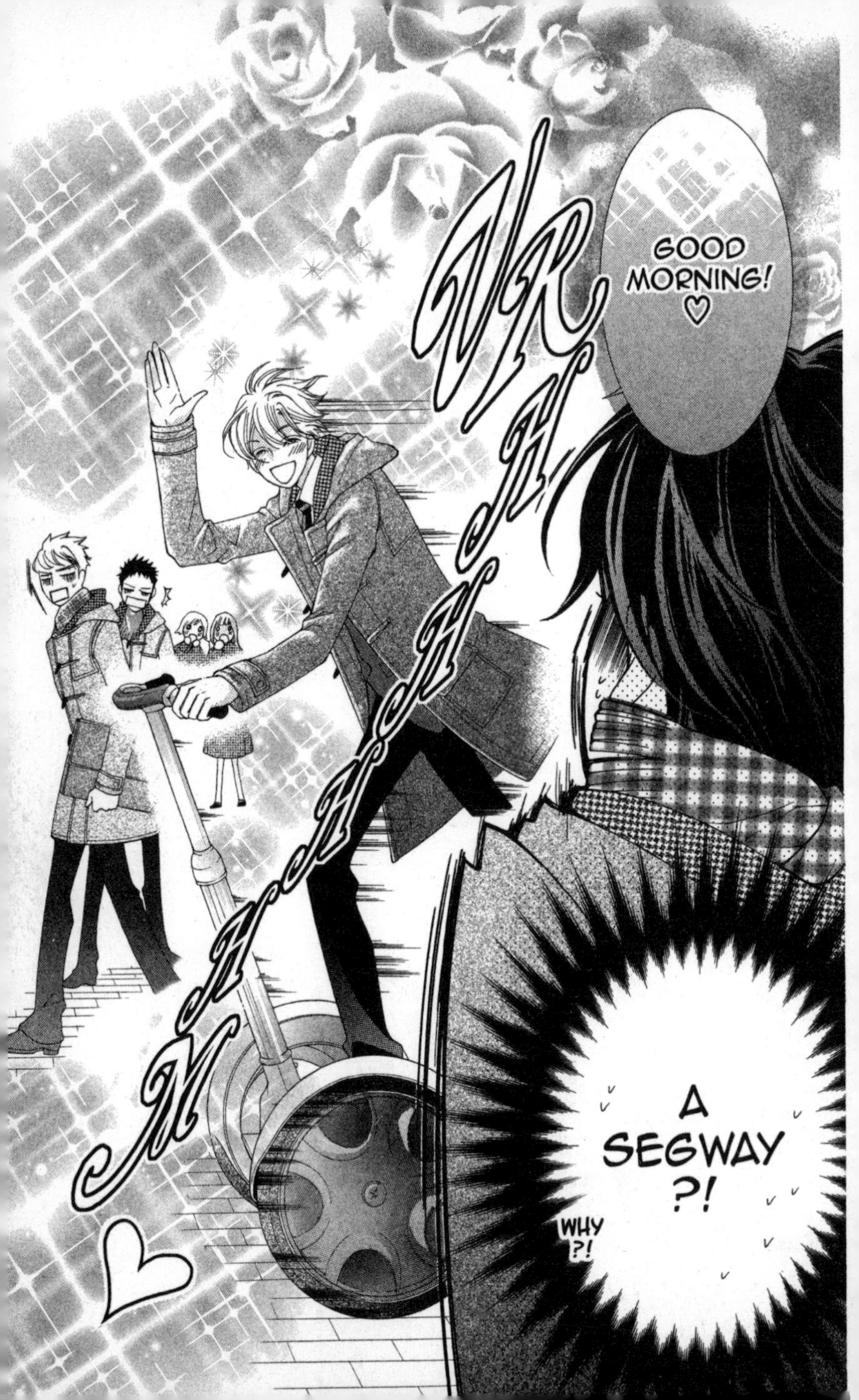
GOOD MORNING! ♡
A SEGWAY ?!
WHY ?!

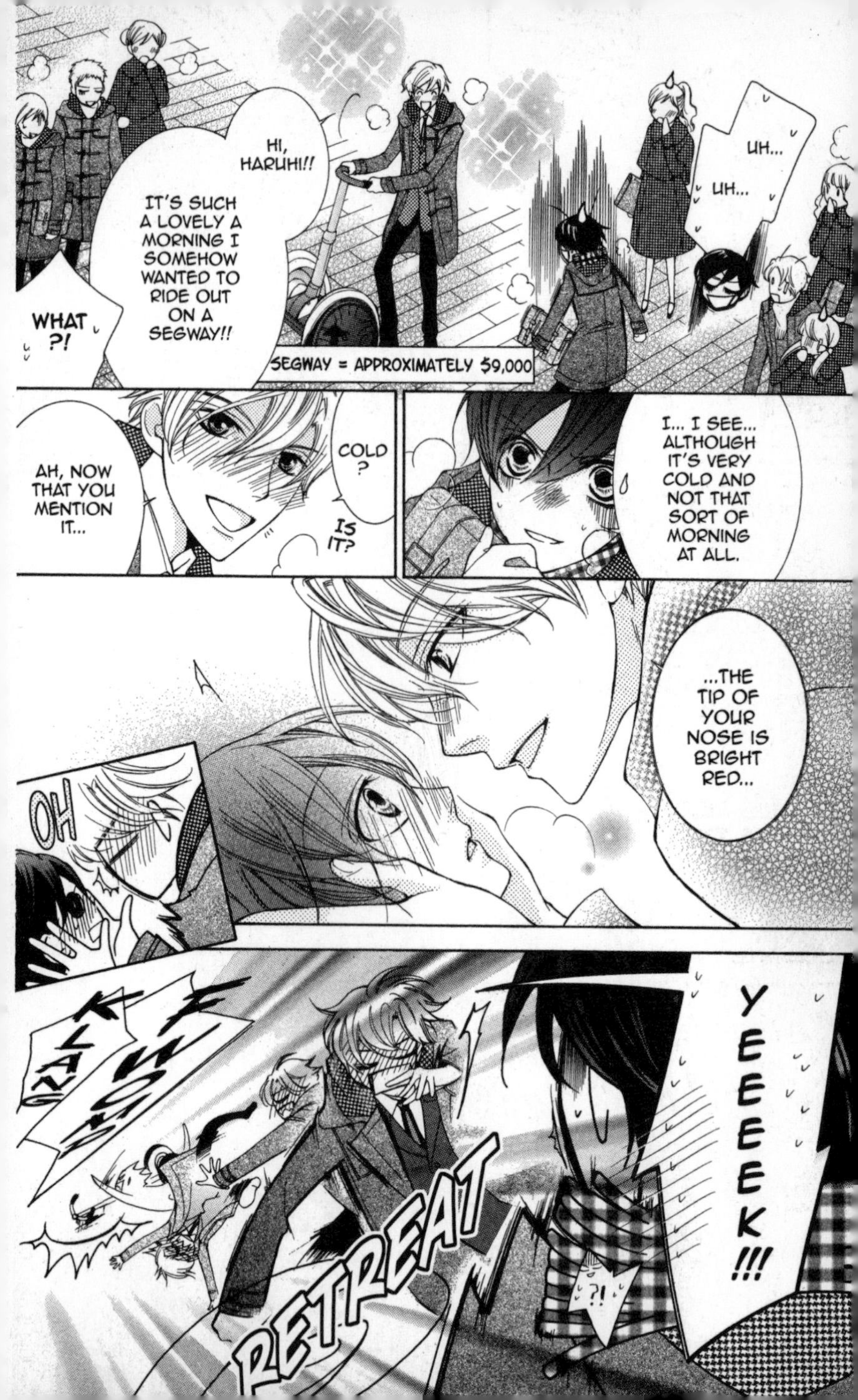
UH... UH...
HI, HARUHI!!
IT'S SUCH A LOVELY A MORNING I SOMEHOW WANTED TO RIDE OUT ON A SEGWAY!!
WHAT ?!
SEGWAY = APPROXIMATELY $9,000
I... I SEE... ALTHOUGH IT'S VERY COLD AND NOT THAT SORT OF MORNING AT ALL.
COLD ?
IS IT?
AH, NOW THAT YOU MENTION IT...
...THE TIP OF YOUR NOSE IS BRIGHT RED...
OH
YEEEEK!!!
?!
FWOOM
KLANG
RETREAT

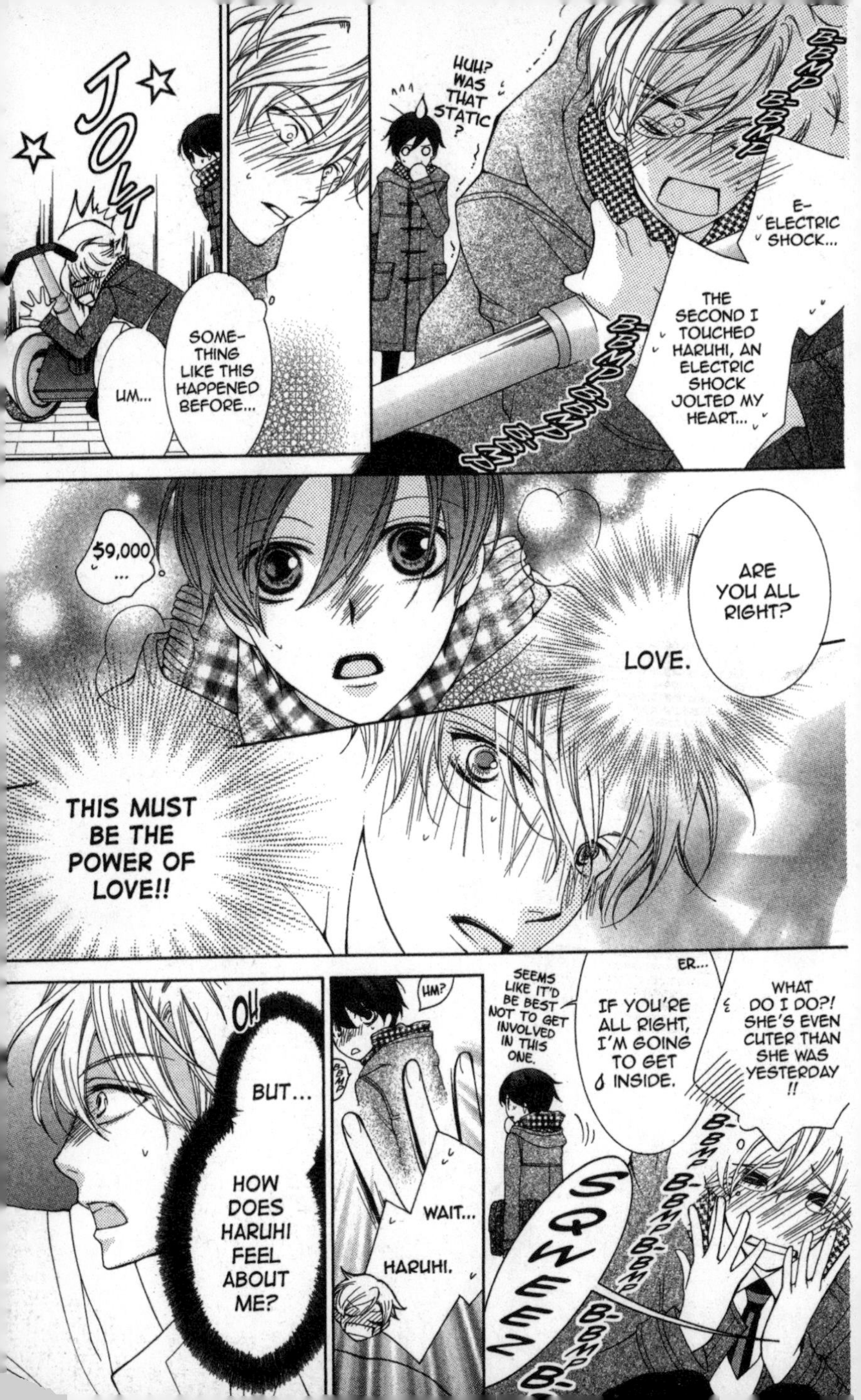
B-BBMP B-BBMP
E-ELECTRIC SHOCK...
THE SECOND I TOUCHED HARUHI, AN ELECTRIC SHOCK JOLTED MY HEART...
B-BBMP B-BBMP B-BBMP
HUH? WAS THAT STATIC?
SOMETHING LIKE THIS HAPPENED BEFORE...
UM...
JOLT
ARE YOU ALL RIGHT?
LOVE.
$9,000...
THIS MUST BE THE POWER OF LOVE!!
WHAT DO I DO?! SHE'S EVEN CUTER THAN SHE WAS YESTERDAY!!
ER...
IF YOU'RE ALL RIGHT, I'M GOING TO GET INSIDE.
SEEMS LIKE IT'D BE BEST NOT TO GET INVOLVED IN THIS ONE.
B-BBMP B-BBMP B-BBMP B-BBMP B-
SQWEEZ
HM?
WAIT...
HARUHI.
OH
BUT...
HOW DOES HARUHI FEEL ABOUT ME?

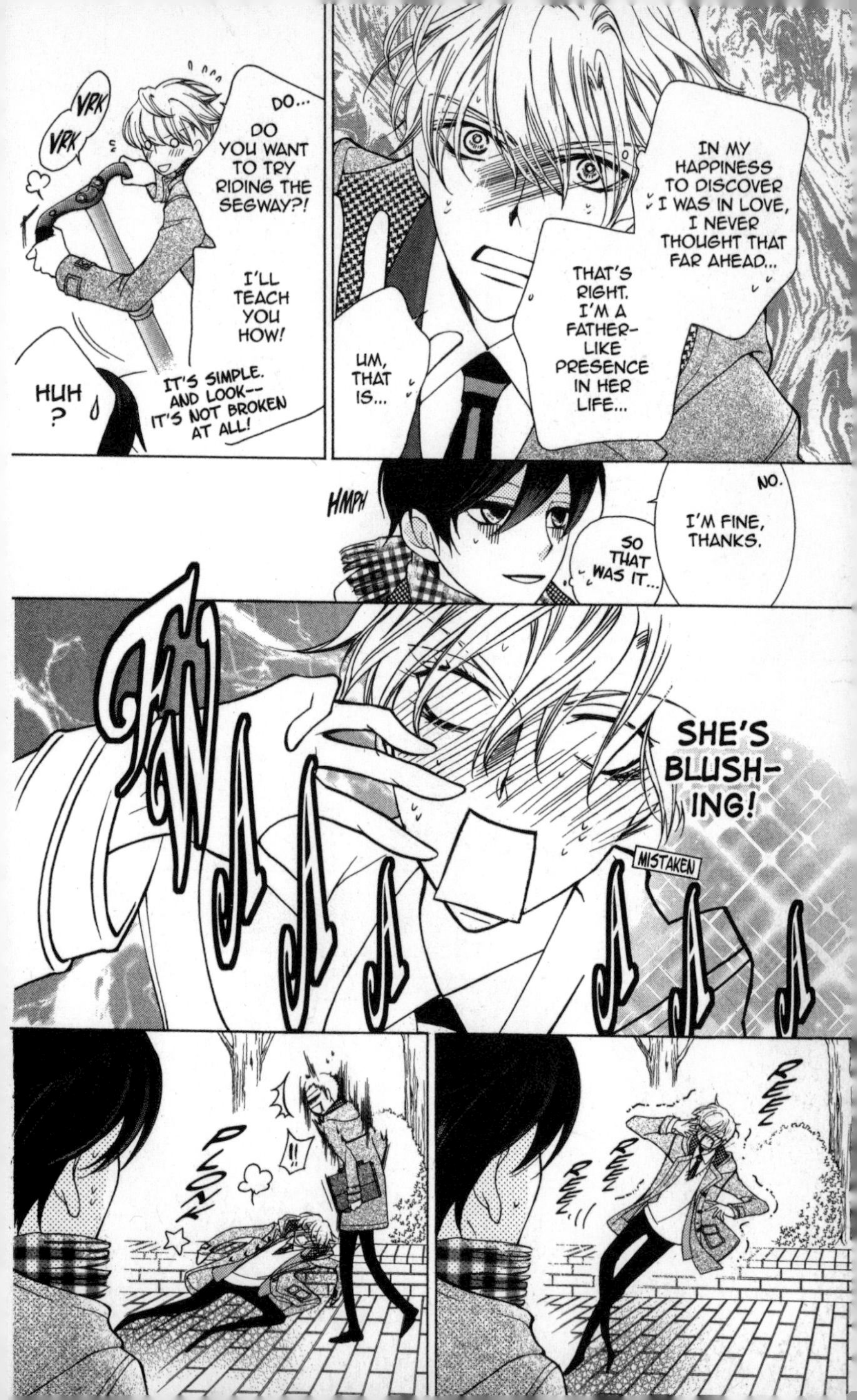
IN MY HAPPINESS TO DISCOVER I WAS IN LOVE, I NEVER THOUGHT THAT FAR AHEAD...
THAT'S RIGHT. I'M A FATHER-LIKE PRESENCE IN HER LIFE...
UM, THAT IS...
DO... DO YOU WANT TO TRY RIDING THE SEGWAY?!
VRK
VRK
I'LL TEACH YOU HOW!
IT'S SIMPLE. AND LOOK-- IT'S NOT BROKEN AT ALL!
HUH?
NO.
I'M FINE, THANKS.
SO THAT WAS IT...
HMPH
SHE'S BLUSH-ING!
MISTAKEN
!!
PLONK
REEL
REEL
REEL

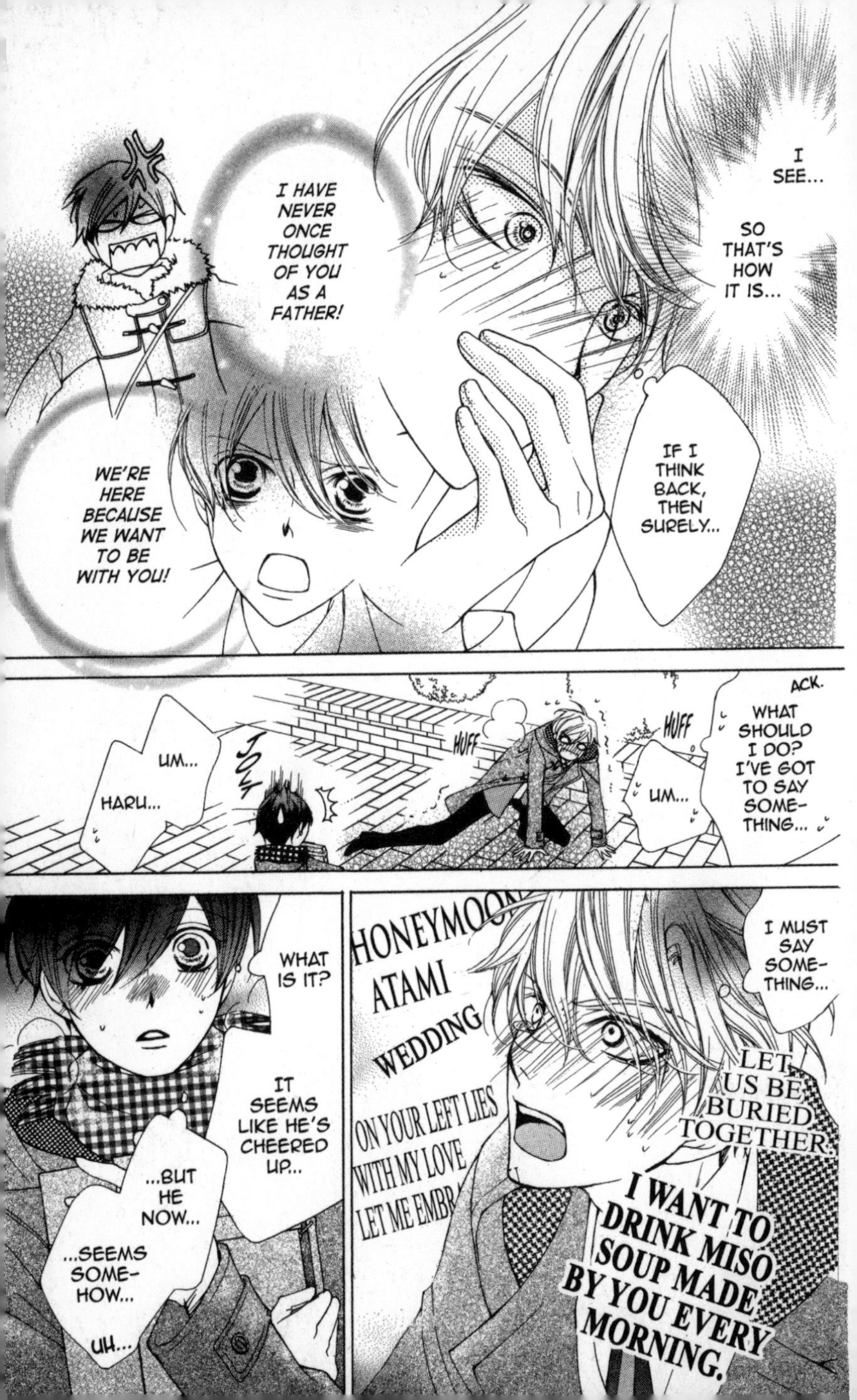
I SEE...
SO THAT'S HOW IT IS...
IF I THINK BACK, THEN SURELY...
I HAVE NEVER ONCE THOUGHT OF YOU AS A FATHER!
WE'RE HERE BECAUSE WE WANT TO BE WITH YOU!
ACK.
WHAT SHOULD I DO? I'VE GOT TO SAY SOME-THING...
UM...
HUFF
HUFF
UM...
HARU...
I MUST SAY SOME-THING...
HONEYMOO
ATAMI
WEDDING
ON YOUR LEFT LIES
WITH MY LOVE
LET ME EMBR
LET US BE BURIED TOGETHER.
I WANT TO DRINK MISO SOUP MADE BY YOU EVERY MORNING.
WHAT IS IT?
IT SEEMS LIKE HE'S CHEERED UP...
...BUT HE NOW...
...SEEMS SOME-HOW...
UH...

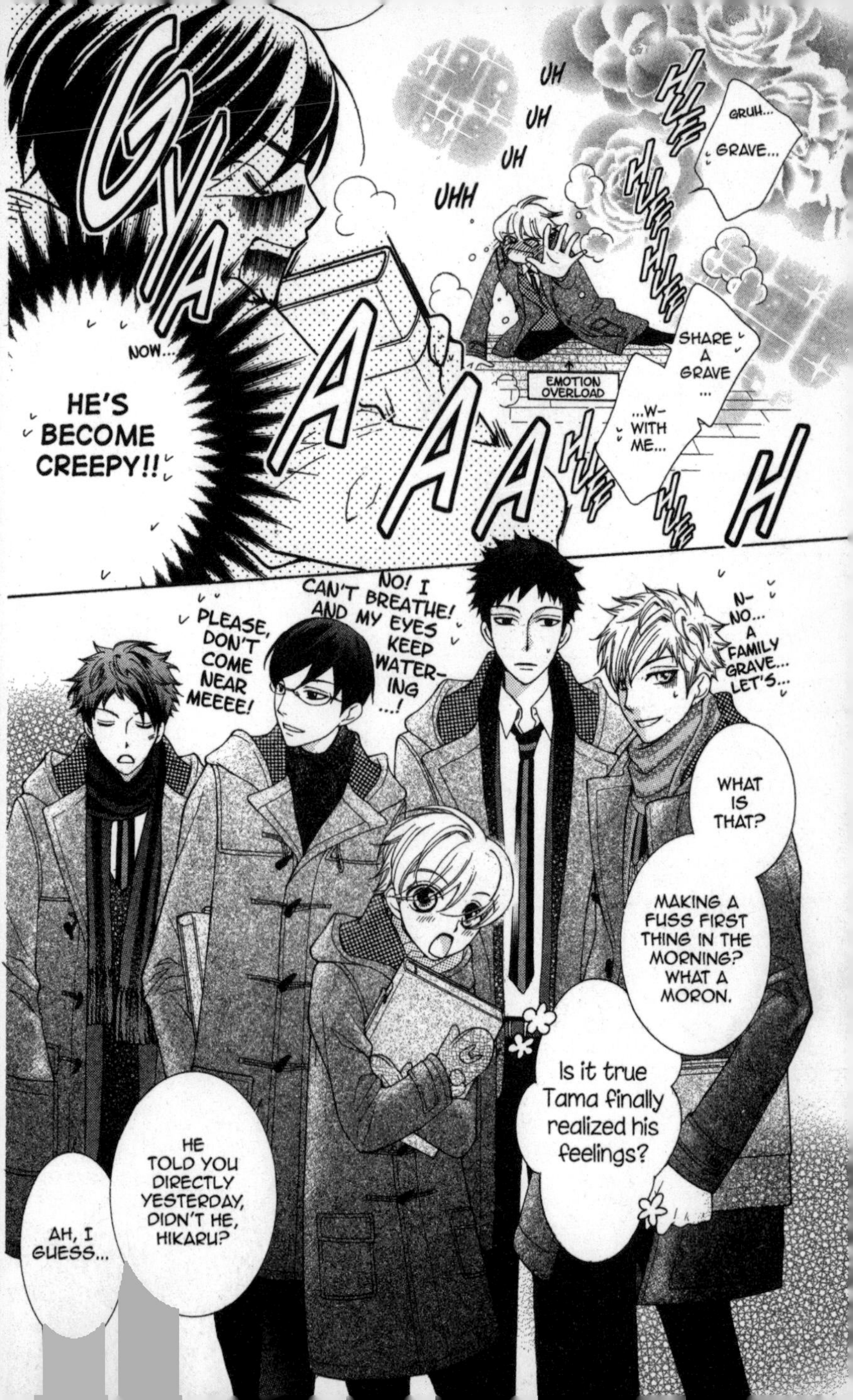
UH
UH
UH
UHH
GRUH... GRAVE...
SHARE A GRAVE...
...W-WITH ME...
EMOTION OVERLOAD
GYAAAAAH
NOW...
HE'S BECOME CREEPY!!
N-NO... A FAMILY GRAVE... LET'S...
WHAT IS THAT?
MAKING A FUSS FIRST THING IN THE MORNING? WHAT A MORON.
NO! I CAN'T BREATHE! AND MY EYES KEEP WATERING...!
Is it true Tama finally realized his feelings?
PLEASE, DON'T COME NEAR MEEEE!
HE TOLD YOU DIRECTLY YESTERDAY, DIDN'T HE, HIKARU?
AH, I GUESS...

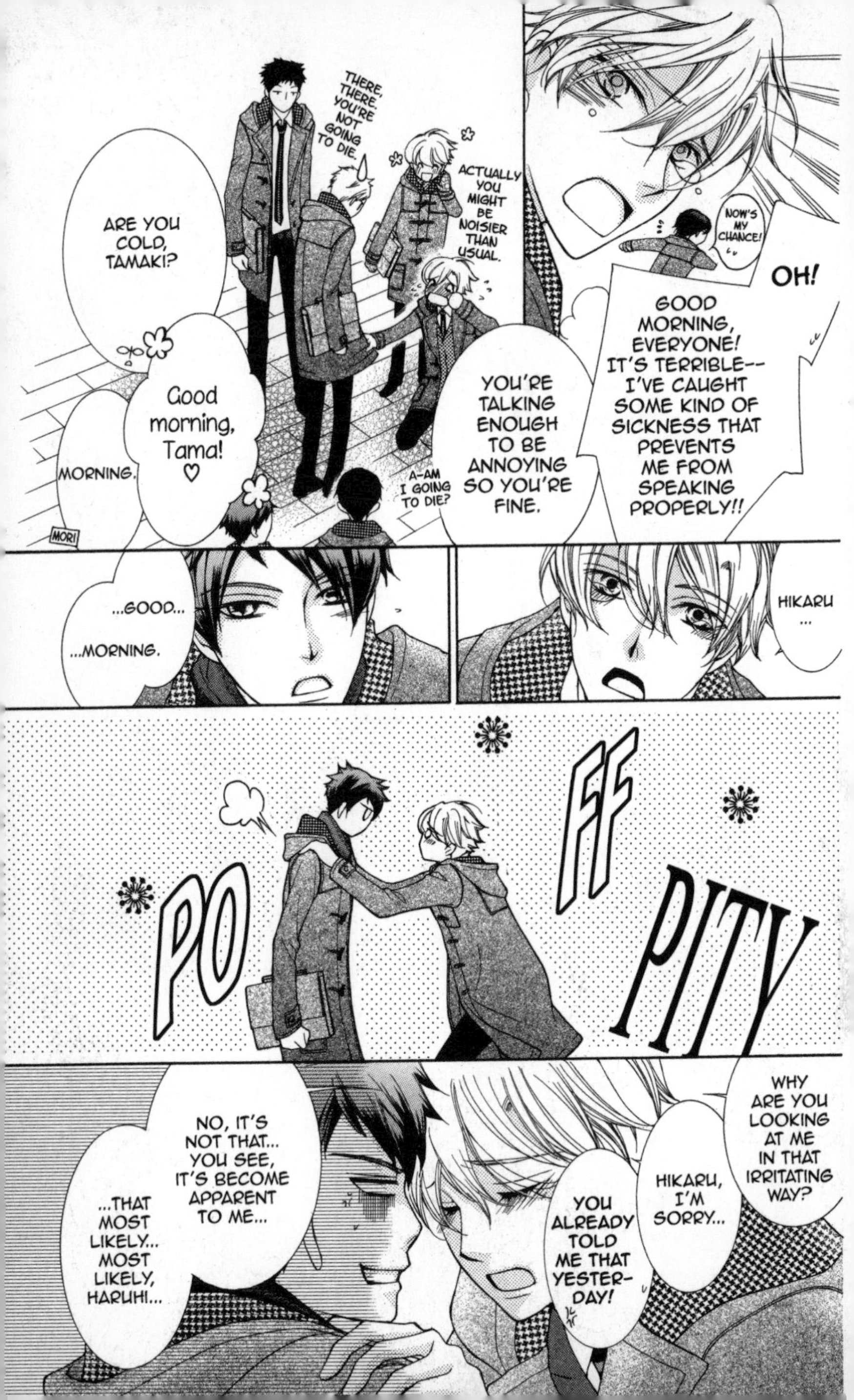
NOW'S MY CHANCE!
OH!
GOOD MORNING, EVERYONE! IT'S TERRIBLE--I'VE CAUGHT SOME KIND OF SICKNESS THAT PREVENTS ME FROM SPEAKING PROPERLY!!
A-AM I GOING TO DIE?
THERE, THERE. YOU'RE NOT GOING TO DIE.
ACTUALLY YOU MIGHT BE NOISIER THAN USUAL.
YOU'RE TALKING ENOUGH TO BE ANNOYING SO YOU'RE FINE.
ARE YOU COLD, TAMAKI?
Good morning, Tama! ♡
MORNING.
MORI
HIKARU ...
...GOOD...
...MORNING.
POFF
PITY
WHY ARE YOU LOOKING AT ME IN THAT IRRITATING WAY?
HIKARU, I'M SORRY...
YOU ALREADY TOLD ME THAT YESTER-DAY!
NO, IT'S NOT THAT... YOU SEE, IT'S BECOME APPARENT TO ME...
...THAT MOST LIKELY... MOST LIKELY, HARUHI...

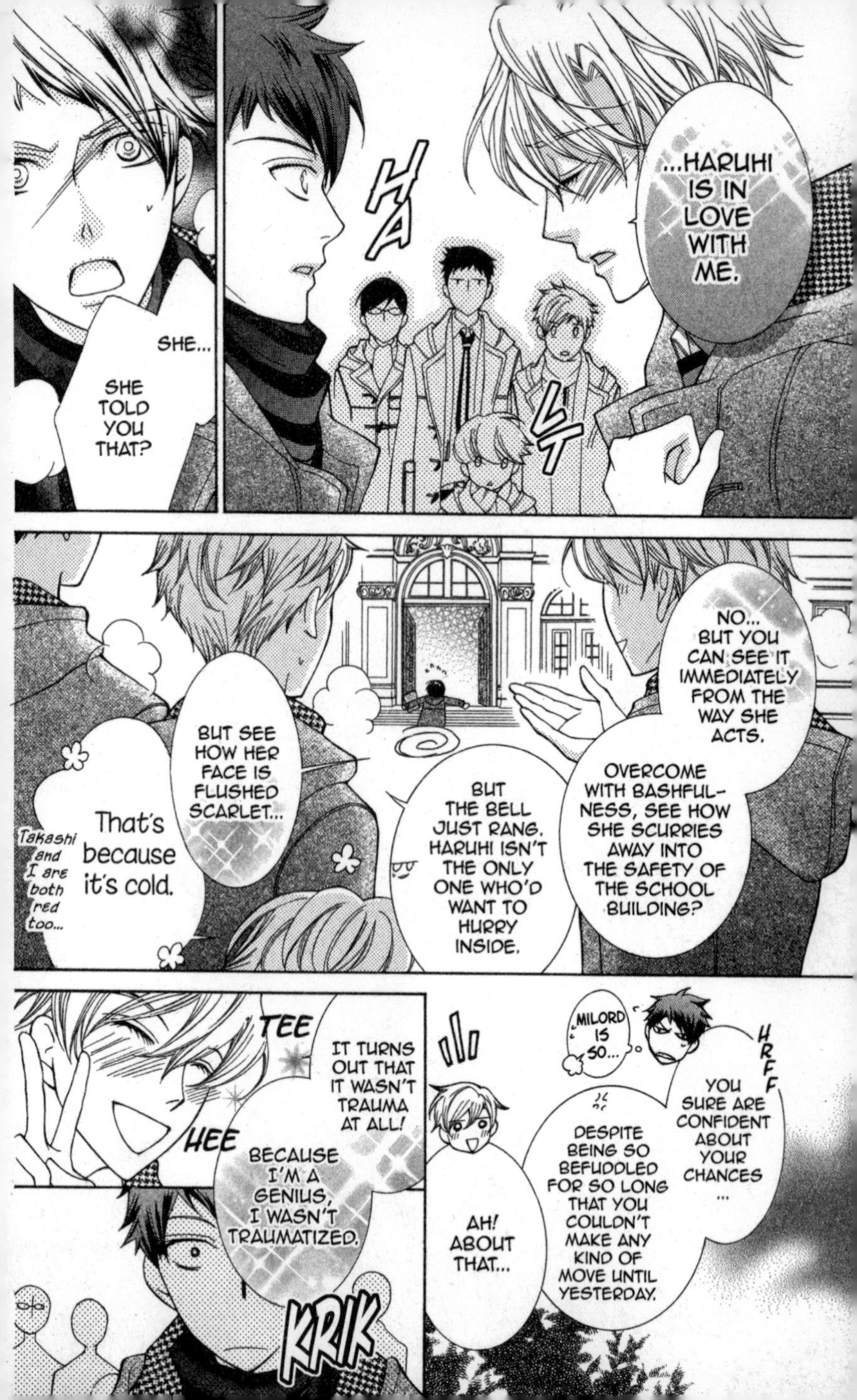
...HARUHI IS IN LOVE WITH ME.
HA
LT
SHE...
SHE TOLD YOU THAT?
NO... BUT YOU CAN SEE IT IMMEDIATELY FROM THE WAY SHE ACTS.
OVERCOME WITH BASHFUL-NESS, SEE HOW SHE SCURRIES AWAY INTO THE SAFETY OF THE SCHOOL BUILDING?
BUT THE BELL JUST RANG. HARUHI ISN'T THE ONLY ONE WHO'D WANT TO HURRY INSIDE.
BUT SEE HOW HER FACE IS FLUSHED SCARLET...
That's because it's cold.
Takashi and I are both red too...
MILORD IS SO...
HRFF
YOU SURE ARE CONFIDENT ABOUT YOUR CHANCES ...
DESPITE BEING SO BEFUDDLED FOR SO LONG THAT YOU COULDN'T MAKE ANY KIND OF MOVE UNTIL YESTERDAY.
AH! ABOUT THAT...
TEE
HEE
IT TURNS OUT THAT IT WASN'T TRAUMA AT ALL!
BECAUSE I'M A GENIUS, I WASN'T TRAUMATIZED.
KRIK

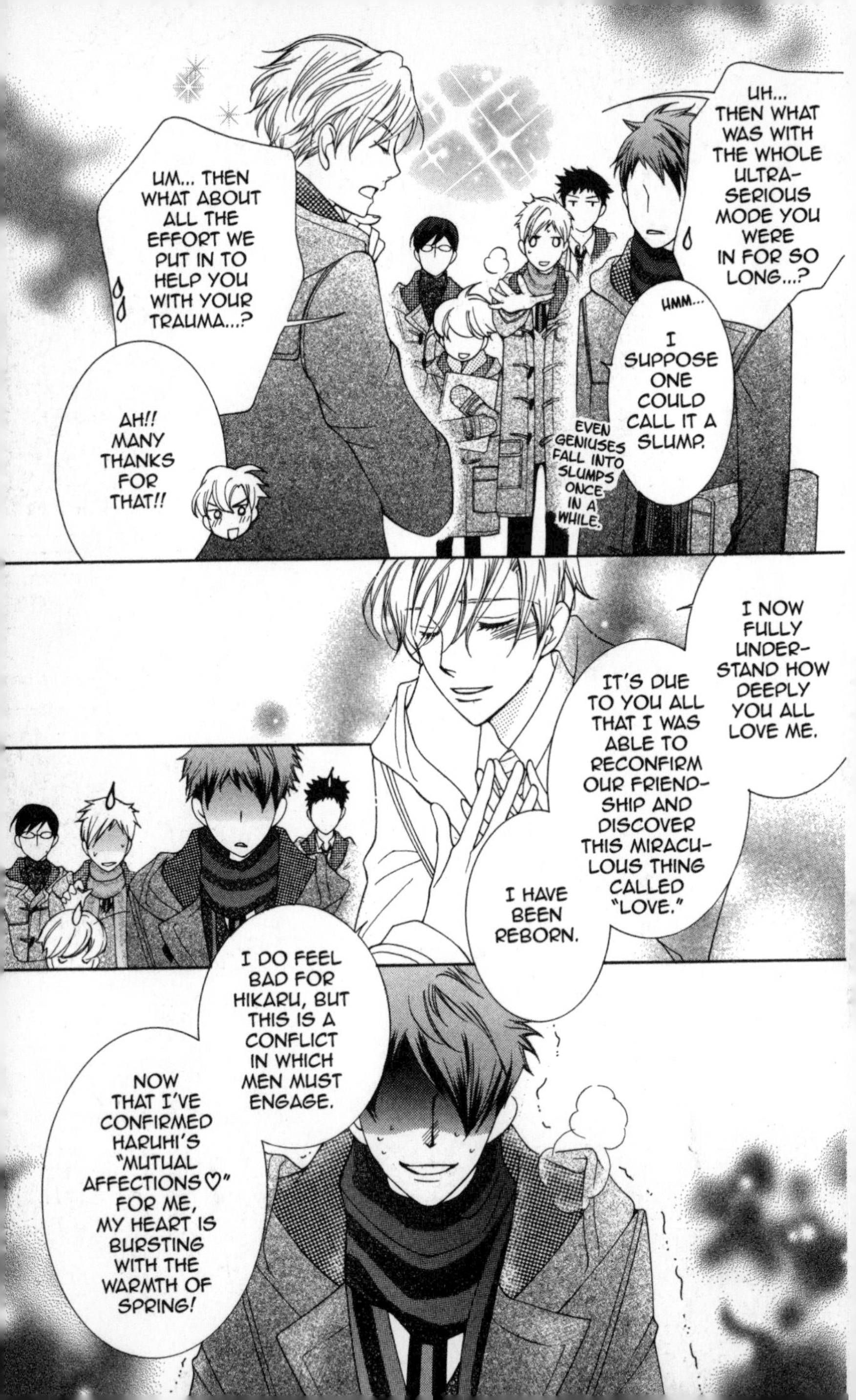
UH... THEN WHAT WAS WITH THE WHOLE ULTRA-SERIOUS MODE YOU WERE IN FOR SO LONG...?
HMM... I SUPPOSE ONE COULD CALL IT A SLUMP.
EVEN GENIUSES FALL INTO SLUMPS ONCE IN A WHILE.
UM... THEN WHAT ABOUT ALL THE EFFORT WE PUT IN TO HELP YOU WITH YOUR TRAUMA...?
AH!! MANY THANKS FOR THAT!!
I NOW FULLY UNDER-STAND HOW DEEPLY YOU ALL LOVE ME.
IT'S DUE TO YOU ALL THAT I WAS ABLE TO RECONFIRM OUR FRIEND-SHIP AND DISCOVER THIS MIRACU-LOUS THING CALLED "LOVE."
I HAVE BEEN REBORN.
I DO FEEL BAD FOR HIKARU, BUT THIS IS A CONFLICT IN WHICH MEN MUST ENGAGE.
NOW THAT I'VE CONFIRMED HARUHI'S "MUTUAL AFFECTIONS♡" FOR ME, MY HEART IS BURSTING WITH THE WARMTH OF SPRING!

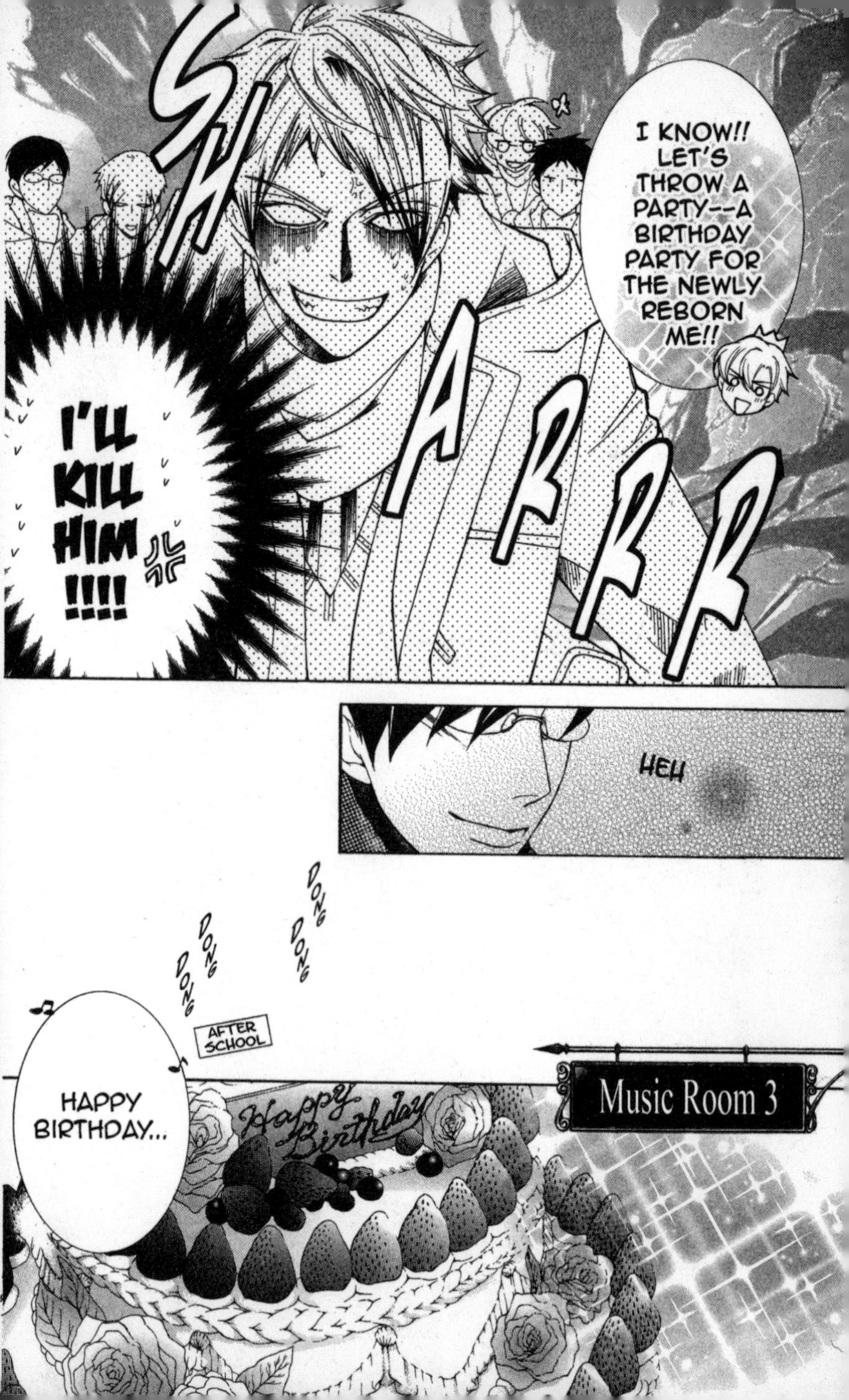
I KNOW!! LET'S THROW A PARTY--A BIRTHDAY PARTY FOR THE NEWLY REBORN ME!!
SHARRR
I'LL KILL HIM!!!!
HEH
DONG DONG
DONG DONG
AFTER SCHOOL
Music Room 3
HAPPY BIRTHDAY...
Happy Birthday

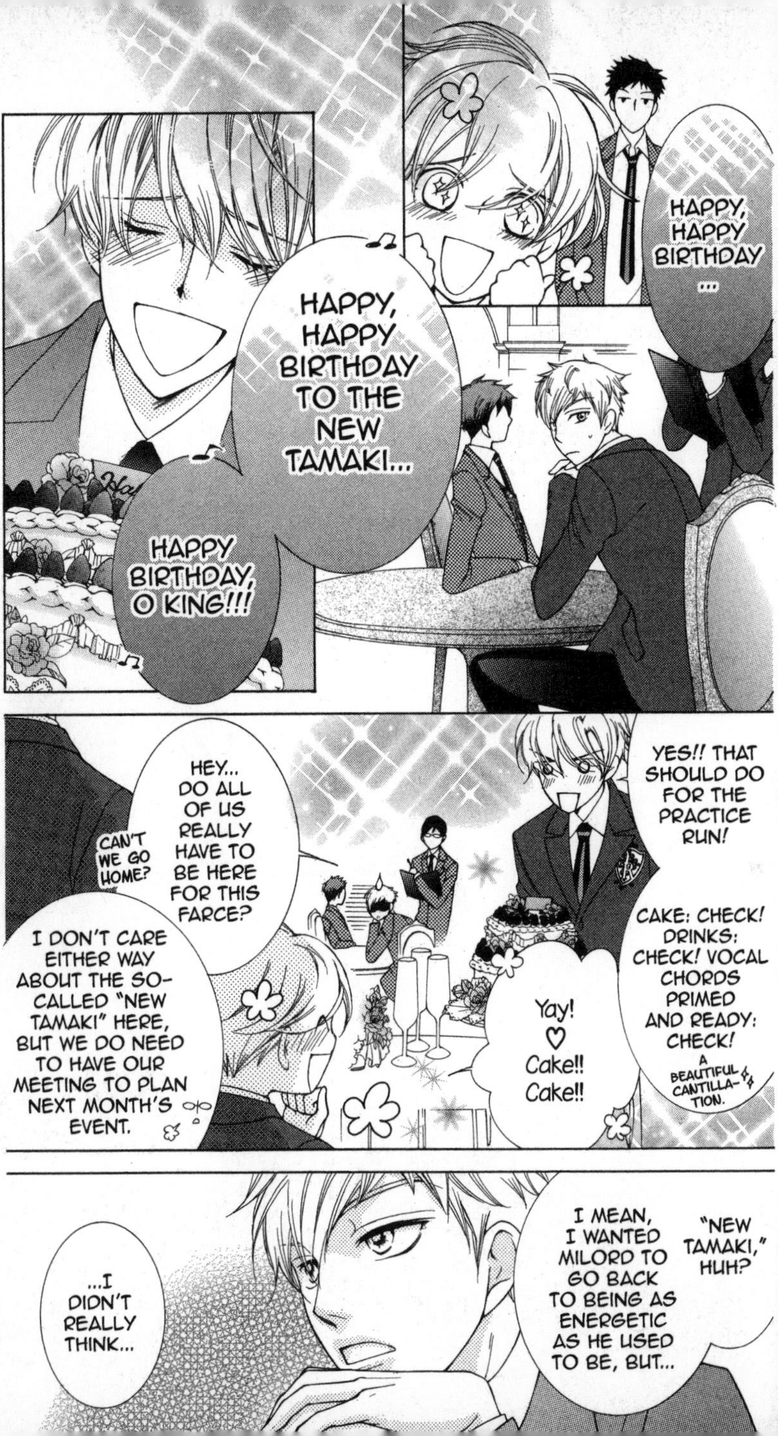
HAPPY, HAPPY BIRTHDAY ...
HAPPY, HAPPY BIRTHDAY TO THE NEW TAMAKI...
HAPPY BIRTHDAY, O KING!!!
YES!! THAT SHOULD DO FOR THE PRACTICE RUN!
CAKE: CHECK! DRINKS: CHECK! VOCAL CHORDS PRIMED AND READY: CHECK!
A BEAUTIFUL CANTILLATION.
Yay! ♡ Cake!! Cake!!
HEY... DO ALL OF US REALLY HAVE TO BE HERE FOR THIS FARCE?
CAN'T WE GO HOME?
I DON'T CARE EITHER WAY ABOUT THE SO-CALLED "NEW TAMAKI" HERE, BUT WE DO NEED TO HAVE OUR MEETING TO PLAN NEXT MONTH'S EVENT.
"NEW TAMAKI," HUH?
I MEAN, I WANTED MILORD TO GO BACK TO BEING AS ENERGETIC AS HE USED TO BE, BUT...
...I DIDN'T REALLY THINK...

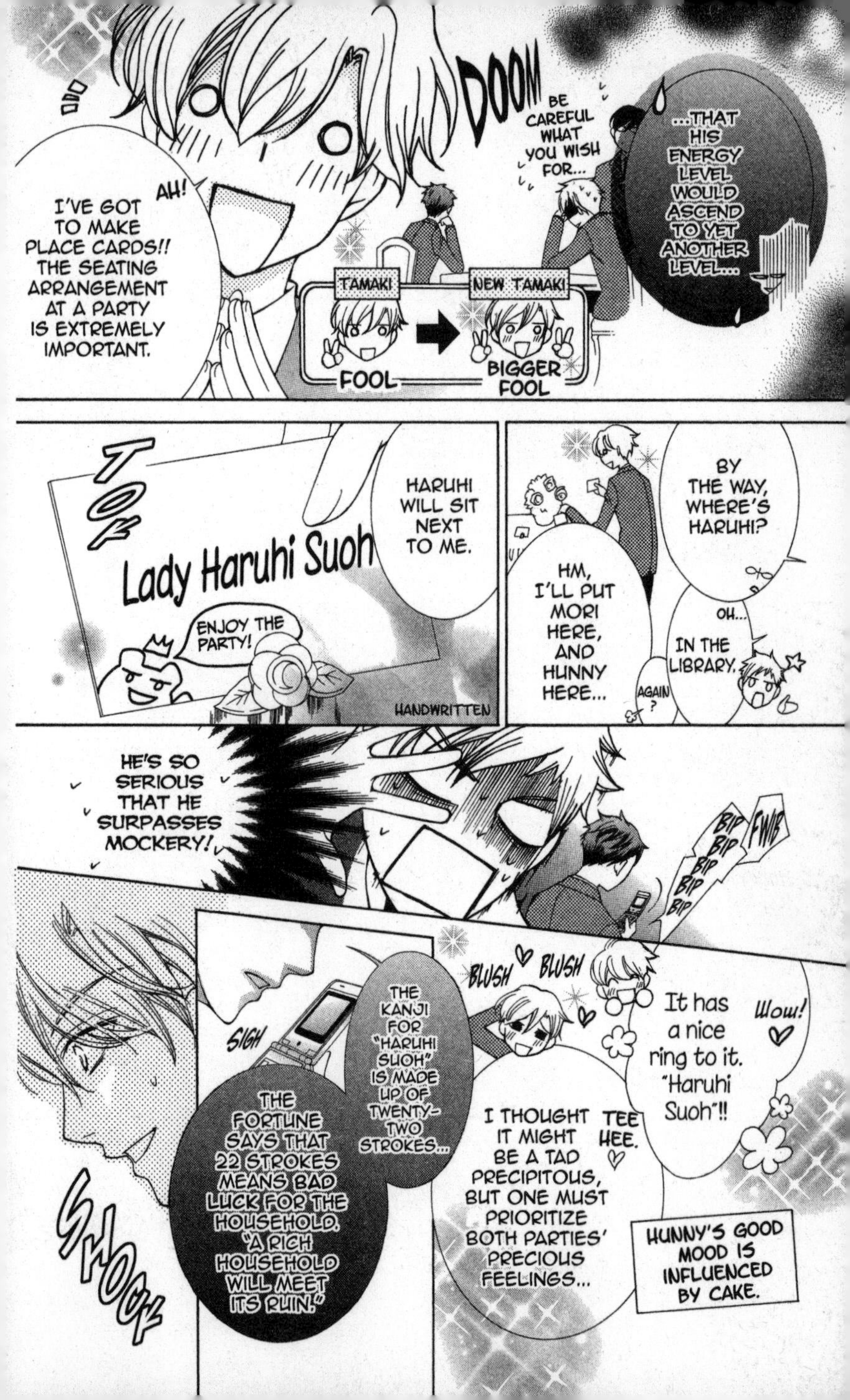
...THAT HIS ENERGY LEVEL WOULD ASCEND TO YET ANOTHER LEVEL...
BE CAREFUL WHAT YOU WISH FOR...
DOOM
NEW TAMAKI
BIGGER FOOL
TAMAKI
FOOL
AH!
I'VE GOT TO MAKE PLACE CARDS!! THE SEATING ARRANGEMENT AT A PARTY IS EXTREMELY IMPORTANT.
BY THE WAY, WHERE'S HARUHI?
OH... IN THE LIBRARY.
AGAIN?
HM, I'LL PUT MORI HERE, AND HUNNY HERE...
HARUHI WILL SIT NEXT TO ME.
TOK
Lady Haruhi Suoh
ENJOY THE PARTY!
HANDWRITTEN
FWIP
BIP BIP BIP BIP BIP
HE'S SO SERIOUS THAT HE SURPASSES MOCKERY!
Wow!
It has a nice ring to it. "Haruhi Suoh"!!
BLUSH BLUSH
TEE HEE.
I THOUGHT IT MIGHT BE A TAD PRECIPITOUS, BUT ONE MUST PRIORITIZE BOTH PARTIES' PRECIOUS FEELINGS...
HUNNY'S GOOD MOOD IS INFLUENCED BY CAKE.
THE KANJI FOR "HARUHI SUOH" IS MADE UP OF TWENTY-TWO STROKES...
SIGH
THE FORTUNE SAYS THAT 22 STROKES MEANS BAD LUCK FOR THE HOUSEHOLD. "A RICH HOUSEHOLD WILL MEET ITS RUIN."
SHOOK

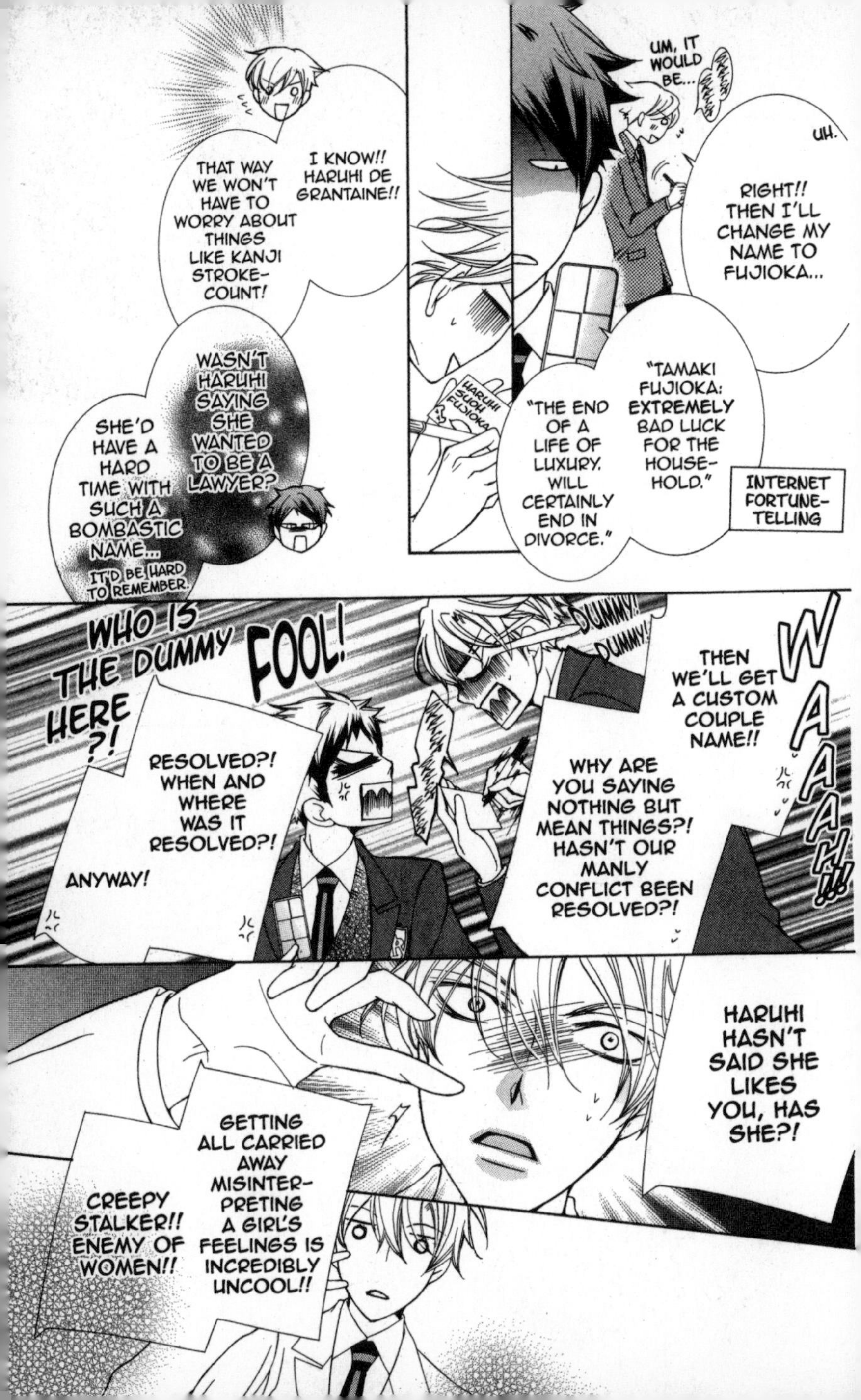
UM, IT WOULD BE...
UH.
RIGHT!! THEN I'LL CHANGE MY NAME TO FUJIOKA...
INTERNET FORTUNE-TELLING
"TAMAKI FUJIOKA: EXTREMELY BAD LUCK FOR THE HOUSEHOLD."
"THE END OF A LIFE OF LUXURY. WILL CERTAINLY END IN DIVORCE."
HARUHI SUOH FUJIOKA
I KNOW!! HARUHI DE GRANTAINE!!
THAT WAY WE WON'T HAVE TO WORRY ABOUT THINGS LIKE KANJI STROKE-COUNT!
WASN'T HARUHI SAYING SHE WANTED TO BE A LAWYER?
SHE'D HAVE A HARD TIME WITH SUCH A BOMBASTIC NAME...
IT'D BE HARD TO REMEMBER.
WAAAH!!
THEN WE'LL GET A CUSTOM COUPLE NAME!!
DUMMY! DUMMY!
WHY ARE YOU SAYING NOTHING BUT MEAN THINGS?! HASN'T OUR MANLY CONFLICT BEEN RESOLVED?!
FOOL!
RESOLVED?! WHEN AND WHERE WAS IT RESOLVED?!
ANYWAY!
WHO IS THE DUMMY HERE?!
HARUHI HASN'T SAID SHE LIKES YOU, HAS SHE?!
GETTING ALL CARRIED AWAY MISINTERPRETING A GIRL'S FEELINGS IS INCREDIBLY UNCOOL!!
CREEPY STALKER!! ENEMY OF WOMEN!!

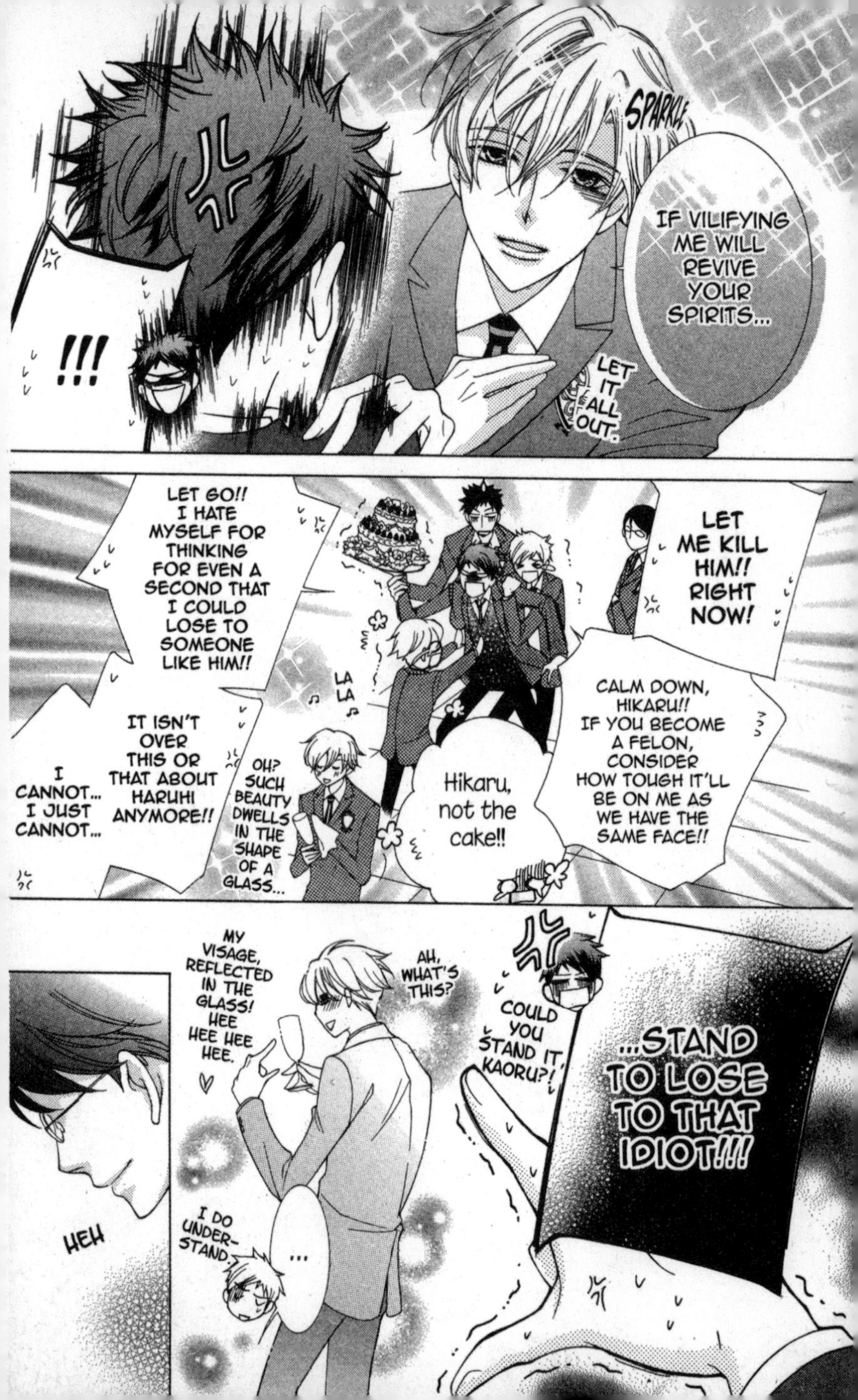
SPARKLE
IF VILIFYING ME WILL REVIVE YOUR SPIRITS...
LET IT ALL OUT.
!!!
LET ME KILL HIM!! RIGHT NOW!
CALM DOWN, HIKARU!! IF YOU BECOME A FELON, CONSIDER HOW TOUGH IT'LL BE ON ME AS WE HAVE THE SAME FACE!!
Hikaru, not the cake!!
LA LA
OH? SUCH BEAUTY DWELLS IN THE SHAPE OF A GLASS...
LET GO!! I HATE MYSELF FOR THINKING FOR EVEN A SECOND THAT I COULD LOSE TO SOMEONE LIKE HIM!!
IT ISN'T OVER THIS OR THAT ABOUT HARUHI ANYMORE!!
I CANNOT... I JUST CANNOT...
...STAND TO LOSE TO THAT IDIOT!!!
COULD YOU STAND IT, KAORU?!
AH, WHAT'S THIS?
MY VISAGE, REFLECTED IN THE GLASS! HEE HEE HEE HEE.
...
I DO UNDERSTAND.
HEH

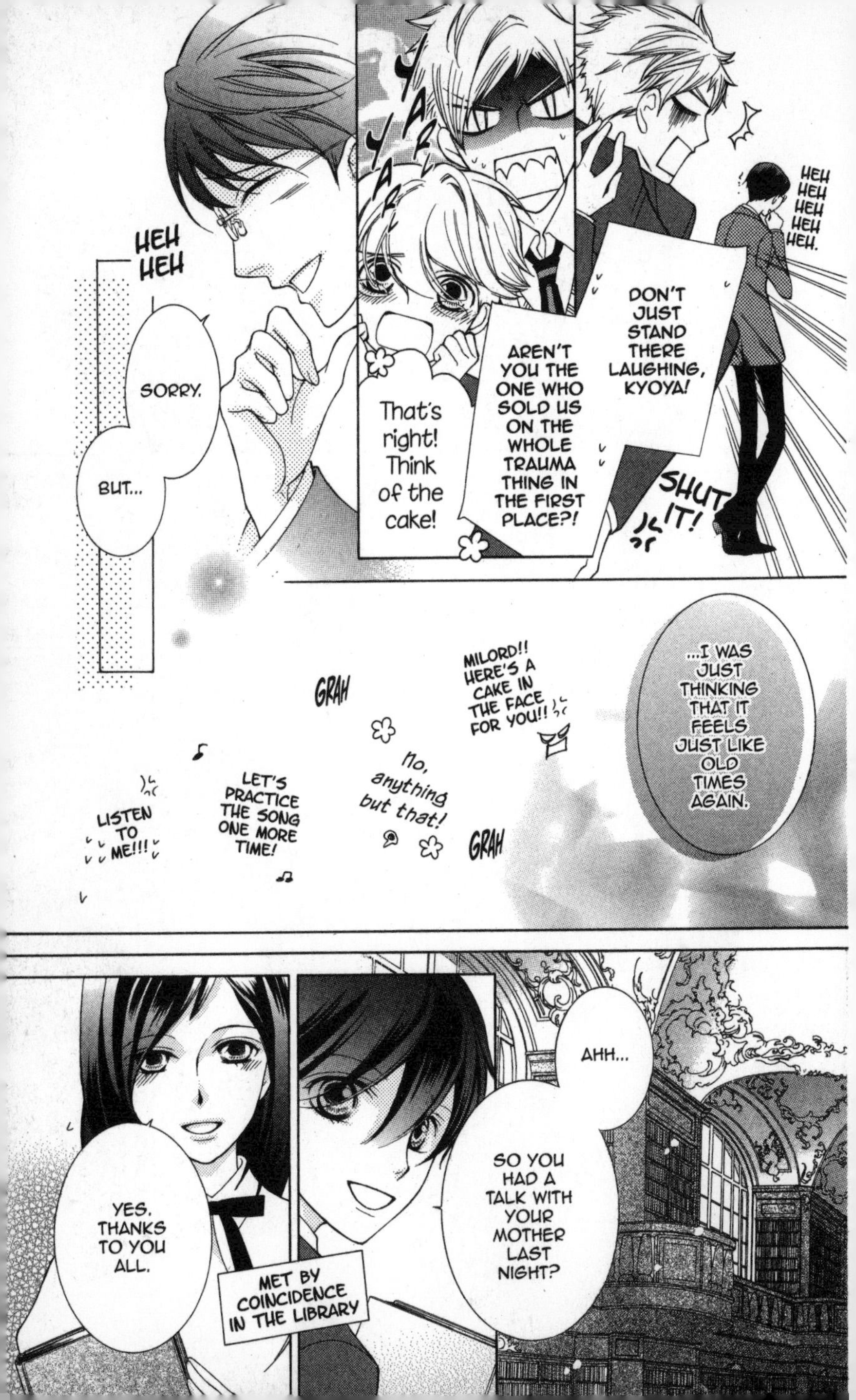
HEH HEH HEH HEH HEH.
DON'T JUST STAND THERE LAUGHING, KYOYA!
SHUT IT!
AREN'T YOU THE ONE WHO SOLD US ON THE WHOLE TRAUMA THING IN THE FIRST PLACE?!
That's right! Think of the cake!
HEH HEH
SORRY.
BUT...
...I WAS JUST THINKING THAT IT FEELS JUST LIKE OLD TIMES AGAIN.
MILORD!! HERE'S A CAKE IN THE FACE FOR YOU!!
GRAH
No, anything but that!
GRAH
LET'S PRACTICE THE SONG ONE MORE TIME!
LISTEN TO ME!!!
AHH...
SO YOU HAD A TALK WITH YOUR MOTHER LAST NIGHT?
MET BY COINCIDENCE IN THE LIBRARY
YES. THANKS TO YOU ALL.

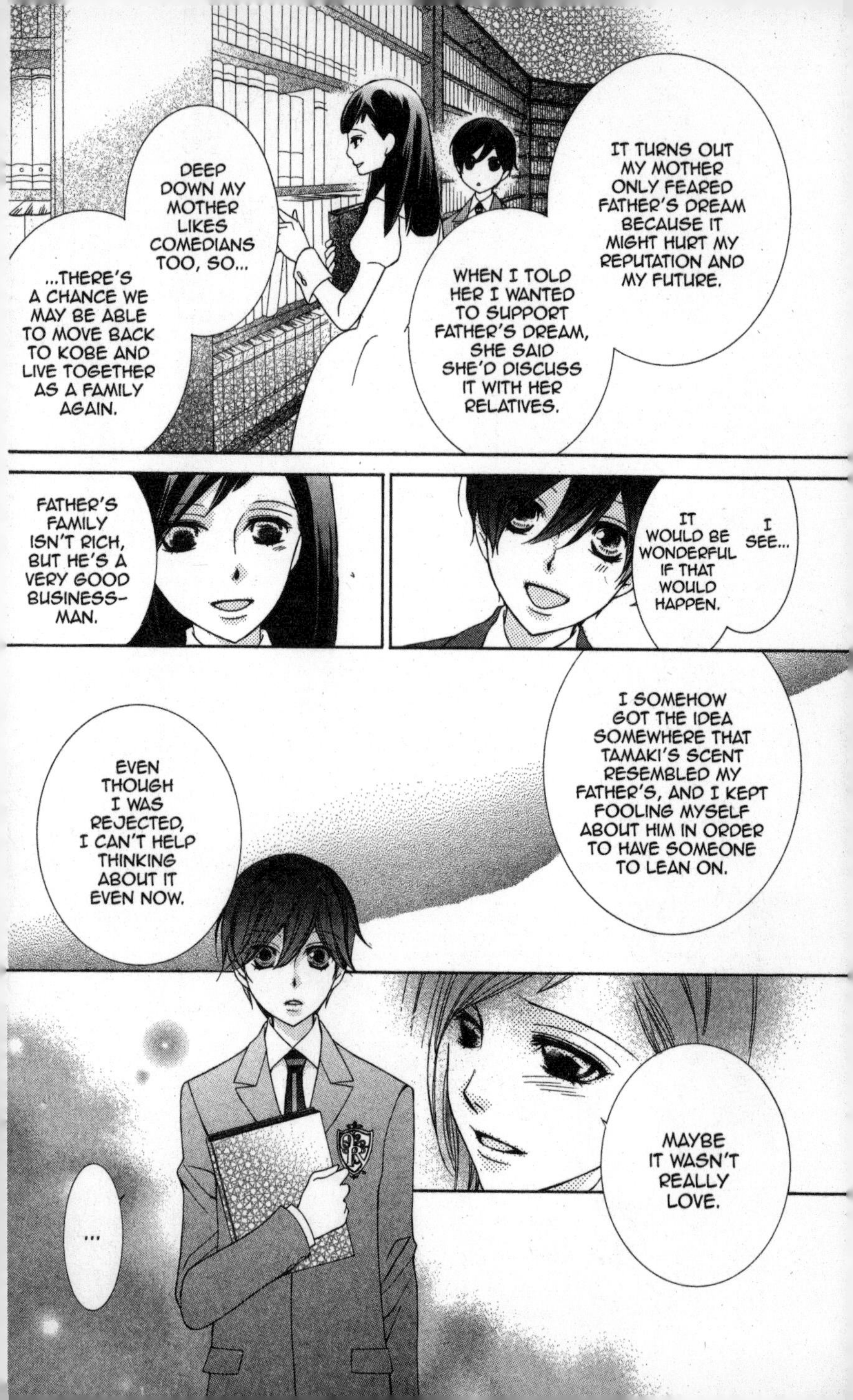
IT TURNS OUT MY MOTHER ONLY FEARED FATHER'S DREAM BECAUSE IT MIGHT HURT MY REPUTATION AND MY FUTURE.
WHEN I TOLD HER I WANTED TO SUPPORT FATHER'S DREAM, SHE SAID SHE'D DISCUSS IT WITH HER RELATIVES.
DEEP DOWN MY MOTHER LIKES COMEDIANS TOO, SO...
...THERE'S A CHANCE WE MAY BE ABLE TO MOVE BACK TO KOBE AND LIVE TOGETHER AS A FAMILY AGAIN.
I SEE...
IT WOULD BE WONDERFUL IF THAT WOULD HAPPEN.
FATHER'S FAMILY ISN'T RICH, BUT HE'S A VERY GOOD BUSINESS-MAN.
I SOMEHOW GOT THE IDEA SOMEWHERE THAT TAMAKI'S SCENT RESEMBLED MY FATHER'S, AND I KEPT FOOLING MYSELF ABOUT HIM IN ORDER TO HAVE SOMEONE TO LEAN ON.
EVEN THOUGH I WAS REJECTED, I CAN'T HELP THINKING ABOUT IT EVEN NOW.
MAYBE IT WASN'T REALLY LOVE.
...

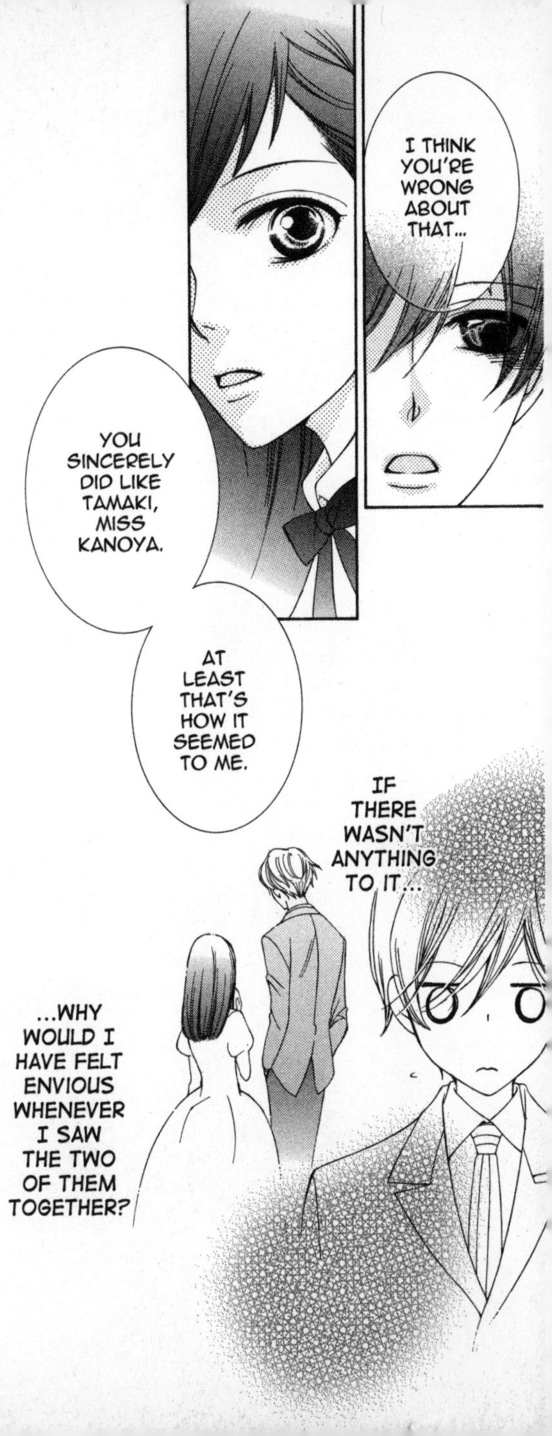
I THINK YOU'RE WRONG ABOUT THAT...
YOU SINCERELY DID LIKE TAMAKI, MISS KANOYA.
AT LEAST THAT'S HOW IT SEEMED TO ME.
IF THERE WASN'T ANYTHING TO IT...
...WHY WOULD I HAVE FELT ENVIOUS WHENEVER I SAW THE TWO OF THEM TOGETHER?

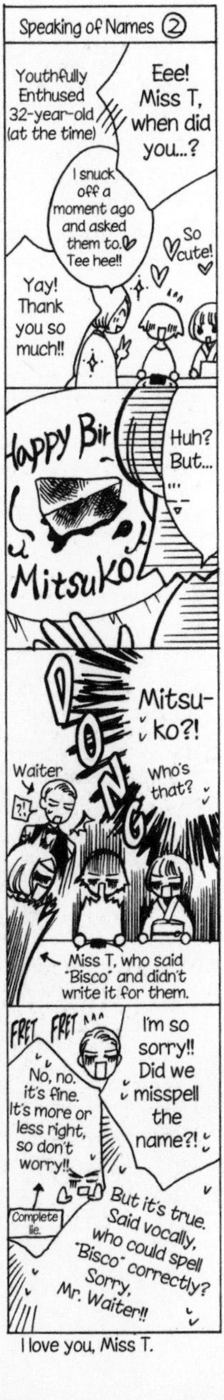
Speaking of Names ②
Eee! Miss T, when did you...?
Youthfully Enthused 32-year-old (at the time)
I snuck off a moment ago and asked them to. Tee hee!!
So cute!
Yay! Thank you so much!!
Happy Bir
Mitsuko
Huh? But...
Mitsu-ko?!
DOONG
Who's that?
Waiter
Miss T, who said "Bisco" and didn't write it for them.
I'm so sorry!! Did we misspell the name?!
FRET FRET
No, no. it's fine. It's more or less right, so don't worry!!
Complete lie.
But it's true. Said vocally, who could spell "Bisco" correctly? Sorry, Mr. Waiter!!

I love you, Miss T.

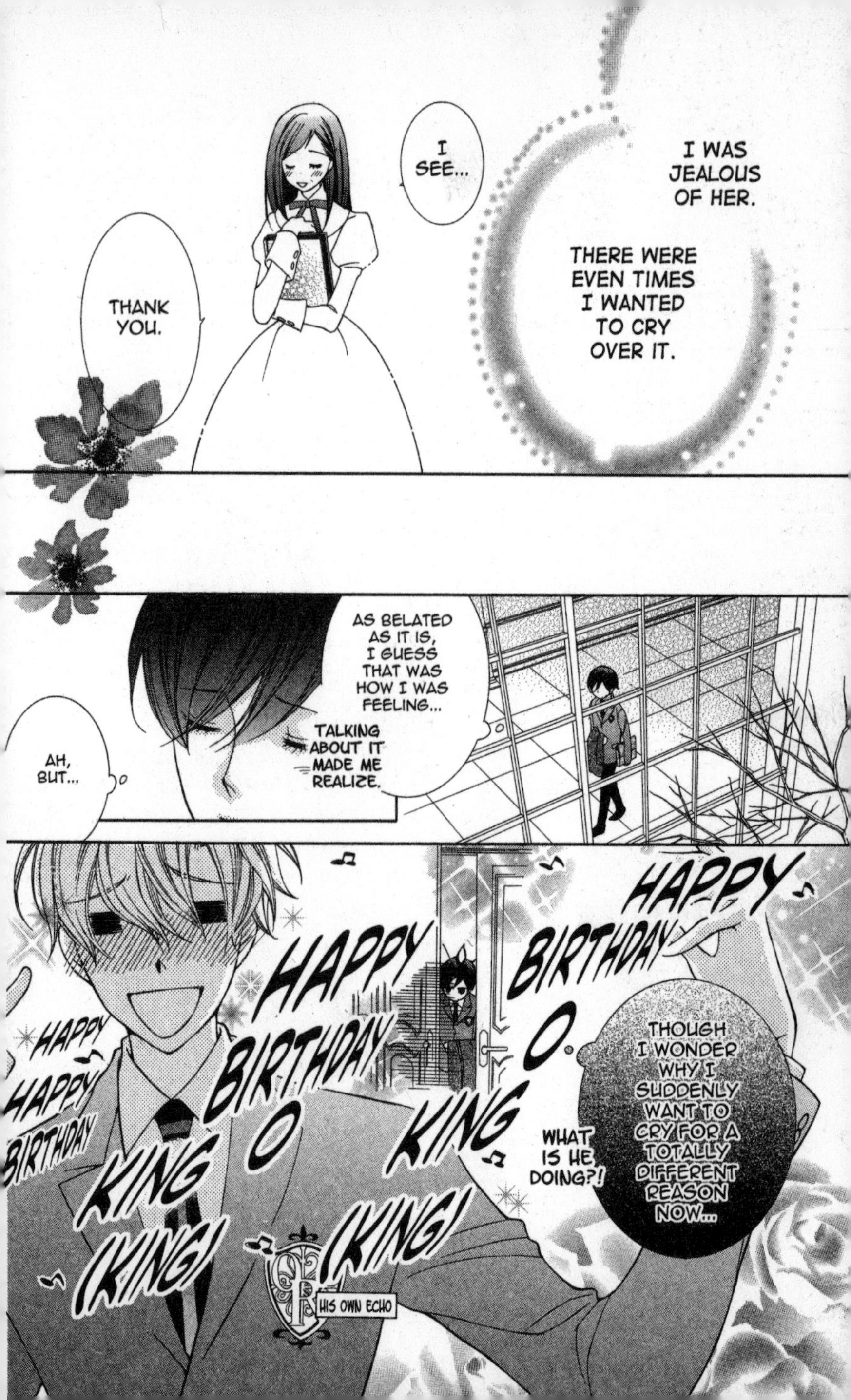
I WAS JEALOUS OF HER.
THERE WERE EVEN TIMES I WANTED TO CRY OVER IT.
I SEE...
THANK YOU.
AS BELATED AS IT IS, I GUESS THAT WAS HOW I WAS FEELING...
TALKING ABOUT IT MADE ME REALIZE.
AH, BUT...
THOUGH I WONDER WHY I SUDDENLY WANT TO CRY FOR A TOTALLY DIFFERENT REASON NOW...
WHAT IS HE DOING?!
HAPPY BIRTHDAY O KING (KING)
HAPPY BIRTHDAY O KING (KING)
HAPPY HAPPY BIRTHDAY
HIS OWN ECHO

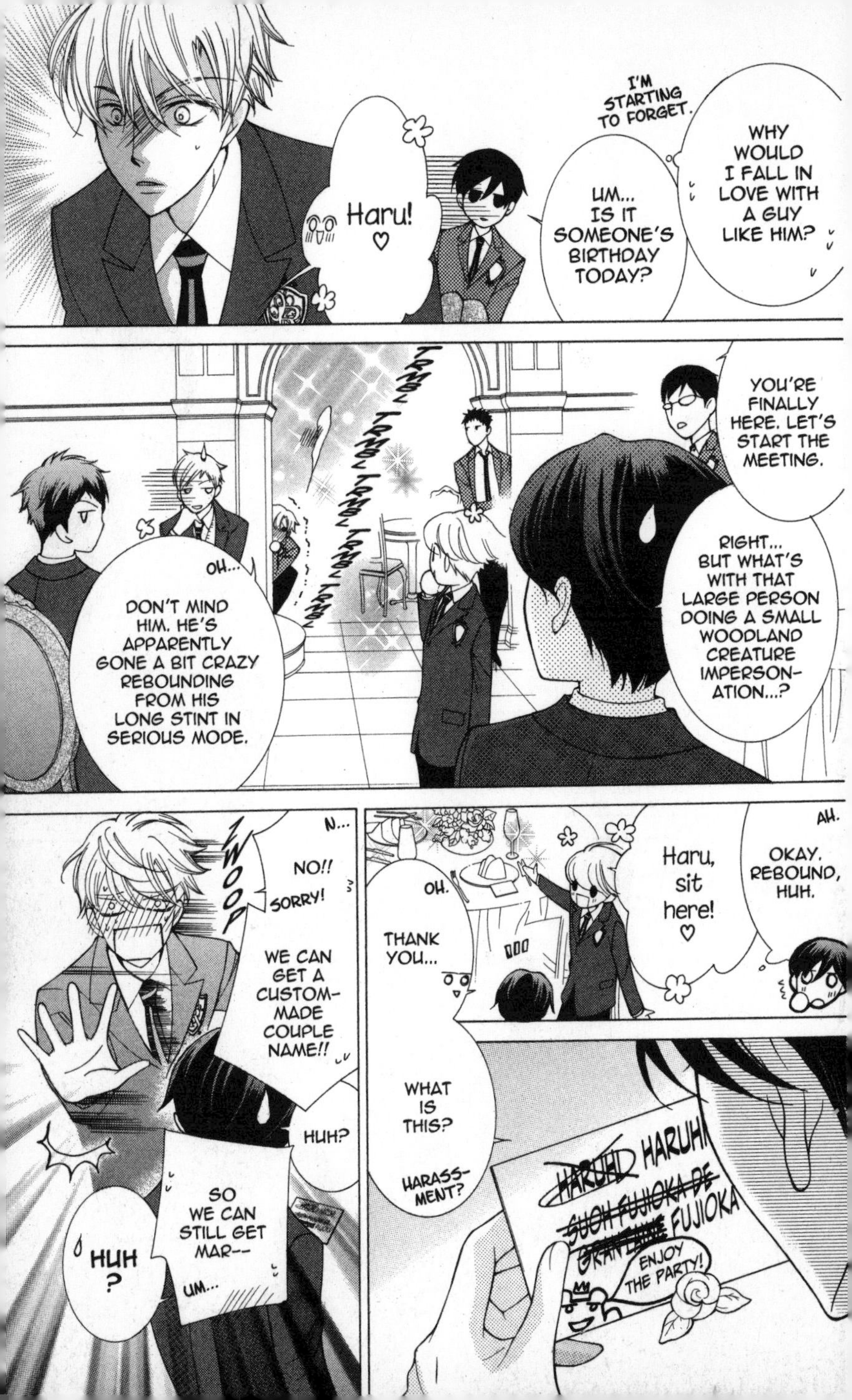
I'M STARTING TO FORGET.
WHY WOULD I FALL IN LOVE WITH A GUY LIKE HIM?
UM... IS IT SOMEONE'S BIRTHDAY TODAY?
Haru! ♡
YOU'RE FINALLY HERE. LET'S START THE MEETING.
RIGHT... BUT WHAT'S WITH THAT LARGE PERSON DOING A SMALL WOODLAND CREATURE IMPERSONATION...?
TRMBL TRMBL TRMBL TRMBL TRMBL
OH...
DON'T MIND HIM. HE'S APPARENTLY GONE A BIT CRAZY REBOUNDING FROM HIS LONG STINT IN SERIOUS MODE.
AH.
OKAY. REBOUND, HUH.
Haru, sit here! ♡
OH.
THANK YOU...
WHAT IS THIS?
HARASSMENT?
HARUHI HARUHI
SUOH FUJIOKA DE FUJIOKA
ENJOY THE PARTY!
N...
NO!!
SORRY!
WOOP
WE CAN GET A CUSTOM-MADE COUPLE NAME!!
HUH?
SO WE CAN STILL GET MAR--
UM...
HUH?

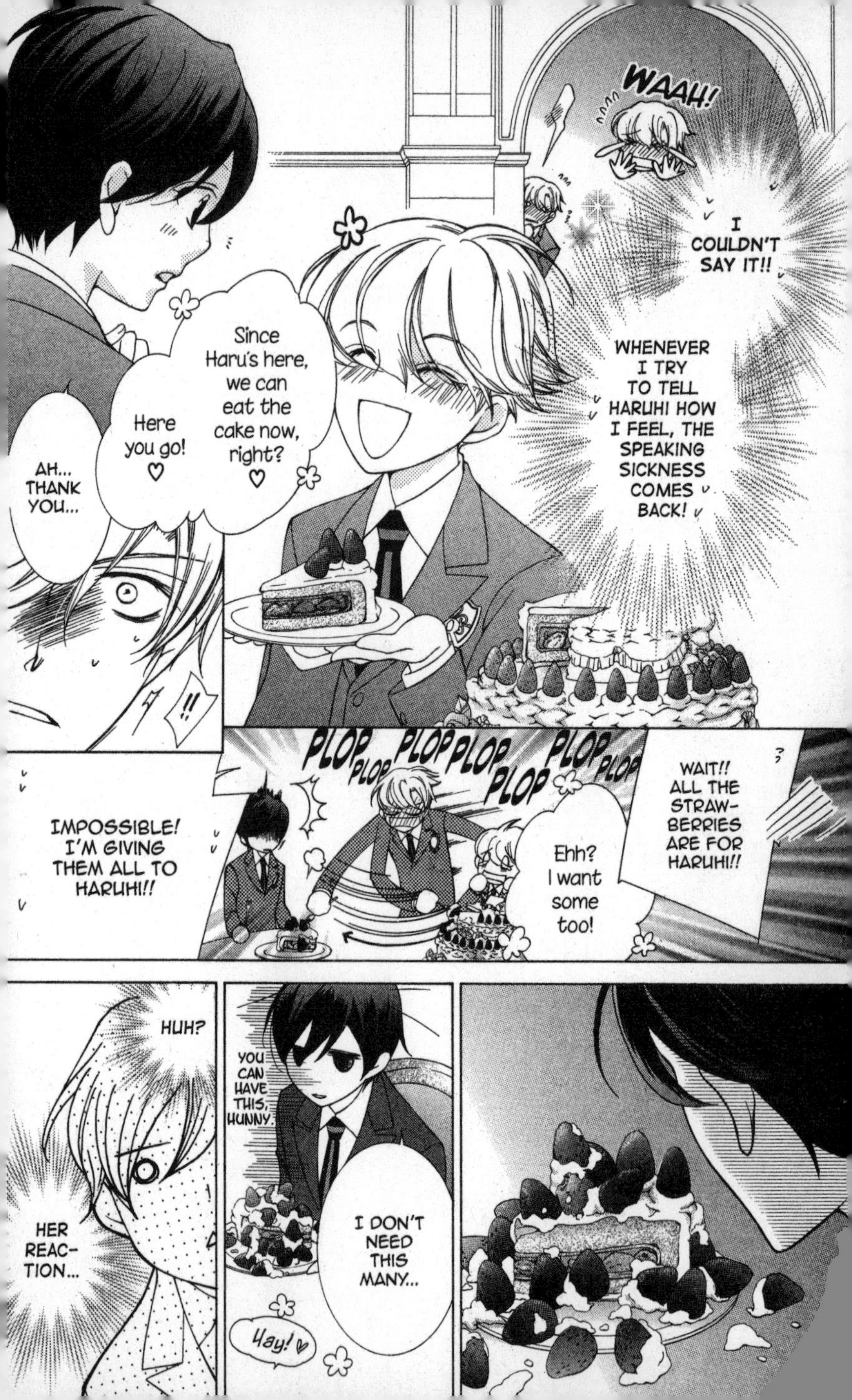
WAAH!
I COULDN'T SAY IT!!
WHENEVER I TRY TO TELL HARUHI HOW I FEEL, THE SPEAKING SICKNESS COMES BACK!
Since Haru's here, we can eat the cake now, right? ♡
Here you go! ♡
AH... THANK YOU...
!!
WAIT!! ALL THE STRAW-BERRIES ARE FOR HARUHI!!
Ehh? I want some too!
PLOP PLOP PLOP PLOP PLOP PLOP PLOP
IMPOSSIBLE! I'M GIVING THEM ALL TO HARUHI!!
YOU CAN HAVE THIS, HUNNY.
I DON'T NEED THIS MANY...
Yay! ♡
HUH?
HER REAC-TION...

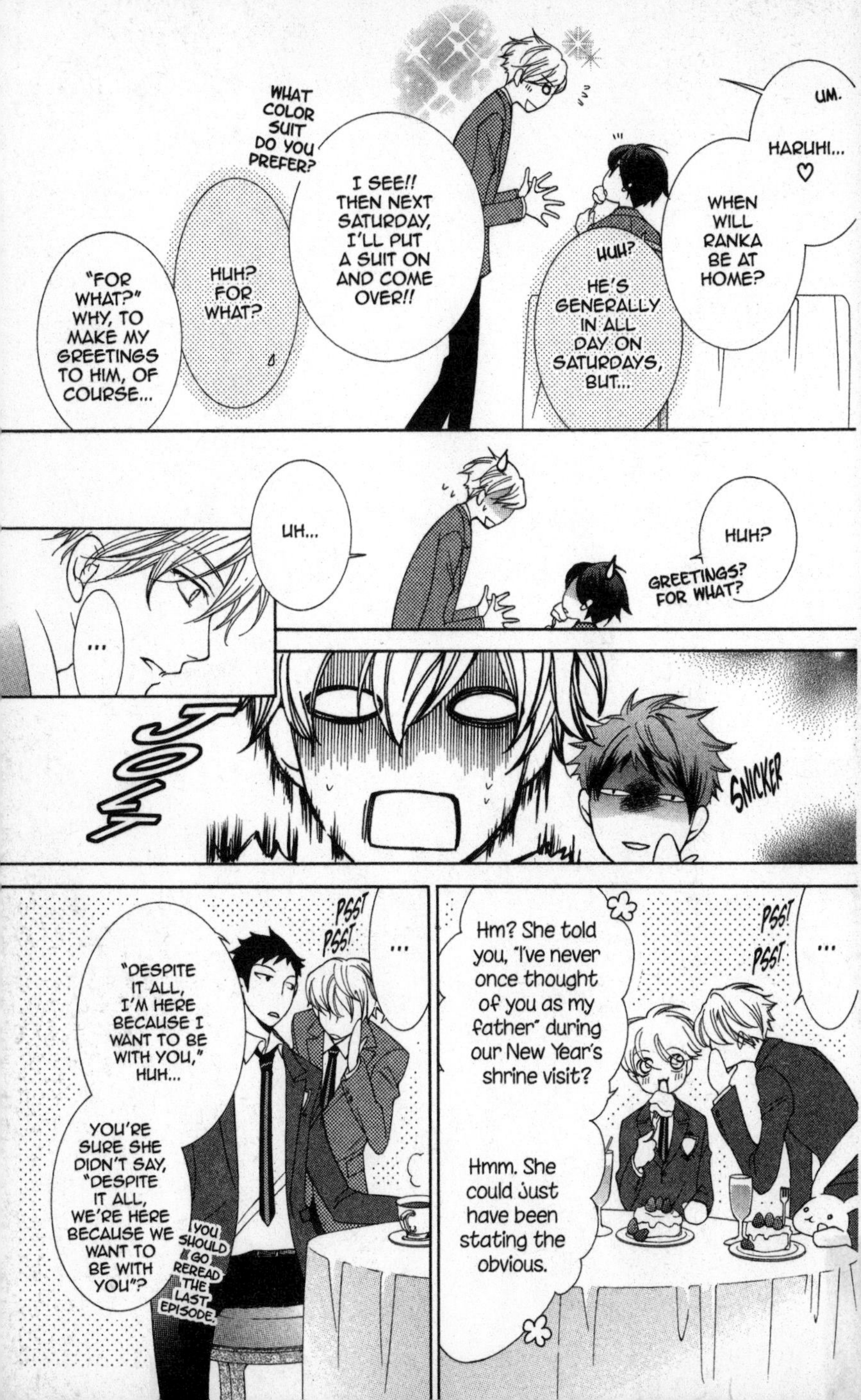
UM. HARUHI... ♡
WHEN WILL RANKA BE AT HOME?
HUH?
HE'S GENERALLY IN ALL DAY ON SATURDAYS, BUT...
I SEE!! THEN NEXT SATURDAY, I'LL PUT A SUIT ON AND COME OVER!!
WHAT COLOR SUIT DO YOU PREFER?
HUH? FOR WHAT?
"FOR WHAT?" WHY, TO MAKE MY GREETINGS TO HIM, OF COURSE...
HUH?
GREETINGS? FOR WHAT?
UH...
...
SNICKER
JOLT
...
PSST PSST
Hm? She told you, "I've never once thought of you as my father" during our New Year's shrine visit?
Hmm. She could just have been stating the obvious.
...
PSST PSST
"DESPITE IT ALL, I'M HERE BECAUSE I WANT TO BE WITH YOU," HUH...
YOU'RE SURE SHE DIDN'T SAY, "DESPITE IT ALL, WE'RE HERE BECAUSE WE WANT TO BE WITH YOU"?
YOU SHOULD GO REREAD THE LAST EPISODE.

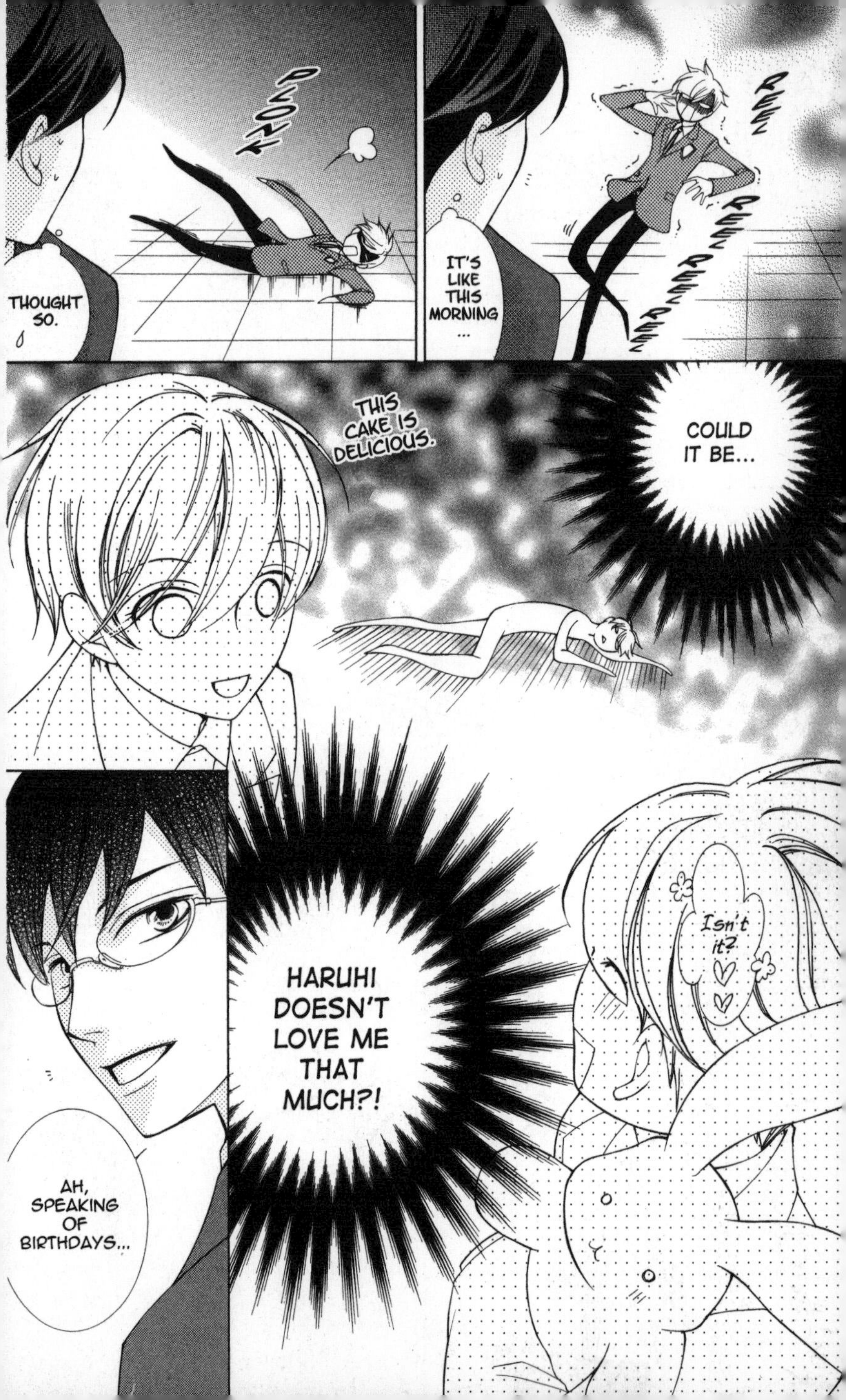
REEL REEL REEL REEL REEL
IT'S LIKE THIS MORNING...
PLONK
THOUGHT SO.
COULD IT BE...
THIS CAKE IS DELICIOUS.
Isn't it?
HARUHI DOESN'T LOVE ME THAT MUCH?!
AH, SPEAKING OF BIRTHDAYS...

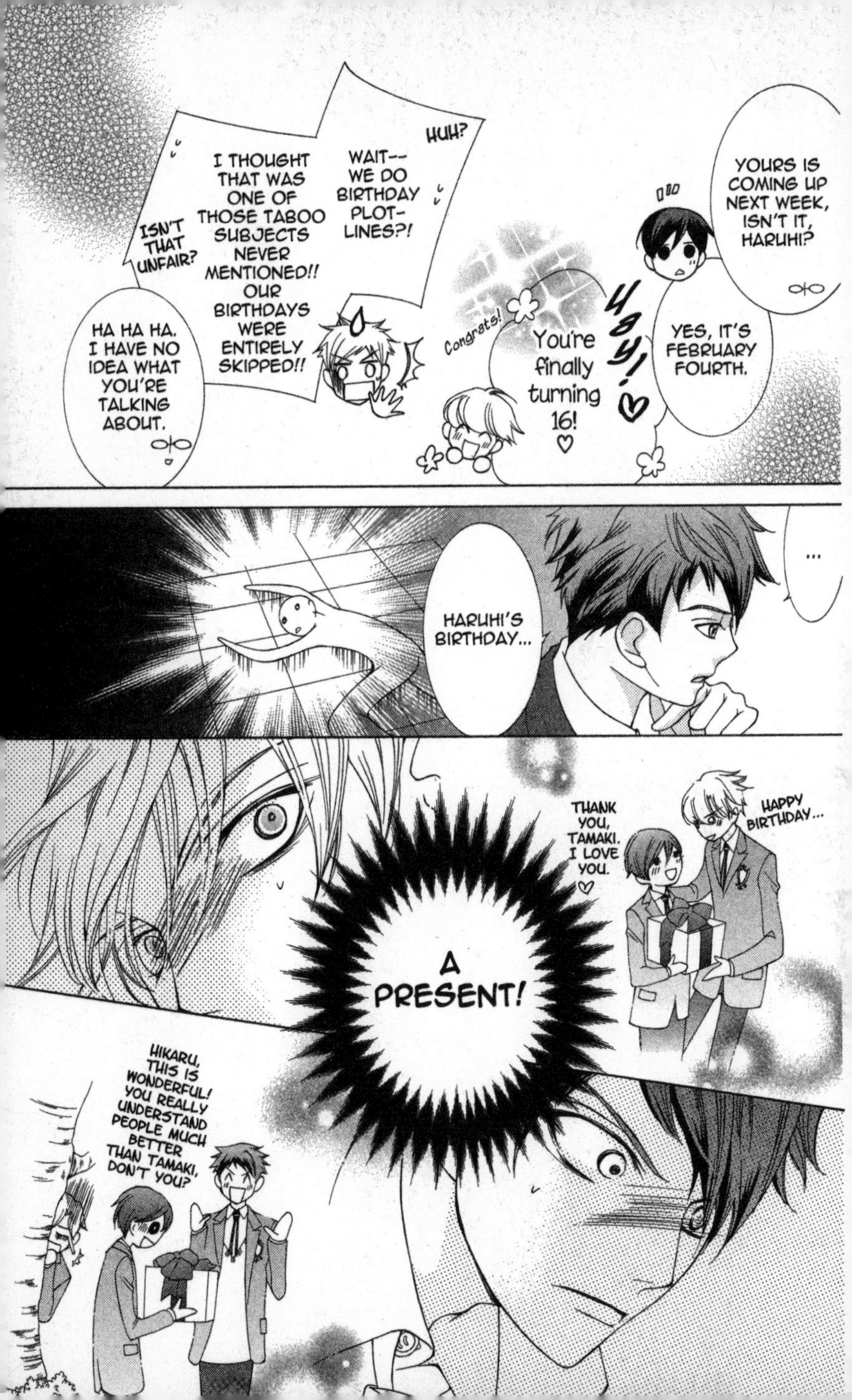
YOURS IS COMING UP NEXT WEEK, ISN'T IT, HARUHI?
YES, IT'S FEBRUARY FOURTH.
YAY!
You're finally turning 16!
Congrats!
HUH?
WAIT-- WE DO BIRTHDAY PLOT-LINES?!
I THOUGHT THAT WAS ONE OF THOSE TABOO SUBJECTS NEVER MENTIONED!! OUR BIRTHDAYS WERE ENTIRELY SKIPPED!!
ISN'T THAT UNFAIR?
HA HA HA. I HAVE NO IDEA WHAT YOU'RE TALKING ABOUT.
...
HARUHI'S BIRTHDAY...
HAPPY BIRTHDAY...
THANK YOU, TAMAKI. I LOVE YOU.
A PRESENT!
HIKARU, THIS IS WONDERFUL! YOU REALLY UNDERSTAND PEOPLE MUCH BETTER THAN TAMAKI, DON'T YOU?

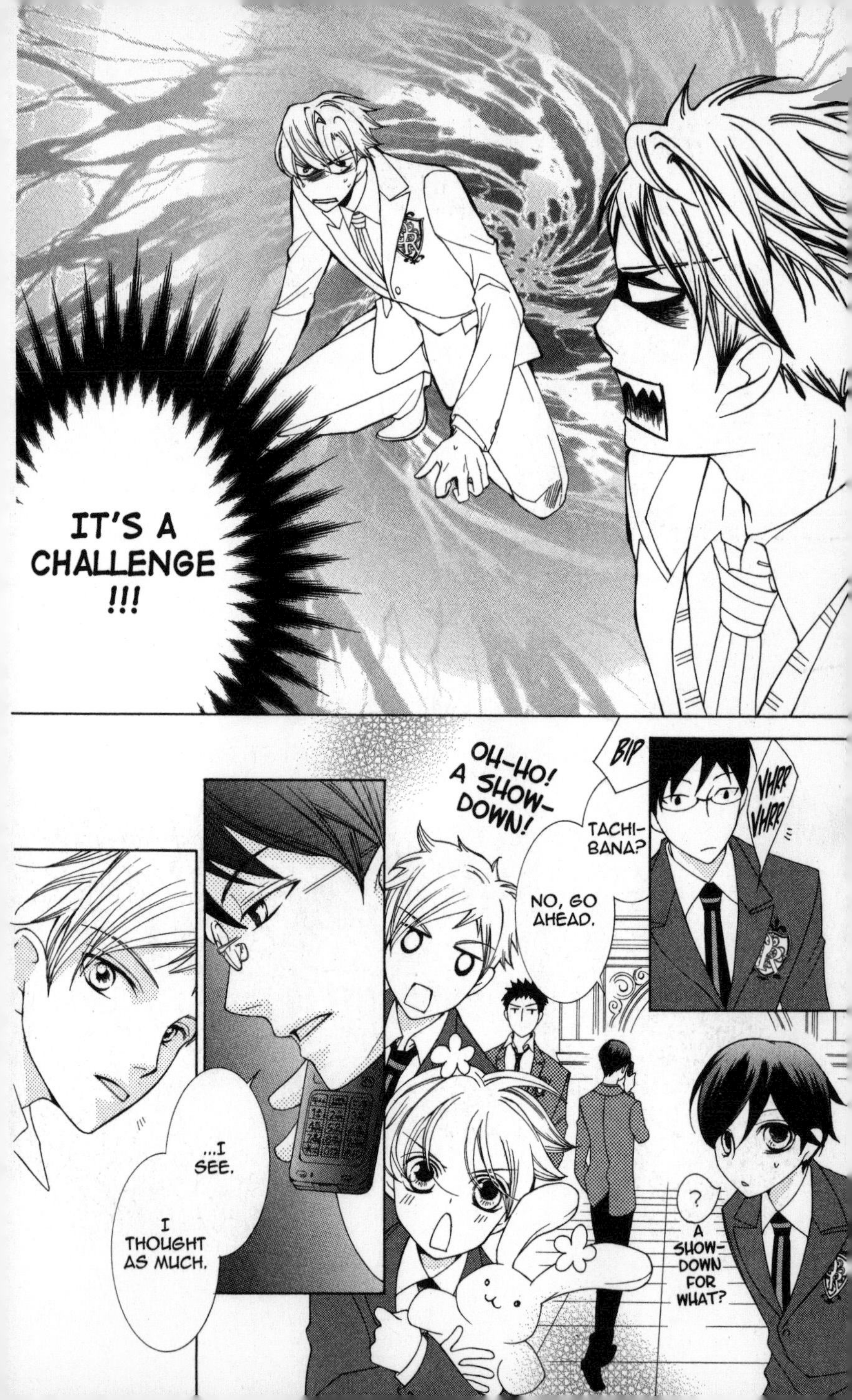
IT'S A CHALLENGE !!!
BIP
VHRR VHRR
TACHI-BANA?
NO, GO AHEAD.
OH-HO! A SHOW-DOWN!
?
A SHOW-DOWN FOR WHAT?
...I SEE.
I THOUGHT AS MUCH.

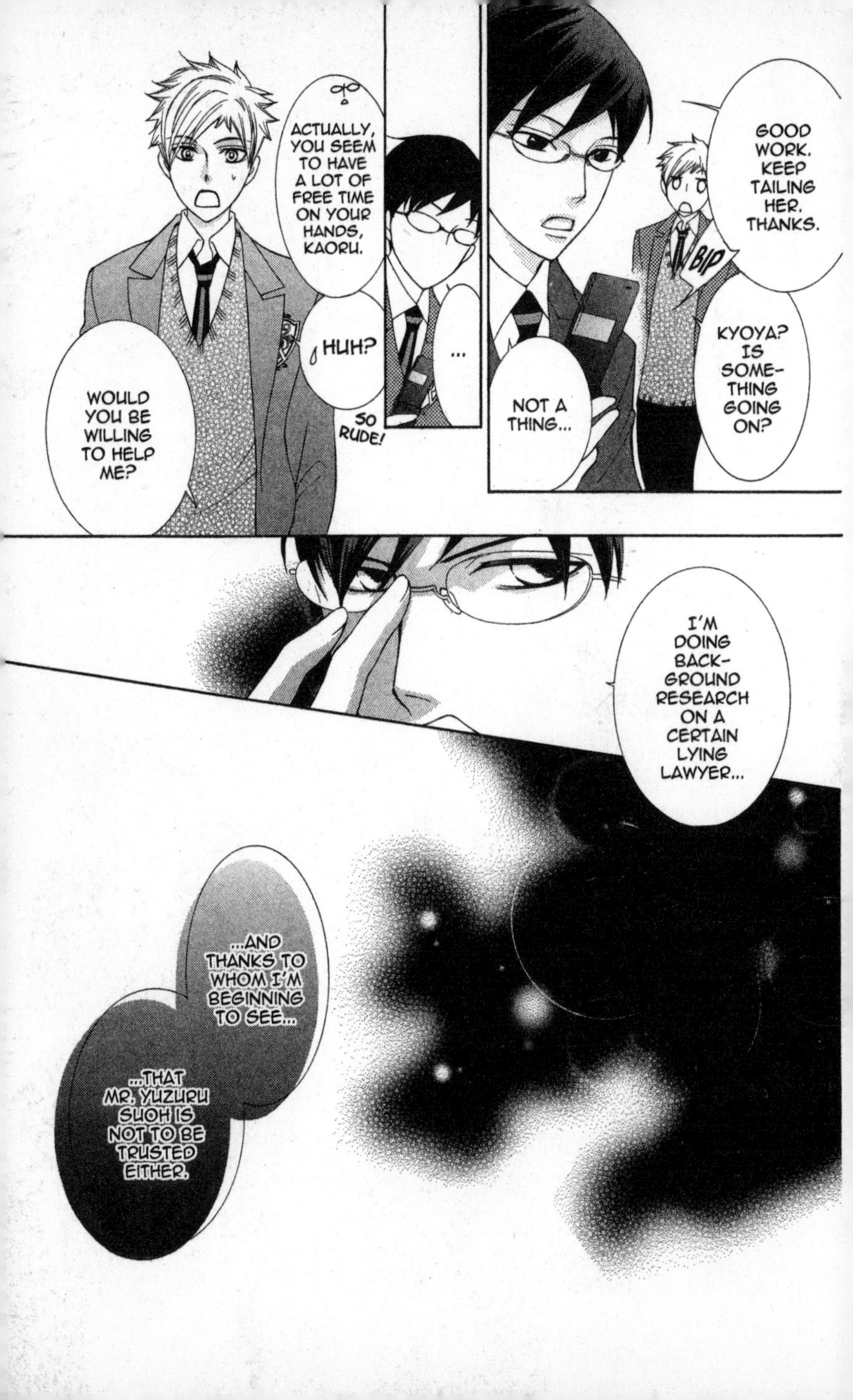
GOOD WORK. KEEP TAILING HER. THANKS.
BIP
KYOYA? IS SOME-THING GOING ON?
NOT A THING...
...
ACTUALLY, YOU SEEM TO HAVE A LOT OF FREE TIME ON YOUR HANDS, KAORU.
HUH?
SO RUDE!
WOULD YOU BE WILLING TO HELP ME?
I'M DOING BACK-GROUND RESEARCH ON A CERTAIN LYING LAWYER...
...AND THANKS TO WHOM I'M BEGINNING TO SEE...
...THAT MR. YUZURU SUOH IS NOT TO BE TRUSTED EITHER.

GUEST ROOM: FAXES

SPECIAL THANKS TO
EMIKO NAKANO!!

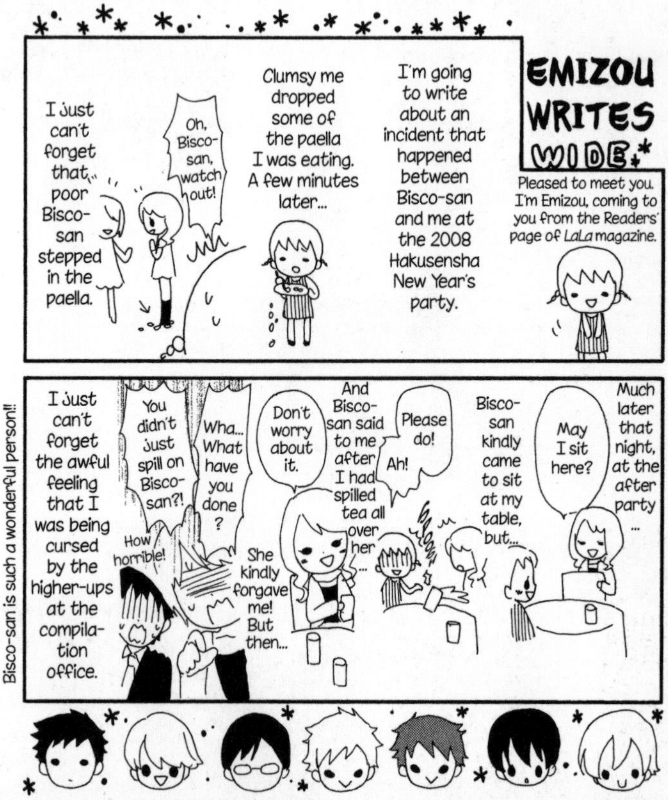
EMIZOU WRITES WIDE
Pleased to meet you. I'm Emizou, coming to you from the Readers' page of *LaLa* magazine.
I'm going to write about an incident that happened between Bisco-san and me at the 2008 Hakusensha New Year's party.
Clumsy me dropped some of the paella I was eating. A few minutes later...
Oh, Bisco-san, watch out!
I just can't forget that poor Bisco-san stepped in the paella.
Much later that night, at the after party...
May I sit here?
Bisco-san kindly came to sit at my table, but...
Ah!
Please do!
And Bisco-san said to me after I had spilled tea all over her...
Don't worry about it.
She kindly forgave me! But then...
Wha... What have you done?
You didn't just spill on Bisco-san?!
How horrible!
I just can't forget the awful feeling that I was being cursed by the higher-ups at the compilation office.
Bisco-san is such a wonderful person!!

MY OLD BUDDY FROM THE READERS' PAGE OF *LALA* MAGAZINE, EMIKO NAKANO HAS DRAWN A BONUS MANGA FOR ME!! AHH, THE LITTLE CHIBI HOSTS ALONG THE BOTTOM ARE SO UTTERLY CUTE...! SO CUTE THAT I WISH THEY'D MAKE MERCHANDISE USING THOSE IMAGES. THANK YOU SO VERY MUCH!

BY THE WAY, FROM MY PERSPECTIVE, THE PAELLA EPISODE WAS MORE A SHOW-CASE OF MY OWN IDIOCY, I THINK... WHY DON'T I WATCH WHERE I'M GOING? I REALLY MADE A MESS ON THAT FLOOR--I'M SO SORRY! (CRIES) ALSO, ACCORDING TO MY MEMORY OF THE TEA-SPILLING EPISODE, I THINK I WAS ACTUALLY A LOT LESS CALM, GOING, "WAAH! GYAH! GYAH!" AND EVERYONE AT THE TABLE WAS KIND OF IN AN UPROAR. THE POOR WAITRESS BROUGHT US A CLOTH TO WIPE IT UP AND ABSOLUTELY FLEW AWAY AFTERWARDS... BASICALLY, WE WERE ALL KIND OF PANICKING. (LAUGHS) MY BEST WISHES TO EMIZOU, WHO IS AS CLUMSY AS A MANGA CHARACTER!!

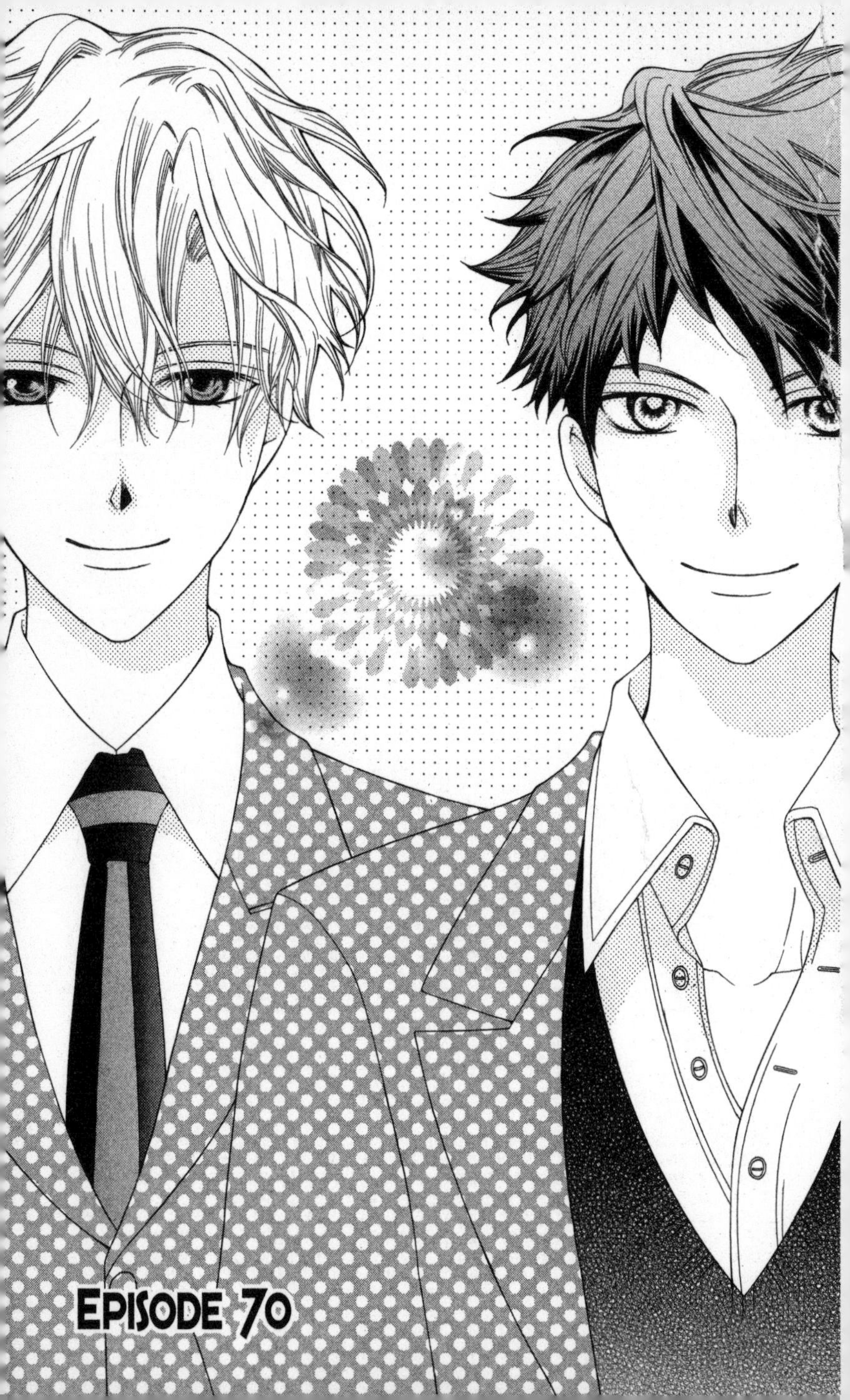
EPISODE 70

FLUP
THIS PHOTO WAS TAKEN THIS YEAR ON JANUARY 6.
AND THIS ONE ON JANUARY 15.
JANUARY 23.
EACH TIME, YUKO KOSAKA HEADS FOR THE MAIN SUOH MANSION TO MEET IN SECRET WITH THE DIRECTOR OF THE BOARD-- THAT IS, TAMAKI'S GRANDMOTHER.
JUDGING BY THIS PATTERN, I'D SAY JANUARY 6 WASN'T THE FIRST TIME SHE'D GONE TO MEET HER.
SECRET MEETINGS?
SORRY, KYOYA, BUT I DON'T REALLY UNDERSTAND THIS.

✿ SUPPORTING CHARACTERS INTRODUCTION ✿

Takeshi Kuze. Blood Type A.

CAPTAIN OF THE FOOTBALL CLUB, THIRD-YEAR, CLASS A.

HIDDEN BENEATH HIS DISAGREEABLE FACADE, IT'S HARD TO TELL, BUT HE REALLY IS A RED-BLOODED TEAM CAPTAIN WHO IS PASSIONATE ABOUT SPORTS. HATORI LIKES THIS SORT OF PERSON VERY MUCH. HIS HAIRSTYLE IS SIMILAR TO THE TWINS'. HE IS THE KING OF THE LOWER EYELASHES.

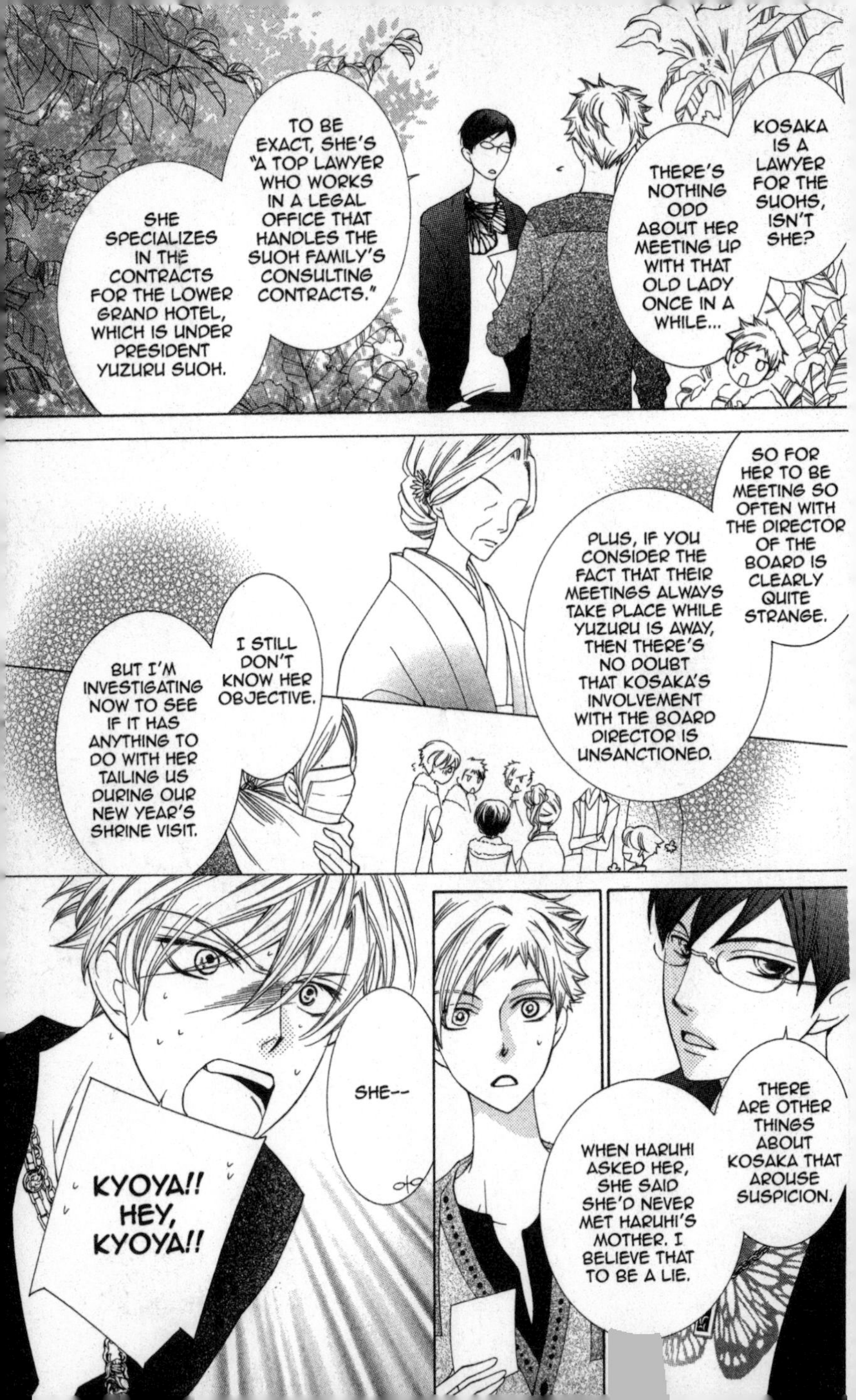
KOSAKA IS A LAWYER FOR THE SUOHS, ISN'T SHE?
THERE'S NOTHING ODD ABOUT HER MEETING UP WITH THAT OLD LADY ONCE IN A WHILE...
TO BE EXACT, SHE'S "A TOP LAWYER WHO WORKS IN A LEGAL OFFICE THAT HANDLES THE SUOH FAMILY'S CONSULTING CONTRACTS."
SHE SPECIALIZES IN THE CONTRACTS FOR THE LOWER GRAND HOTEL, WHICH IS UNDER PRESIDENT YUZURU SUOH.
SO FOR HER TO BE MEETING SO OFTEN WITH THE DIRECTOR OF THE BOARD IS CLEARLY QUITE STRANGE.
PLUS, IF YOU CONSIDER THE FACT THAT THEIR MEETINGS ALWAYS TAKE PLACE WHILE YUZURU IS AWAY, THEN THERE'S NO DOUBT THAT KOSAKA'S INVOLVEMENT WITH THE BOARD DIRECTOR IS UNSANCTIONED.
I STILL DON'T KNOW HER OBJECTIVE.
BUT I'M INVESTIGATING NOW TO SEE IF IT HAS ANYTHING TO DO WITH HER TAILING US DURING OUR NEW YEAR'S SHRINE VISIT.
THERE ARE OTHER THINGS ABOUT KOSAKA THAT AROUSE SUSPICION.
WHEN HARUHI ASKED HER, SHE SAID SHE'D NEVER MET HARUHI'S MOTHER. I BELIEVE THAT TO BE A LIE.
SHE--
KYOYA!! HEY, KYOYA!!

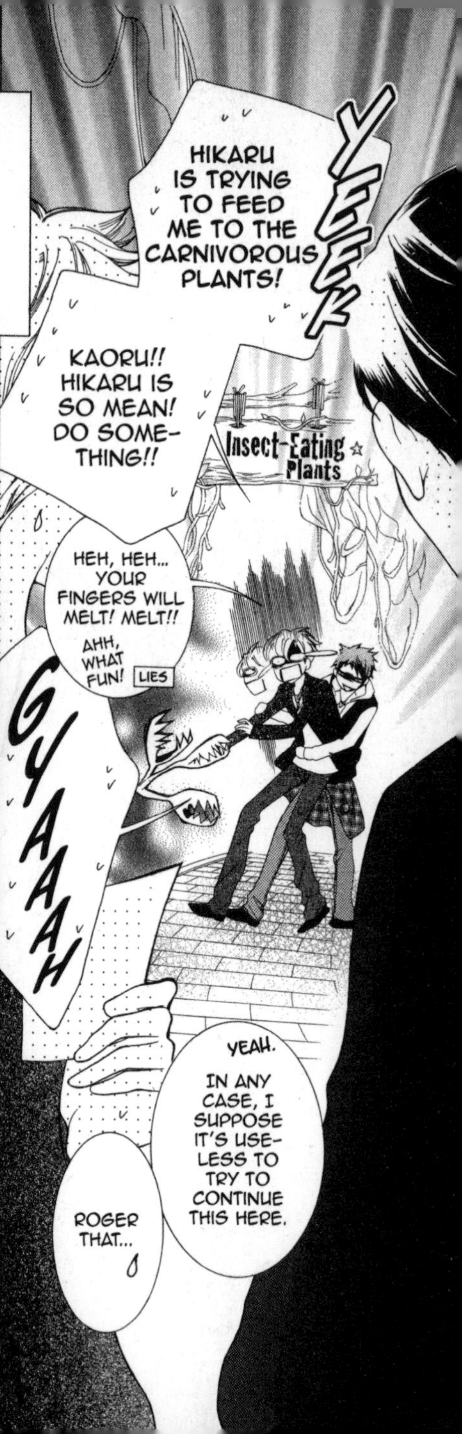
HIKARU IS TRYING TO FEED ME TO THE CARNIVOROUS PLANTS!
KAORU!! HIKARU IS SO MEAN! DO SOME-THING!!
Insect-Eating ☆ Plants
HEH, HEH... YOUR FINGERS WILL MELT! MELT!!
AHH, WHAT FUN!
LIES
GYAAAH
YEAH.
IN ANY CASE, I SUPPOSE IT'S USE-LESS TO TRY TO CONTINUE THIS HERE.
ROGER THAT...
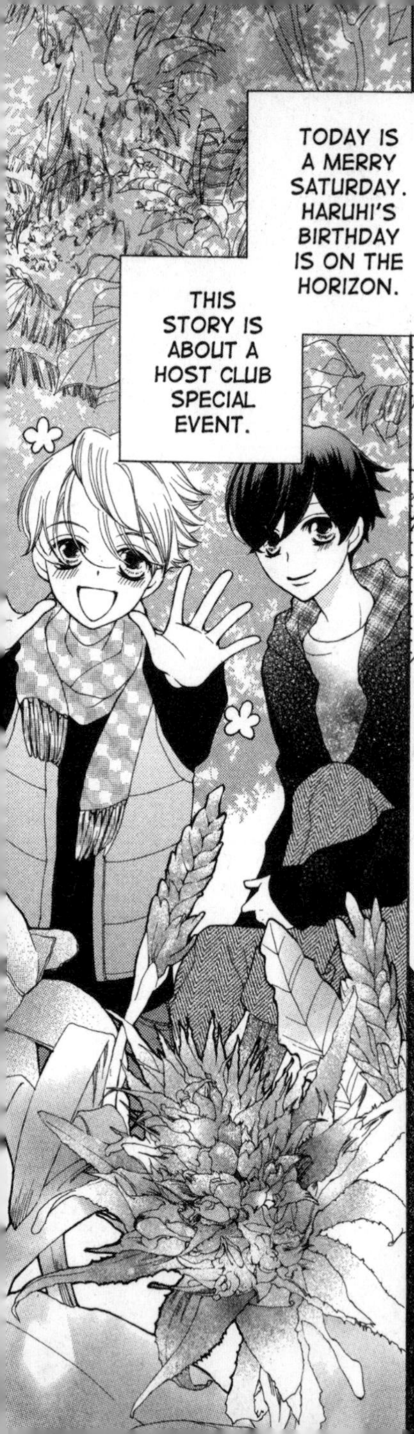
TODAY IS A MERRY SATURDAY. HARUHI'S BIRTHDAY IS ON THE HORIZON.
THIS STORY IS ABOUT A HOST CLUB SPECIAL EVENT.

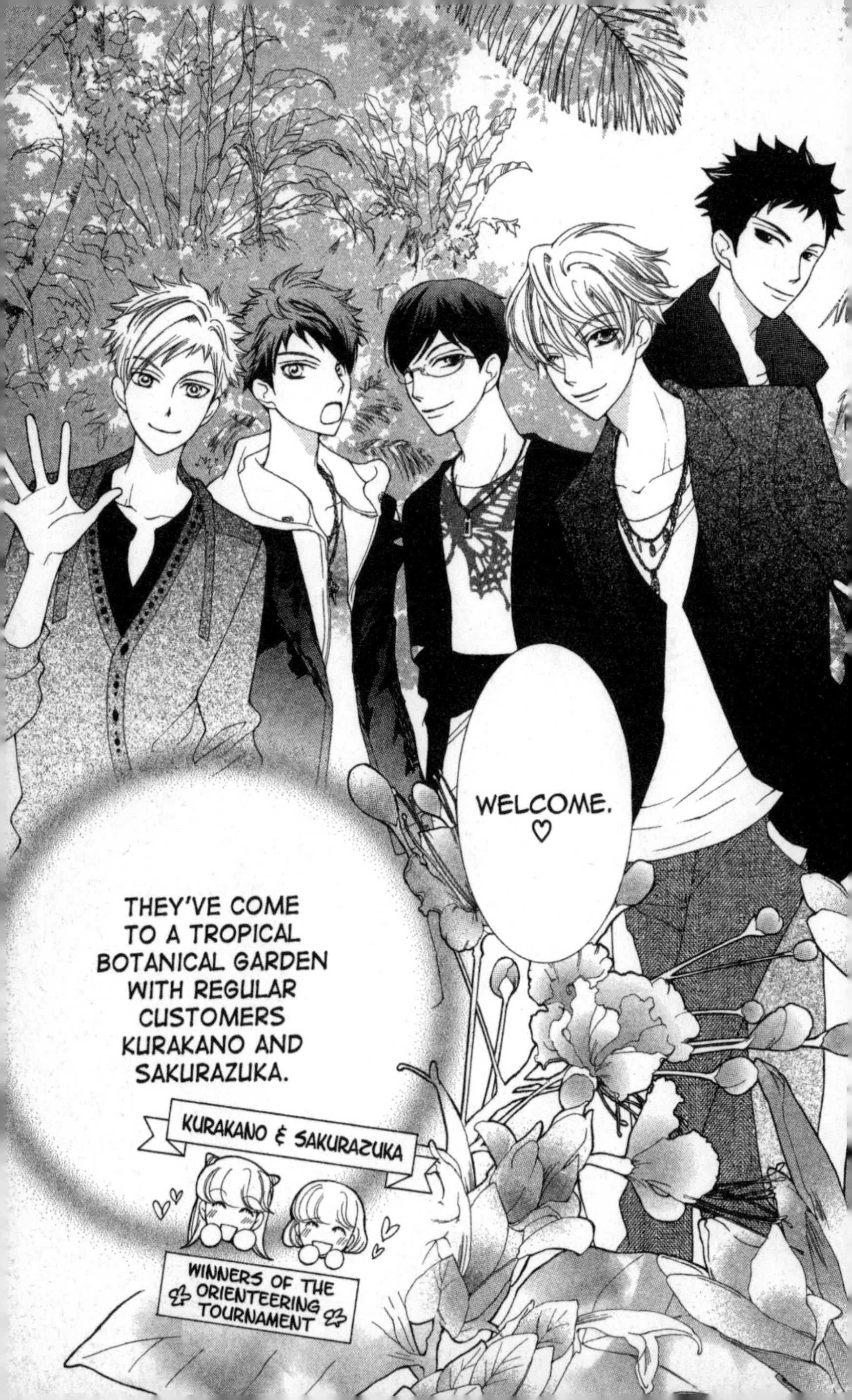
WELCOME. ♡
THEY'VE COME TO A TROPICAL BOTANICAL GARDEN WITH REGULAR CUSTOMERS KURAKANO AND SAKURAZUKA.
KURAKANO & SAKURAZUKA
WINNERS OF THE ORIENTEERING TOURNAMENT

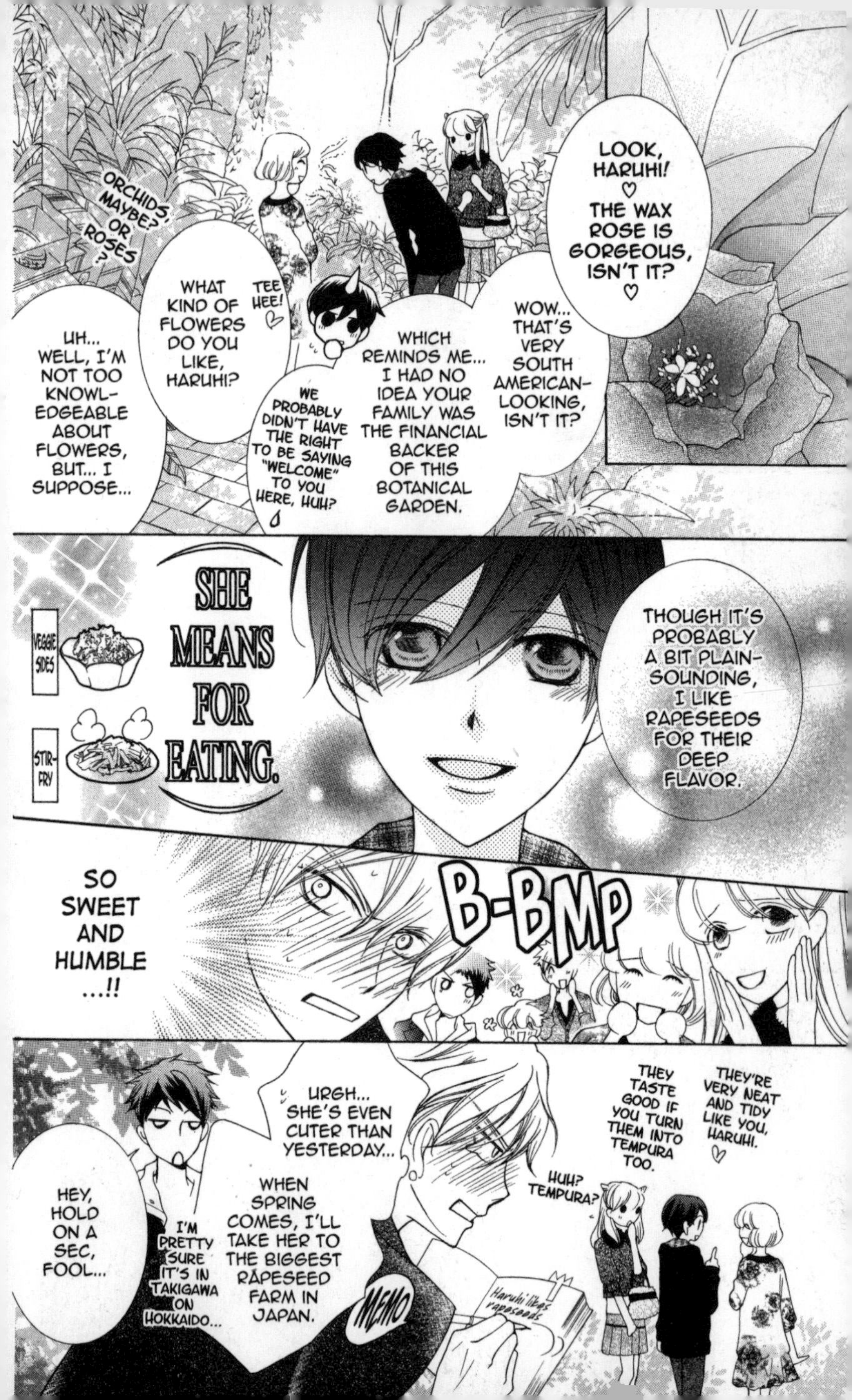

LOOK, HARUHI! ♡ THE WAX ROSE IS GORGEOUS, ISN'T IT? ♡
WOW... THAT'S VERY SOUTH AMERICAN-LOOKING, ISN'T IT?
WHICH REMINDS ME... I HAD NO IDEA YOUR FAMILY WAS THE FINANCIAL BACKER OF THIS BOTANICAL GARDEN.
WE PROBABLY DIDN'T HAVE THE RIGHT TO BE SAYING "WELCOME" TO YOU HERE, HUH?
TEE HEE!
ORCHIDS, MAYBE? OR ROSES?
WHAT KIND OF FLOWERS DO YOU LIKE, HARUHI?
UH... WELL, I'M NOT TOO KNOWLEDGEABLE ABOUT FLOWERS, BUT... I SUPPOSE...
THOUGH IT'S PROBABLY A BIT PLAIN-SOUNDING, I LIKE RAPESEEDS FOR THEIR DEEP FLAVOR.
SHE MEANS FOR EATING.
VEGGIE SIDES
STIR-FRY
B-BMP
SO SWEET AND HUMBLE ...!!
THEY'RE VERY NEAT AND TIDY LIKE YOU, HARUHI. ♡
THEY TASTE GOOD IF YOU TURN THEM INTO TEMPURA TOO.
HUH? TEMPURA?
URGH... SHE'S EVEN CUTER THAN YESTERDAY...
WHEN SPRING COMES, I'LL TAKE HER TO THE BIGGEST RAPESEED FARM IN JAPAN.
Haruhi likes rapeseeds
MEMO
I'M PRETTY SURE IT'S IN TAKIGAWA ON HOKKAIDO...
HEY, HOLD ON A SEC, FOOL...

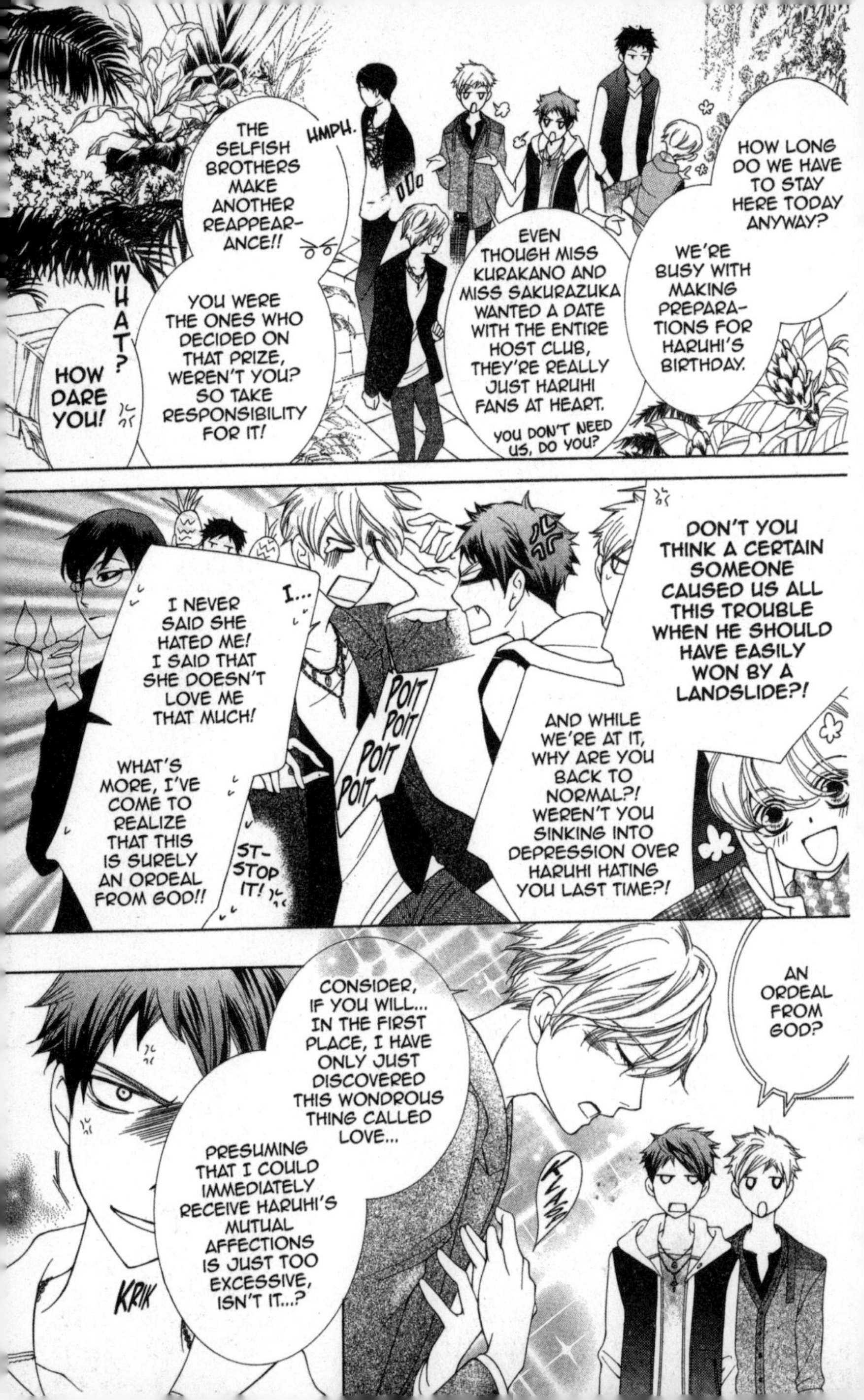
HOW LONG DO WE HAVE TO STAY HERE TODAY ANYWAY?
WE'RE BUSY WITH MAKING PREPARATIONS FOR HARUHI'S BIRTHDAY.
EVEN THOUGH MISS KURAKANO AND MISS SAKURAZUKA WANTED A DATE WITH THE ENTIRE HOST CLUB, THEY'RE REALLY JUST HARUHI FANS AT HEART.
YOU DON'T NEED US, DO YOU?
HMPH.
THE SELFISH BROTHERS MAKE ANOTHER REAPPEARANCE!!
YOU WERE THE ONES WHO DECIDED ON THAT PRIZE, WEREN'T YOU? SO TAKE RESPONSIBILITY FOR IT!
WHAT?
HOW DARE YOU!
DON'T YOU THINK A CERTAIN SOMEONE CAUSED US ALL THIS TROUBLE WHEN HE SHOULD HAVE EASILY WON BY A LANDSLIDE?!
AND WHILE WE'RE AT IT, WHY ARE YOU BACK TO NORMAL?! WEREN'T YOU SINKING INTO DEPRESSION OVER HARUHI HATING YOU LAST TIME?!
POIT POIT POIT POIT
I...
ST-STOP IT!
I NEVER SAID SHE HATED ME! I SAID THAT SHE DOESN'T LOVE ME THAT MUCH!
WHAT'S MORE, I'VE COME TO REALIZE THAT THIS IS SURELY AN ORDEAL FROM GOD!!
AN ORDEAL FROM GOD?
CONSIDER, IF YOU WILL... IN THE FIRST PLACE, I HAVE ONLY JUST DISCOVERED THIS WONDROUS THING CALLED LOVE...
PRESUMING THAT I COULD IMMEDIATELY RECEIVE HARUHI'S MUTUAL AFFECTIONS IS JUST TOO EXCESSIVE, ISN'T IT...?
KRIK

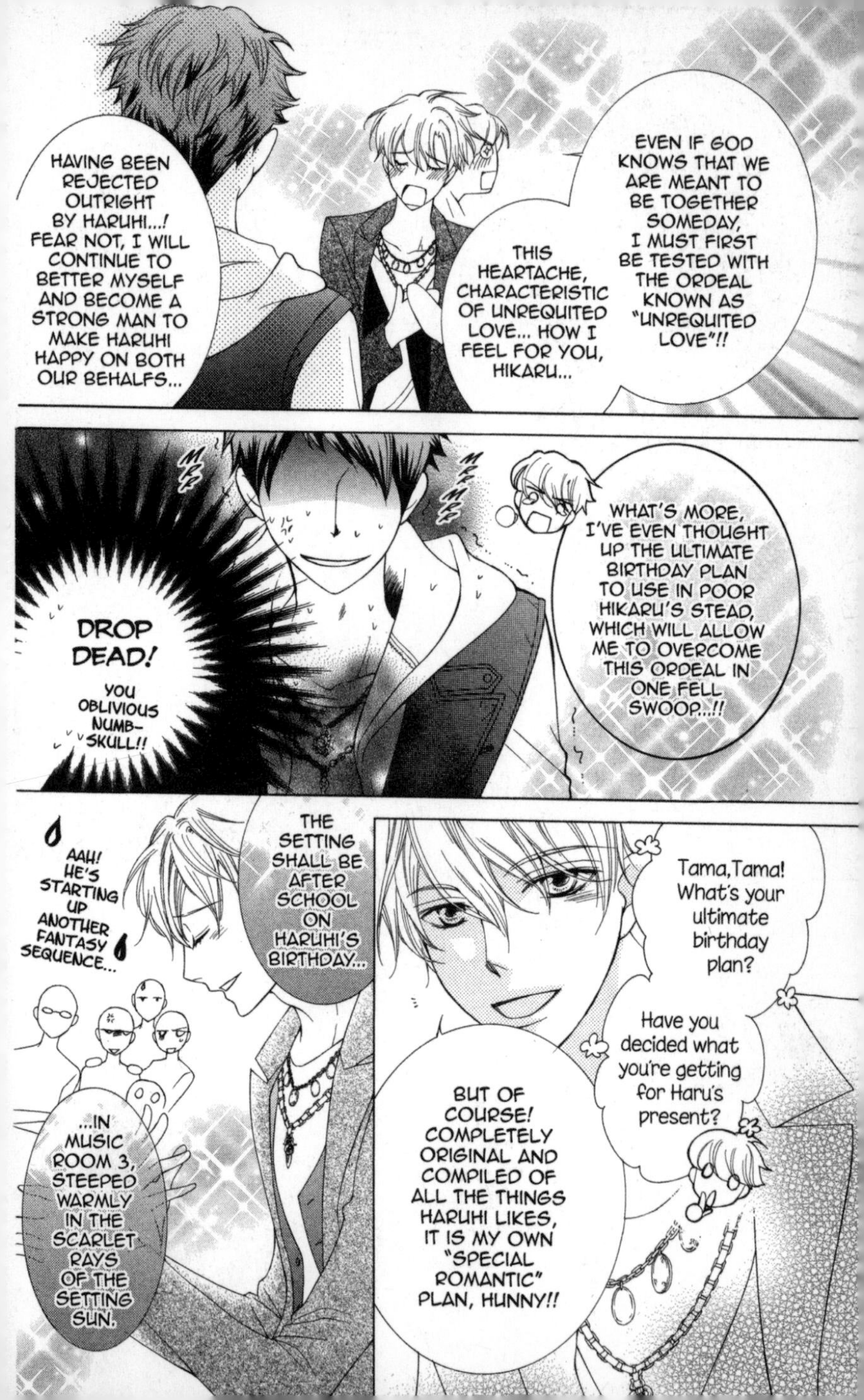
EVEN IF GOD KNOWS THAT WE ARE MEANT TO BE TOGETHER SOMEDAY, I MUST FIRST BE TESTED WITH THE ORDEAL KNOWN AS "UNREQUITED LOVE"!!
THIS HEARTACHE, CHARACTERISTIC OF UNREQUITED LOVE... HOW I FEEL FOR YOU, HIKARU...
HAVING BEEN REJECTED OUTRIGHT BY HARUHI...! FEAR NOT, I WILL CONTINUE TO BETTER MYSELF AND BECOME A STRONG MAN TO MAKE HARUHI HAPPY ON BOTH OUR BEHALFS...
WHAT'S MORE, I'VE EVEN THOUGHT UP THE ULTIMATE BIRTHDAY PLAN TO USE IN POOR HIKARU'S STEAD, WHICH WILL ALLOW ME TO OVERCOME THIS ORDEAL IN ONE FELL SWOOP...!!
MRR MRR
MRR
DROP DEAD!
YOU OBLIVIOUS NUMB-SKULL!!
Tama,Tama! What's your ultimate birthday plan?
Have you decided what you're getting for Haru's present?
BUT OF COURSE! COMPLETELY ORIGINAL AND COMPILED OF ALL THE THINGS HARUHI LIKES, IT IS MY OWN "SPECIAL ROMANTIC" PLAN, HUNNY!!
THE SETTING SHALL BE AFTER SCHOOL ON HARUHI'S BIRTHDAY...
AAH! HE'S STARTING UP ANOTHER FANTASY SEQUENCE...
...IN MUSIC ROOM 3, STEEPED WARMLY IN THE SCARLET RAYS OF THE SETTING SUN.

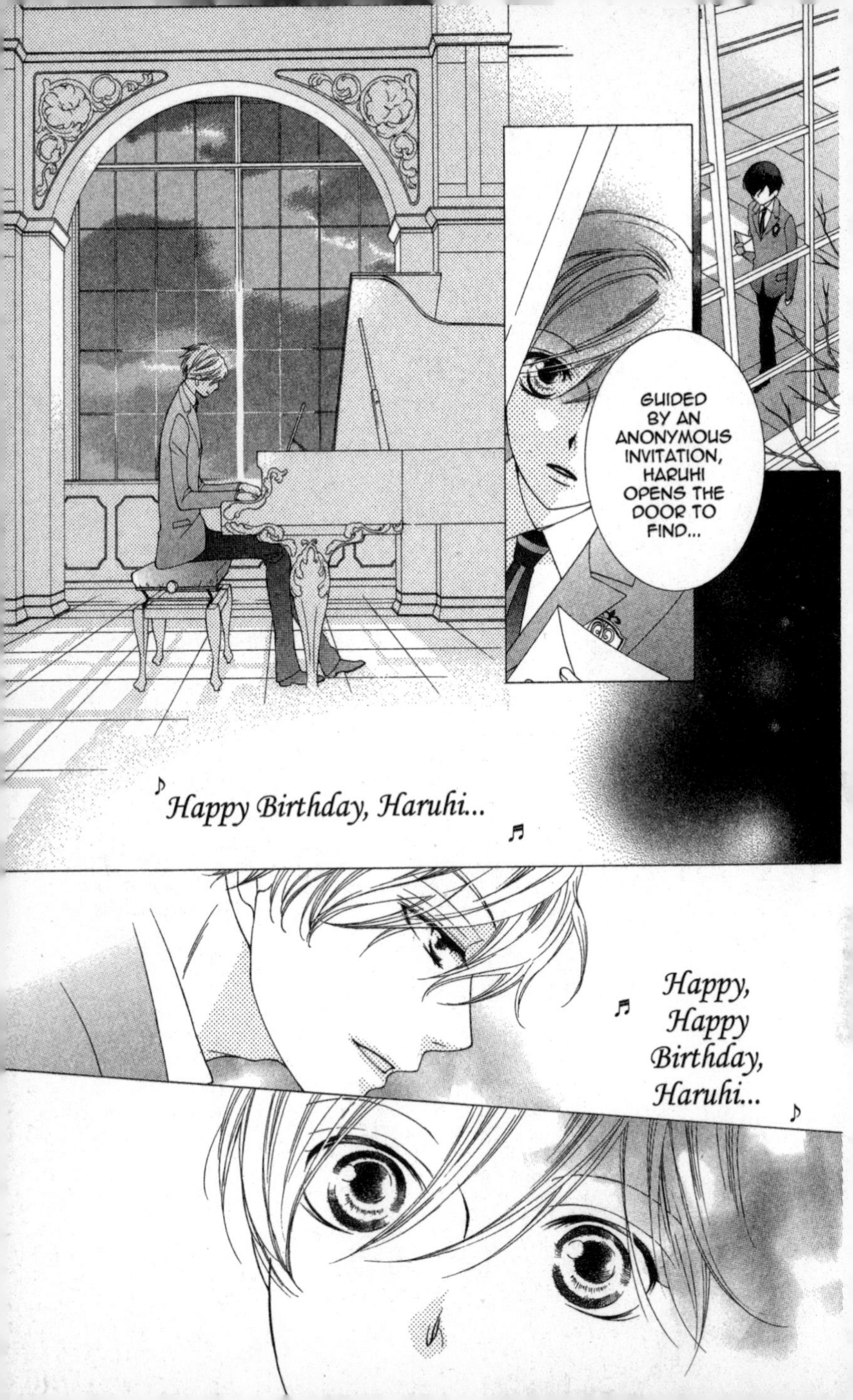
GUIDED BY AN ANONYMOUS INVITATION, HARUHI OPENS THE DOOR TO FIND...
♪ Happy Birthday, Haruhi... ♬
♬ Happy, Happy Birthday, Haruhi... ♪

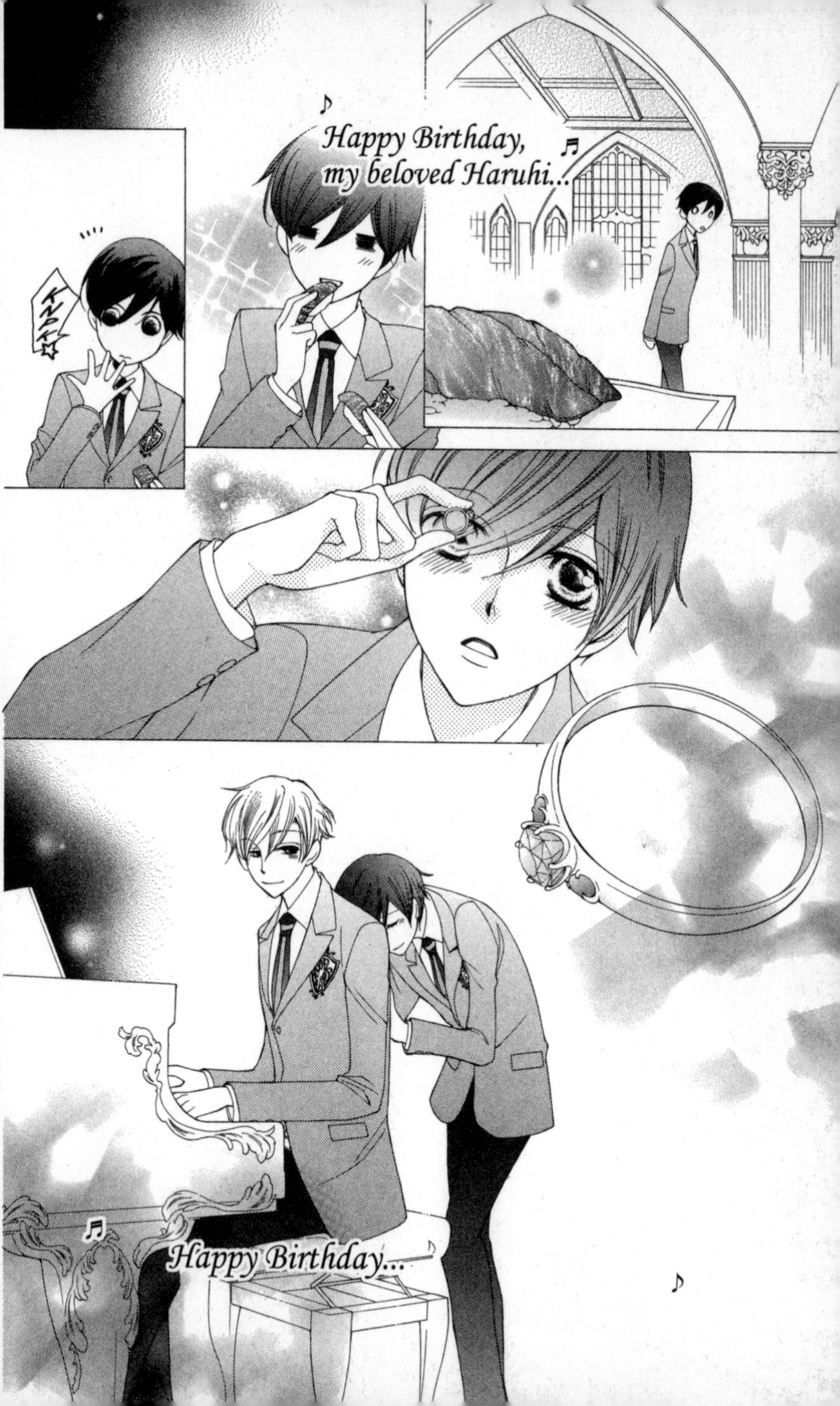

Happy Birthday, my beloved Haruhi...
Happy Birthday...

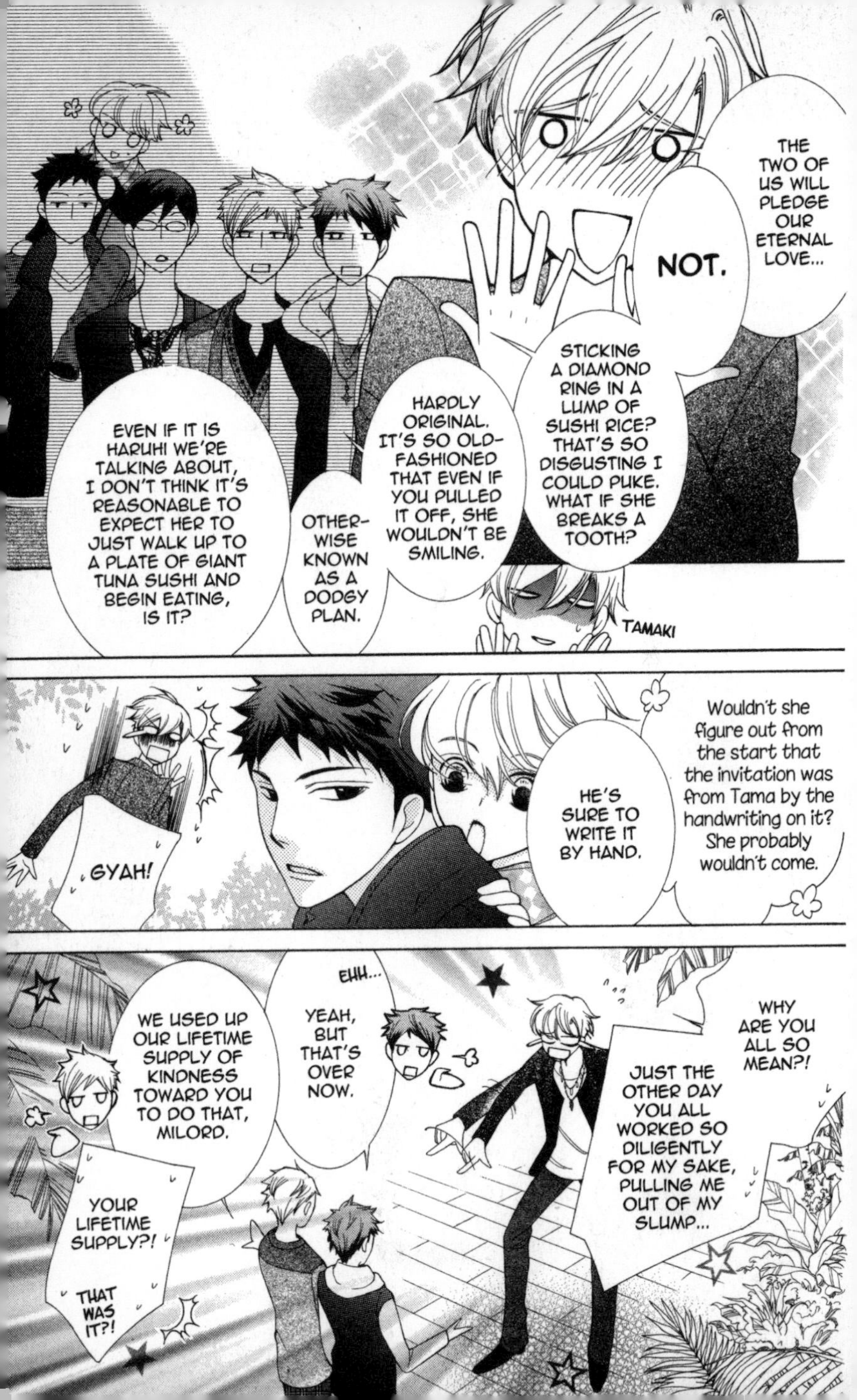
THE TWO OF US WILL PLEDGE OUR ETERNAL LOVE...
NOT.
STICKING A DIAMOND RING IN A LUMP OF SUSHI RICE? THAT'S SO DISGUSTING I COULD PUKE. WHAT IF SHE BREAKS A TOOTH?
HARDLY ORIGINAL. IT'S SO OLD-FASHIONED THAT EVEN IF YOU PULLED IT OFF, SHE WOULDN'T BE SMILING.
OTHER-WISE KNOWN AS A DODGY PLAN.
EVEN IF IT IS HARUHI WE'RE TALKING ABOUT, I DON'T THINK IT'S REASONABLE TO EXPECT HER TO JUST WALK UP TO A PLATE OF GIANT TUNA SUSHI AND BEGIN EATING, IS IT?
TAMAKI
Wouldn't she figure out from the start that the invitation was from Tama by the handwriting on it? She probably wouldn't come.
HE'S SURE TO WRITE IT BY HAND.
GYAH!
WHY ARE YOU ALL SO MEAN?!
JUST THE OTHER DAY YOU ALL WORKED SO DILIGENTLY FOR MY SAKE, PULLING ME OUT OF MY SLUMP...
EHH...
YEAH, BUT THAT'S OVER NOW.
WE USED UP OUR LIFETIME SUPPLY OF KINDNESS TOWARD YOU TO DO THAT, MILORD.
YOUR LIFETIME SUPPLY?!
THAT WAS IT?!

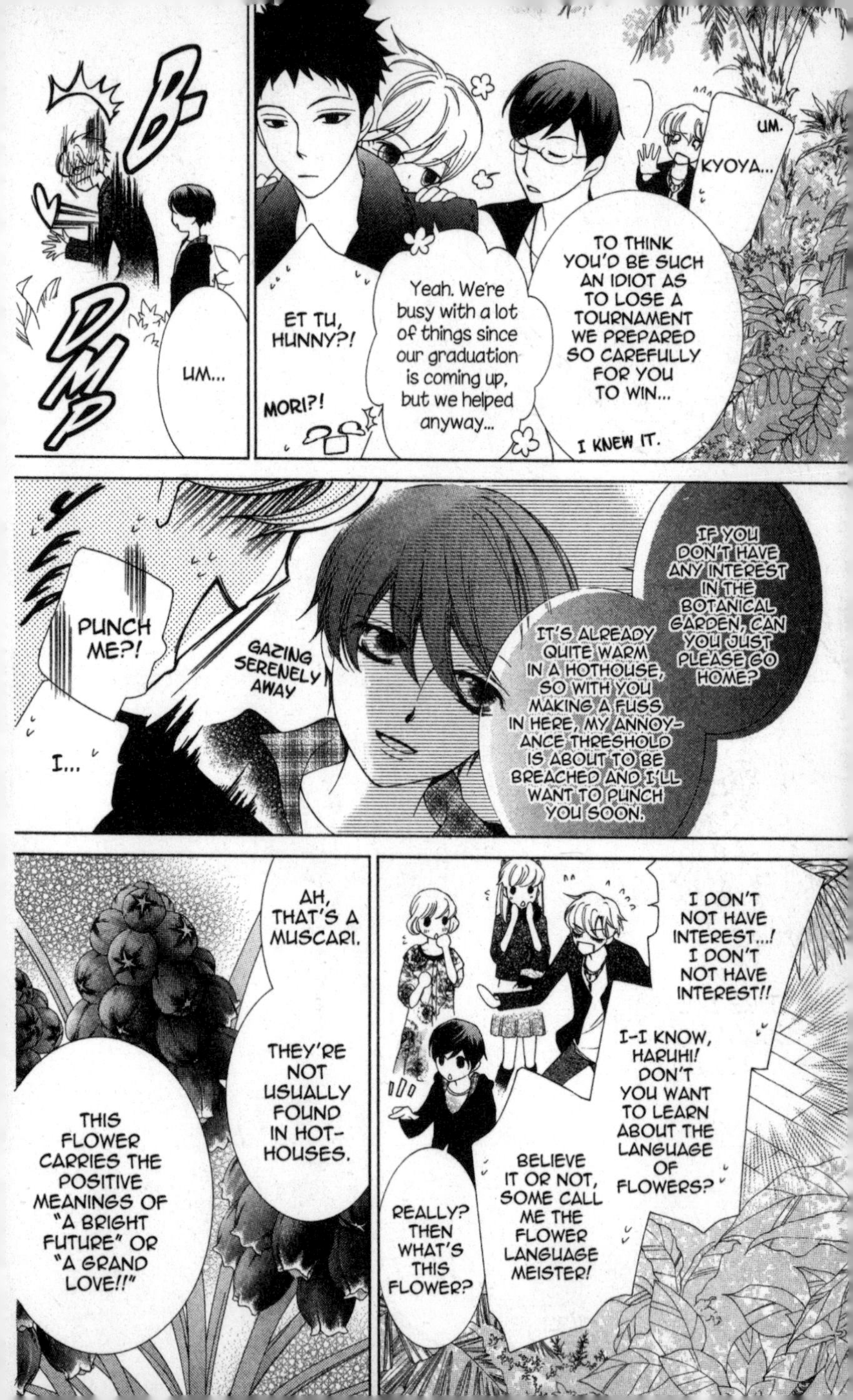
UM.
KYOYA...
TO THINK YOU'D BE SUCH AN IDIOT AS TO LOSE A TOURNAMENT WE PREPARED SO CAREFULLY FOR YOU TO WIN...
I KNEW IT.
Yeah. We're busy with a lot of things since our graduation is coming up, but we helped anyway...
ET TU, HUNNY?!
MORI?!
B
DMP
UM...
IF YOU DON'T HAVE ANY INTEREST IN THE BOTANICAL GARDEN, CAN YOU JUST PLEASE GO HOME?
IT'S ALREADY QUITE WARM IN A HOTHOUSE, SO WITH YOU MAKING A FUSS IN HERE, MY ANNOYANCE THRESHOLD IS ABOUT TO BE BREACHED AND I'LL WANT TO PUNCH YOU SOON.
GAZING SERENELY AWAY
PUNCH ME?!
I...
I DON'T NOT HAVE INTEREST...! I DON'T NOT HAVE INTEREST!!
I-I KNOW, HARUHI! DON'T YOU WANT TO LEARN ABOUT THE LANGUAGE OF FLOWERS?
BELIEVE IT OR NOT, SOME CALL ME THE FLOWER LANGUAGE MEISTER!
REALLY? THEN WHAT'S THIS FLOWER?
AH, THAT'S A MUSCARI.
THEY'RE NOT USUALLY FOUND IN HOTHOUSES.
THIS FLOWER CARRIES THE POSITIVE MEANINGS OF "A BRIGHT FUTURE" OR "A GRAND LOVE!!"

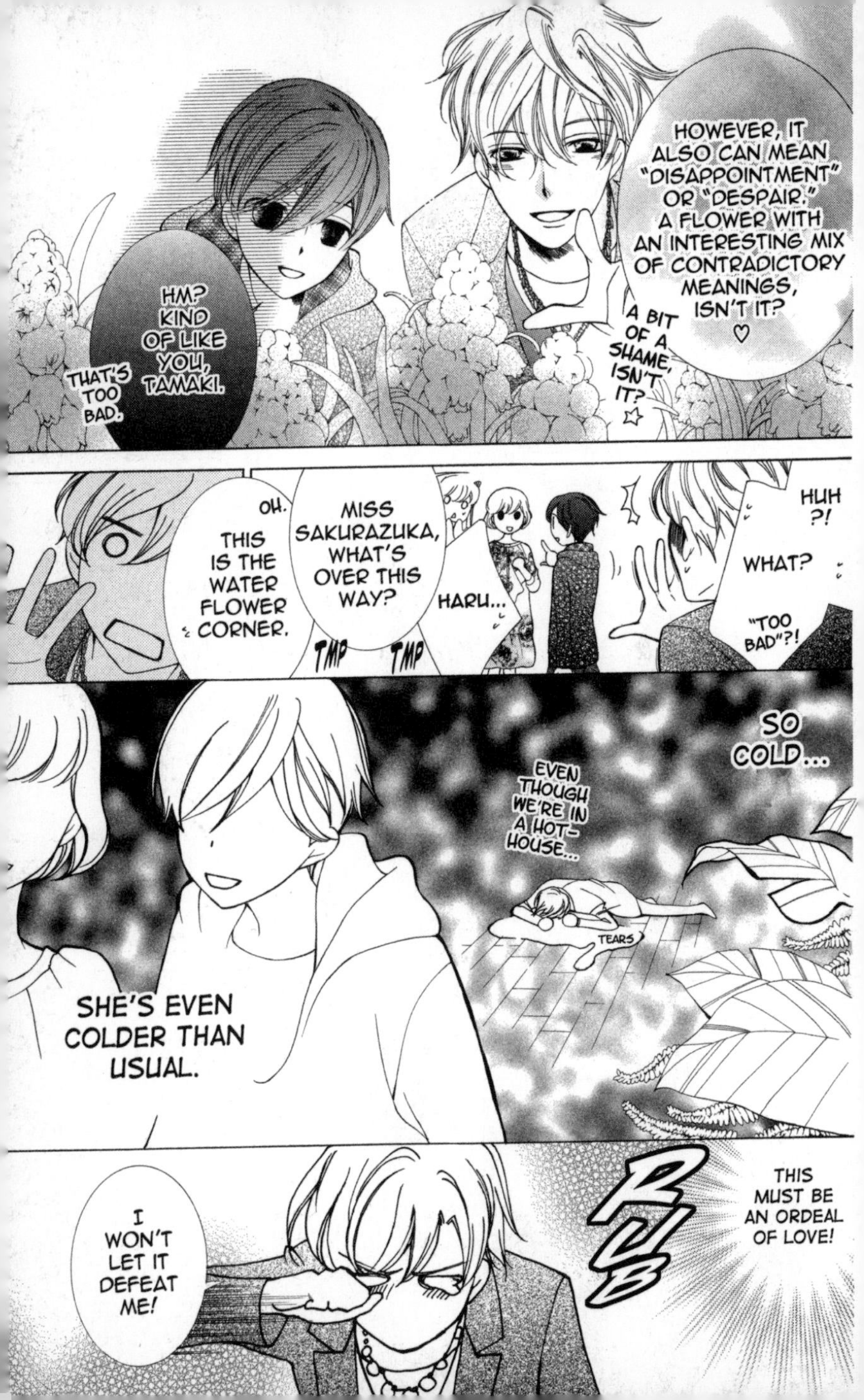
HOWEVER, IT ALSO CAN MEAN "DISAPPOINTMENT" OR "DESPAIR." A FLOWER WITH AN INTERESTING MIX OF CONTRADICTORY MEANINGS, ISN'T IT? ♡
A BIT OF A SHAME, ISN'T IT? ☆
HM? KIND OF LIKE YOU, TAMAKI.
THAT'S TOO BAD.
HUH?!
WHAT?
"TOO BAD"?!
HARU...
MISS SAKURAZUKA, WHAT'S OVER THIS WAY?
TMP TMP
OH.
THIS IS THE WATER FLOWER CORNER.
SO COLD...
EVEN THOUGH WE'RE IN A HOT-HOUSE...
TEARS
SHE'S EVEN COLDER THAN USUAL.
THIS MUST BE AN ORDEAL OF LOVE!
RUB
I WON'T LET IT DEFEAT ME!

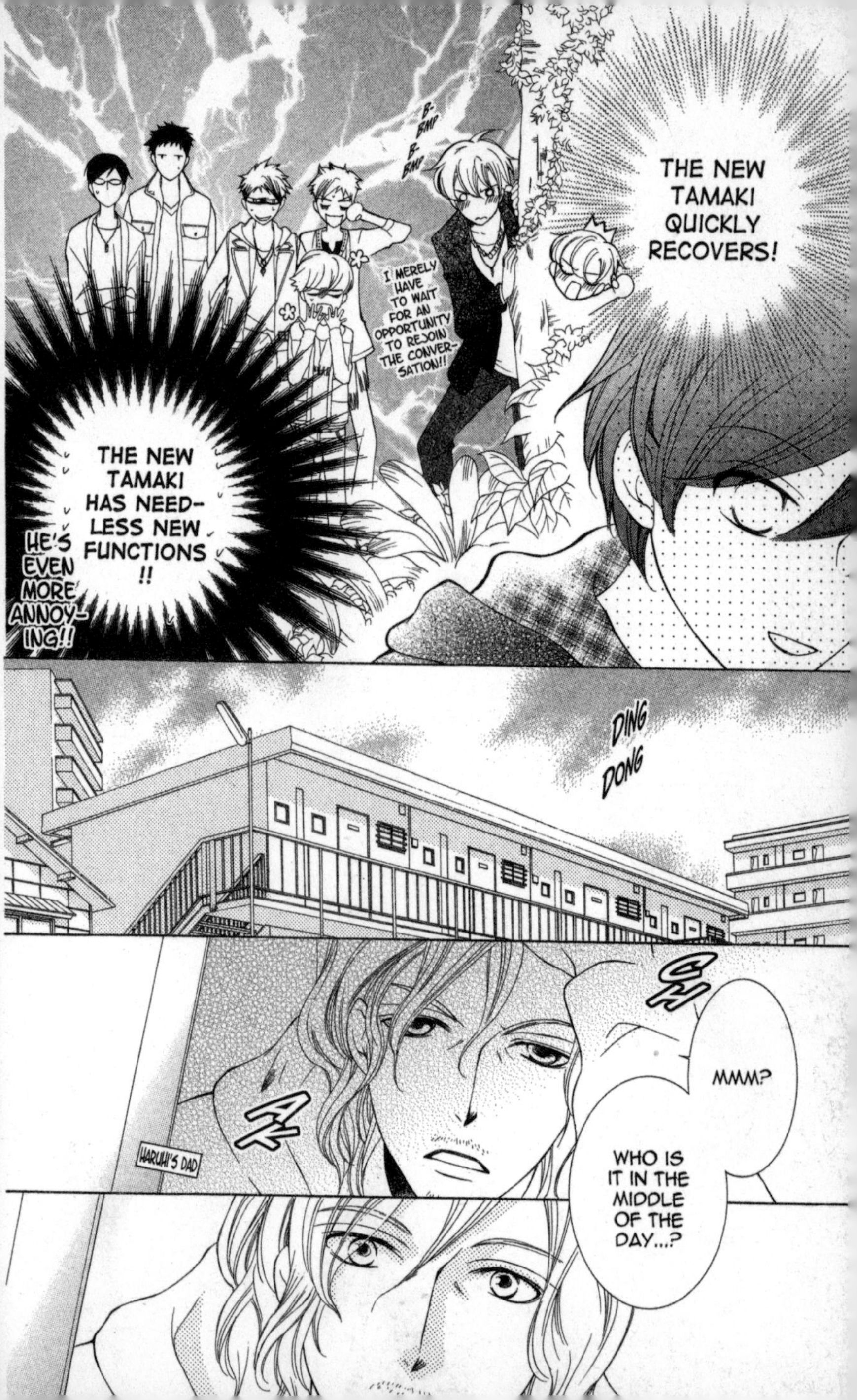
THE NEW TAMAKI QUICKLY RECOVERS!
B-BMP B-BMP
I MERELY HAVE TO WAIT FOR AN OPPORTUNITY TO REJOIN THE CONVERSATION!!
THE NEW TAMAKI HAS NEEDLESS NEW FUNCTIONS!!
HE'S EVEN MORE ANNOYING!!
DING DONG
GH
AH
HARUHI'S DAD
MMM?
WHO IS IT IN THE MIDDLE OF THE DAY...?

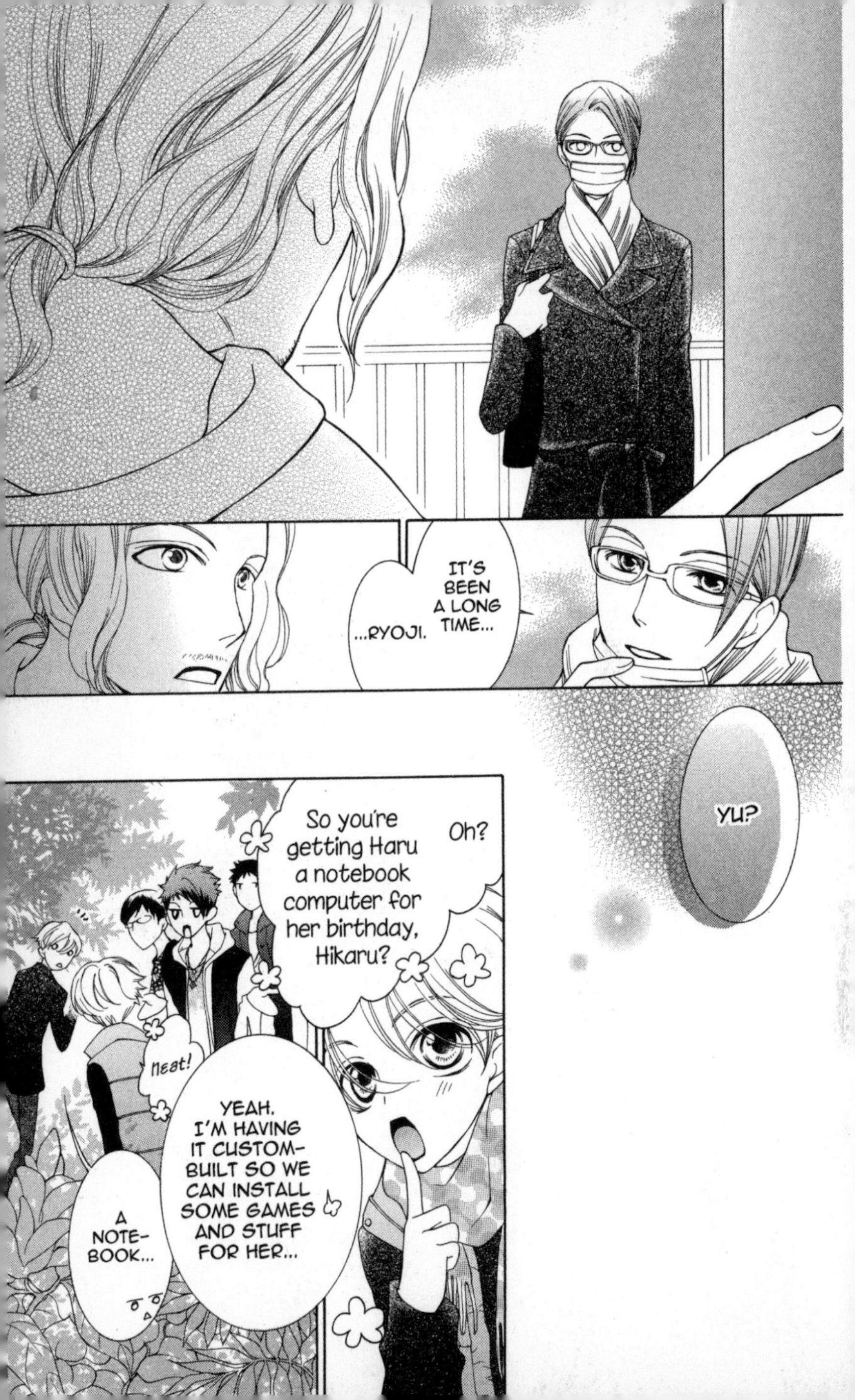
IT'S BEEN A LONG TIME...
...RYOJI.
YU?
Oh?
So you're getting Haru a notebook computer for her birthday, Hikaru?
Neat!
YEAH. I'M HAVING IT CUSTOM-BUILT SO WE CAN INSTALL SOME GAMES AND STUFF FOR HER...
A NOTE-BOOK...

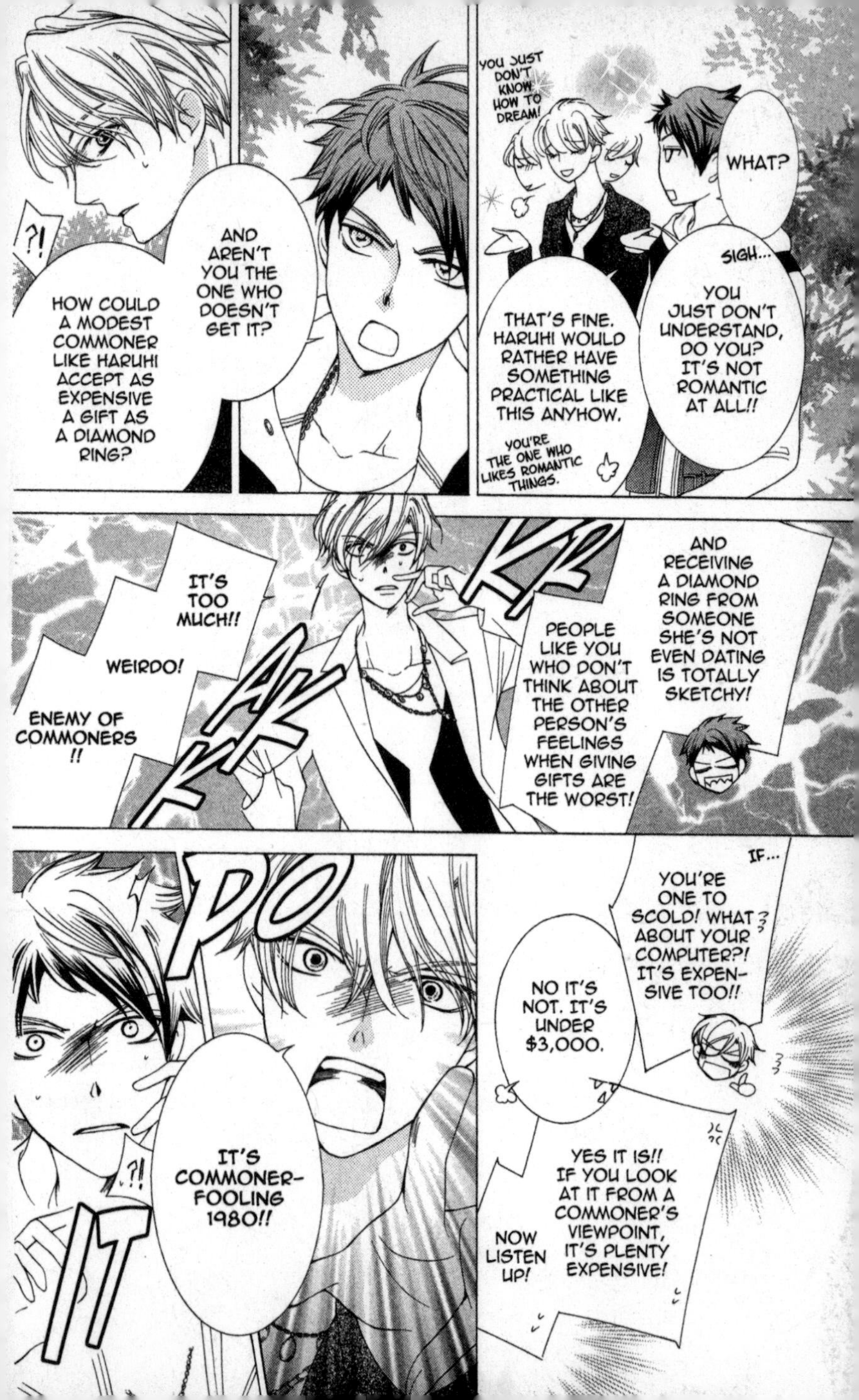
WHAT?
SIGH...
YOU JUST DON'T UNDERSTAND, DO YOU? IT'S NOT ROMANTIC AT ALL!!
YOU JUST DON'T KNOW HOW TO DREAM!
THAT'S FINE. HARUHI WOULD RATHER HAVE SOMETHING PRACTICAL LIKE THIS ANYHOW.
YOU'RE THE ONE WHO LIKES ROMANTIC THINGS.
AND AREN'T YOU THE ONE WHO DOESN'T GET IT?
?!
HOW COULD A MODEST COMMONER LIKE HARUHI ACCEPT AS EXPENSIVE A GIFT AS A DIAMOND RING?
AND RECEIVING A DIAMOND RING FROM SOMEONE SHE'S NOT EVEN DATING IS TOTALLY SKETCHY!
PEOPLE LIKE YOU WHO DON'T THINK ABOUT THE OTHER PERSON'S FEELINGS WHEN GIVING GIFTS ARE THE WORST!
KR
AK
K
IT'S TOO MUCH!!
WEIRDO!
ENEMY OF COMMONERS!!
IF...
YOU'RE ONE TO SCOLD! WHAT ABOUT YOUR COMPUTER?! IT'S EXPENSIVE TOO!!
NO IT'S NOT. IT'S UNDER $3,000.
YES IT IS!! IF YOU LOOK AT IT FROM A COMMONER'S VIEWPOINT, IT'S PLENTY EXPENSIVE!
NOW LISTEN UP!
PO
IT
IT'S COMMONER-FOOLING 1980!!
?!

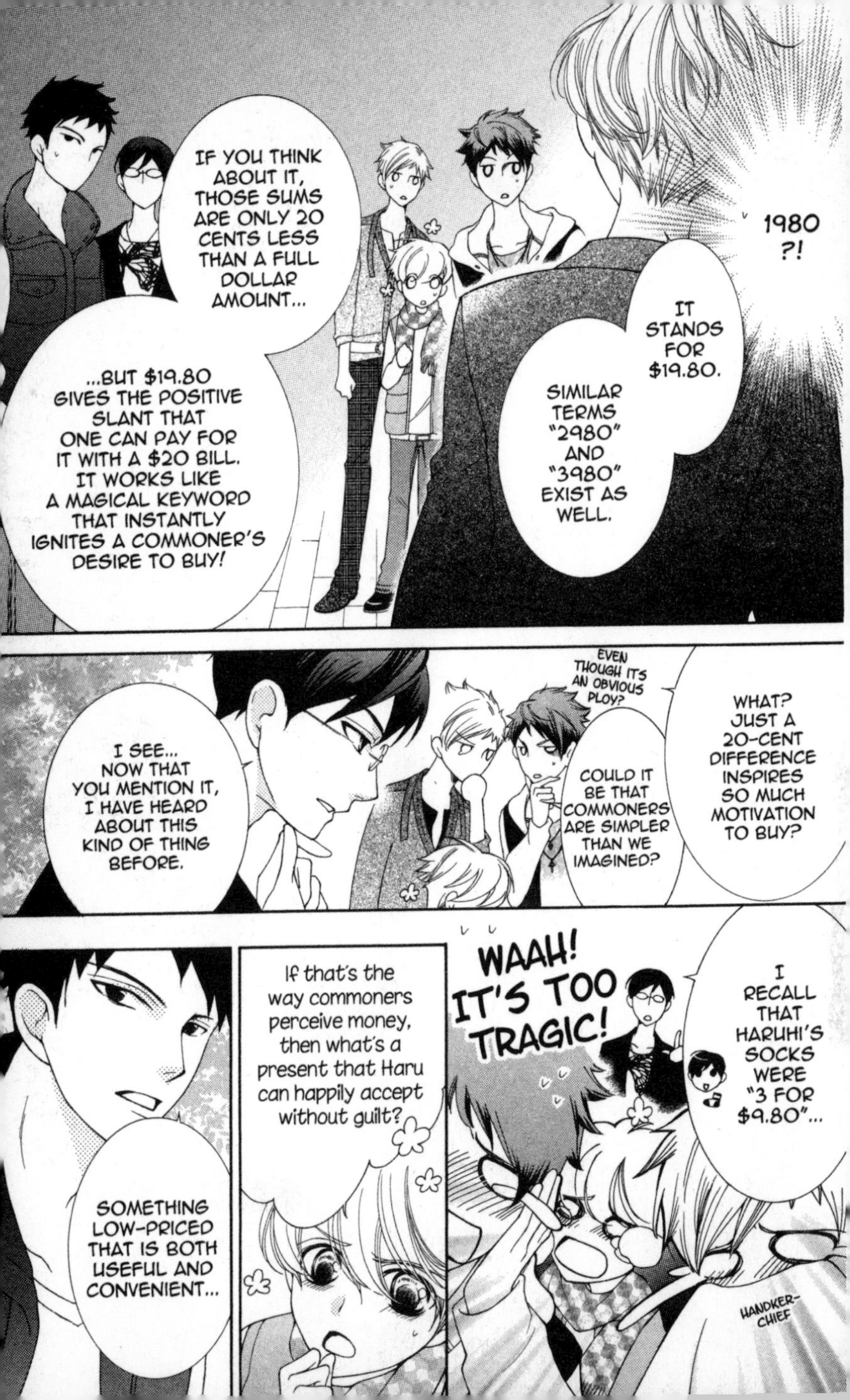
1980 ?!
IT STANDS FOR $19.80.
SIMILAR TERMS "2980" AND "3980" EXIST AS WELL.
IF YOU THINK ABOUT IT, THOSE SUMS ARE ONLY 20 CENTS LESS THAN A FULL DOLLAR AMOUNT...
...BUT $19.80 GIVES THE POSITIVE SLANT THAT ONE CAN PAY FOR IT WITH A $20 BILL. IT WORKS LIKE A MAGICAL KEYWORD THAT INSTANTLY IGNITES A COMMONER'S DESIRE TO BUY!
WHAT? JUST A 20-CENT DIFFERENCE INSPIRES SO MUCH MOTIVATION TO BUY?
EVEN THOUGH ITS AN OBVIOUS PLOY?
COULD IT BE THAT COMMONERS ARE SIMPLER THAN WE IMAGINED?
I SEE... NOW THAT YOU MENTION IT, I HAVE HEARD ABOUT THIS KIND OF THING BEFORE.
I RECALL THAT HARUHI'S SOCKS WERE "3 FOR $9.80"...
WAAH! IT'S TOO TRAGIC!
HANDKER-CHIEF
If that's the way commoners perceive money, then what's a present that Haru can happily accept without guilt?
SOMETHING LOW-PRICED THAT IS BOTH USEFUL AND CONVENIENT...

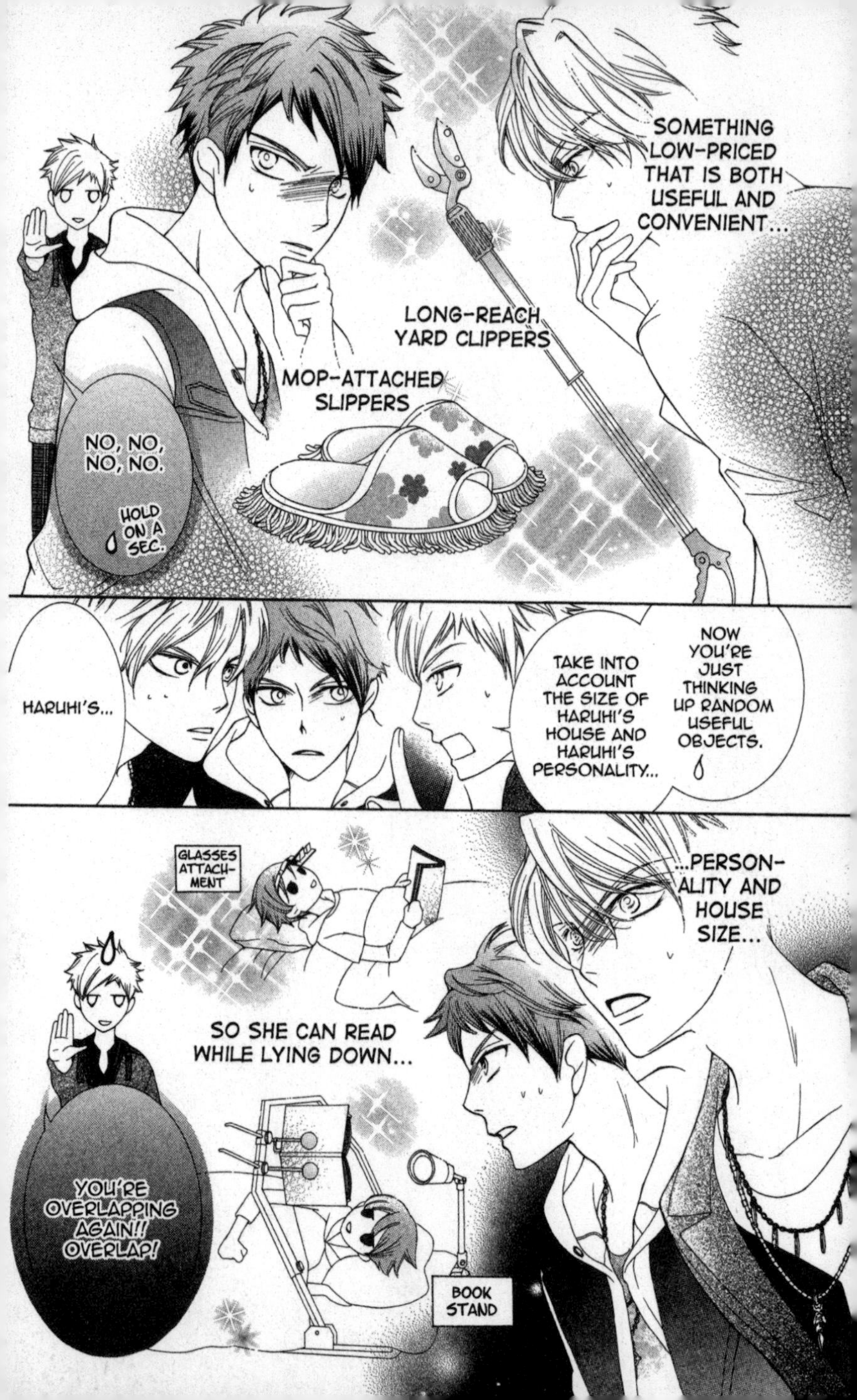
SOMETHING LOW-PRICED THAT IS BOTH USEFUL AND CONVENIENT...
LONG-REACH YARD CLIPPERS
MOP-ATTACHED SLIPPERS
NO, NO, NO, NO.
HOLD ON A SEC.
NOW YOU'RE JUST THINKING UP RANDOM USEFUL OBJECTS.
TAKE INTO ACCOUNT THE SIZE OF HARUHI'S HOUSE AND HARUHI'S PERSONALITY...
HARUHI'S...
...PERSONALITY AND HOUSE SIZE...
GLASSES ATTACHMENT
SO SHE CAN READ WHILE LYING DOWN...
BOOK STAND
YOU'RE OVERLAPPING AGAIN!! OVERLAP!

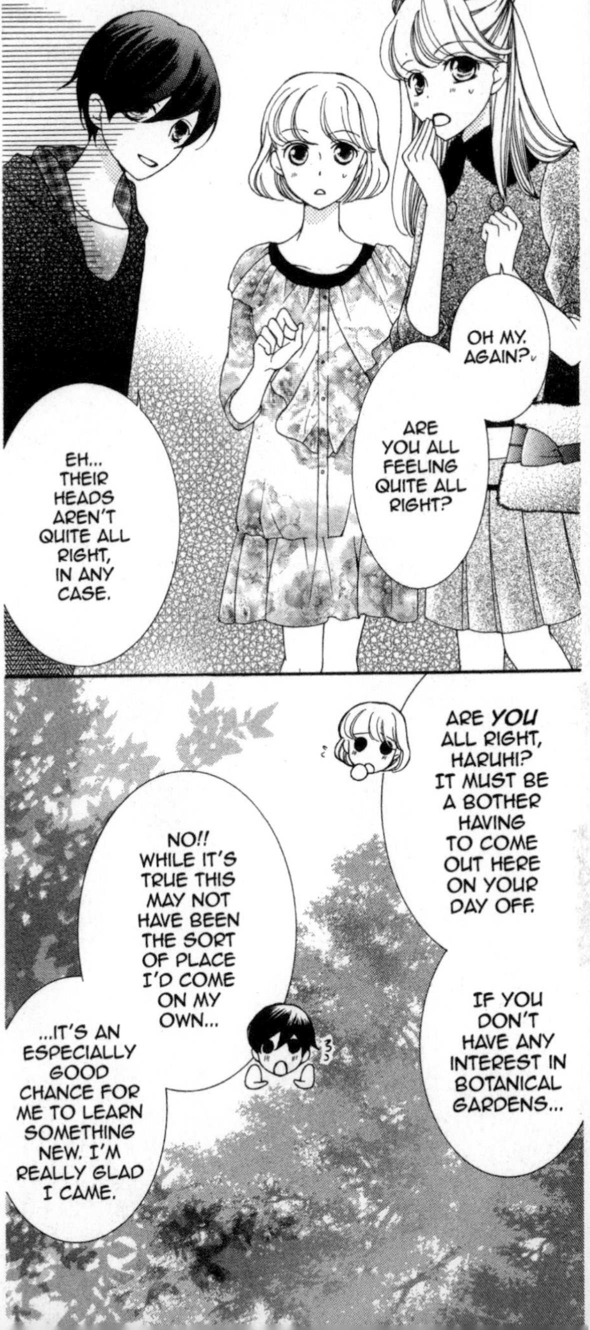
OH MY. AGAIN?
ARE YOU ALL FEELING QUITE ALL RIGHT?
EH... THEIR HEADS AREN'T QUITE ALL RIGHT, IN ANY CASE.
ARE *YOU* ALL RIGHT, HARUHI? IT MUST BE A BOTHER HAVING TO COME OUT HERE ON YOUR DAY OFF.
IF YOU DON'T HAVE ANY INTEREST IN BOTANICAL GARDENS...
NO!! WHILE IT'S TRUE THIS MAY NOT HAVE BEEN THE SORT OF PLACE I'D COME ON MY OWN...
...IT'S AN ESPECIALLY GOOD CHANCE FOR ME TO LEARN SOMETHING NEW. I'M REALLY GLAD I CAME.

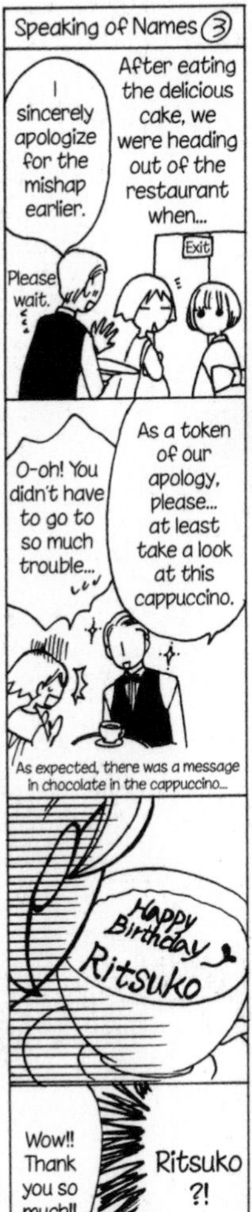
Speaking of Names 3
After eating the delicious cake, we were heading out of the restaurant when...
I sincerely apologize for the mishap earlier.
Exit
Please wait.
As a token of our apology, please... at least take a look at this cappuccino.
O-oh! You didn't have to go to so much trouble...
As expected, there was a message in chocolate in the cappuccino...
Happy Birthday Ritsuko
Ritsuko?!
Wow!! Thank you so much!!
I'm so glad I was able to catch you before you left.
Naturally, I went with the flow of the situation and enjoyed the cup gratefully. And I just love that kind of waiter. Thank you so much!!

But try to confirm the spelling next time, huh?!

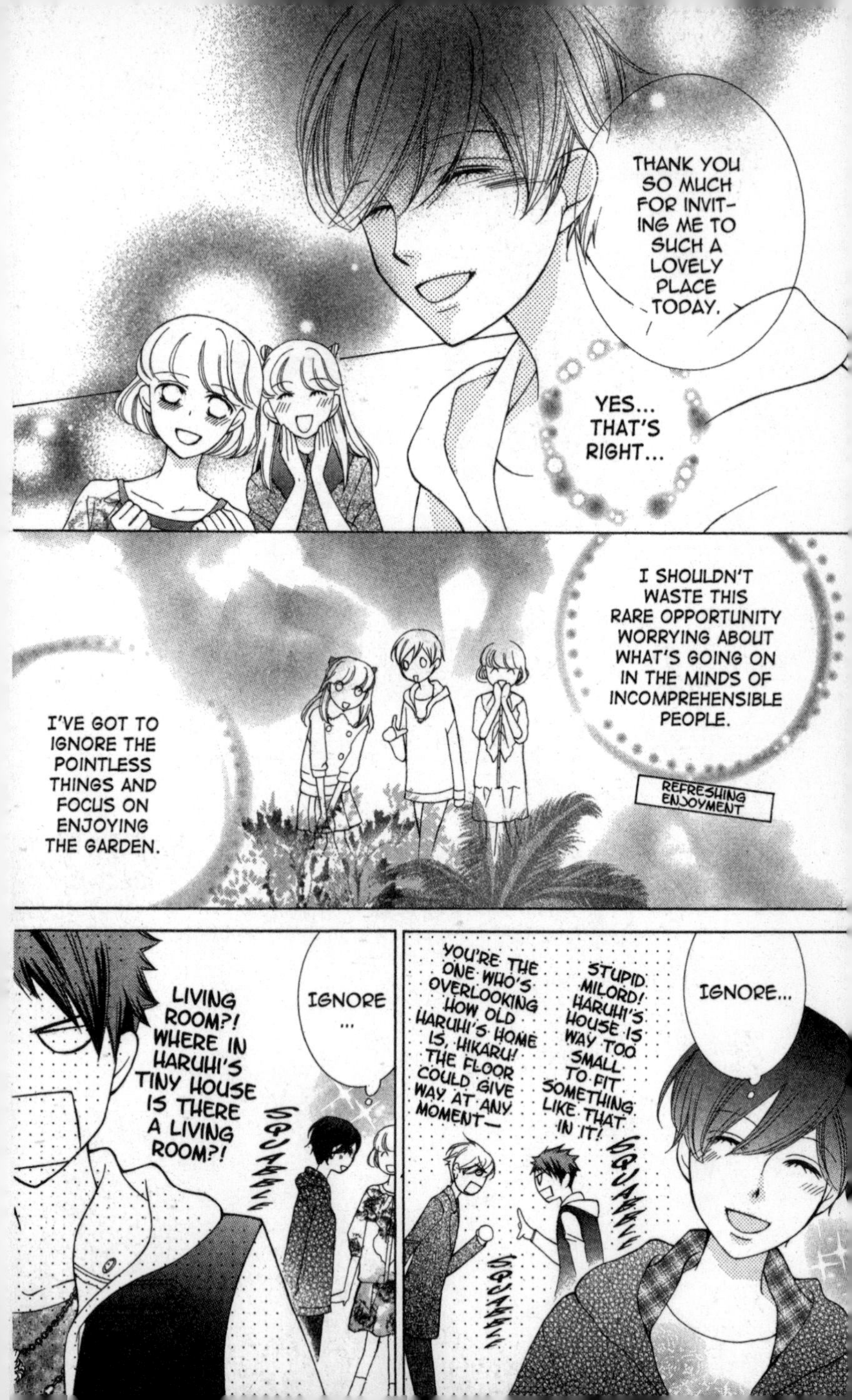
THANK YOU SO MUCH FOR INVITING ME TO SUCH A LOVELY PLACE TODAY.
YES... THAT'S RIGHT...
I SHOULDN'T WASTE THIS RARE OPPORTUNITY WORRYING ABOUT WHAT'S GOING ON IN THE MINDS OF INCOMPREHENSIBLE PEOPLE.
REFRESHING ENJOYMENT
I'VE GOT TO IGNORE THE POINTLESS THINGS AND FOCUS ON ENJOYING THE GARDEN.
IGNORE...
STUPID MILORD! HARUHI'S HOUSE IS WAY TOO SMALL TO FIT SOMETHING LIKE THAT IN IT!
YOU'RE THE ONE WHO'S OVERLOOKING HOW OLD HARUHI'S HOME IS, HIKARU! THE FLOOR COULD GIVE WAY AT ANY MOMENT—
IGNORE ...
LIVING ROOM?! WHERE IN HARUHI'S TINY HOUSE IS THERE A LIVING ROOM?!

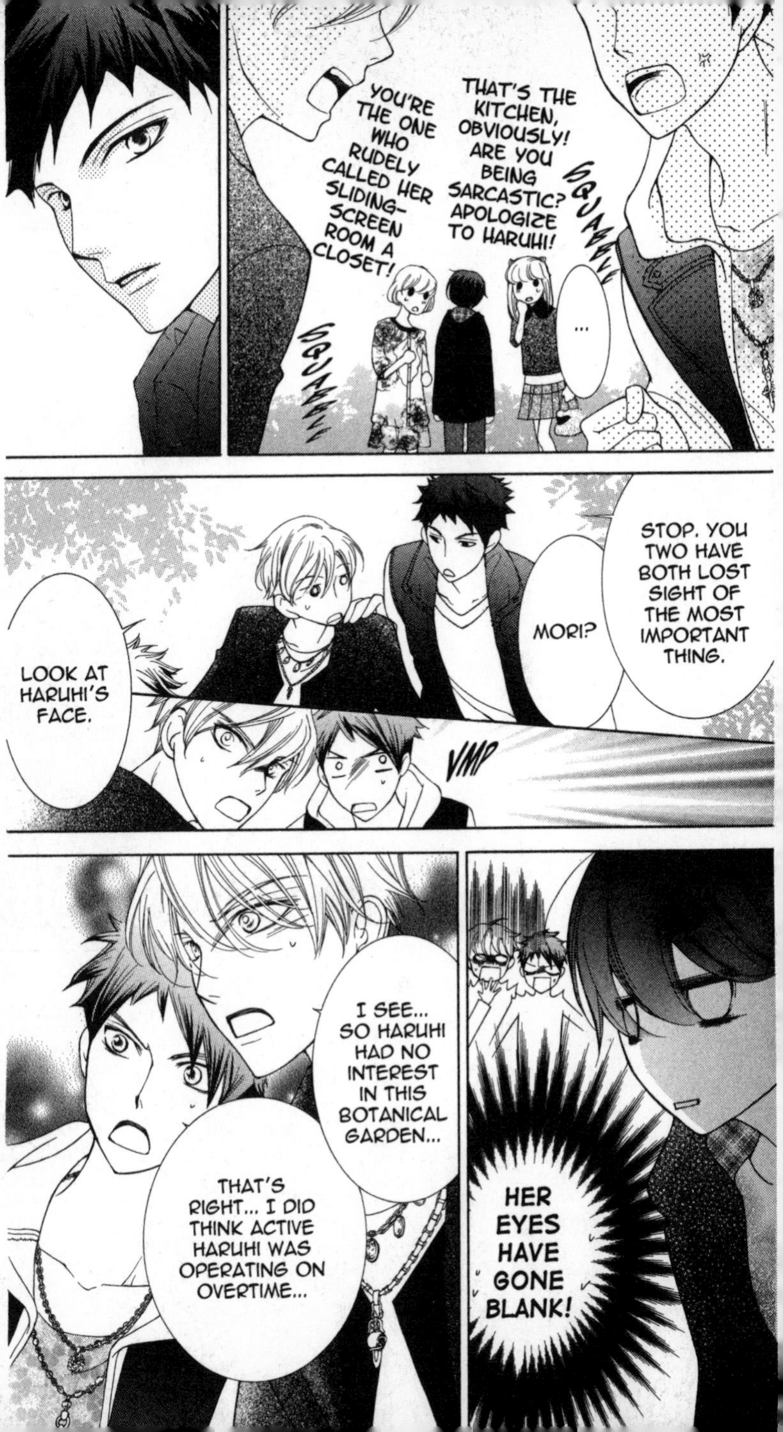

SQUAWK
THAT'S THE KITCHEN, OBVIOUSLY! ARE YOU BEING SARCASTIC? APOLOGIZE TO HARUHI!
...
YOU'RE THE ONE WHO RUDELY CALLED HER SLIDING-SCREEN ROOM A CLOSET!
SQUAWK
STOP. YOU TWO HAVE BOTH LOST SIGHT OF THE MOST IMPORTANT THING.
MORI?
LOOK AT HARUHI'S FACE.
VMP
HER EYES HAVE GONE BLANK!
I SEE... SO HARUHI HAD NO INTEREST IN THIS BOTANICAL GARDEN...
THAT'S RIGHT... I DID THINK ACTIVE HARUHI WAS OPERATING ON OVERTIME...

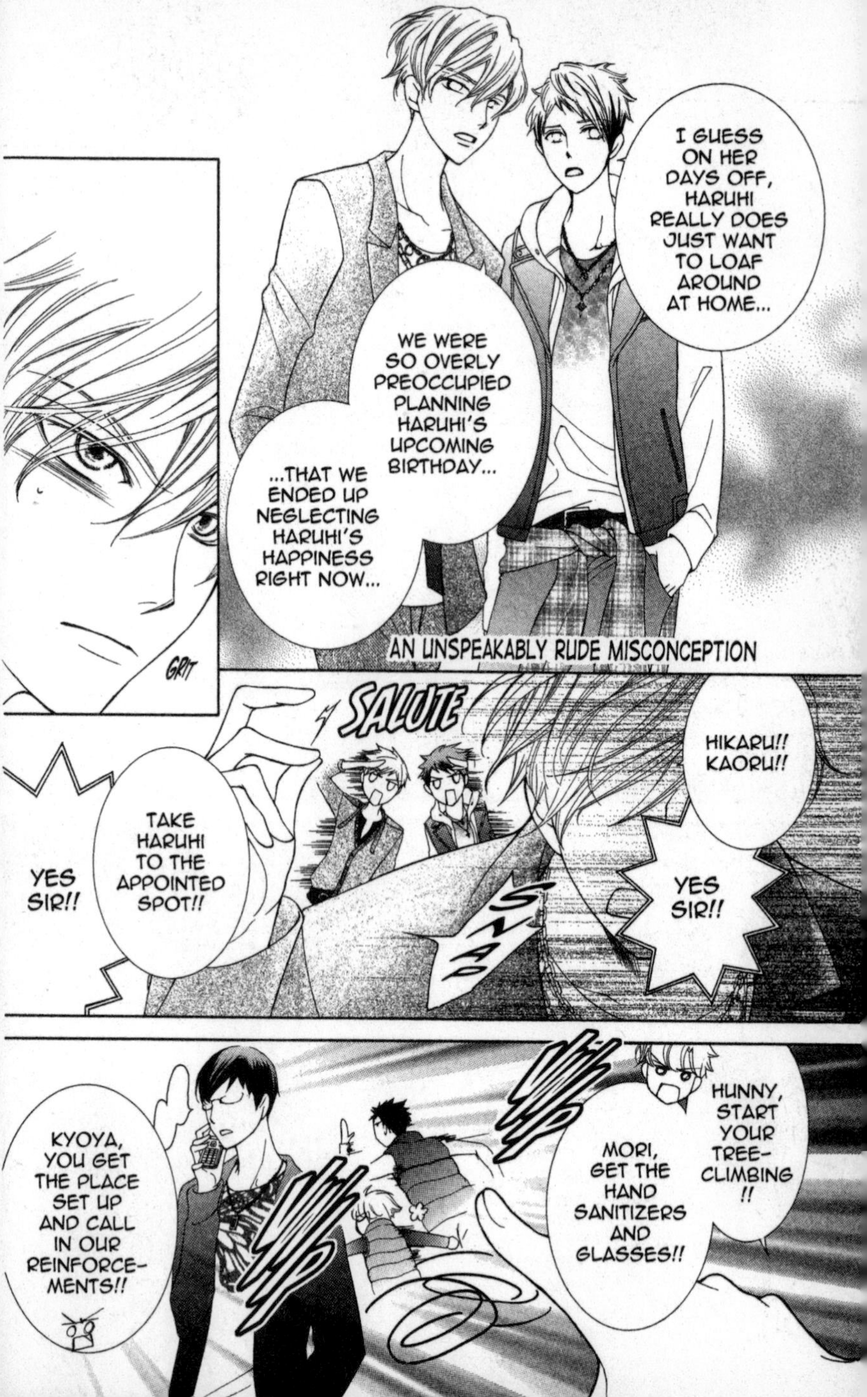
I GUESS ON HER DAYS OFF, HARUHI REALLY DOES JUST WANT TO LOAF AROUND AT HOME...
WE WERE SO OVERLY PREOCCUPIED PLANNING HARUHI'S UPCOMING BIRTHDAY...
...THAT WE ENDED UP NEGLECTING HARUHI'S HAPPINESS RIGHT NOW...
AN UNSPEAKABLY RUDE MISCONCEPTION
GRIT
SALUTE
HIKARU!! KAORU!!
YES SIR!!
SNAP
TAKE HARUHI TO THE APPOINTED SPOT!!
YES SIR!!
HUNNY, START YOUR TREE-CLIMBING!!
MORI, GET THE HAND SANITIZERS AND GLASSES!!
KYOYA, YOU GET THE PLACE SET UP AND CALL IN OUR REINFORCE-MENTS!!

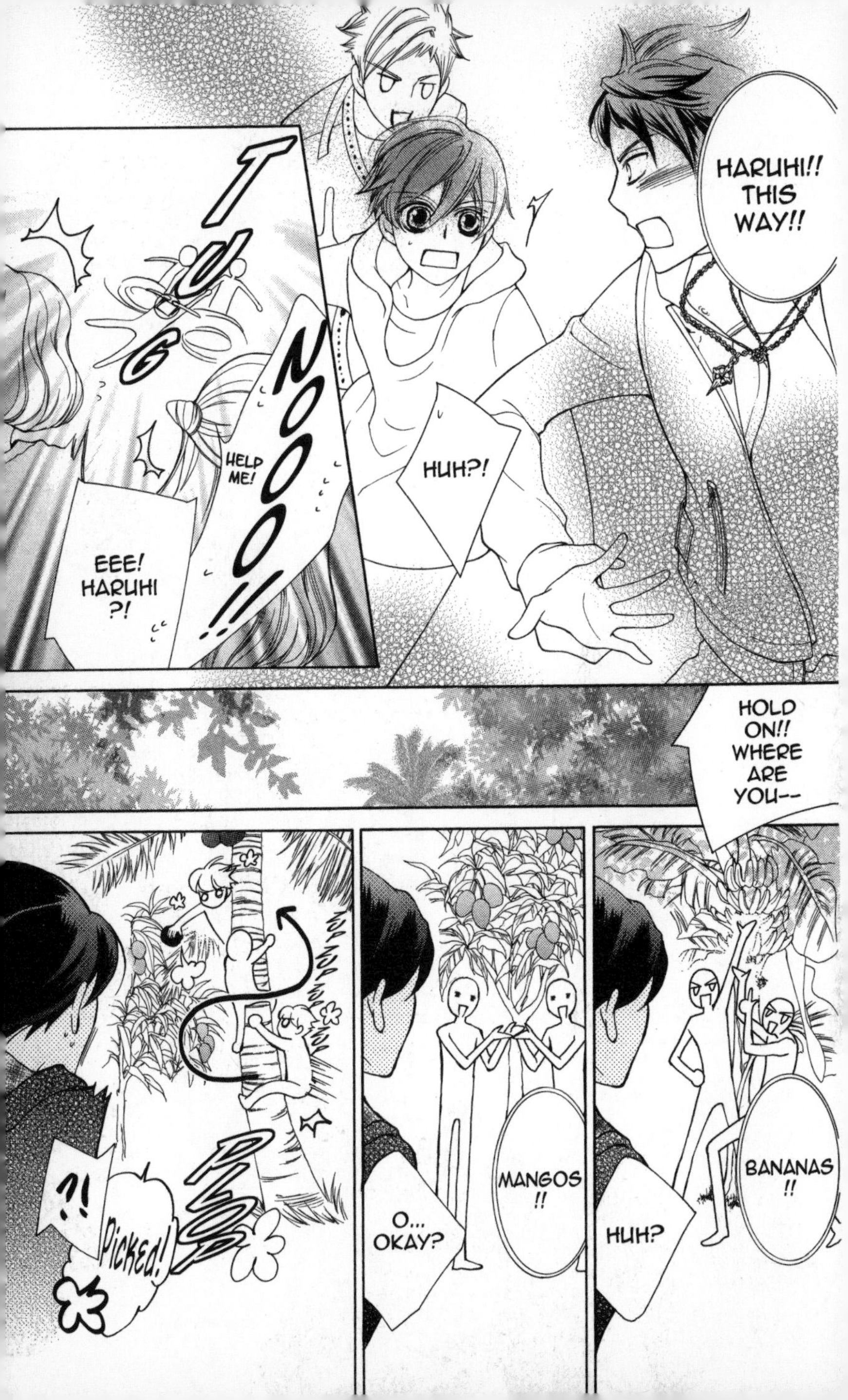
HARUHI!! THIS WAY!!
HUH?!
TUG
NOOOO!!
HELP ME!
EEE! HARUHI ?!
HOLD ON!! WHERE ARE YOU--
BANANAS !!
HUH?
MANGOS !!
O... OKAY?
?!
PLOOP
Picked!

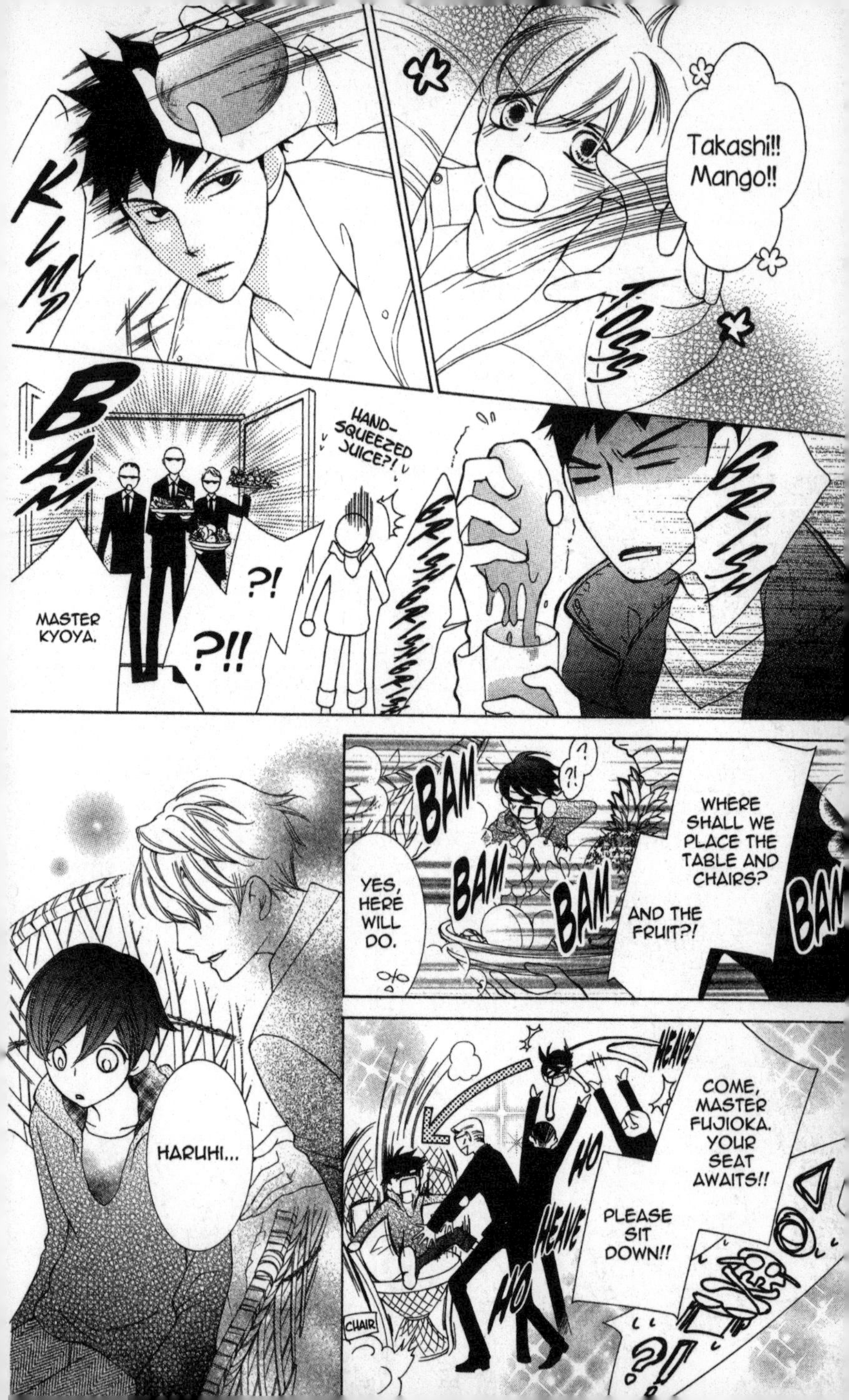
Takashi!! Mango!!
TOSS
KLUMP
GRISH
GRISH GRISH GRISH GRISH
HAND-SQUEEZED JUICE?!
BAM
?!
?!!
MASTER KYOYA.
BAM
WHERE SHALL WE PLACE THE TABLE AND CHAIRS?
AND THE FRUIT?!
BAM
BAM
BAM
?!
YES, HERE WILL DO.
HEAVE
COME, MASTER FUJIOKA. YOUR SEAT AWAITS!!
PLEASE SIT DOWN!!
HO
HEAVE
HO
CHAIR
?!
HARUHI...

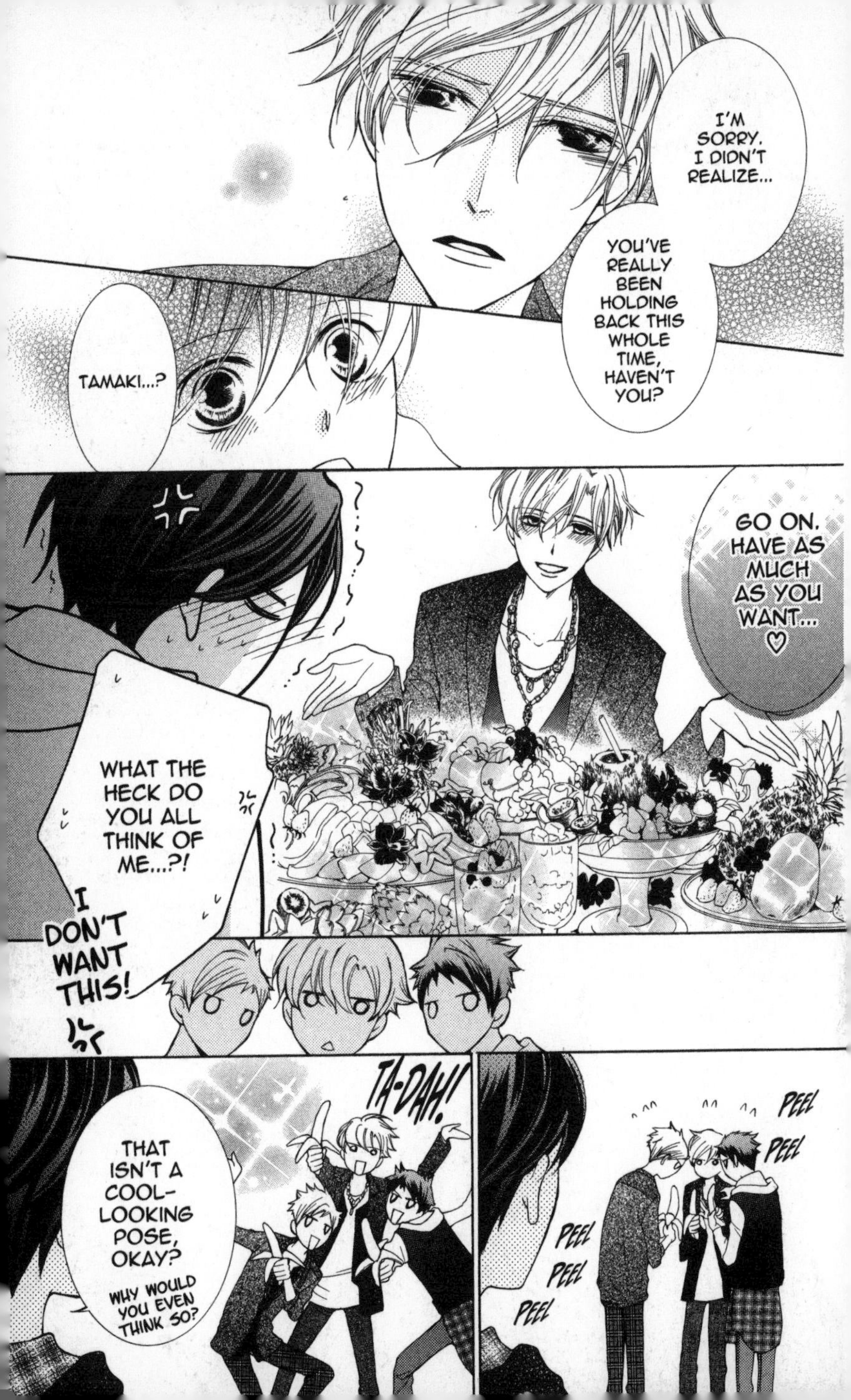
I'M SORRY. I DIDN'T REALIZE...
YOU'VE REALLY BEEN HOLDING BACK THIS WHOLE TIME, HAVEN'T YOU?
TAMAKI...?
GO ON. HAVE AS MUCH AS YOU WANT... ♡
WHAT THE HECK DO YOU ALL THINK OF ME...?!
I DON'T WANT THIS!
PEEL
PEEL
PEEL
PEEL
PEEL
TA-DAH!
THAT ISN'T A COOL-LOOKING POSE, OKAY?
WHY WOULD YOU EVEN THINK SO?

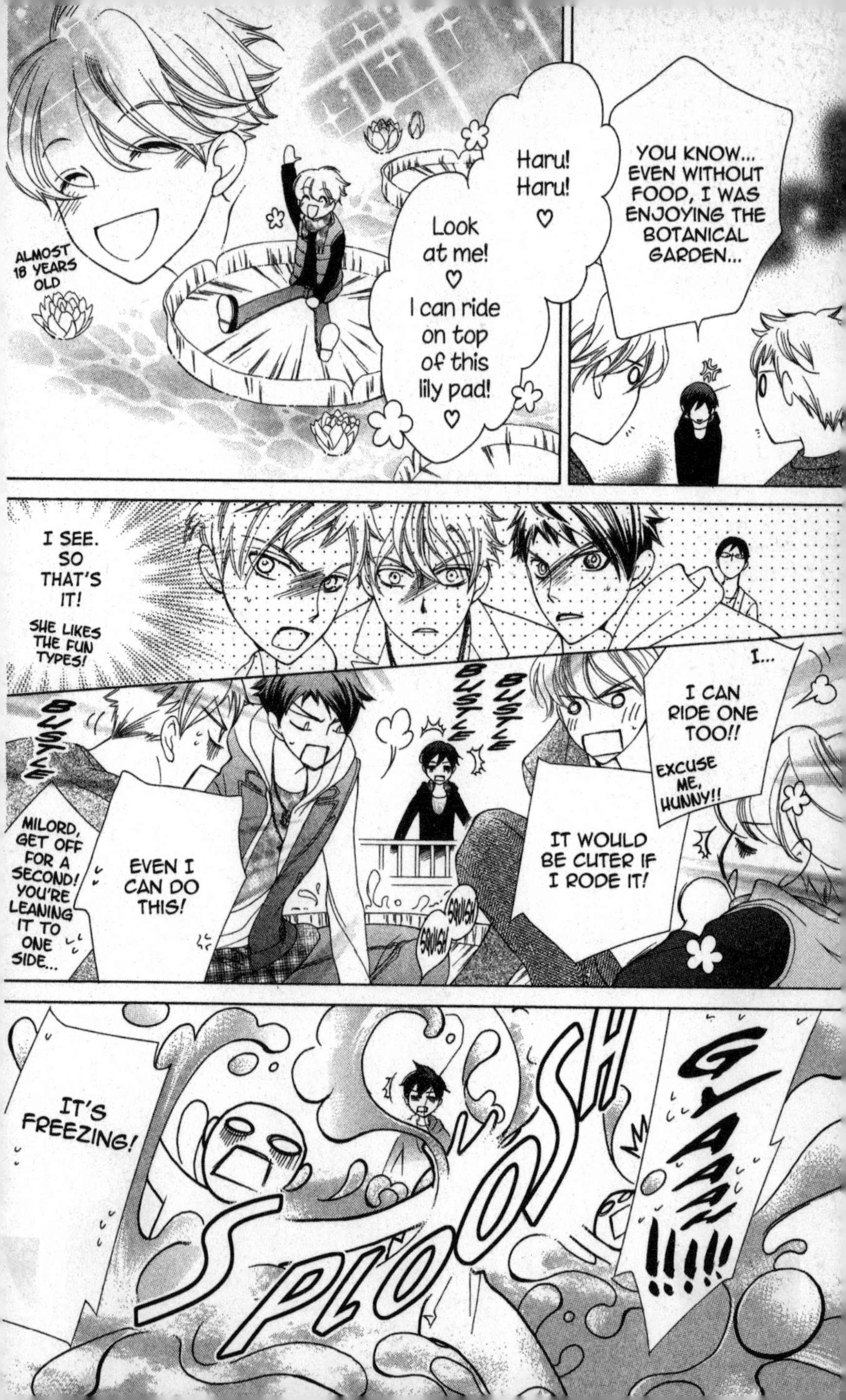
YOU KNOW... EVEN WITHOUT FOOD, I WAS ENJOYING THE BOTANICAL GARDEN...
Haru! Haru! ♡
Look at me! ♡ I can ride on top of this lily pad! ♡
ALMOST 18 YEARS OLD
I SEE. SO THAT'S IT!
SHE LIKES THE FUN TYPES!
I...
I CAN RIDE ONE TOO!!
EXCUSE ME, HUNNY!!
BUSTLE
BUSTLE
IT WOULD BE CUTER IF I RODE IT!
SQUISH
SQUISH
EVEN I CAN DO THIS!
BUSTLE
MILORD, GET OFF FOR A SECOND! YOU'RE LEANING IT TO ONE SIDE...
GYAAAH!!!!!!
SPLOOSH
IT'S FREEZING!

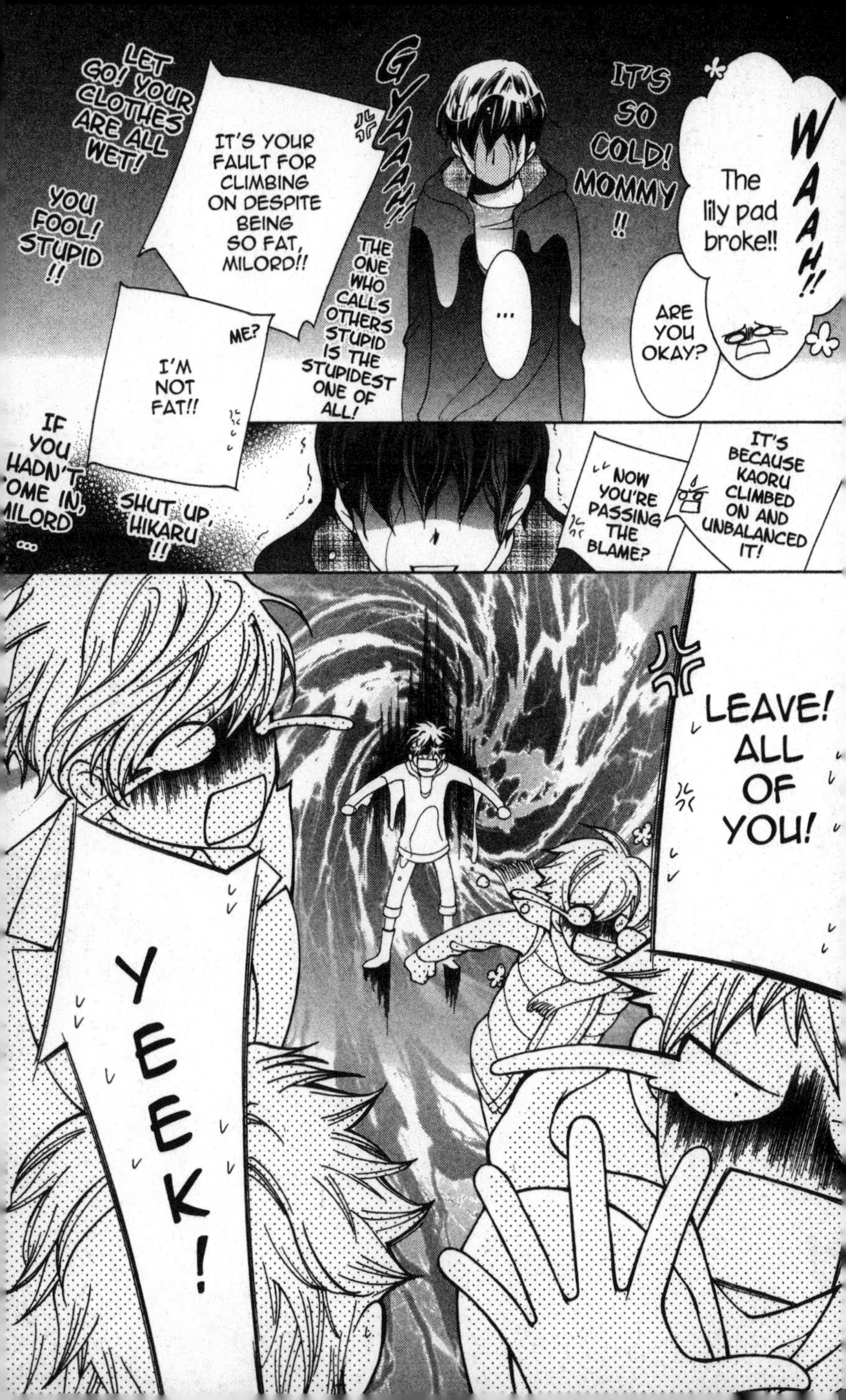
The lily pad broke!!
WAAAH!!
ARE YOU OKAY?
IT'S SO COLD! MOMMY!!
GYAAAAH!!
...
THE ONE WHO CALLS OTHERS STUPID IS THE STUPIDEST ONE OF ALL!
IT'S YOUR FAULT FOR CLIMBING ON DESPITE BEING SO FAT, MILORD!!
ME?
I'M NOT FAT!!
LET GO! YOUR CLOTHES ARE ALL WET!
YOU FOOL! STUPID!!
IT'S BECAUSE KAORU CLIMBED ON AND UNBALANCED IT!
NOW YOU'RE PASSING THE BLAME?
SHUT UP, HIKARU!!
IF YOU HADN'T OME IN, ILORD ...
LEAVE! ALL OF YOU!
YEEK!

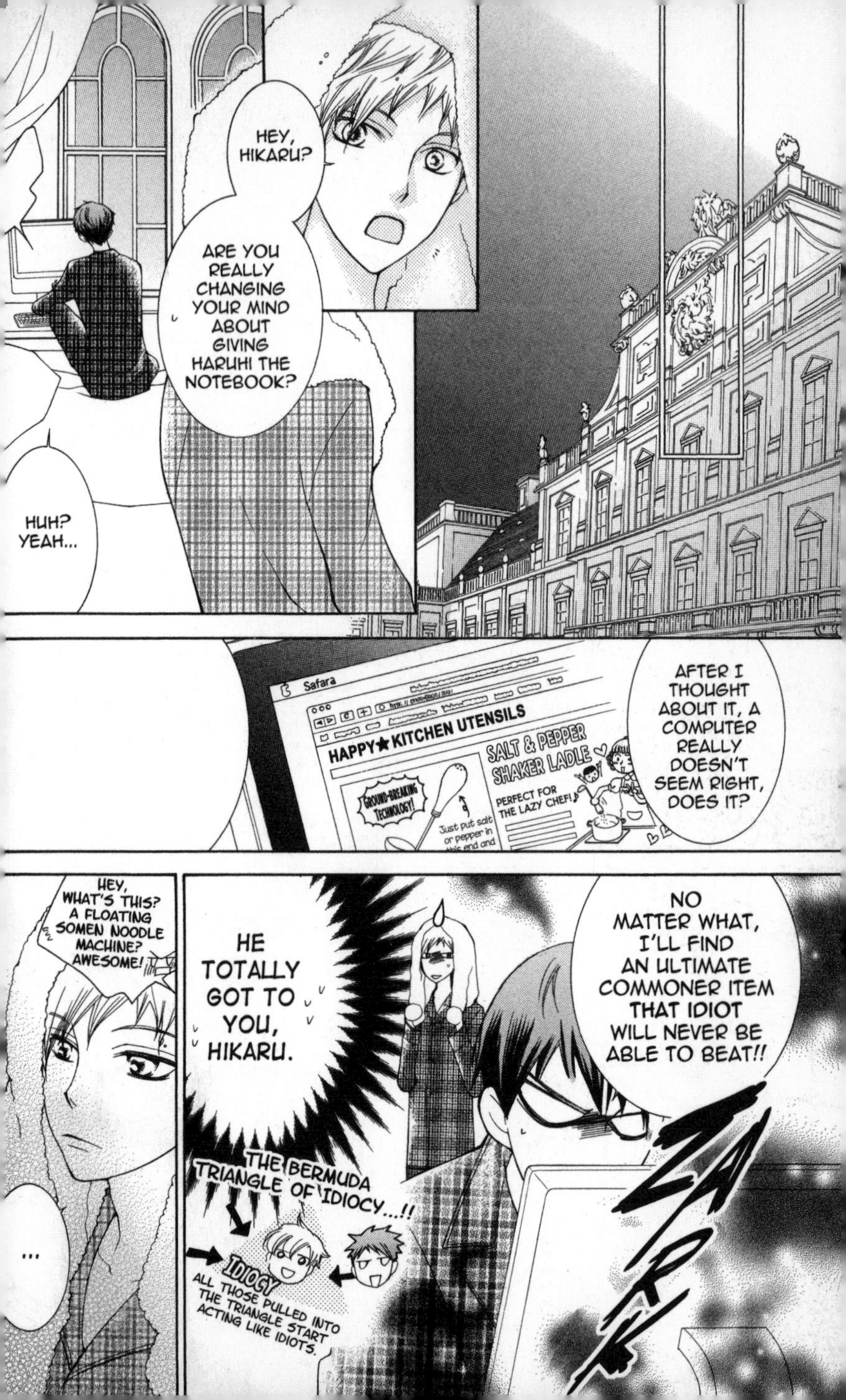
HEY, HIKARU?
ARE YOU REALLY CHANGING YOUR MIND ABOUT GIVING HARUHI THE NOTEBOOK?
HUH? YEAH...
AFTER I THOUGHT ABOUT IT, A COMPUTER REALLY DOESN'T SEEM RIGHT, DOES IT?
Safara
HAPPY★KITCHEN UTENSILS
SALT & PEPPER SHAKER LADLE
PERFECT FOR THE LAZY CHEF!
GROUND-BREAKING TECHNOLOGY!
Just put salt or pepper in
NO MATTER WHAT, I'LL FIND AN ULTIMATE COMMONER ITEM THAT IDIOT WILL NEVER BE ABLE TO BEAT!!
HE TOTALLY GOT TO YOU, HIKARU.
THE BERMUDA TRIANGLE OF IDIOCY...!!
IDIOCY
ALL THOSE PULLED INTO THE TRIANGLE START ACTING LIKE IDIOTS.
HEY, WHAT'S THIS? A FLOATING SOMEN NOODLE MACHINE? AWESOME!
...

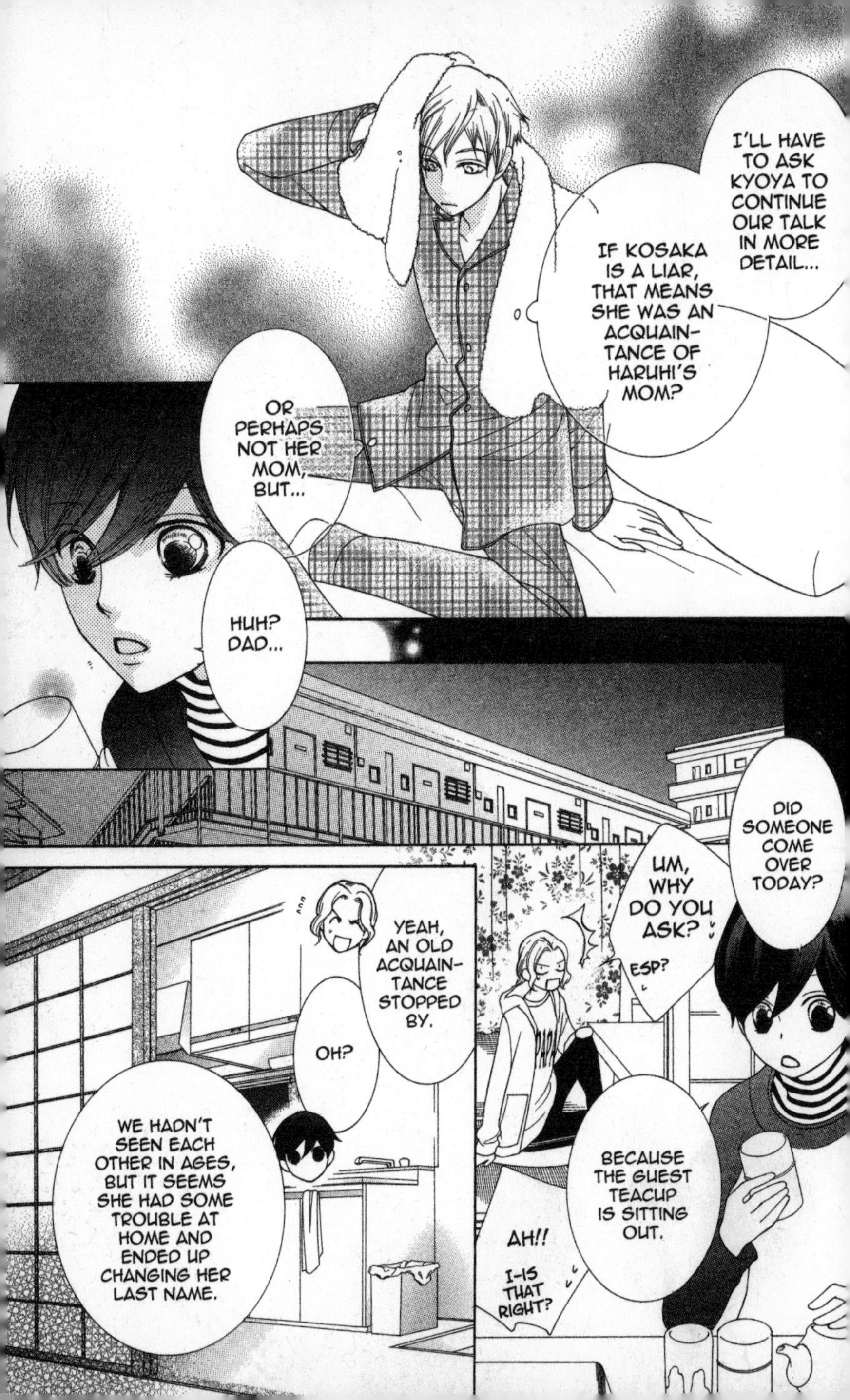
I'LL HAVE TO ASK KYOYA TO CONTINUE OUR TALK IN MORE DETAIL...
IF KOSAKA IS A LIAR, THAT MEANS SHE WAS AN ACQUAINTANCE OF HARUHI'S MOM?
OR PERHAPS NOT HER MOM, BUT...
HUH? DAD...
DID SOMEONE COME OVER TODAY?
UM, WHY DO YOU ASK?
ESP?
BECAUSE THE GUEST TEACUP IS SITTING OUT.
AH!!
I-IS THAT RIGHT?
YEAH, AN OLD ACQUAINTANCE STOPPED BY.
OH?
WE HADN'T SEEN EACH OTHER IN AGES, BUT IT SEEMS SHE HAD SOME TROUBLE AT HOME AND ENDED UP CHANGING HER LAST NAME.

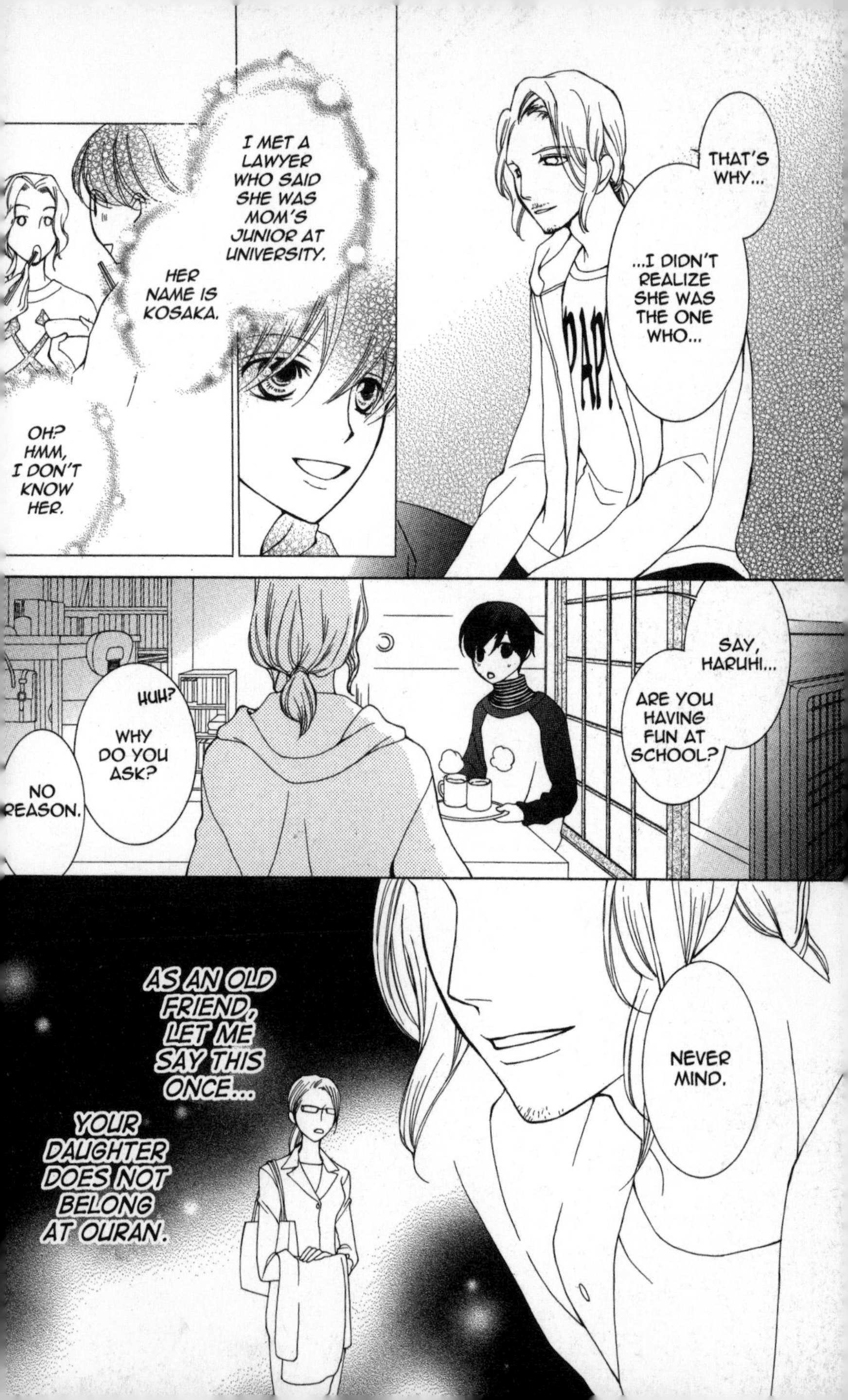
THAT'S WHY...
...I DIDN'T REALIZE SHE WAS THE ONE WHO...
I MET A LAWYER WHO SAID SHE WAS MOM'S JUNIOR AT UNIVERSITY.
HER NAME IS KOSAKA.
OH? HMM, I DON'T KNOW HER.
SAY, HARUHI...
ARE YOU HAVING FUN AT SCHOOL?
HUH?
WHY DO YOU ASK?
NO REASON.
NEVER MIND.
AS AN OLD FRIEND, LET ME SAY THIS ONCE...
YOUR DAUGHTER DOES NOT BELONG AT OURAN.

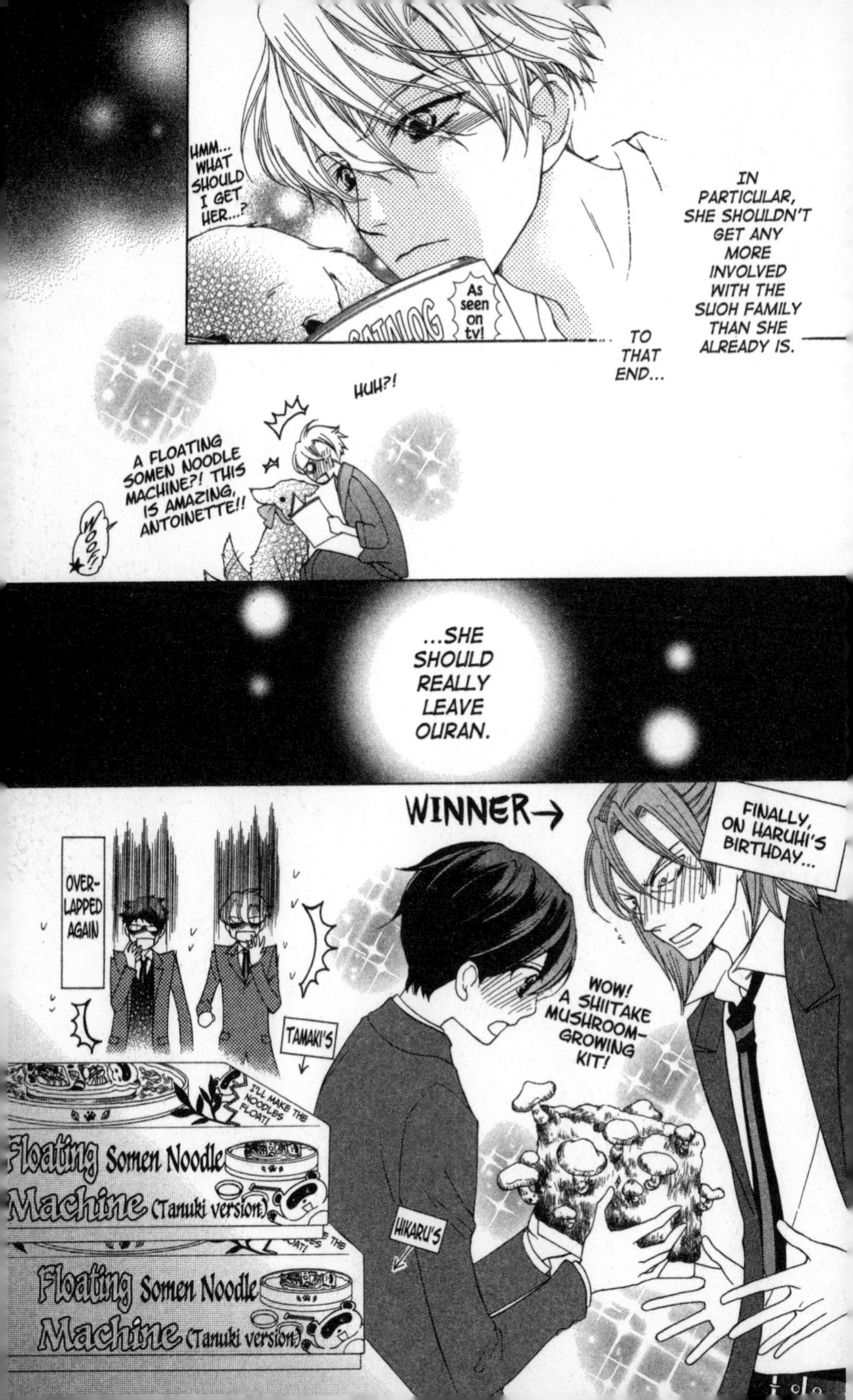
IN PARTICULAR, SHE SHOULDN'T GET ANY MORE INVOLVED WITH THE SUOH FAMILY THAN SHE ALREADY IS.
TO THAT END...
HMM... WHAT SHOULD I GET HER...?
As seen on tv!
HUH?!
A FLOATING SOMEN NOODLE MACHINE?! THIS IS AMAZING, ANTOINETTE!!
WOOF!
...SHE SHOULD REALLY LEAVE OURAN.
FINALLY, ON HARUHI'S BIRTHDAY...
WINNER→
WOW! A SHIITAKE MUSHROOM-GROWING KIT!
TAMAKI'S
HIKARU'S
OVER-LAPPED AGAIN
I'LL MAKE THE NOODLES FLOAT!
Floating Somen Noodle Machine (Tanuki version)
Floating Somen Noodle Machine (Tanuki version)

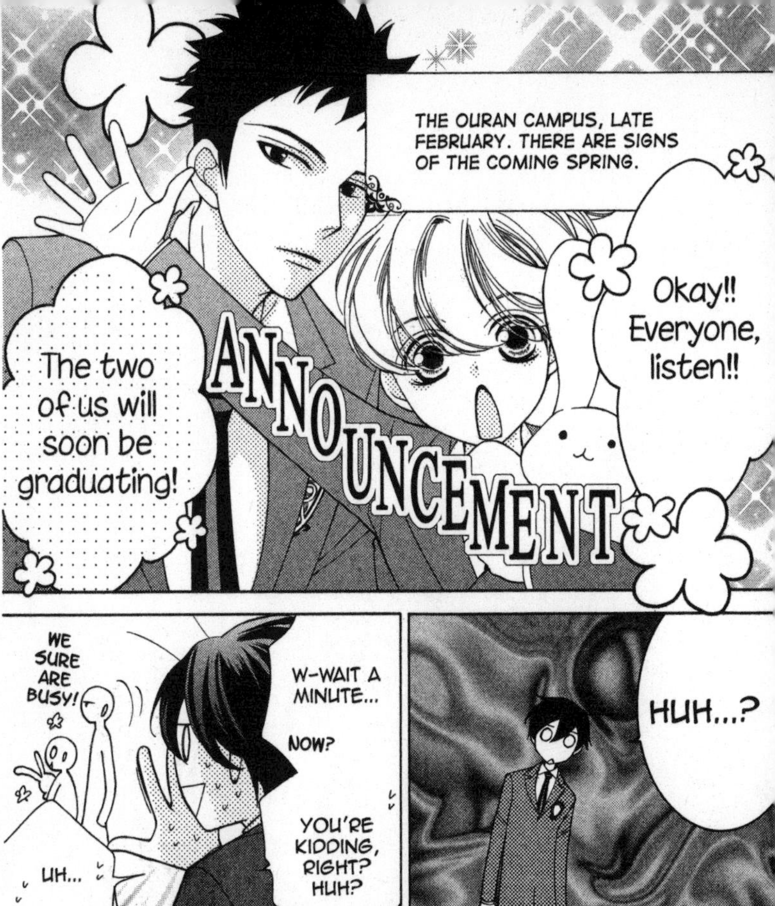
THE OURAN CAMPUS, LATE FEBRUARY. THERE ARE SIGNS OF THE COMING SPRING.
Okay!! Everyone, listen!!
ANNOUNCEMENT
The two of us will soon be graduating!
HUH...?
W-WAIT A MINUTE...
NOW?
YOU'RE KIDDING, RIGHT? HUH?
WE SURE ARE BUSY!
UH...
AND WITH THAT, TODAY'S HOST CLUB EVENT IS...

✿ SUPPORTING CHARACTERS INTRODUCTION ✿

Kanan Matsuyama. Blood Type O.

STUDENT COUNCIL SECRETARY. KUZE'S FIANCÉE.

SHE HAS THE SORT OF PERSONALITY HATORI REALLY LOVES. PLEASE ALWAYS BE ALL LOVEY-DOVEY WITH KUZE.

SHE APPEARED IN THE ORIENTEERING ARC BECAUSE, THINKING AHEAD TO THIS GRADUATION ARC, I WANTED ALL THE THIRD-YEARS TO APPEAR AS MUCH AS POSSIBLE.

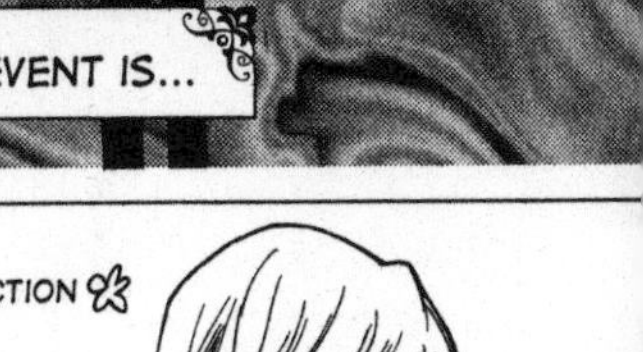

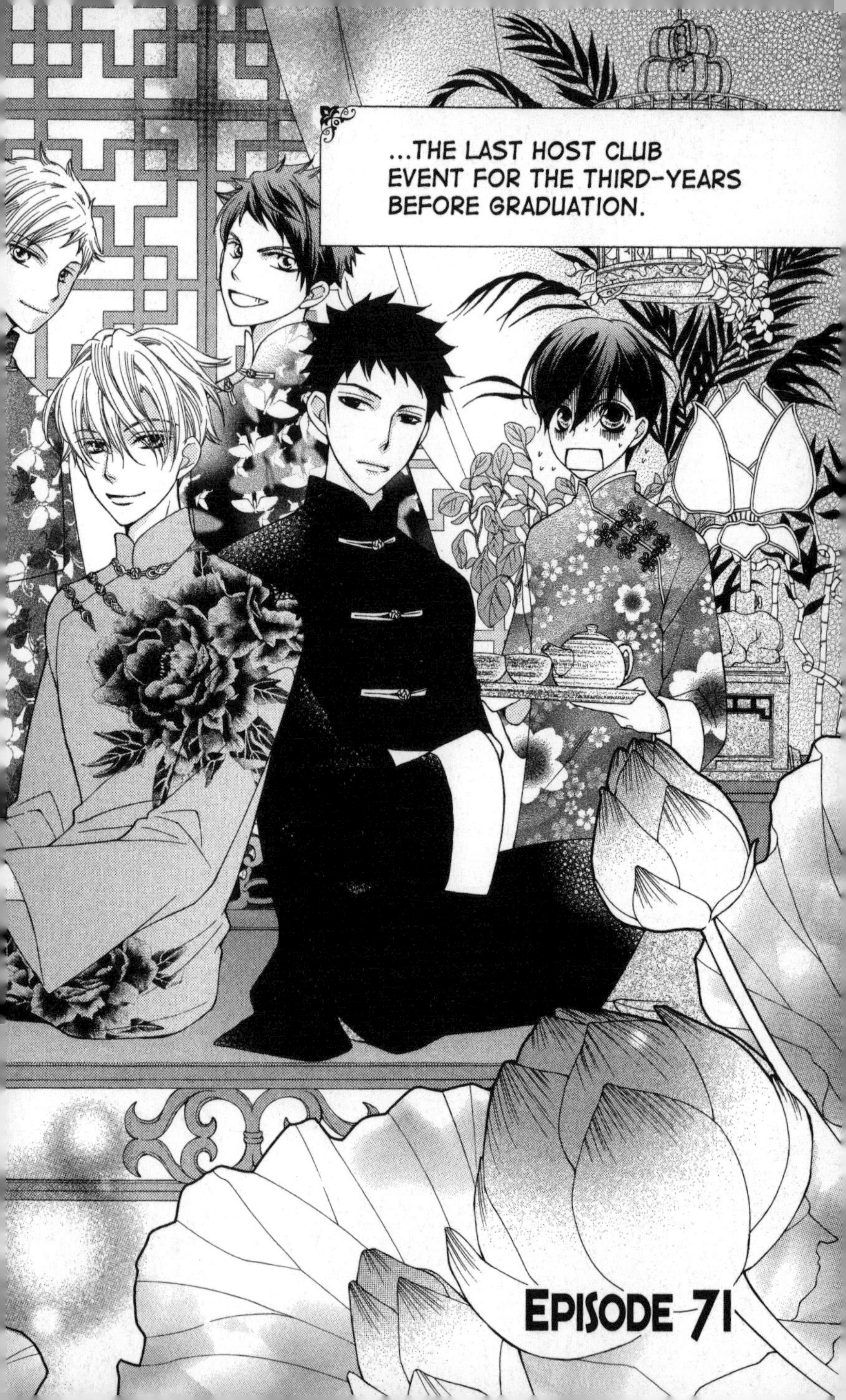
...THE LAST HOST CLUB
EVENT FOR THE THIRD-YEARS
BEFORE GRADUATION.
EPISODE 71

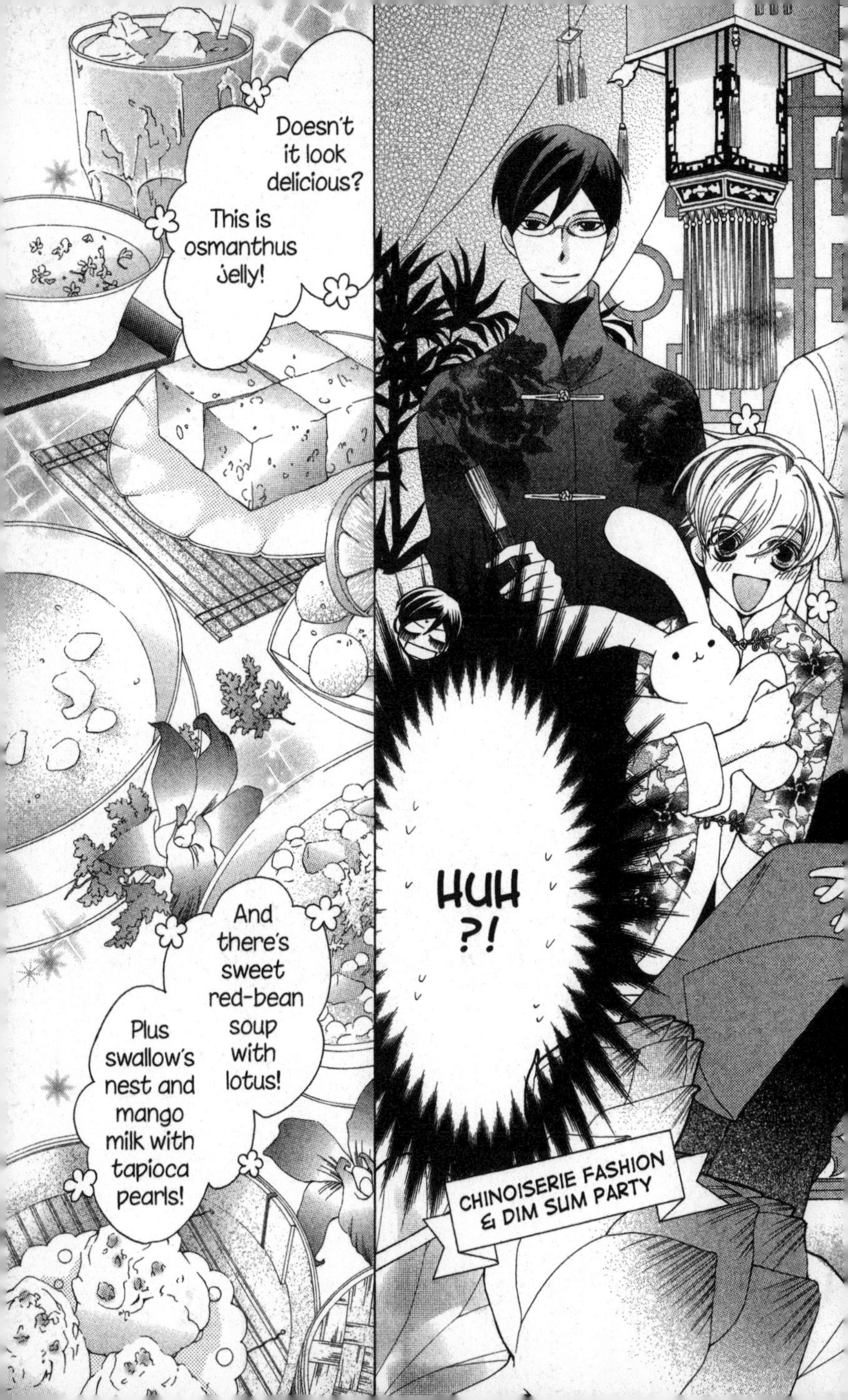
HUH ?!
CHINOISERIE FASHION & DIM SUM PARTY
Doesn't it look delicious? This is osmanthus jelly!
And there's sweet red-bean soup with lotus!
Plus swallow's nest and mango milk with tapioca pearls!

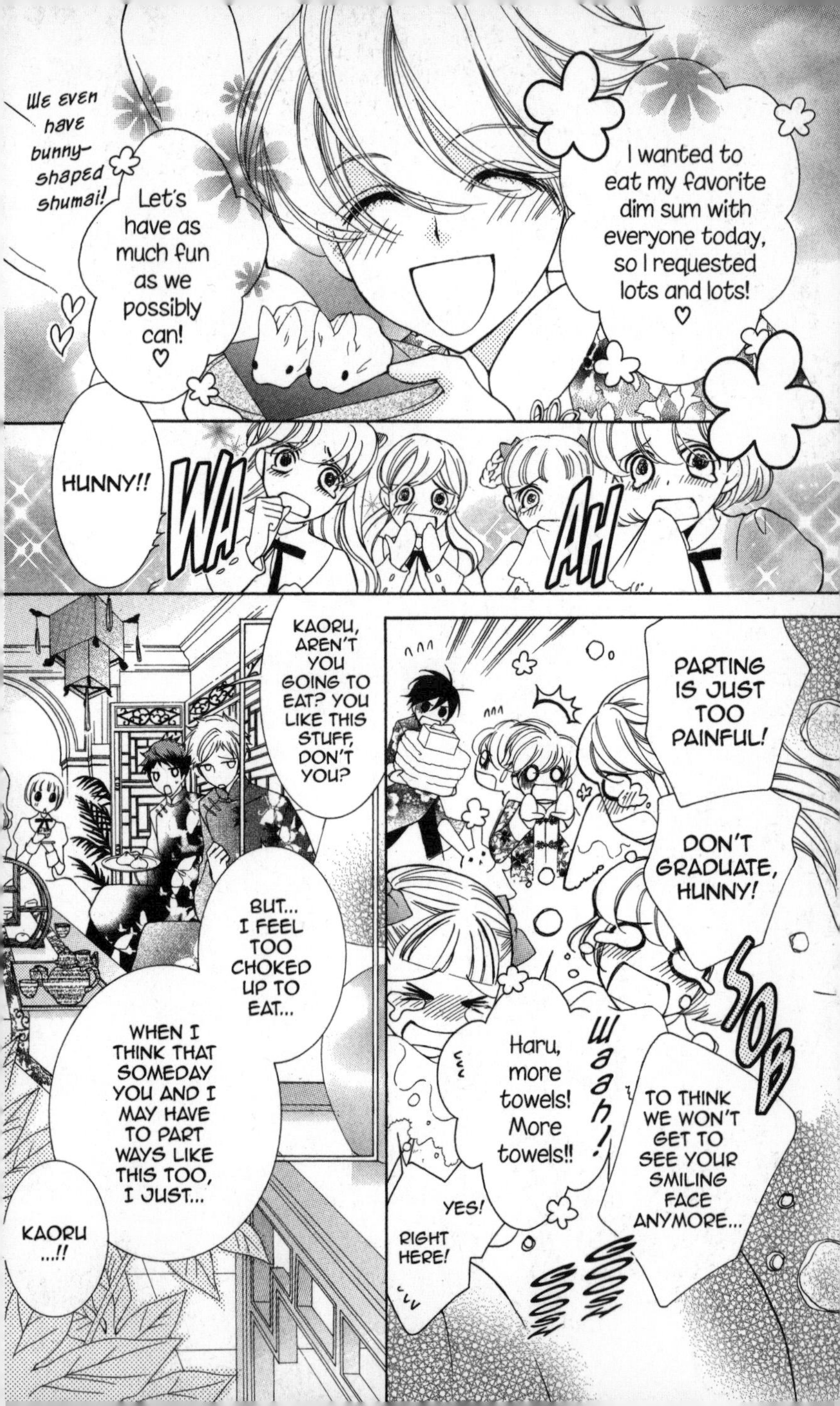
I wanted to eat my favorite dim sum with everyone today, so I requested lots and lots! ♡
Let's have as much fun as we possibly can! ♡
We even have bunny-shaped shumai!
WA AH
HUNNY!!
PARTING IS JUST TOO PAINFUL!
DON'T GRADUATE, HUNNY!
SOB
TO THINK WE WON'T GET TO SEE YOUR SMILING FACE ANYMORE...
Haru, more towels! More towels!!
Waah!
YES! RIGHT HERE!
KAORU, AREN'T YOU GOING TO EAT? YOU LIKE THIS STUFF, DON'T YOU?
BUT... I FEEL TOO CHOKED UP TO EAT...
WHEN I THINK THAT SOMEDAY YOU AND I MAY HAVE TO PART WAYS LIKE THIS TOO, I JUST...
KAORU ...!!

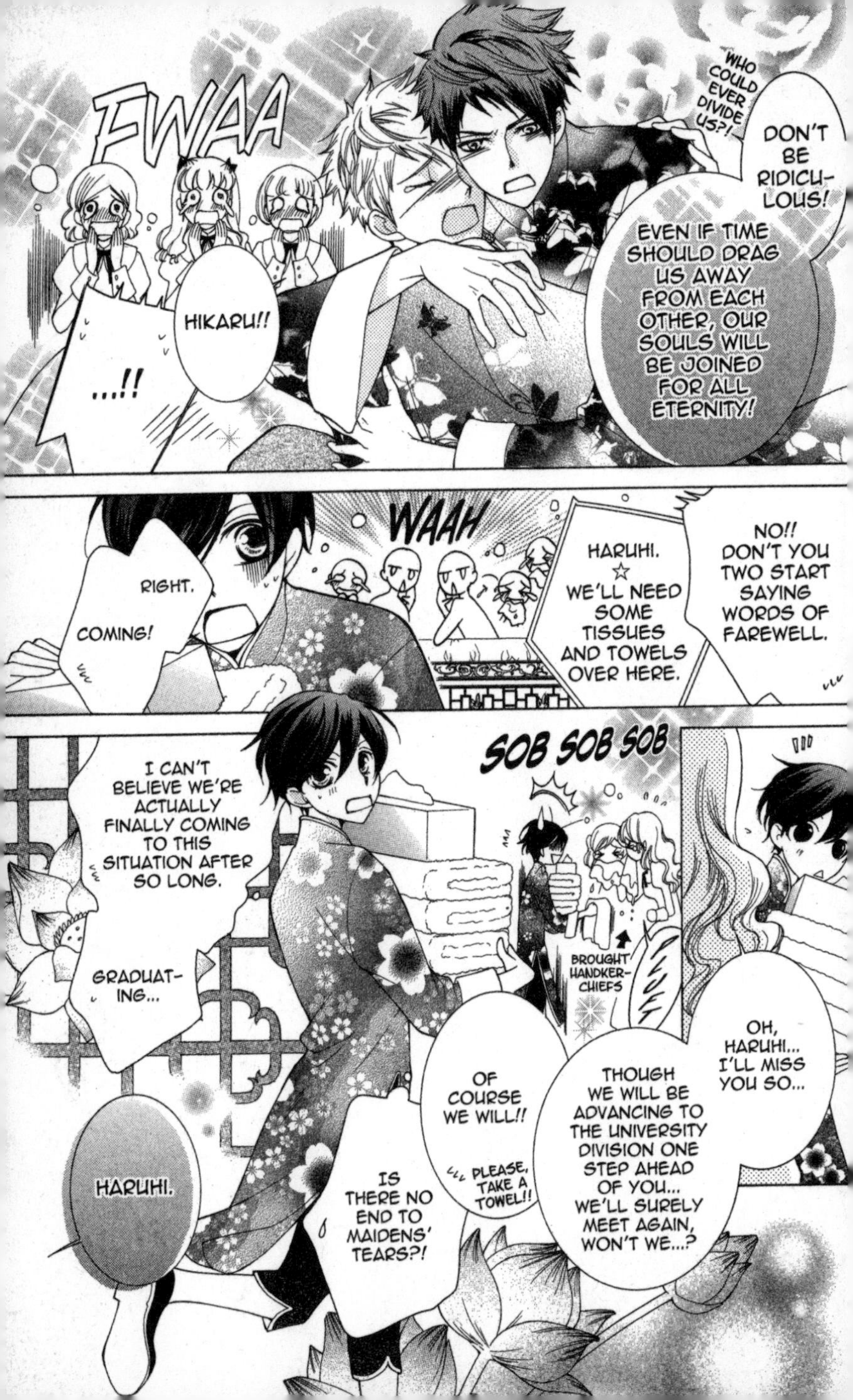
WHO COULD EVER DIVIDE US?!
DON'T BE RIDICULOUS!
EVEN IF TIME SHOULD DRAG US AWAY FROM EACH OTHER, OUR SOULS WILL BE JOINED FOR ALL ETERNITY!
FWAA
HIKARU!!
...!!
NO!! DON'T YOU TWO START SAYING WORDS OF FAREWELL.
HARUHI. ☆ WE'LL NEED SOME TISSUES AND TOWELS OVER HERE.
WAAH
RIGHT.
COMING!
SOB SOB SOB
OH, HARUHI... I'LL MISS YOU SO...
THOUGH WE WILL BE ADVANCING TO THE UNIVERSITY DIVISION ONE STEP AHEAD OF YOU... WE'LL SURELY MEET AGAIN, WON'T WE...?
BROUGHT HANDKERCHIEFS
OF COURSE WE WILL!!
PLEASE, TAKE A TOWEL!!
I CAN'T BELIEVE WE'RE ACTUALLY FINALLY COMING TO THIS SITUATION AFTER SO LONG.
GRADUATING...
IS THERE NO END TO MAIDENS' TEARS?!
HARUHI.

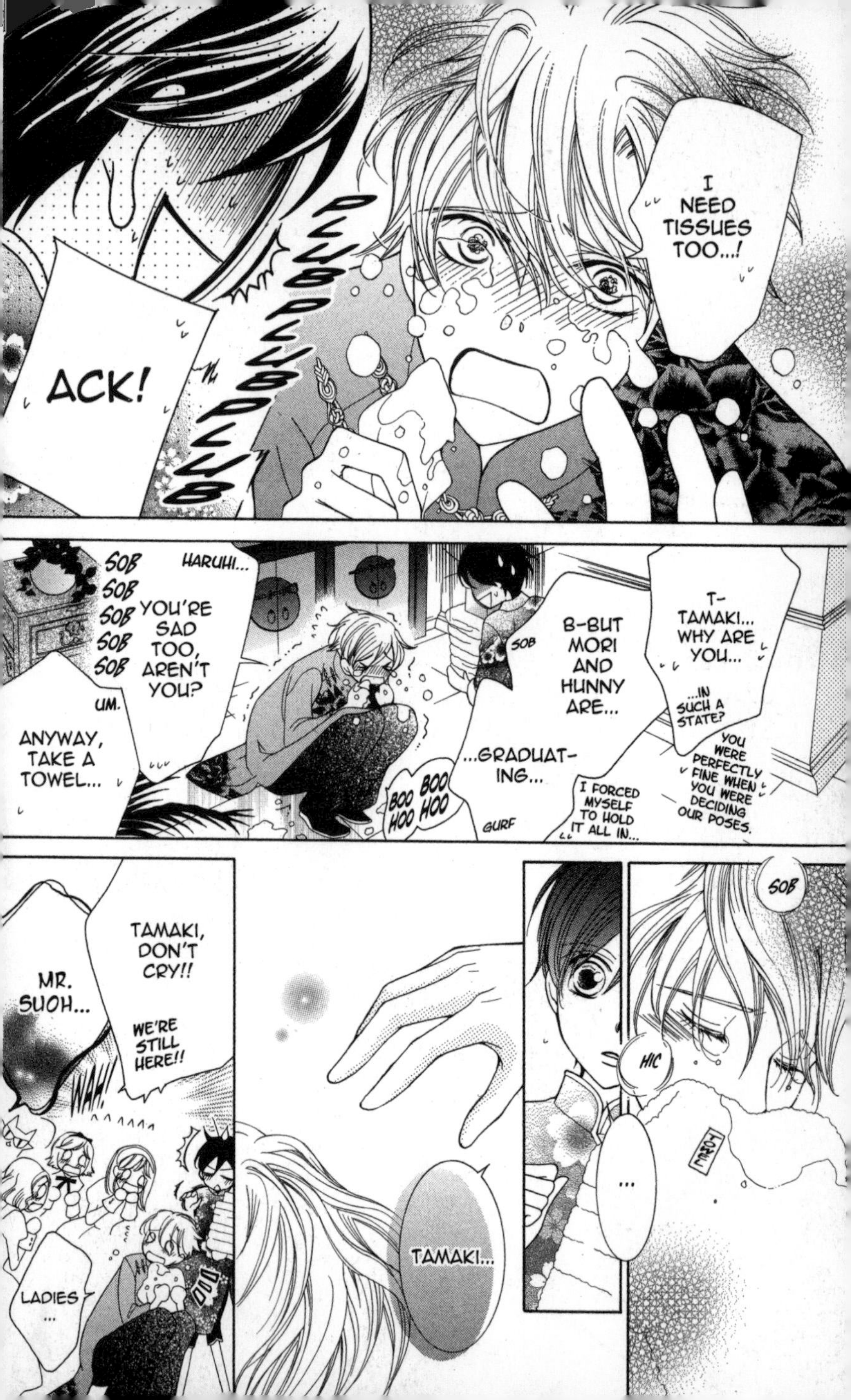
I NEED TISSUES TOO...!
PLUB PLUB PLUB PLUB PLUB
ACK!
T-TAMAKI... WHY ARE YOU...
...IN SUCH A STATE?
YOU WERE PERFECTLY FINE WHEN YOU WERE DECIDING OUR POSES.
I FORCED MYSELF TO HOLD IT ALL IN...
B-BUT MORI AND HUNNY ARE...
...GRADUAT-ING...
SOB
GURF
BOO HOO BOO HOO
HARUHI... YOU'RE SAD TOO, AREN'T YOU?
SOB SOB SOB SOB SOB
UM.
ANYWAY, TAKE A TOWEL...
SOB
HIC
...
TAMAKI...
TAMAKI, DON'T CRY!!
WE'RE STILL HERE!!
MR. SUOH...
WAH!
LADIES ...

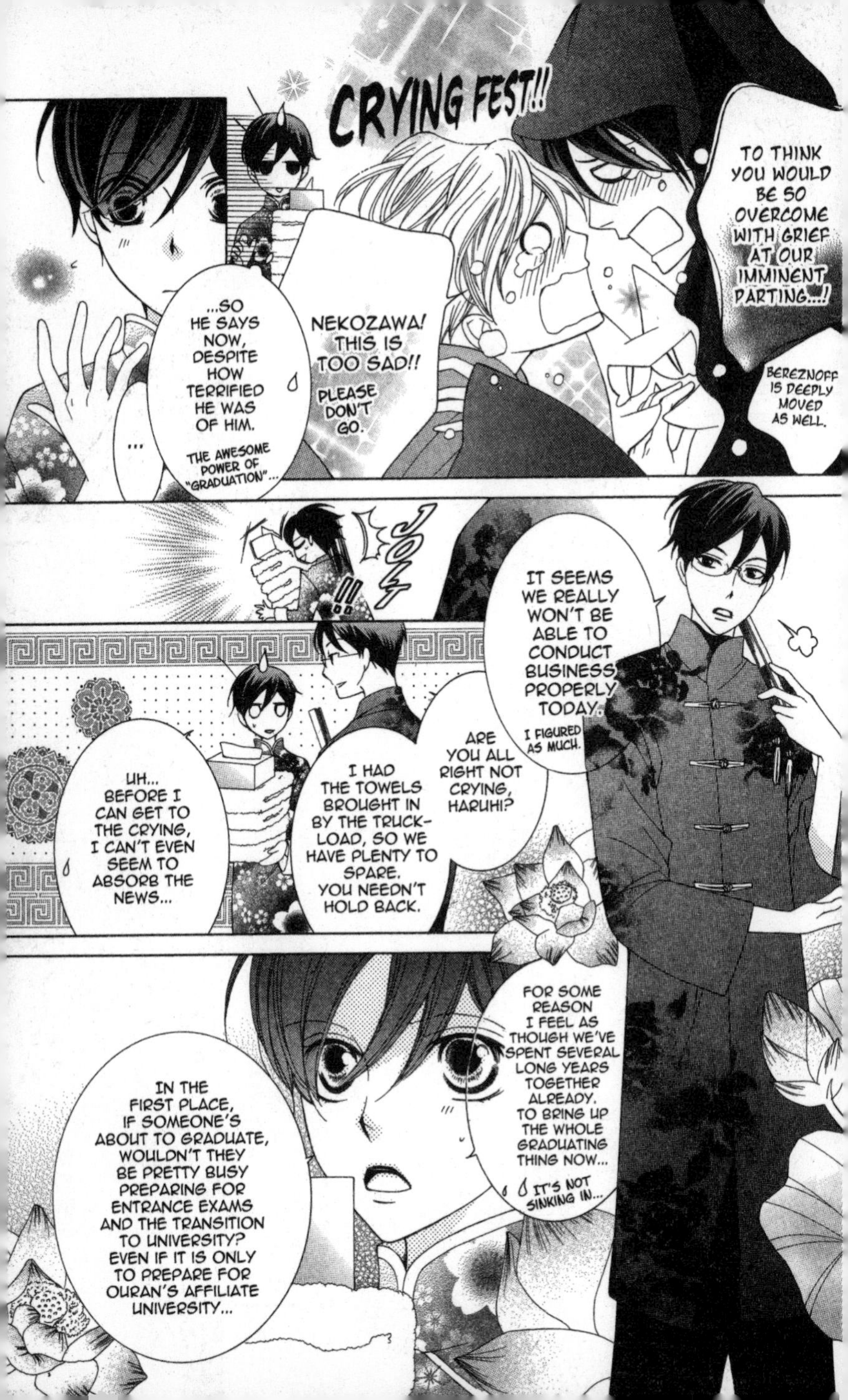
CRYING FEST!!
TO THINK YOU WOULD BE SO OVERCOME WITH GRIEF AT OUR IMMINENT PARTING...!
BEREZNOFF IS DEEPLY MOVED AS WELL.
NEKOZAWA! THIS IS TOO SAD!!
PLEASE DON'T GO.
...SO HE SAYS NOW, DESPITE HOW TERRIFIED HE WAS OF HIM.
THE AWESOME POWER OF "GRADUATION"...
...
IT SEEMS WE REALLY WON'T BE ABLE TO CONDUCT BUSINESS PROPERLY TODAY.
I FIGURED AS MUCH.
JOLT
!!
ARE YOU ALL RIGHT NOT CRYING, HARUHI?
I HAD THE TOWELS BROUGHT IN BY THE TRUCK-LOAD, SO WE HAVE PLENTY TO SPARE. YOU NEEDN'T HOLD BACK.
UH... BEFORE I CAN GET TO THE CRYING, I CAN'T EVEN SEEM TO ABSORB THE NEWS...
FOR SOME REASON I FEEL AS THOUGH WE'VE SPENT SEVERAL LONG YEARS TOGETHER ALREADY. TO BRING UP THE WHOLE GRADUATING THING NOW...
IT'S NOT SINKING IN...
IN THE FIRST PLACE, IF SOMEONE'S ABOUT TO GRADUATE, WOULDN'T THEY BE PRETTY BUSY PREPARING FOR ENTRANCE EXAMS AND THE TRANSITION TO UNIVERSITY? EVEN IF IT IS ONLY TO PREPARE FOR OURAN'S AFFILIATE UNIVERSITY...

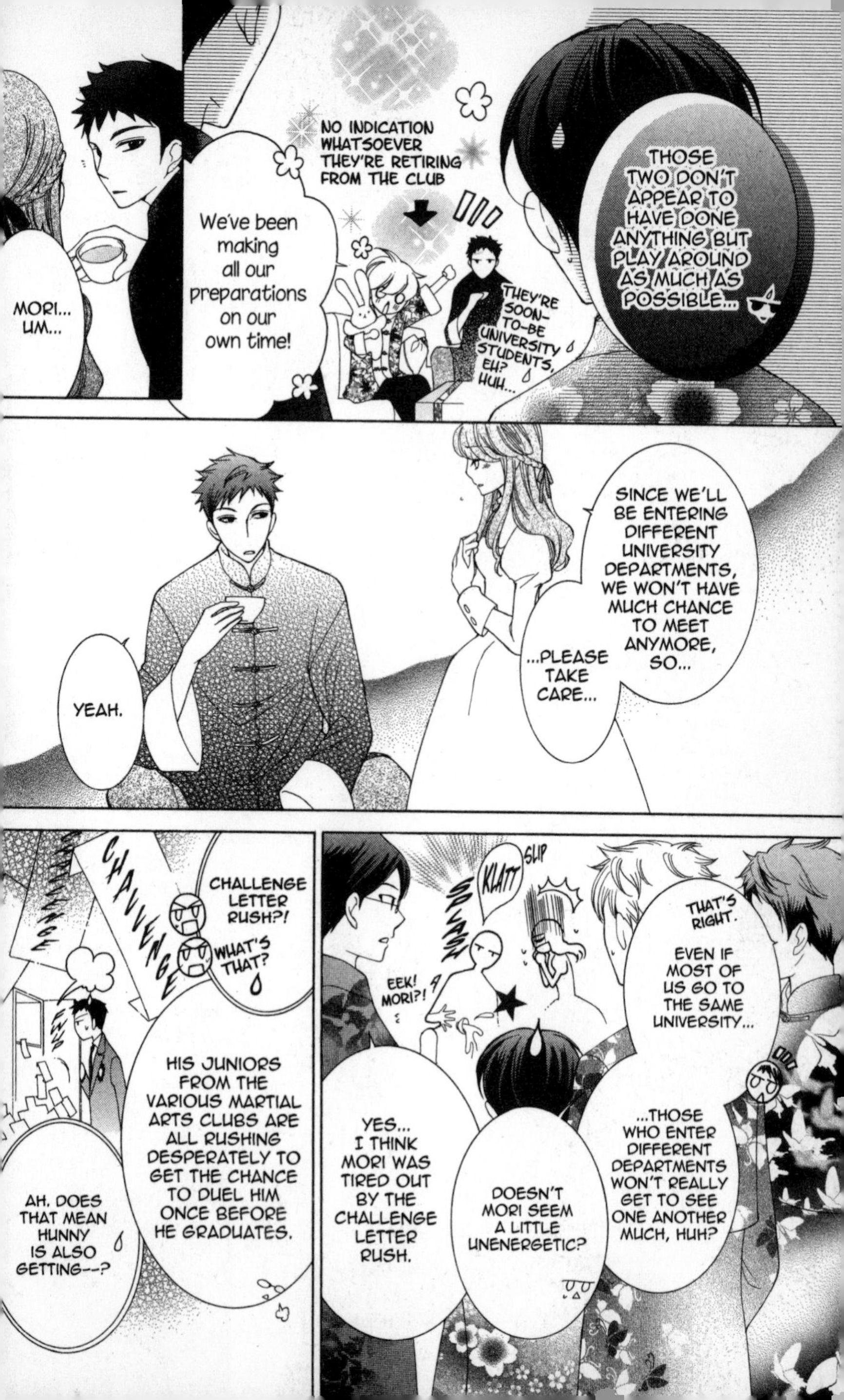
THOSE TWO DON'T APPEAR TO HAVE DONE ANYTHING BUT PLAY AROUND AS MUCH AS POSSIBLE...
THEY'RE SOON-TO-BE UNIVERSITY STUDENTS, EH? HUH...
NO INDICATION WHATSOEVER THEY'RE RETIRING FROM THE CLUB
We've been making all our preparations on our own time!
MORI... UM...
SINCE WE'LL BE ENTERING DIFFERENT UNIVERSITY DEPARTMENTS, WE WON'T HAVE MUCH CHANCE TO MEET ANYMORE, SO...
...PLEASE TAKE CARE...
YEAH.
THAT'S RIGHT.
EVEN IF MOST OF US GO TO THE SAME UNIVERSITY...
...THOSE WHO ENTER DIFFERENT DEPARTMENTS WON'T REALLY GET TO SEE ONE ANOTHER MUCH, HUH?
SLIP
KLATT
EEK! MORI?!
DOESN'T MORI SEEM A LITTLE UNENERGETIC?
YES... I THINK MORI WAS TIRED OUT BY THE CHALLENGE LETTER RUSH.
CHALLENGE LETTER RUSH?!
WHAT'S THAT?
HIS JUNIORS FROM THE VARIOUS MARTIAL ARTS CLUBS ARE ALL RUSHING DESPERATELY TO GET THE CHANCE TO DUEL HIM ONCE BEFORE HE GRADUATES.
AH. DOES THAT MEAN HUNNY IS ALSO GETTING--?

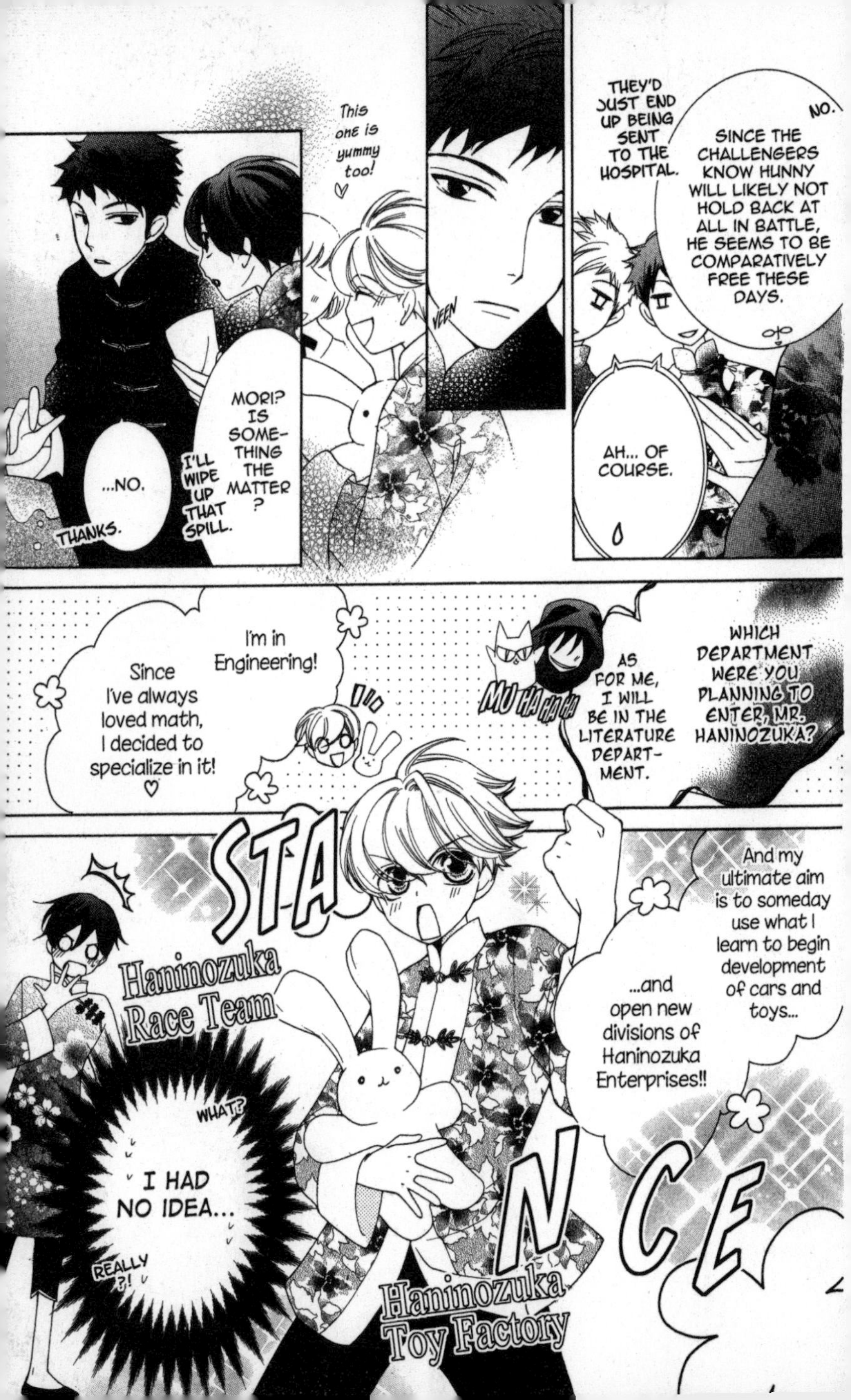
NO.
SINCE THE CHALLENGERS KNOW HUNNY WILL LIKELY NOT HOLD BACK AT ALL IN BATTLE, HE SEEMS TO BE COMPARATIVELY FREE THESE DAYS.
THEY'D JUST END UP BEING SENT TO THE HOSPITAL.
AH... OF COURSE.
This one is yummy too! ♡
VEEN
MORI? IS SOMETHING THE MATTER?
I'LL WIPE UP THAT SPILL.
...NO.
THANKS.
WHICH DEPARTMENT WERE YOU PLANNING TO ENTER, MR. HANINOZUKA?
AS FOR ME, I WILL BE IN THE LITERATURE DEPARTMENT.
MU HA HA HA
I'm in Engineering!
Since I've always loved math, I decided to specialize in it! ♡
And my ultimate aim is to someday use what I learn to begin development of cars and toys...
...and open new divisions of Haninozuka Enterprises!!
STA NCE
Haninozuka Toy Factory
Haninozuka Race Team
WHAT?
I HAD NO IDEA...
REALLY?!

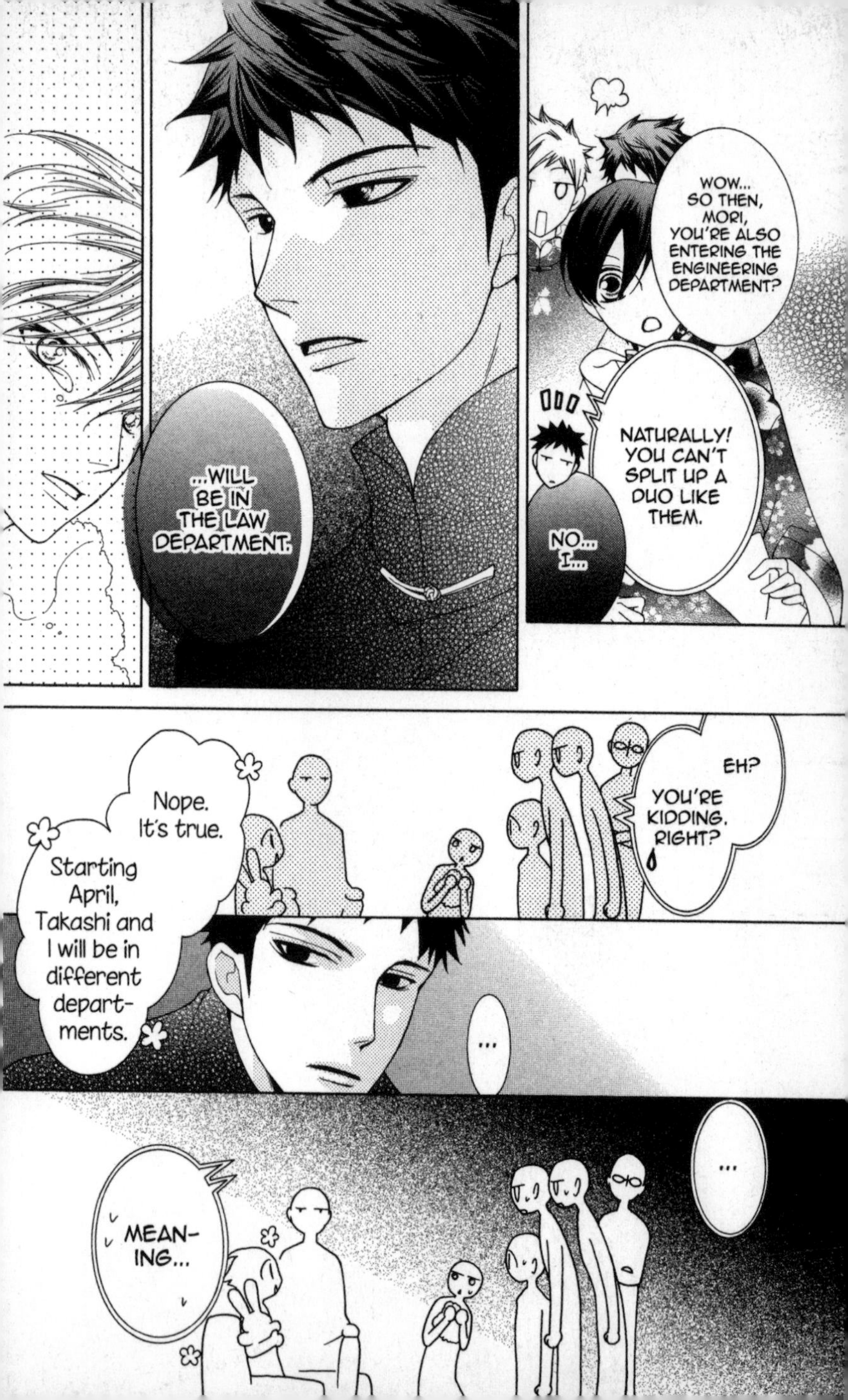
WOW... SO THEN, MORI, YOU'RE ALSO ENTERING THE ENGINEERING DEPARTMENT?
NATURALLY! YOU CAN'T SPLIT UP A DUO LIKE THEM.
NO... I...
...WILL BE IN THE LAW DEPARTMENT.
EH? YOU'RE KIDDING. RIGHT?
Nope. It's true.
Starting April, Takashi and I will be in different depart-ments.
...
...
MEAN-ING...

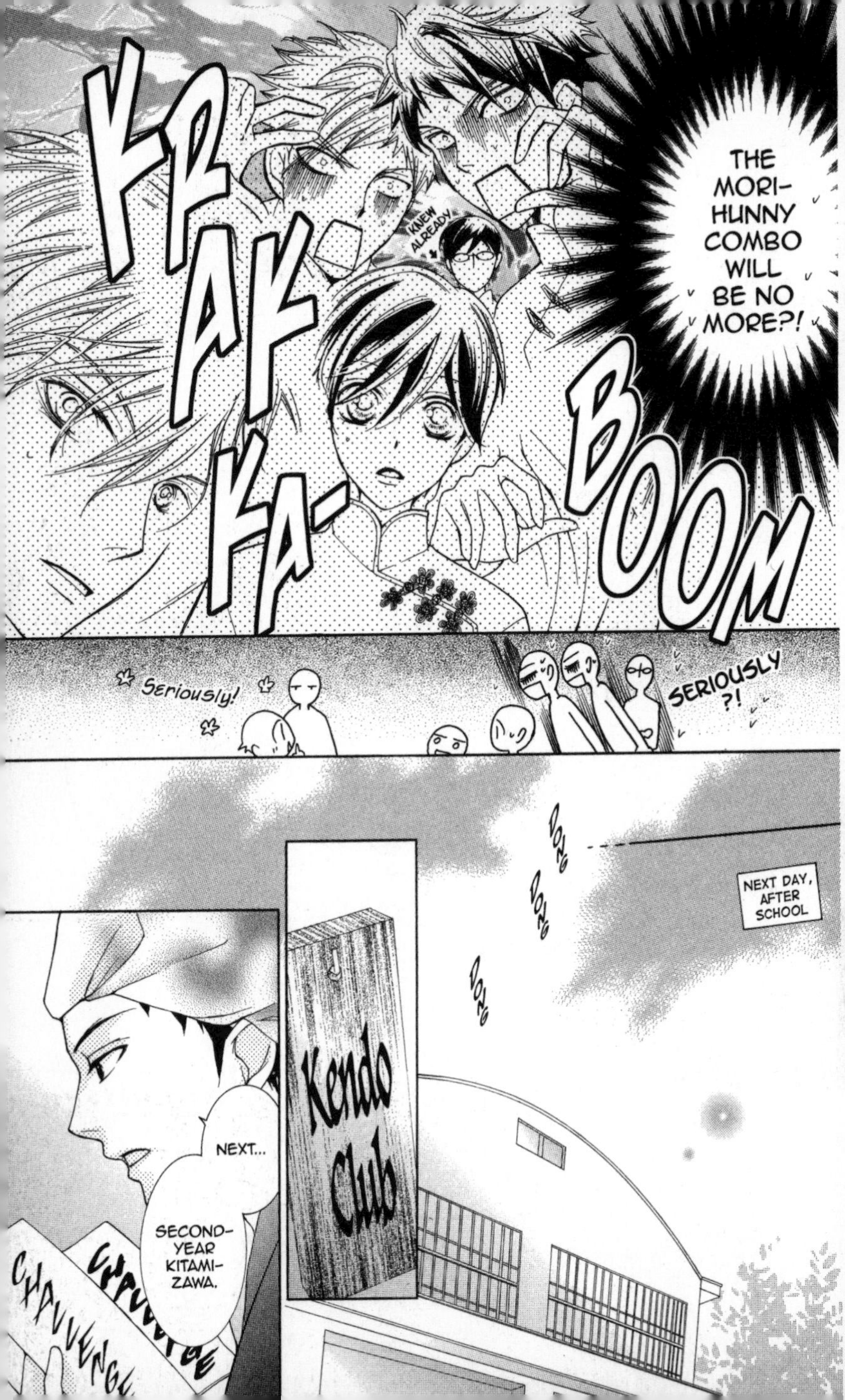

THE MORI-HUNNY COMBO WILL BE NO MORE?!
KNEW ALREADY
KA-KA-KA-BOOM
SERIOUSLY?!
Seriously!
NEXT DAY, AFTER SCHOOL
DONG
DONG
DONG
Kendo Club
NEXT...
SECOND-YEAR KITAMI-ZAWA.
CHALLENGE
CHALLENG

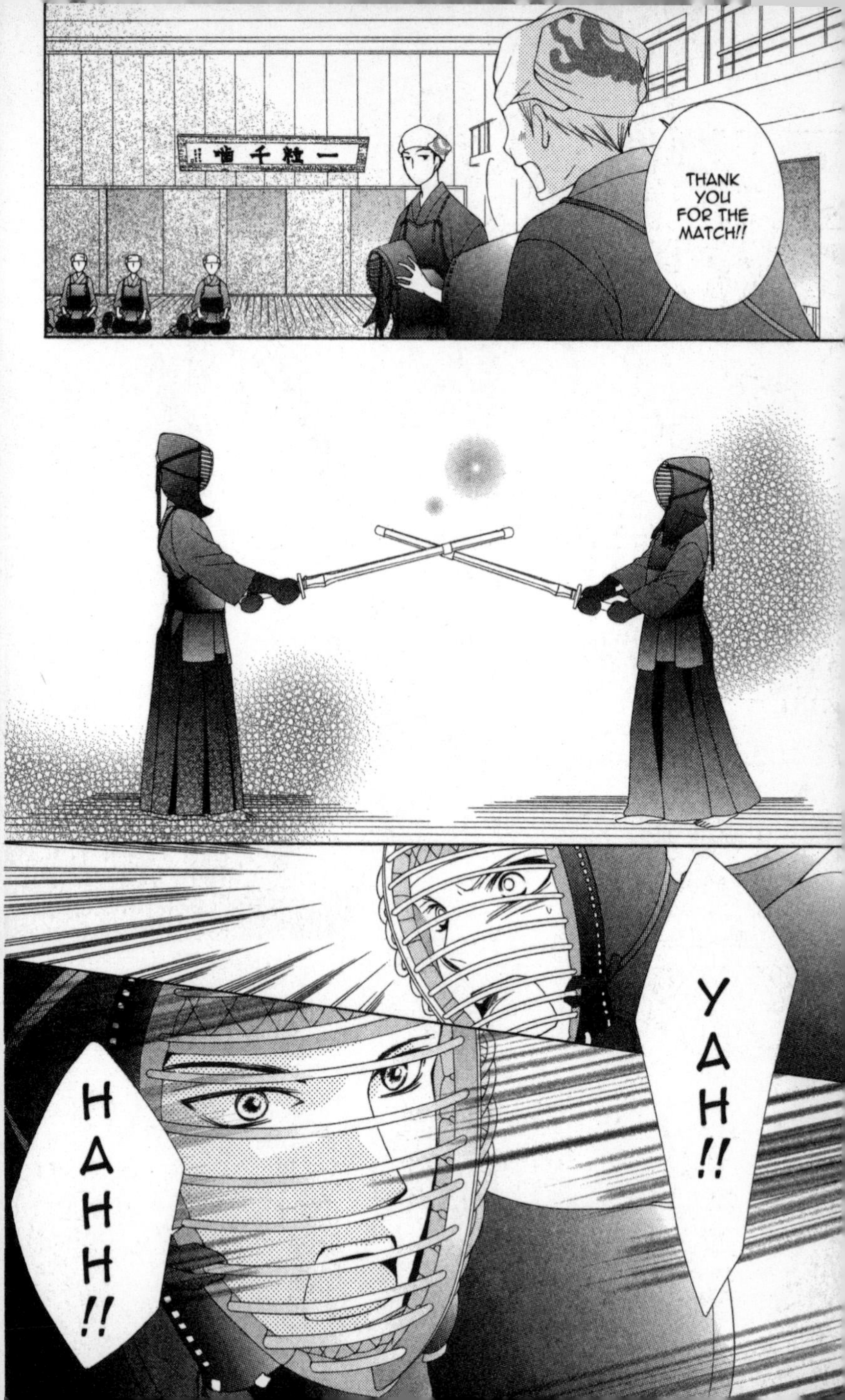
THANK YOU FOR THE MATCH!!
YAH!!
HAHH!!

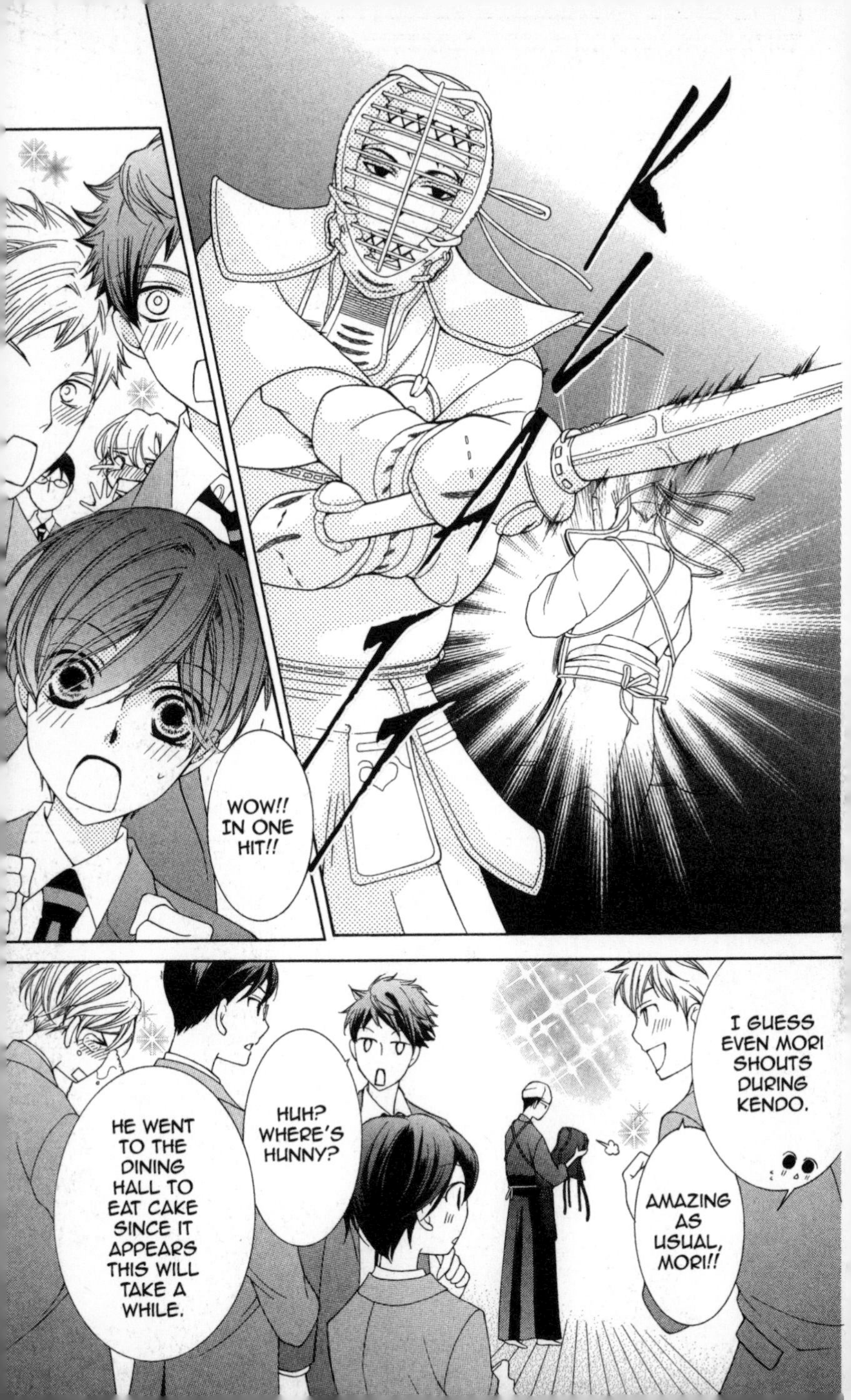
WOW!! IN ONE HIT!!
I GUESS EVEN MORI SHOUTS DURING KENDO.
AMAZING AS USUAL, MORI!!
HUH? WHERE'S HUNNY?
HE WENT TO THE DINING HALL TO EAT CAKE SINCE IT APPEARS THIS WILL TAKE A WHILE.

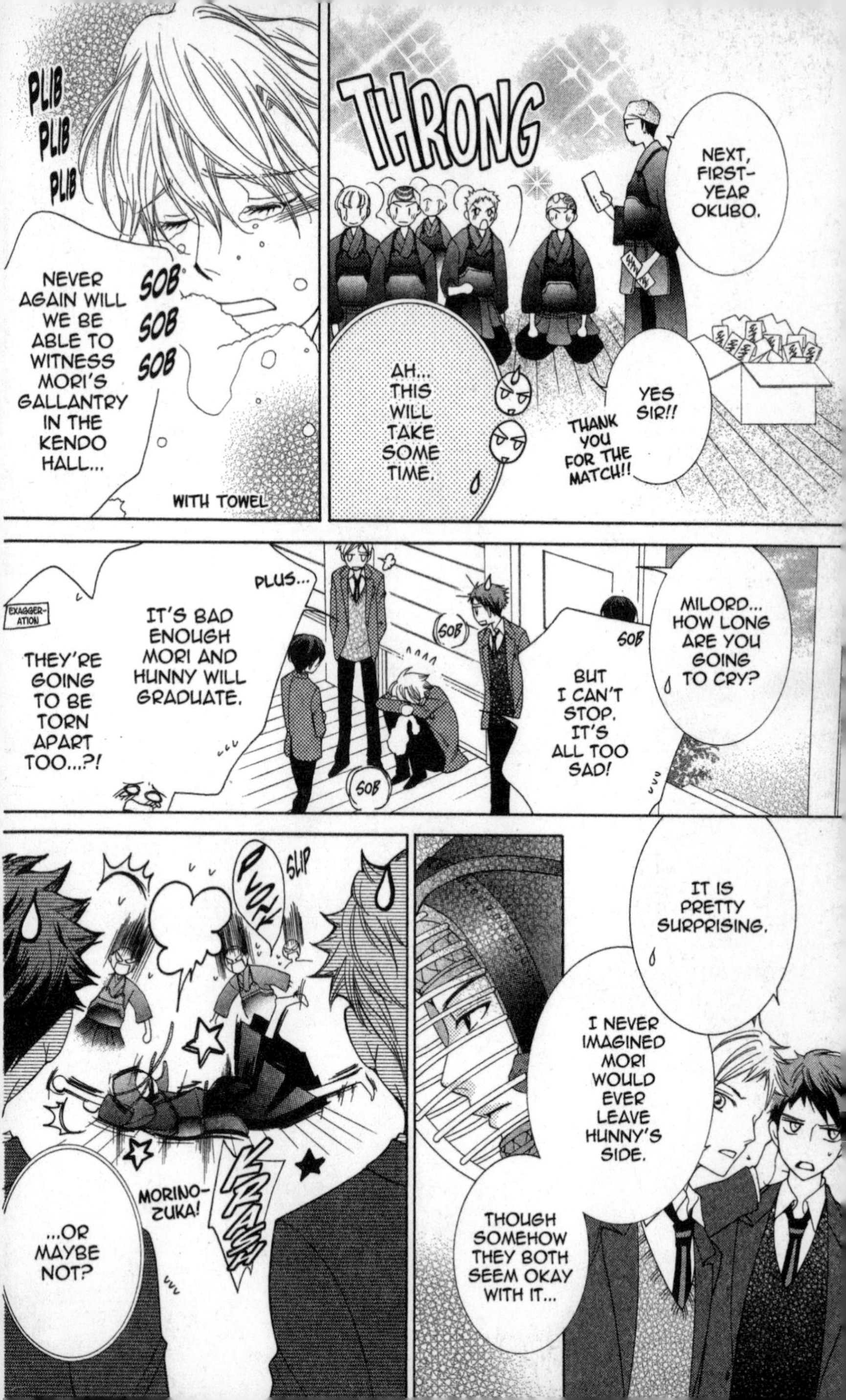
THRONG
NEXT, FIRST-YEAR OKUBO.
YES SIR!!
THANK YOU FOR THE MATCH!!
AH... THIS WILL TAKE SOME TIME.
PLIB PLIB PLIB
SOB SOB SOB
NEVER AGAIN WILL WE BE ABLE TO WITNESS MORI'S GALLANTRY IN THE KENDO HALL...
WITH TOWEL
MILORD... HOW LONG ARE YOU GOING TO CRY?
SOB
BUT I CAN'T STOP. IT'S ALL TOO SAD!
SOB
SOB
PLUS...
IT'S BAD ENOUGH MORI AND HUNNY WILL GRADUATE.
THEY'RE GOING TO BE TORN APART TOO...?!
EXAGGER-ATION
IT IS PRETTY SURPRISING.
I NEVER IMAGINED MORI WOULD EVER LEAVE HUNNY'S SIDE.
THOUGH SOMEHOW THEY BOTH SEEM OKAY WITH IT...
SLIP
MORINO-ZUKA!
...OR MAYBE NOT?

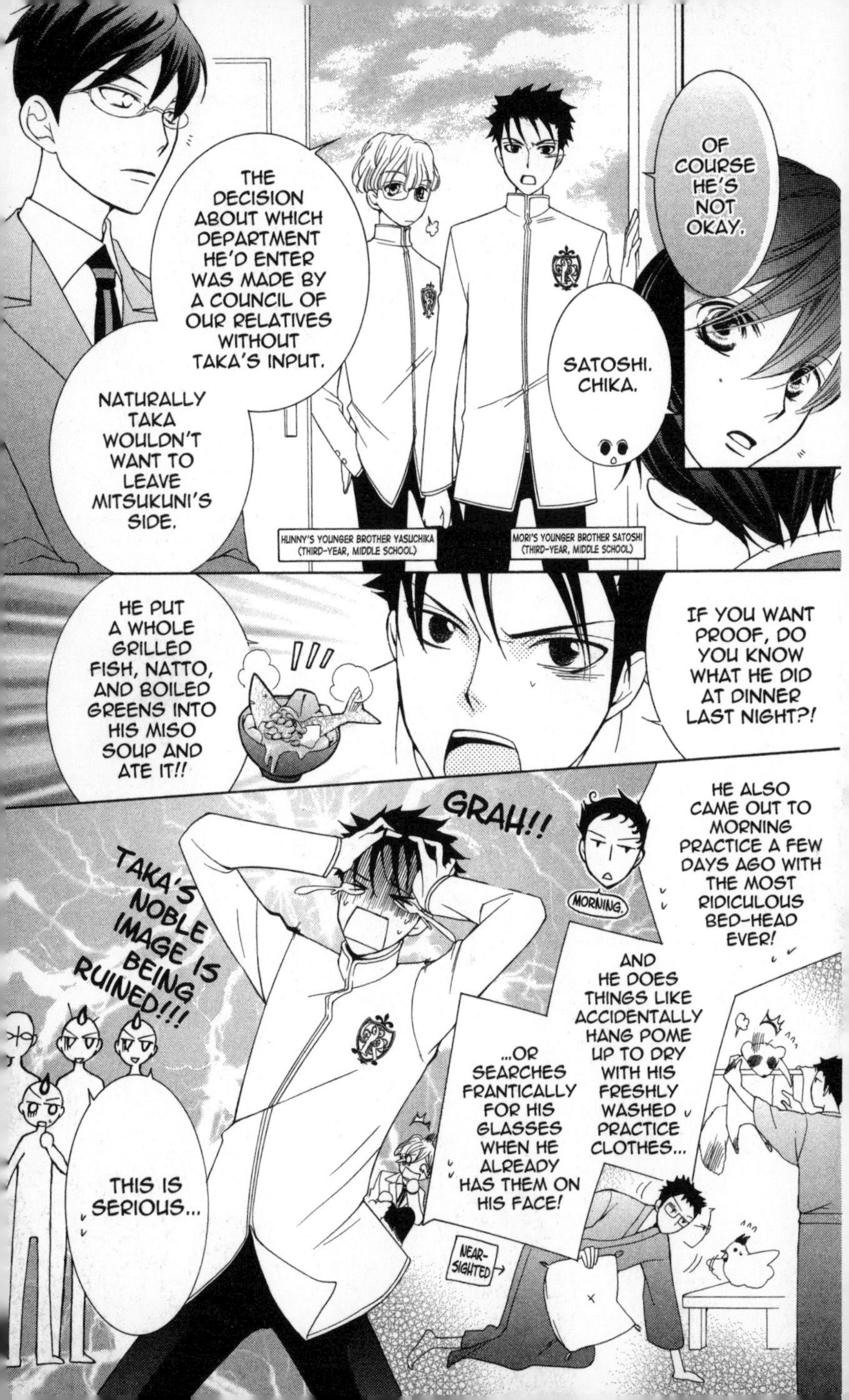
OF COURSE HE'S NOT OKAY.
SATOSHI. CHIKA.
MORI'S YOUNGER BROTHER SATOSHI (THIRD-YEAR, MIDDLE SCHOOL)
HUNNY'S YOUNGER BROTHER YASUCHIKA (THIRD-YEAR, MIDDLE SCHOOL)
THE DECISION ABOUT WHICH DEPARTMENT HE'D ENTER WAS MADE BY A COUNCIL OF OUR RELATIVES WITHOUT TAKA'S INPUT.
NATURALLY TAKA WOULDN'T WANT TO LEAVE MITSUKUNI'S SIDE.
IF YOU WANT PROOF, DO YOU KNOW WHAT HE DID AT DINNER LAST NIGHT?!
HE PUT A WHOLE GRILLED FISH, NATTO, AND BOILED GREENS INTO HIS MISO SOUP AND ATE IT!!
HE ALSO CAME OUT TO MORNING PRACTICE A FEW DAYS AGO WITH THE MOST RIDICULOUS BED-HEAD EVER!
MORNING.
GRAH!!
AND HE DOES THINGS LIKE ACCIDENTALLY HANG POME UP TO DRY WITH HIS FRESHLY WASHED PRACTICE CLOTHES...
...OR SEARCHES FRANTICALLY FOR HIS GLASSES WHEN HE ALREADY HAS THEM ON HIS FACE!
NEAR-SIGHTED
TAKA'S NOBLE IMAGE IS BEING RUINED!!!
THIS IS SERIOUS...

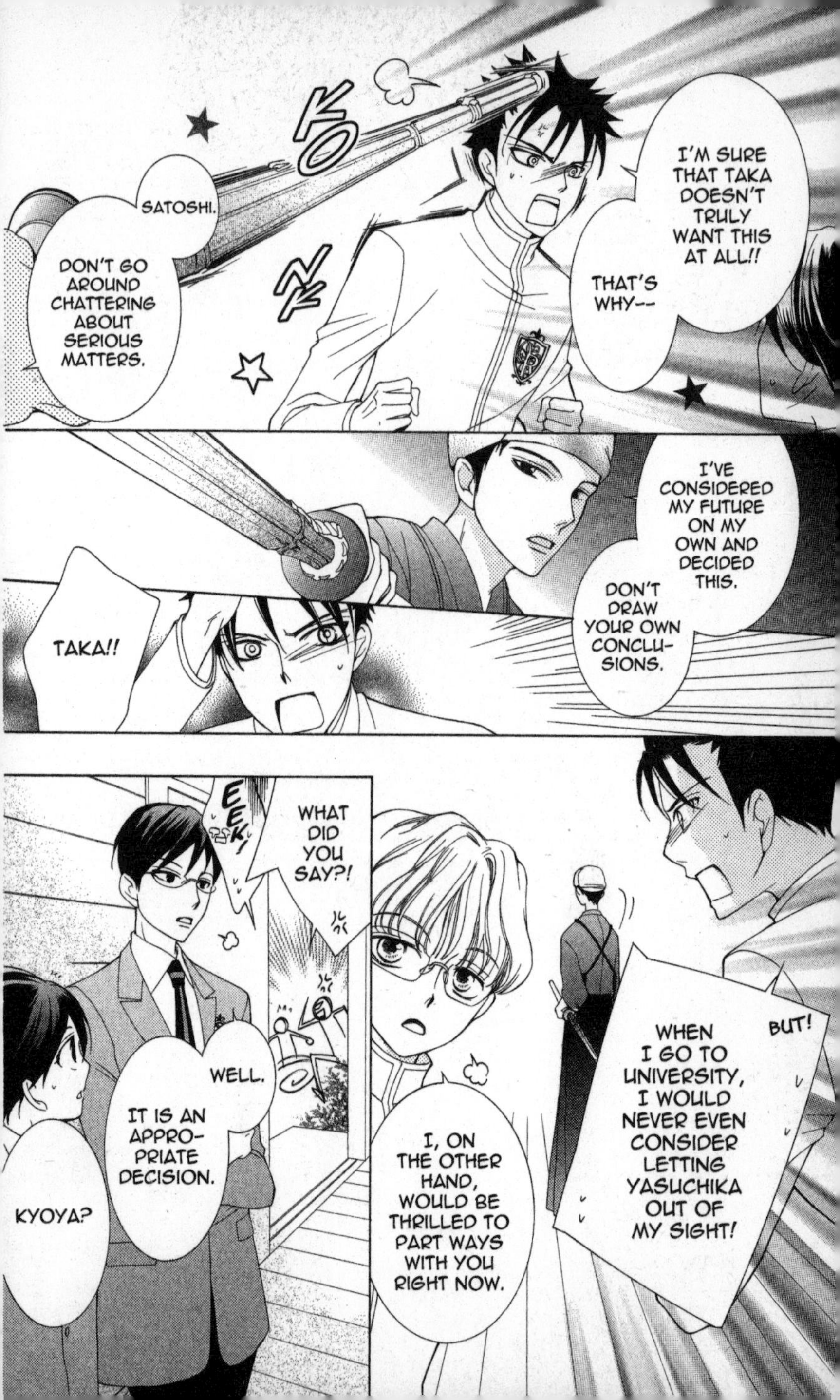
I'M SURE THAT TAKA DOESN'T TRULY WANT THIS AT ALL!!
THAT'S WHY--
SATOSHI.
DON'T GO AROUND CHATTERING ABOUT SERIOUS MATTERS.
I'VE CONSIDERED MY FUTURE ON MY OWN AND DECIDED THIS.
DON'T DRAW YOUR OWN CONCLUSIONS.
TAKA!!
BUT!
WHEN I GO TO UNIVERSITY, I WOULD NEVER EVEN CONSIDER LETTING YASUCHIKA OUT OF MY SIGHT!
I, ON THE OTHER HAND, WOULD BE THRILLED TO PART WAYS WITH YOU RIGHT NOW.
WHAT DID YOU SAY?!
EEK!
WELL.
IT IS AN APPROPRIATE DECISION.
KYOYA?

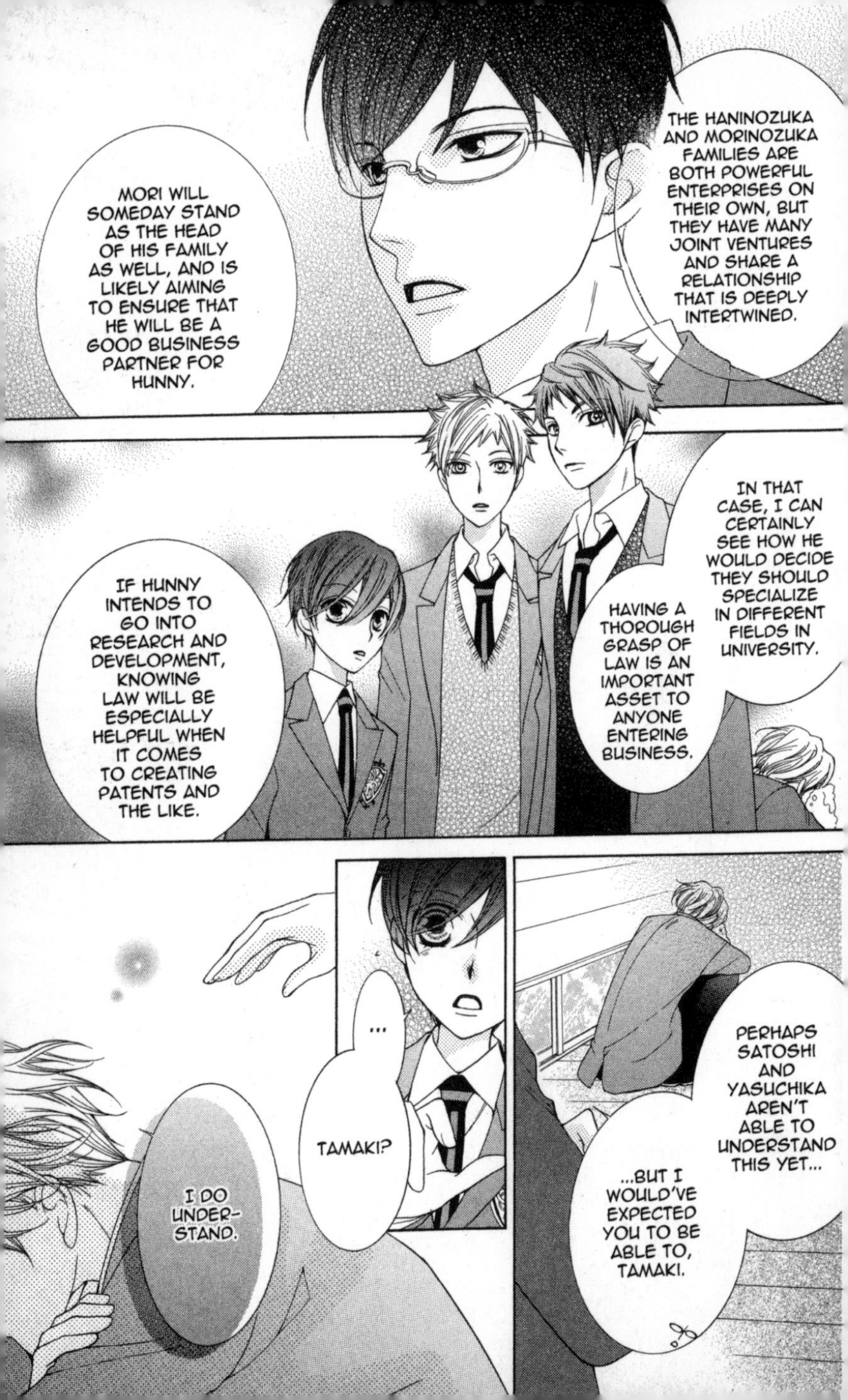
THE HANINOZUKA AND MORINOZUKA FAMILIES ARE BOTH POWERFUL ENTERPRISES ON THEIR OWN, BUT THEY HAVE MANY JOINT VENTURES AND SHARE A RELATIONSHIP THAT IS DEEPLY INTERTWINED.
MORI WILL SOMEDAY STAND AS THE HEAD OF HIS FAMILY AS WELL, AND IS LIKELY AIMING TO ENSURE THAT HE WILL BE A GOOD BUSINESS PARTNER FOR HUNNY.
IN THAT CASE, I CAN CERTAINLY SEE HOW HE WOULD DECIDE THEY SHOULD SPECIALIZE IN DIFFERENT FIELDS IN UNIVERSITY.
HAVING A THOROUGH GRASP OF LAW IS AN IMPORTANT ASSET TO ANYONE ENTERING BUSINESS.
IF HUNNY INTENDS TO GO INTO RESEARCH AND DEVELOPMENT, KNOWING LAW WILL BE ESPECIALLY HELPFUL WHEN IT COMES TO CREATING PATENTS AND THE LIKE.
PERHAPS SATOSHI AND YASUCHIKA AREN'T ABLE TO UNDERSTAND THIS YET...
...BUT I WOULD'VE EXPECTED YOU TO BE ABLE TO, TAMAKI.
...
TAMAKI?
I DO UNDER-STAND.

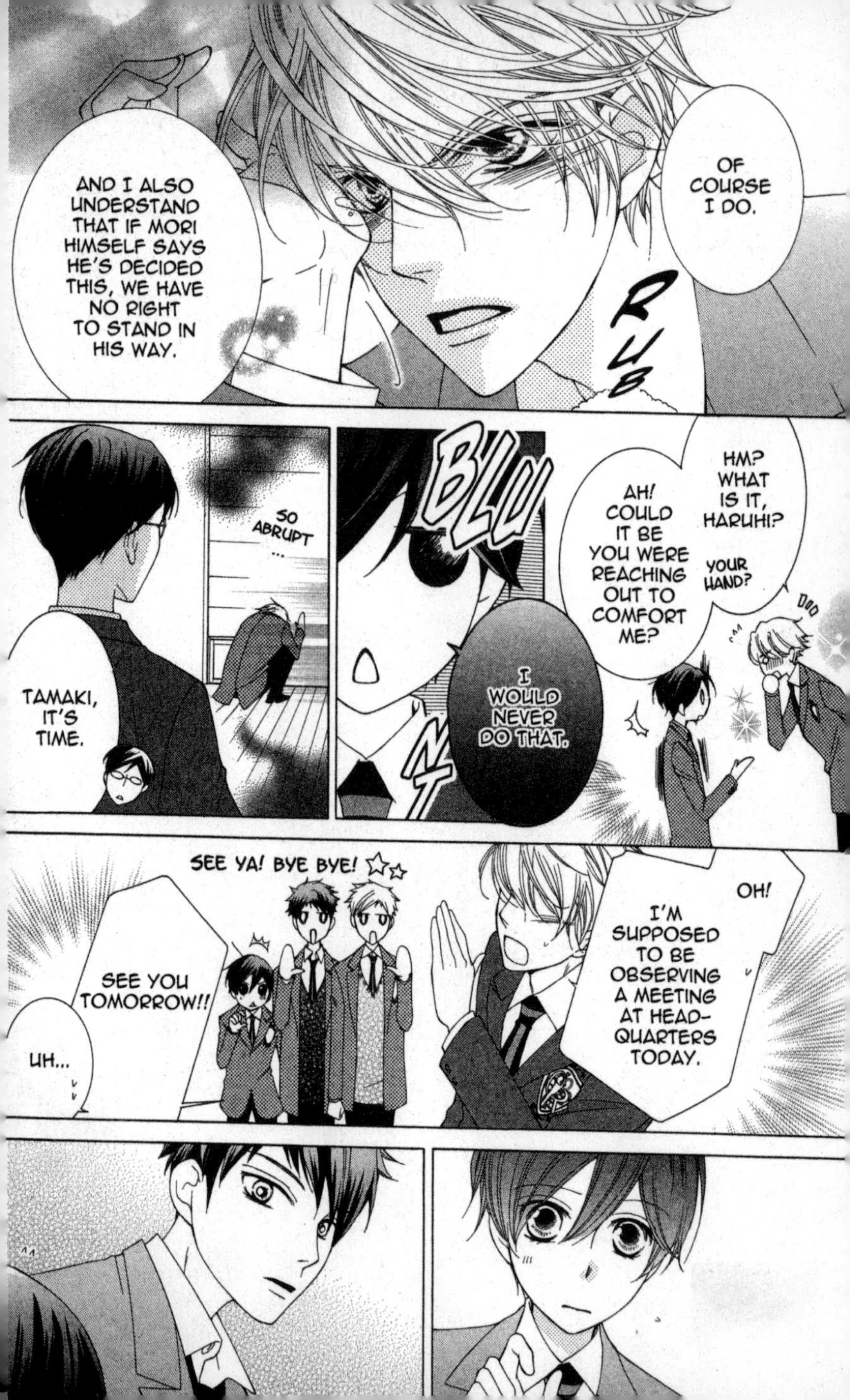
OF COURSE I DO.
RUB
AND I ALSO UNDERSTAND THAT IF MORI HIMSELF SAYS HE'S DECIDED THIS, WE HAVE NO RIGHT TO STAND IN HIS WAY.
HM? WHAT IS IT, HARUHI?
YOUR HAND?
AH! COULD IT BE YOU WERE REACHING OUT TO COMFORT ME?
BLUNT
I WOULD NEVER DO THAT.
SO ABRUPT ...
TAMAKI, IT'S TIME.
OH! I'M SUPPOSED TO BE OBSERVING A MEETING AT HEAD-QUARTERS TODAY.
SEE YA! BYE BYE!
SEE YOU TOMORROW!!
UH...

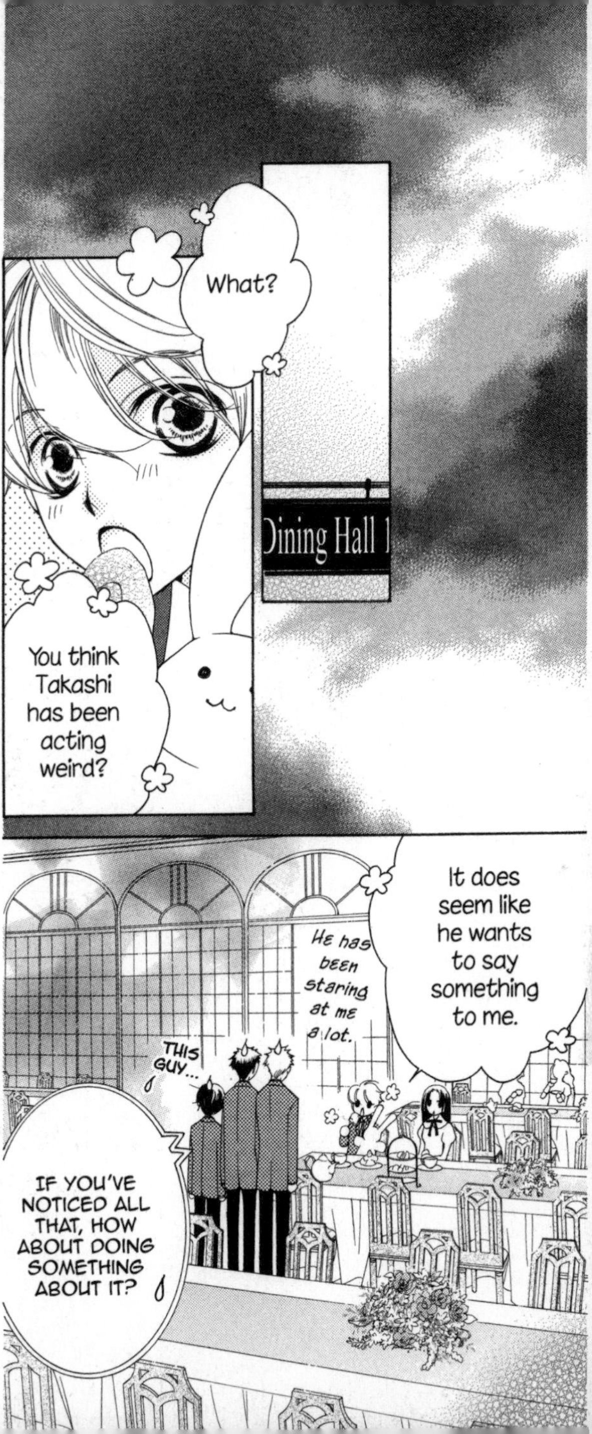
Dining Hall 1
What?
You think Takashi has been acting weird?
It does seem like he wants to say something to me.
He has been staring at me a lot.
THIS GUY...
IF YOU'VE NOTICED ALL THAT, HOW ABOUT DOING SOMETHING ABOUT IT?

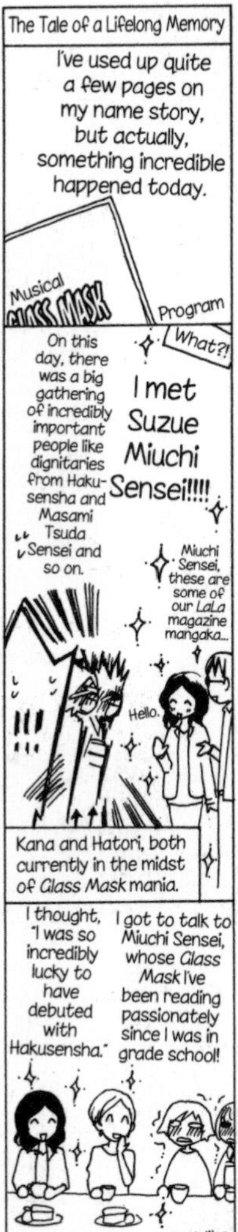
The Tale of a Lifelong Memory
I've used up quite a few pages on my name story, but actually, something incredible happened today.
Musical GLASS MASK
Program
What?!
On this day, there was a big gathering of incredibly important people like dignitaries from Hakusensha and Masami Tsuda Sensei and so on.
I met Suzue Miuchi Sensei!!!!
Miuchi Sensei, these are some of our LaLa magazine mangaka...
Hello.
Kana and Hatori, both currently in the midst of Glass Mask mania.
I thought, "I was so incredibly lucky to have debuted with Hakusensha."
I got to talk to Miuchi Sensei, whose Glass Mask I've been reading passionately since I was in grade school!
It felt like having tea with God.
The person with her was the wife of Tomio Umezawa. Such impressive company! Miuchi Sensei even gave me an autograph! Thank you so very much!!
She was so incredibly nice.

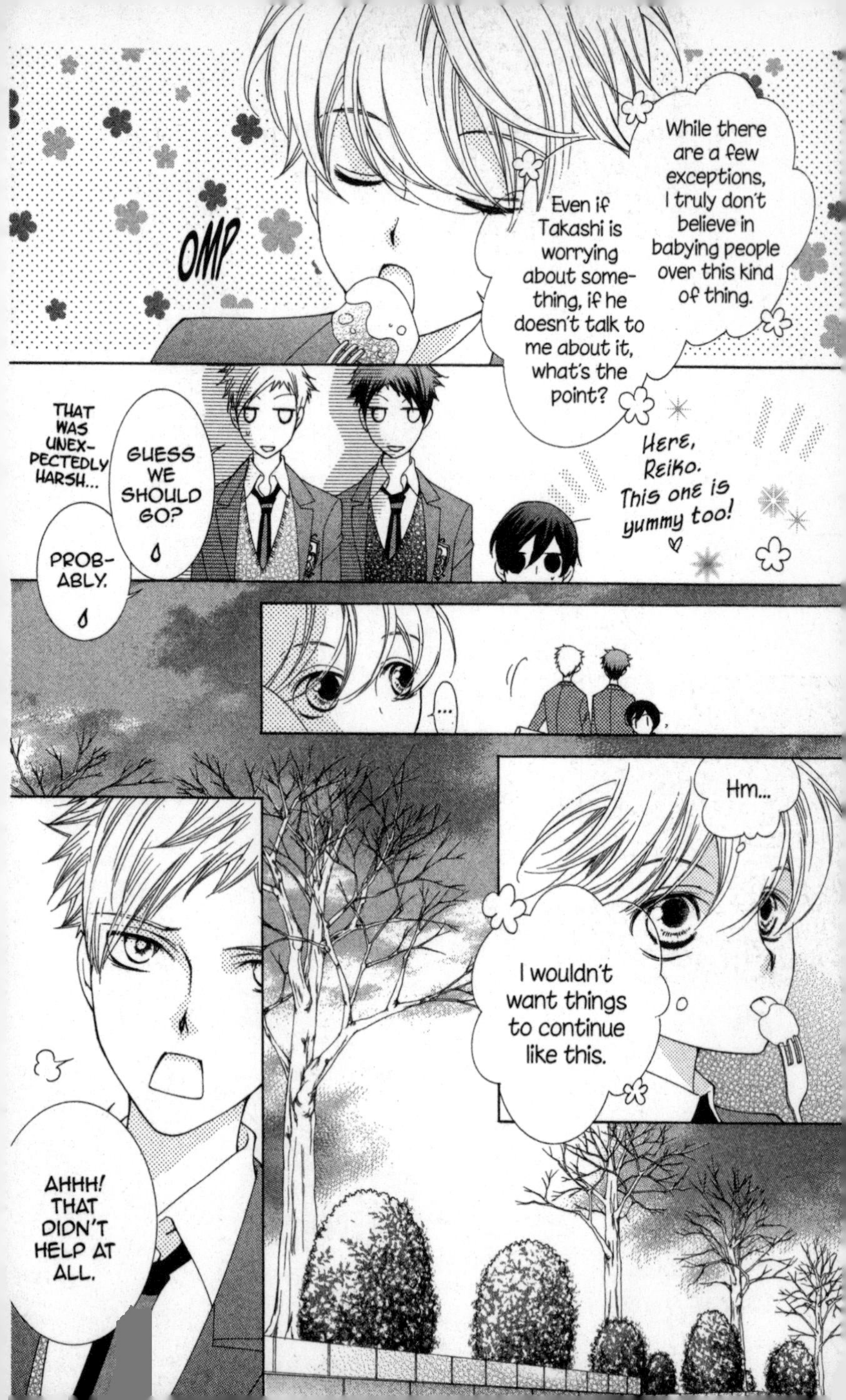
While there are a few exceptions, I truly don't believe in babying people over this kind of thing.
Even if Takashi is worrying about something, if he doesn't talk to me about it, what's the point?
OMP
Here, Reiko. This one is yummy too!
GUESS WE SHOULD GO?
THAT WAS UNEXPECTEDLY HARSH...
PROBABLY.
...
Hm...
I wouldn't want things to continue like this.
AHHH! THAT DIDN'T HELP AT ALL.

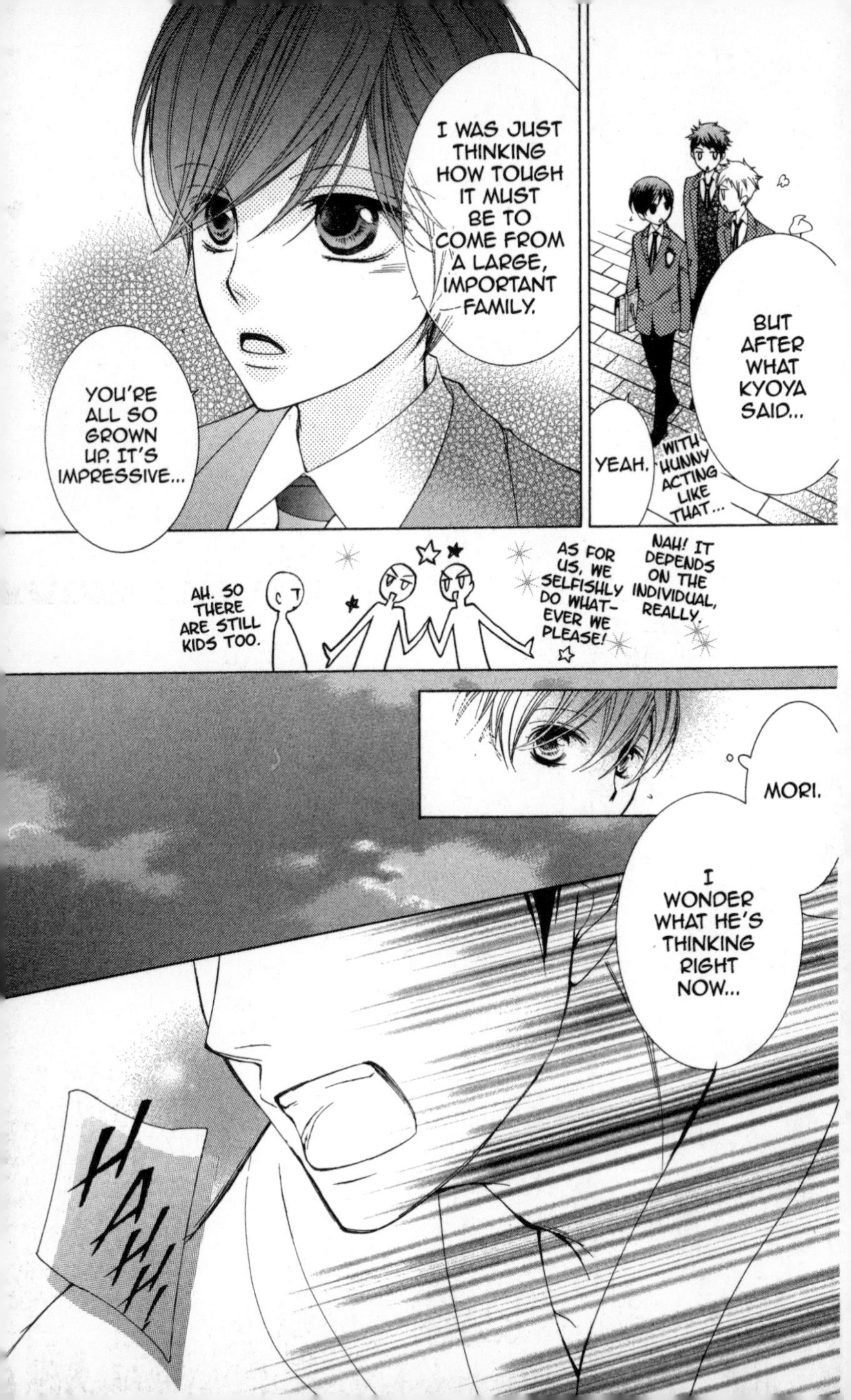
BUT AFTER WHAT KYOYA SAID...
WITH HUNNY ACTING LIKE THAT...
YEAH.
I WAS JUST THINKING HOW TOUGH IT MUST BE TO COME FROM A LARGE, IMPORTANT FAMILY.
YOU'RE ALL SO GROWN UP. IT'S IMPRESSIVE...
NAH! IT DEPENDS ON THE INDIVIDUAL, REALLY.
AS FOR US, WE SELFISHLY DO WHAT-EVER WE PLEASE!
AH. SO THERE ARE STILL KIDS TOO.
MORI.
I WONDER WHAT HE'S THINKING RIGHT NOW...
HAH

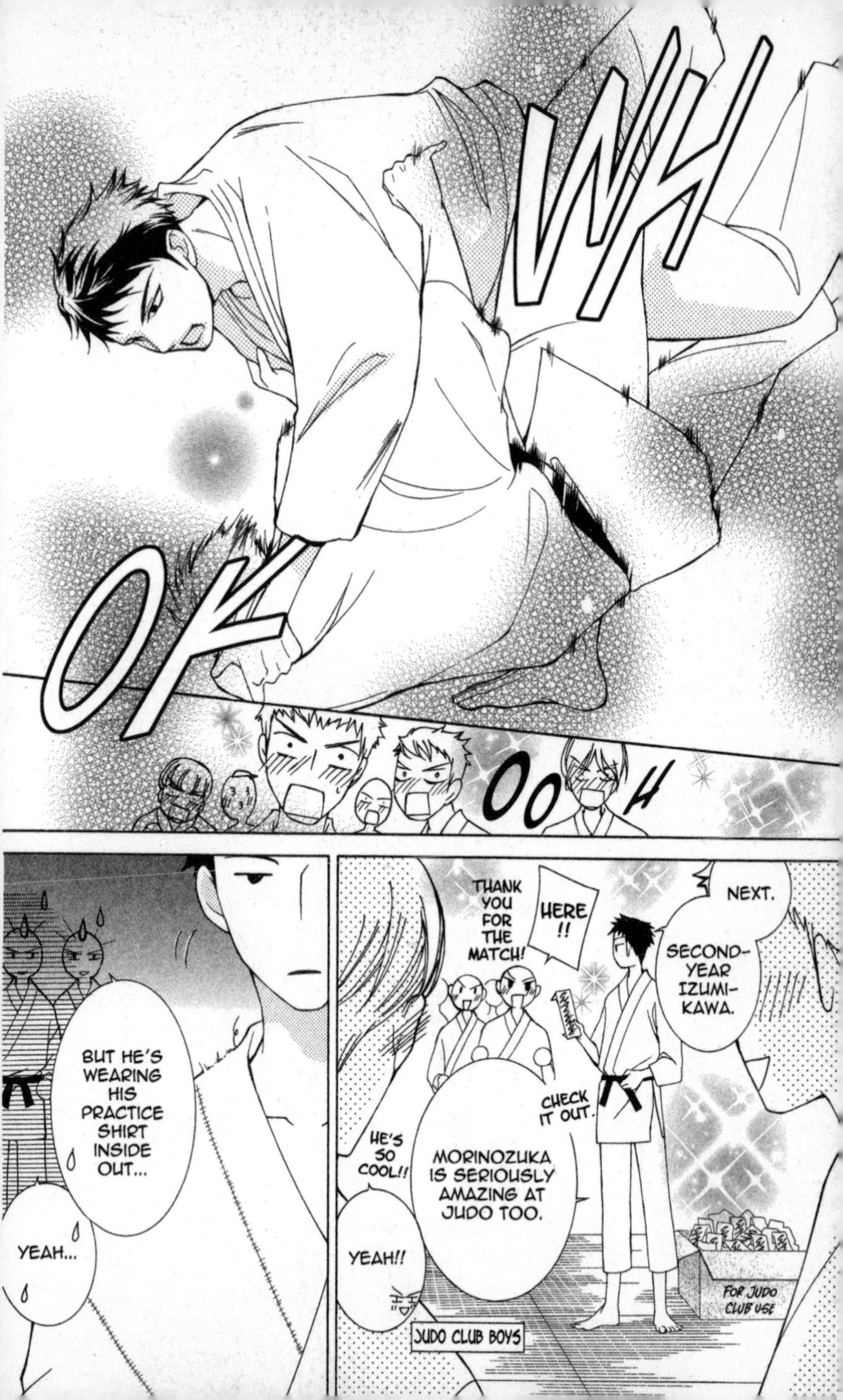
WH
OY
OOH
NEXT.
SECOND-YEAR IZUMI-KAWA.
HERE!!
THANK YOU FOR THE MATCH!
CHECK IT OUT.
MORINOZUKA IS SERIOUSLY AMAZING AT JUDO TOO.
HE'S SO COOL!!
YEAH!!
FOR JUDO CLUB USE
JUDO CLUB BOYS
BUT HE'S WEARING HIS PRACTICE SHIRT INSIDE OUT...
YEAH...

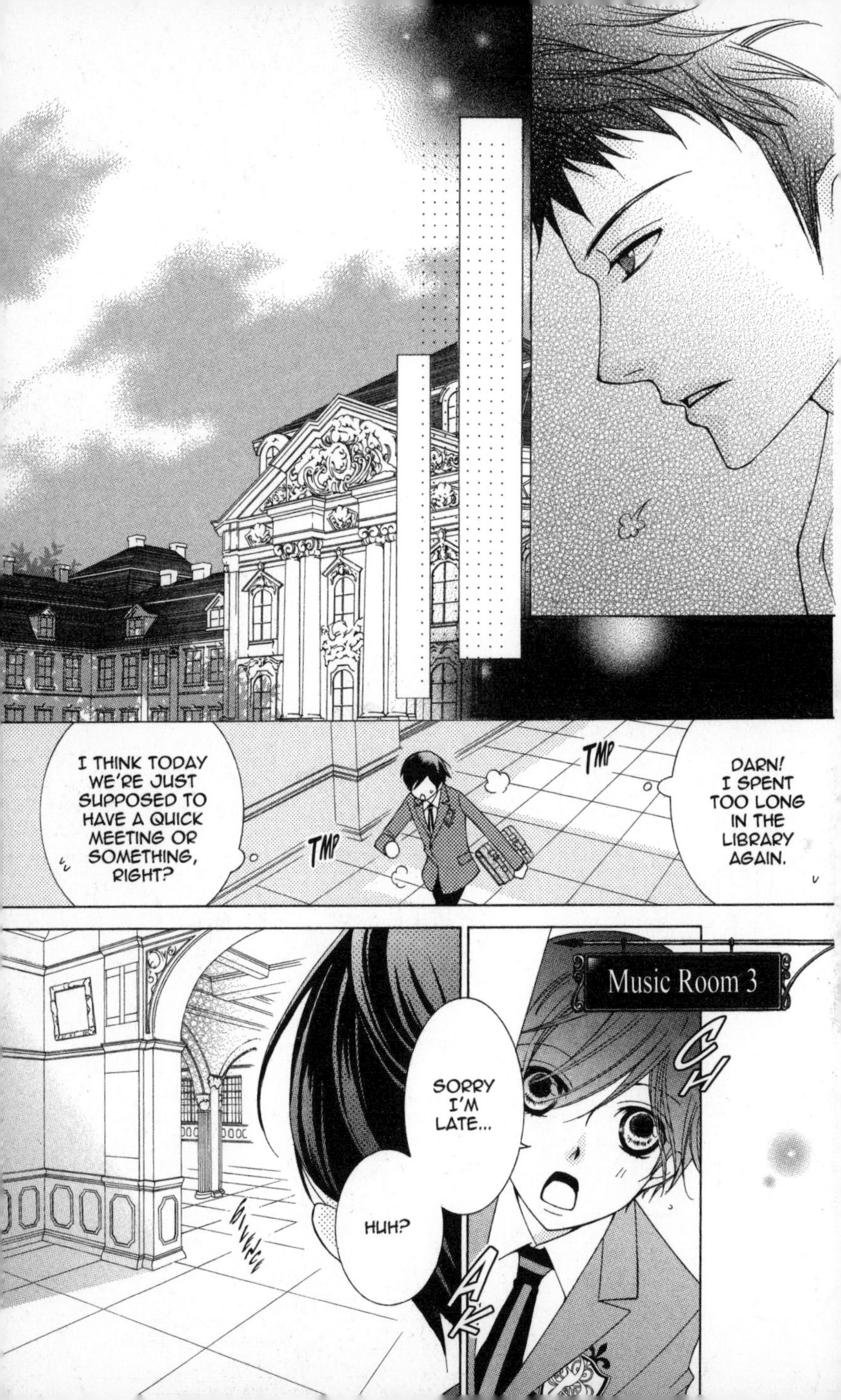
DARN! I SPENT TOO LONG IN THE LIBRARY AGAIN.
TMP
TMP
I THINK TODAY WE'RE JUST SUPPOSED TO HAVE A QUICK MEETING OR SOMETHING, RIGHT?
Music Room 3
CH
AK
SORRY I'M LATE...
HUH?

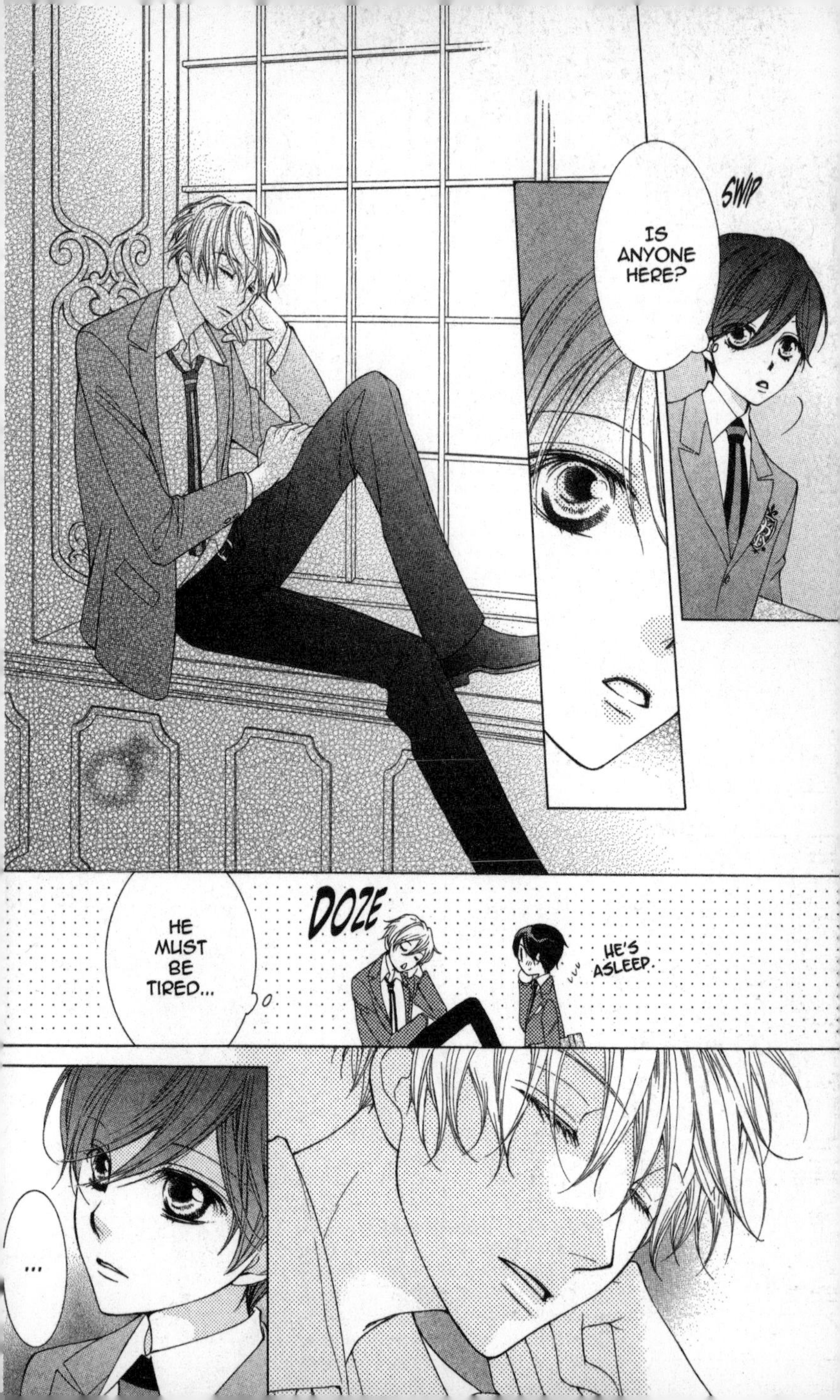
SWIP
IS ANYONE HERE?
HE'S ASLEEP.
DOZE
HE MUST BE TIRED...
...

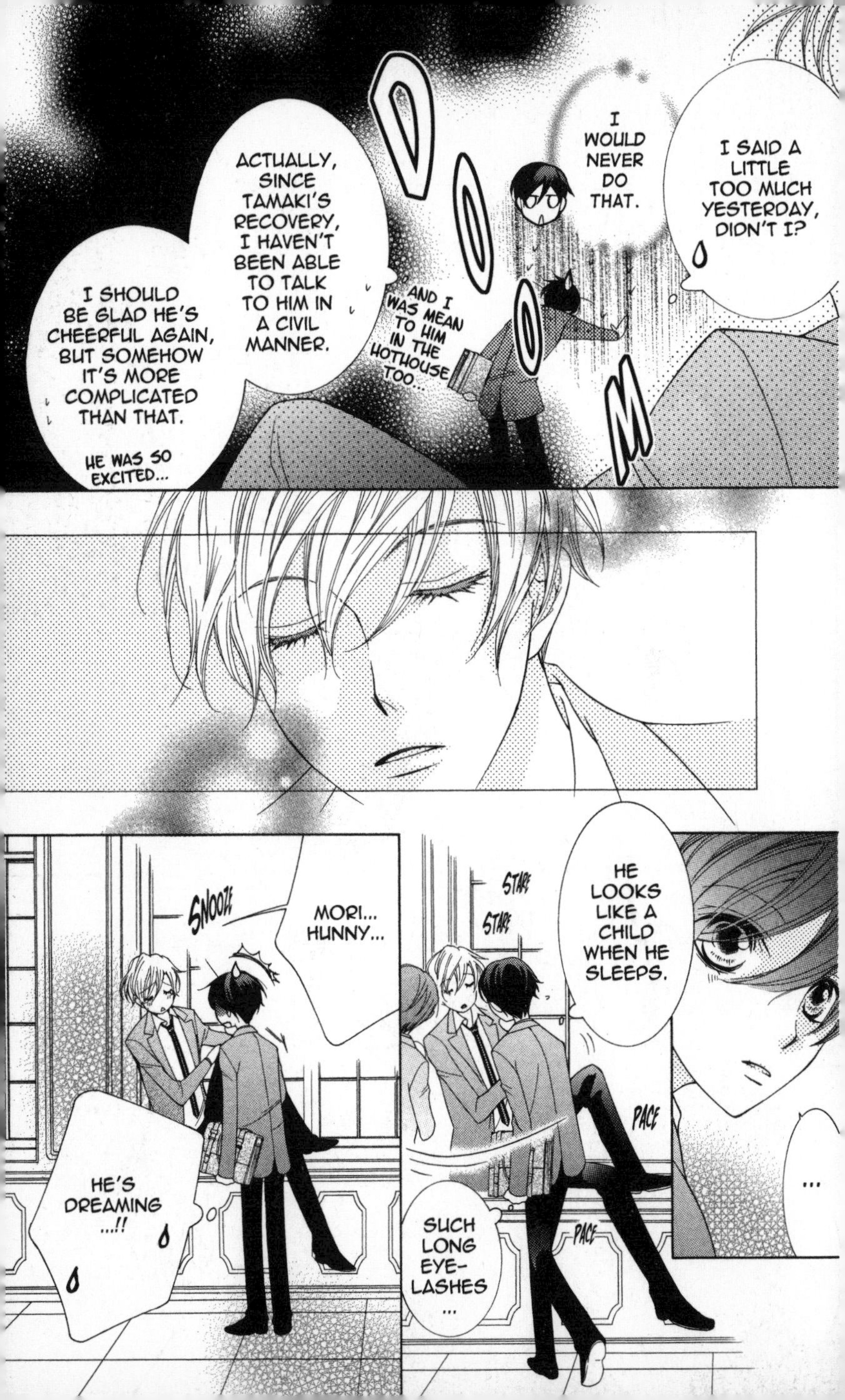
I SAID A LITTLE TOO MUCH YESTERDAY, DIDN'T I?
I WOULD NEVER DO THAT.
DOOOM
AND I WAS MEAN TO HIM IN THE HOTHOUSE TOO...
ACTUALLY, SINCE TAMAKI'S RECOVERY, I HAVEN'T BEEN ABLE TO TALK TO HIM IN A CIVIL MANNER.
I SHOULD BE GLAD HE'S CHEERFUL AGAIN, BUT SOMEHOW IT'S MORE COMPLICATED THAN THAT.
HE WAS SO EXCITED...
...
HE LOOKS LIKE A CHILD WHEN HE SLEEPS.
STARE
STARE
PACE
PACE
SUCH LONG EYE-LASHES...
SNOOZE
MORI... HUNNY...
HE'S DREAMING...!!

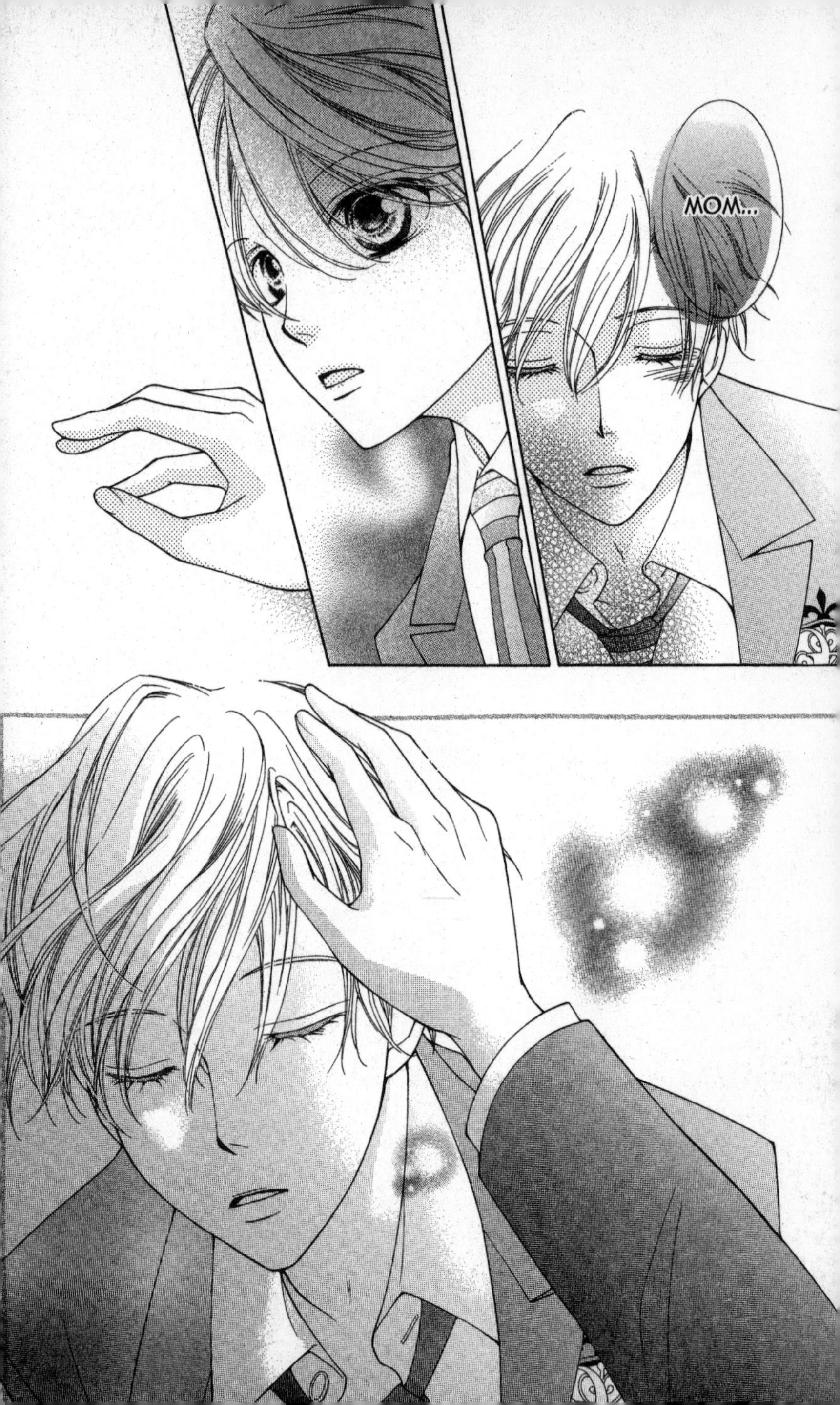
MOM...

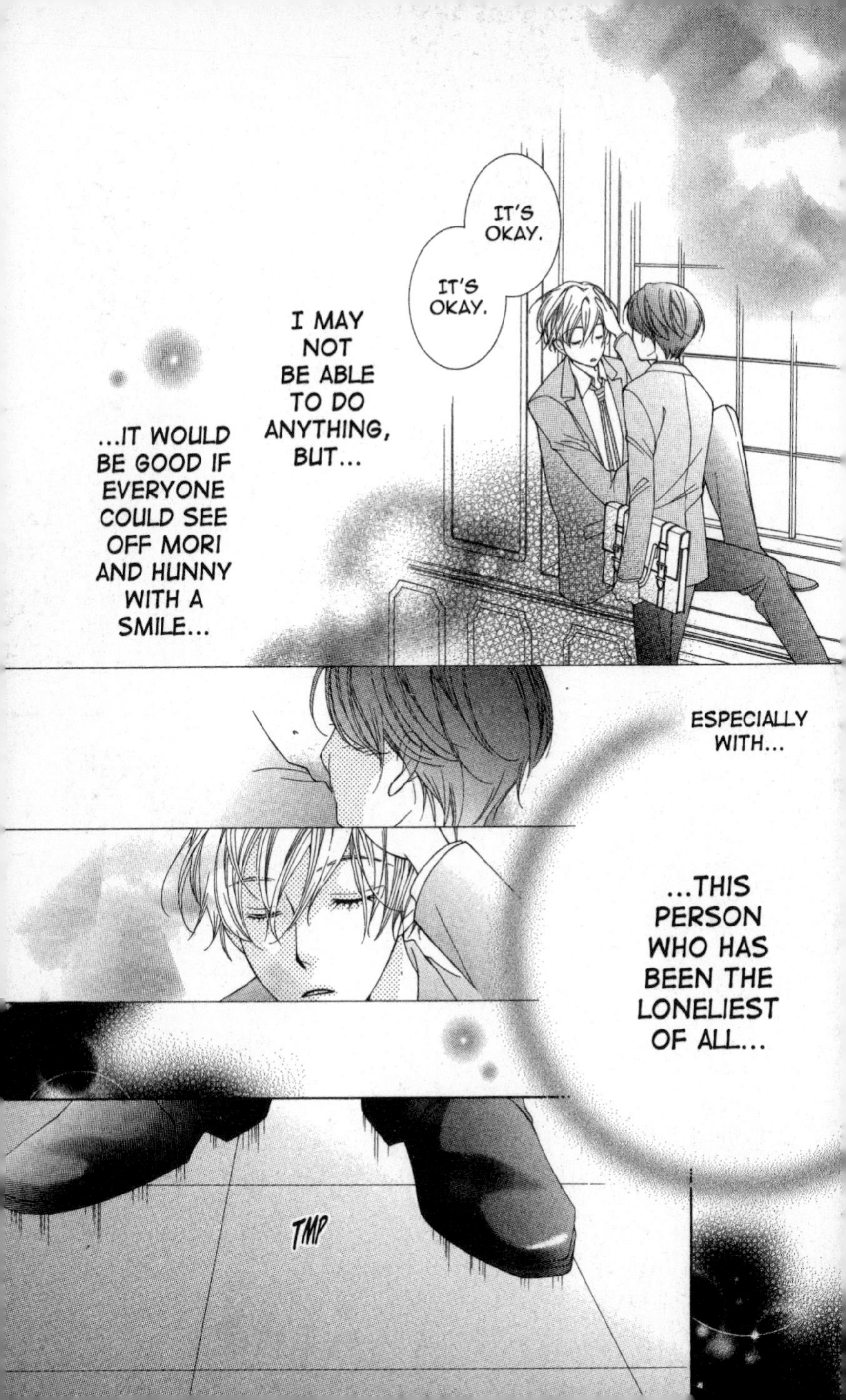
IT'S OKAY.
IT'S OKAY.
I MAY NOT BE ABLE TO DO ANYTHING, BUT...
...IT WOULD BE GOOD IF EVERYONE COULD SEE OFF MORI AND HUNNY WITH A SMILE...
ESPECIALLY WITH...
...THIS PERSON WHO HAS BEEN THE LONELIEST OF ALL...
TMP

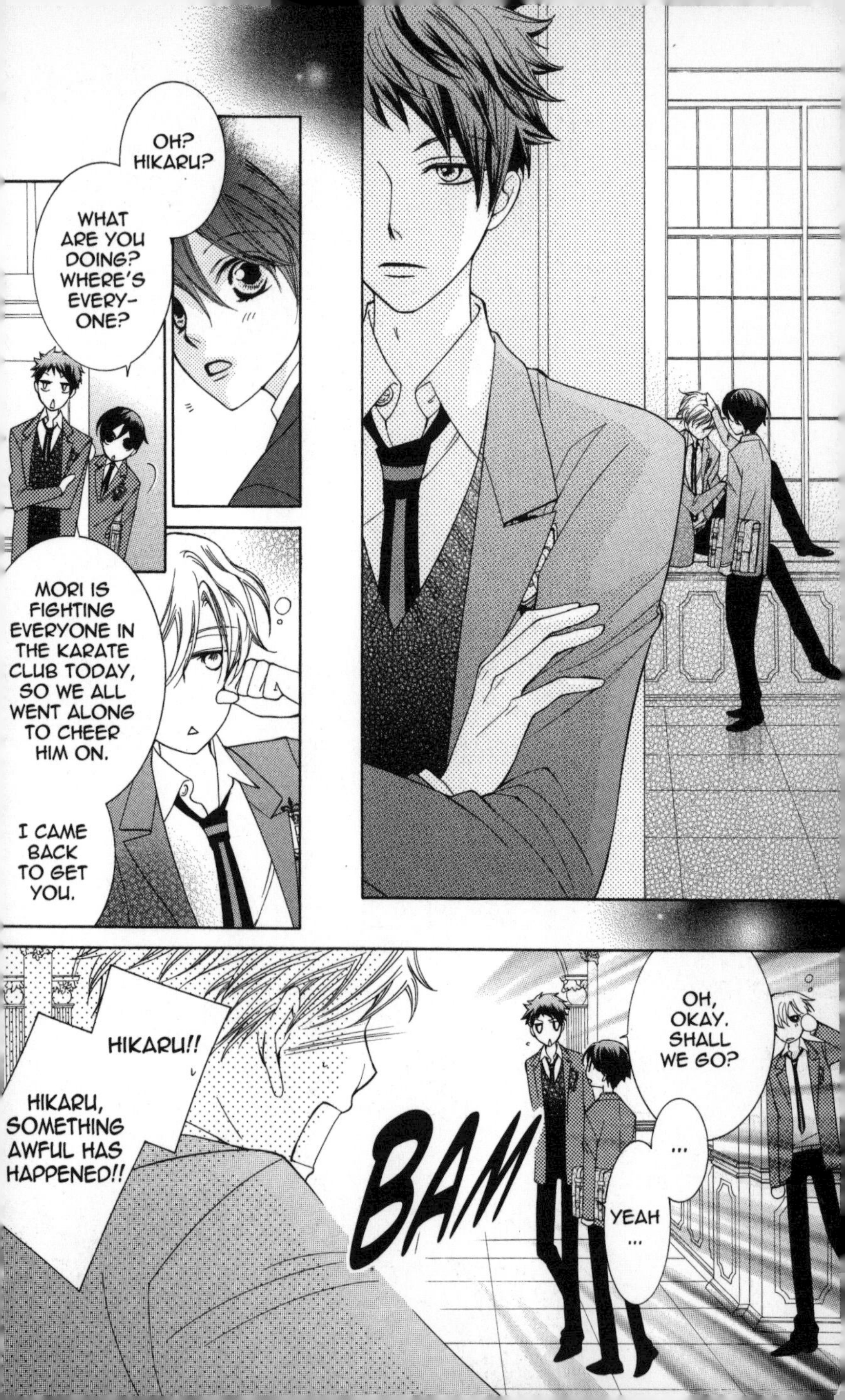
OH? HIKARU?
WHAT ARE YOU DOING? WHERE'S EVERYONE?
MORI IS FIGHTING EVERYONE IN THE KARATE CLUB TODAY, SO WE ALL WENT ALONG TO CHEER HIM ON.
I CAME BACK TO GET YOU.
OH, OKAY. SHALL WE GO?
...
YEAH ...
BAM
HIKARU!!
HIKARU, SOMETHING AWFUL HAS HAPPENED!!

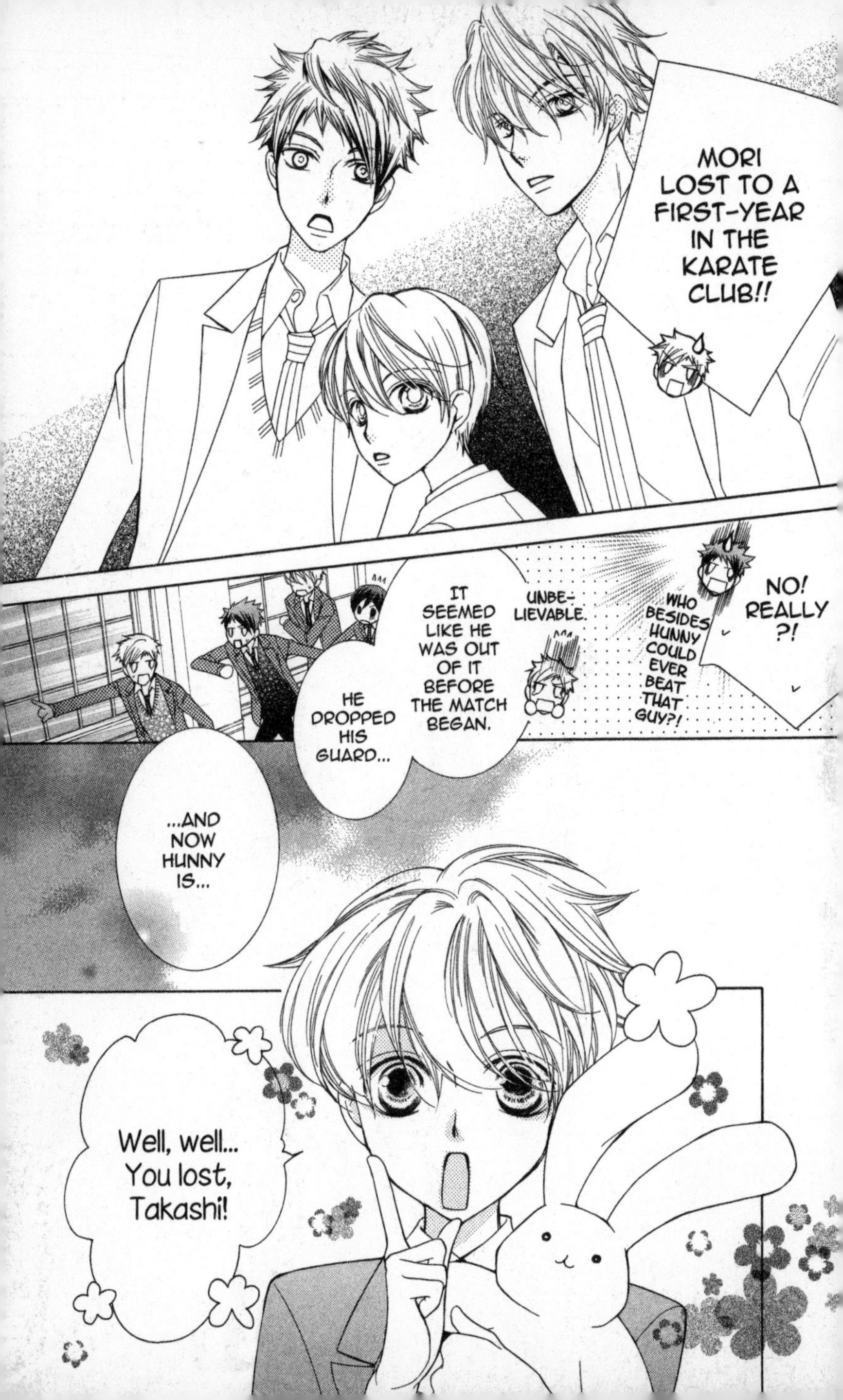
MORI LOST TO A FIRST-YEAR IN THE KARATE CLUB!!
NO! REALLY ?!
WHO BESIDES HUNNY COULD EVER BEAT THAT GUY?!
UNBE-LIEVABLE.
IT SEEMED LIKE HE WAS OUT OF IT BEFORE THE MATCH BEGAN.
HE DROPPED HIS GUARD...
...AND NOW HUNNY IS...
Well, well... You lost, Takashi!

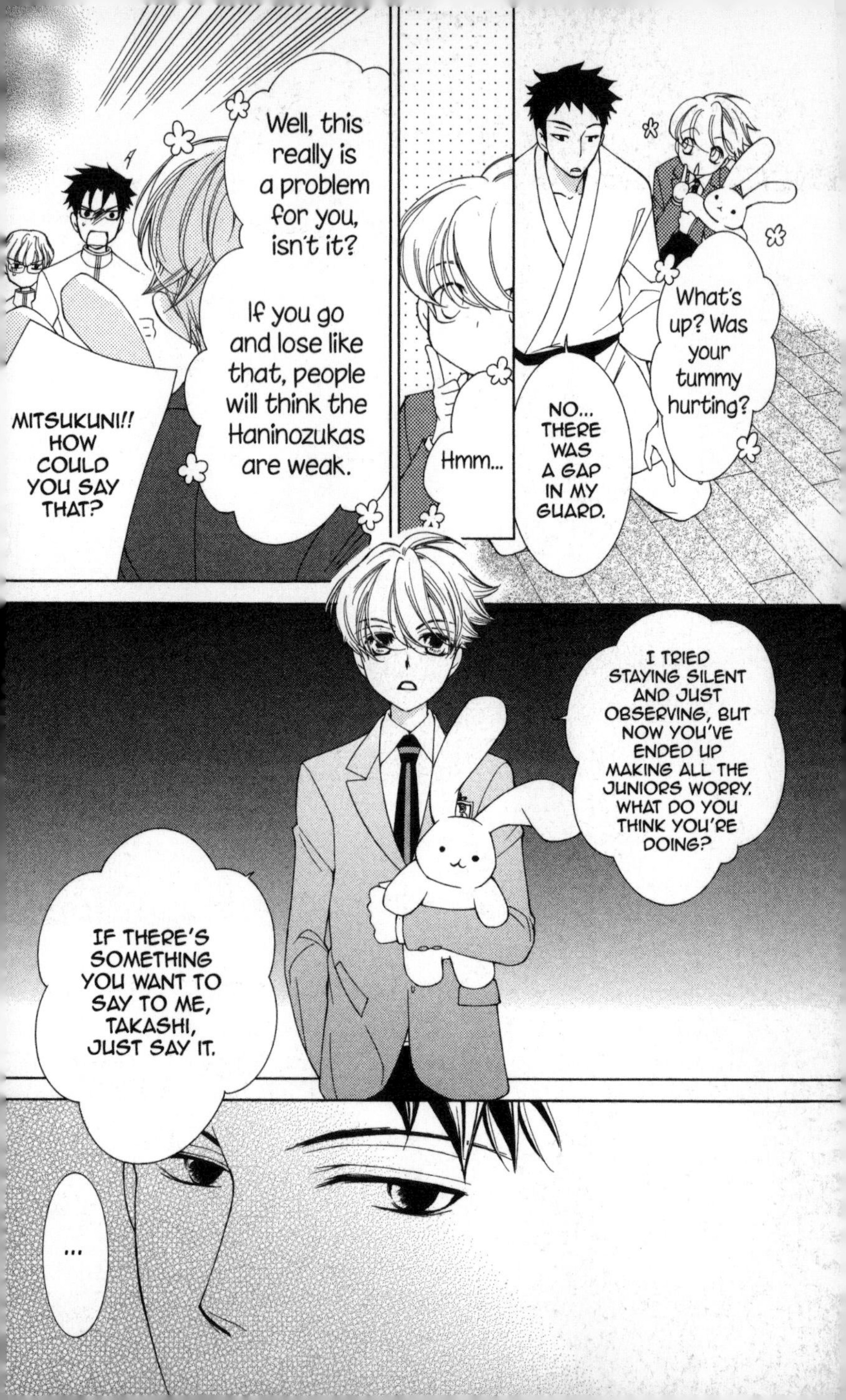

What's up? Was your tummy hurting?
NO... THERE WAS A GAP IN MY GUARD.
Hmm...
Well, this really is a problem for you, isn't it?
If you go and lose like that, people will think the Haninozukas are weak.
MITSUKUNI!! HOW COULD YOU SAY THAT?
I TRIED STAYING SILENT AND JUST OBSERVING, BUT NOW YOU'VE ENDED UP MAKING ALL THE JUNIORS WORRY. WHAT DO YOU THINK YOU'RE DOING?
IF THERE'S SOMETHING YOU WANT TO SAY TO ME, TAKASHI, JUST SAY IT.
...

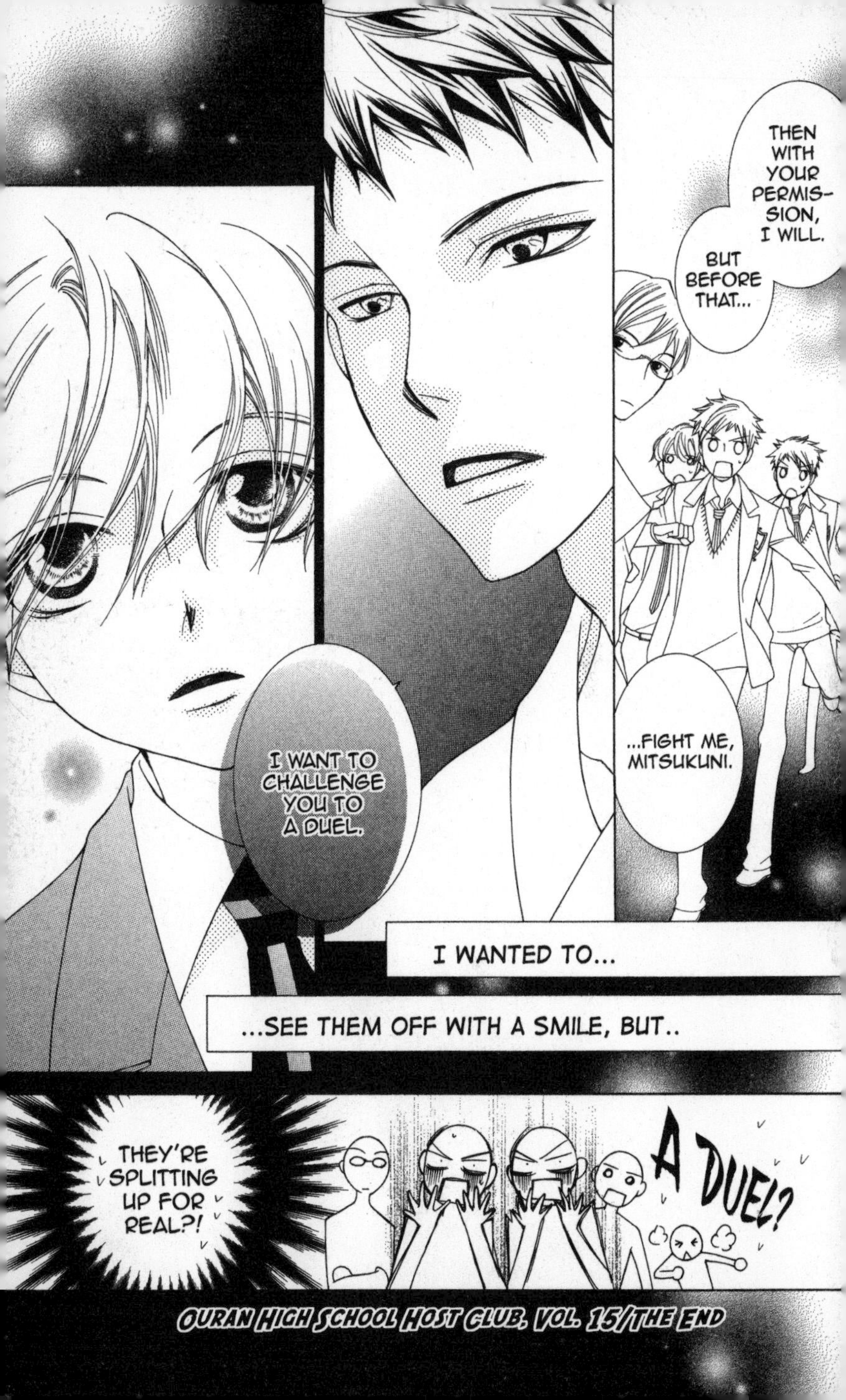
THEN WITH YOUR PERMISSION, I WILL.
BUT BEFORE THAT...
...FIGHT ME, MITSUKUNI.
I WANT TO CHALLENGE YOU TO A DUEL.
I WANTED TO...
...SEE THEM OFF WITH A SMILE, BUT..
A DUEL?
THEY'RE SPLITTING UP FOR REAL?!
OURAN HIGH SCHOOL HOST CLUB, VOL. 15/THE END

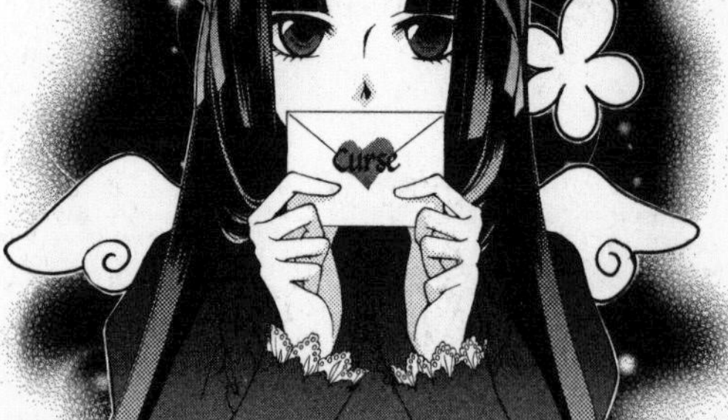
Curse

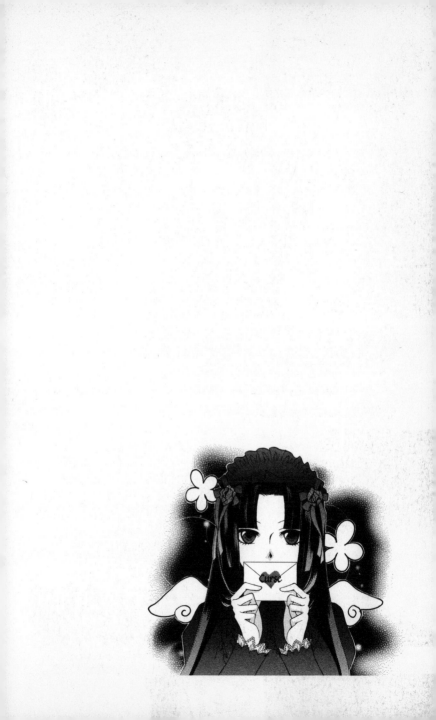

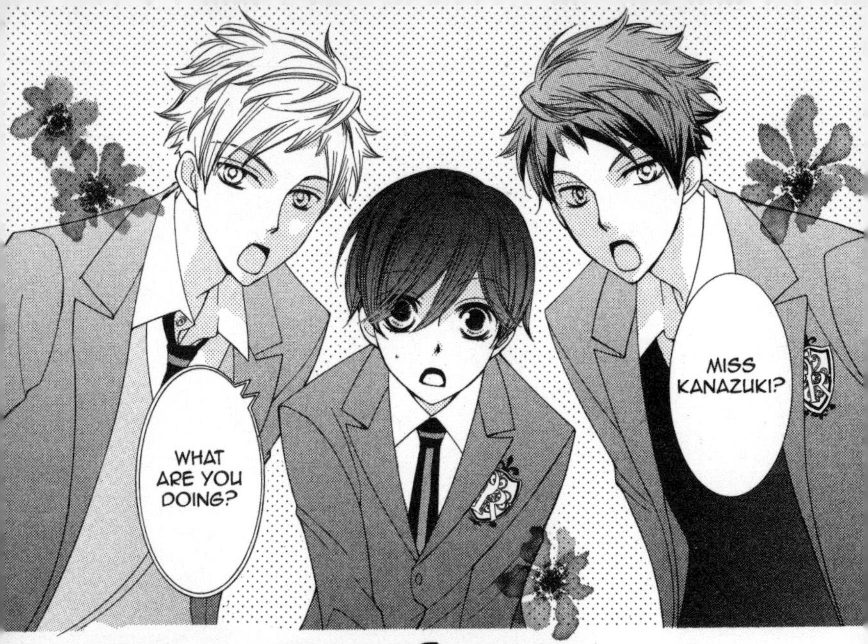
MISS KANAZUKI!?
WHAT ARE YOU DOING?

OURAN HIGH SCHOOL HOST CLUB

EXTRA EPISODE

OPERATION: KANAZUKI'S BIG DATE

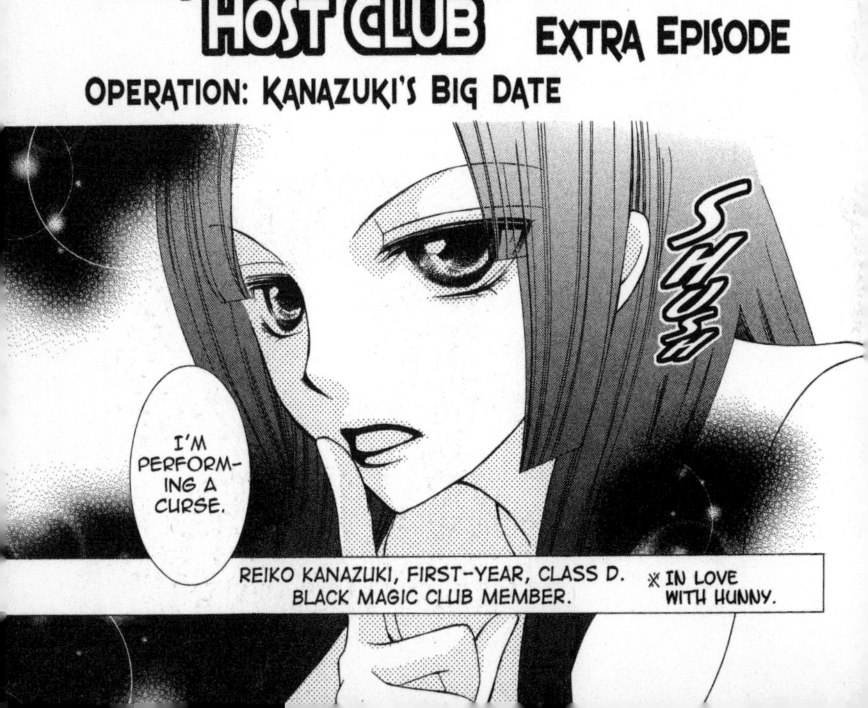
SHUSH
I'M PERFORMING A CURSE.
REIKO KANAZUKI, FIRST-YEAR, CLASS D. BLACK MAGIC CLUB MEMBER.
※IN LOVE WITH HUNNY.

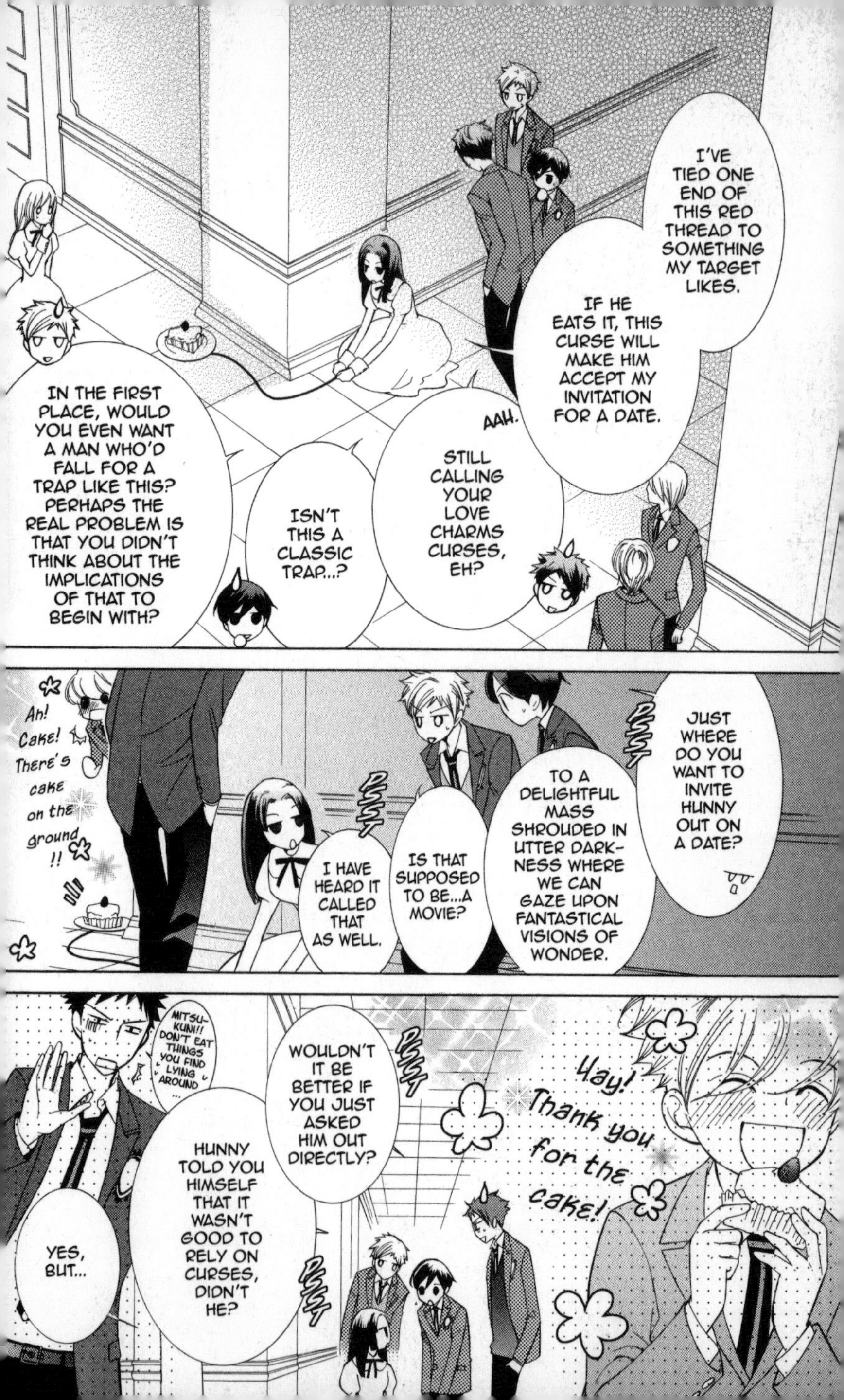
I'VE TIED ONE END OF THIS RED THREAD TO SOMETHING MY TARGET LIKES.
IF HE EATS IT, THIS CURSE WILL MAKE HIM ACCEPT MY INVITATION FOR A DATE.
AAH.
STILL CALLING YOUR LOVE CHARMS CURSES, EH?
ISN'T THIS A CLASSIC TRAP...?
IN THE FIRST PLACE, WOULD YOU EVEN WANT A MAN WHO'D FALL FOR A TRAP LIKE THIS? PERHAPS THE REAL PROBLEM IS THAT YOU DIDN'T THINK ABOUT THE IMPLICATIONS OF THAT TO BEGIN WITH?
JUST WHERE DO YOU WANT TO INVITE HUNNY OUT ON A DATE?
TO A DELIGHTFUL MASS SHROUDED IN UTTER DARKNESS WHERE WE CAN GAZE UPON FANTASTICAL VISIONS OF WONDER.
IS THAT SUPPOSED TO BE...A MOVIE?
I HAVE HEARD IT CALLED THAT AS WELL.
Ah! Cake! There's cake on the ground!!
Yay! Thank you for the cake!
WOULDN'T IT BE BETTER IF YOU JUST ASKED HIM OUT DIRECTLY?
HUNNY TOLD YOU HIMSELF THAT IT WASN'T GOOD TO RELY ON CURSES, DIDN'T HE?
MITSUKUNI!! DON'T EAT THINGS YOU FIND LYING AROUND...
YES, BUT...

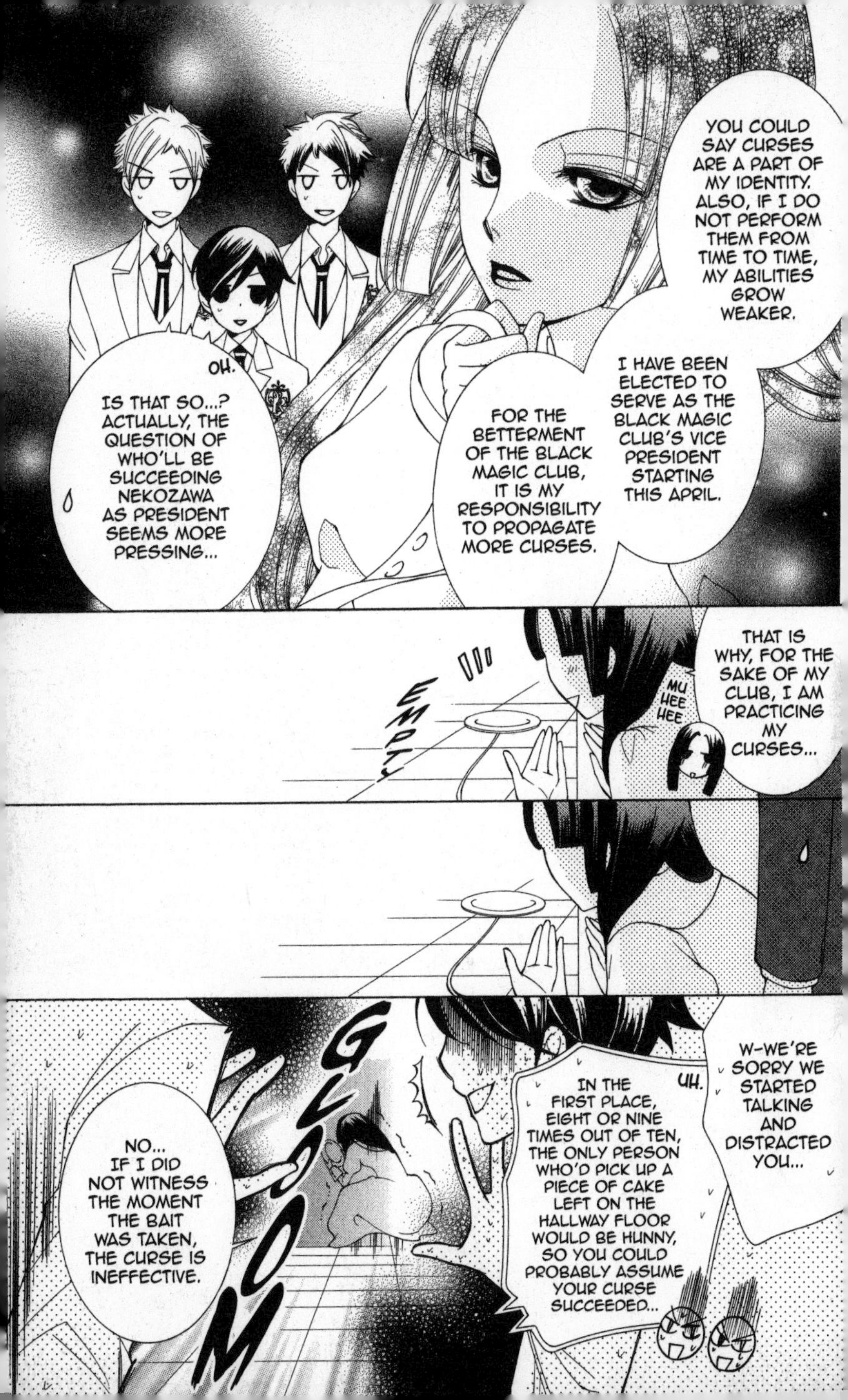
YOU COULD SAY CURSES ARE A PART OF MY IDENTITY. ALSO, IF I DO NOT PERFORM THEM FROM TIME TO TIME, MY ABILITIES GROW WEAKER.
I HAVE BEEN ELECTED TO SERVE AS THE BLACK MAGIC CLUB'S VICE PRESIDENT STARTING THIS APRIL.
FOR THE BETTERMENT OF THE BLACK MAGIC CLUB, IT IS MY RESPONSIBILITY TO PROPAGATE MORE CURSES.
OH.
IS THAT SO...? ACTUALLY, THE QUESTION OF WHO'LL BE SUCCEEDING NEKOZAWA AS PRESIDENT SEEMS MORE PRESSING...
THAT IS WHY, FOR THE SAKE OF MY CLUB, I AM PRACTICING MY CURSES...
MU HEE HEE
EMPTY
W-WE'RE SORRY WE STARTED TALKING AND DISTRACTED YOU...
UH.
IN THE FIRST PLACE, EIGHT OR NINE TIMES OUT OF TEN, THE ONLY PERSON WHO'D PICK UP A PIECE OF CAKE LEFT ON THE HALLWAY FLOOR WOULD BE HUNNY, SO YOU COULD PROBABLY ASSUME YOUR CURSE SUCCEEDED...
GLOOM
NO... IF I DID NOT WITNESS THE MOMENT THE BAIT WAS TAKEN, THE CURSE IS INEFFECTIVE.

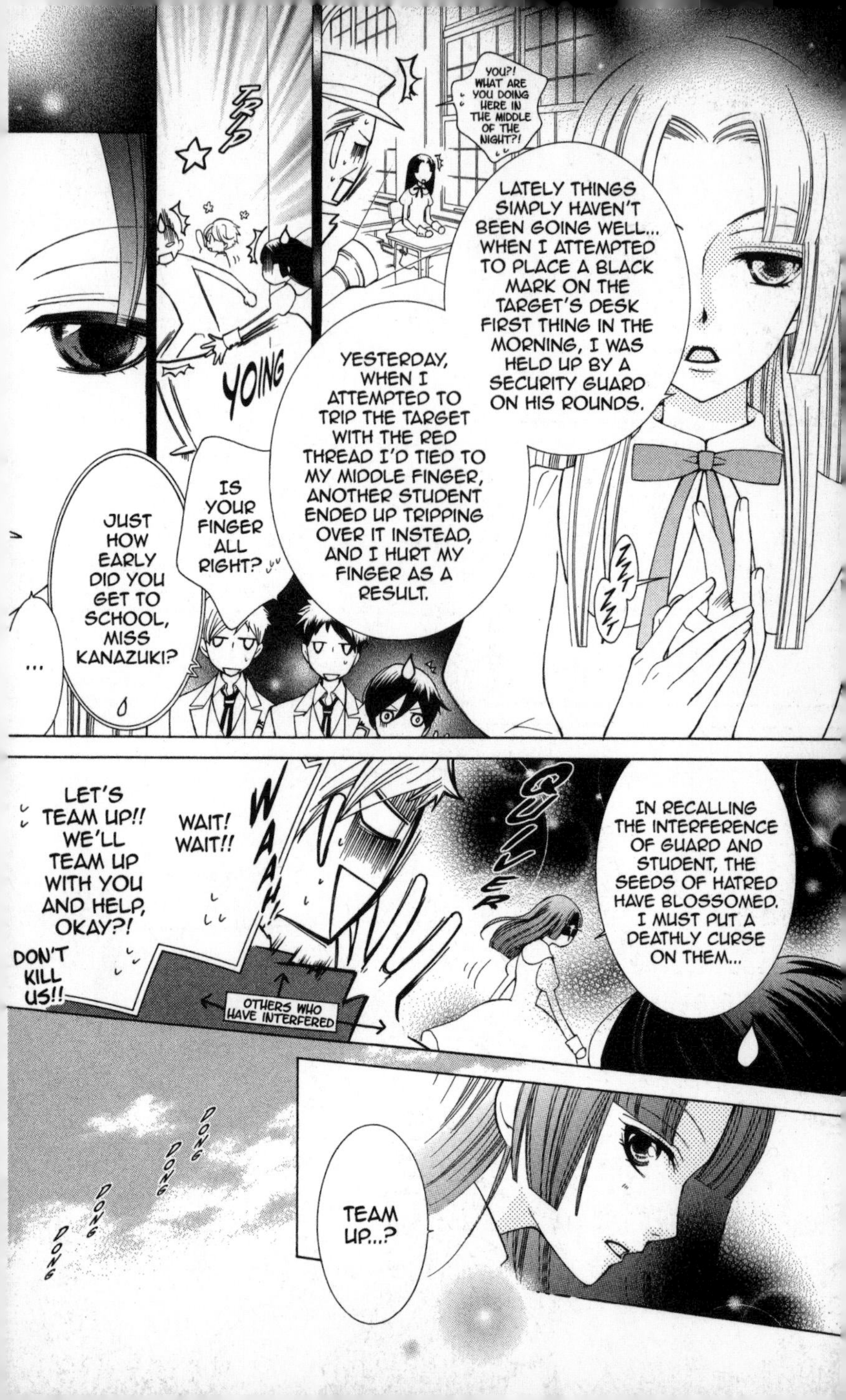
LATELY THINGS SIMPLY HAVEN'T BEEN GOING WELL... WHEN I ATTEMPTED TO PLACE A BLACK MARK ON THE TARGET'S DESK FIRST THING IN THE MORNING, I WAS HELD UP BY A SECURITY GUARD ON HIS ROUNDS.
YOU?! WHAT ARE YOU DOING HERE IN THE MIDDLE OF THE NIGHT?!
YESTERDAY, WHEN I ATTEMPTED TO TRIP THE TARGET WITH THE RED THREAD I'D TIED TO MY MIDDLE FINGER, ANOTHER STUDENT ENDED UP TRIPPING OVER IT INSTEAD, AND I HURT MY FINGER AS A RESULT.
TRIP
YOING
IS YOUR FINGER ALL RIGHT?
JUST HOW EARLY DID YOU GET TO SCHOOL, MISS KANAZUKI?
...
QUIVER
IN RECALLING THE INTERFERENCE OF GUARD AND STUDENT, THE SEEDS OF HATRED HAVE BLOSSOMED. I MUST PUT A DEATHLY CURSE ON THEM...
WAAAH
WAIT! WAIT!!
LET'S TEAM UP!! WE'LL TEAM UP WITH YOU AND HELP, OKAY?!
DON'T KILL US!!
OTHERS WHO HAVE INTERFERED
TEAM UP...?
DONG DONG DONG DONG

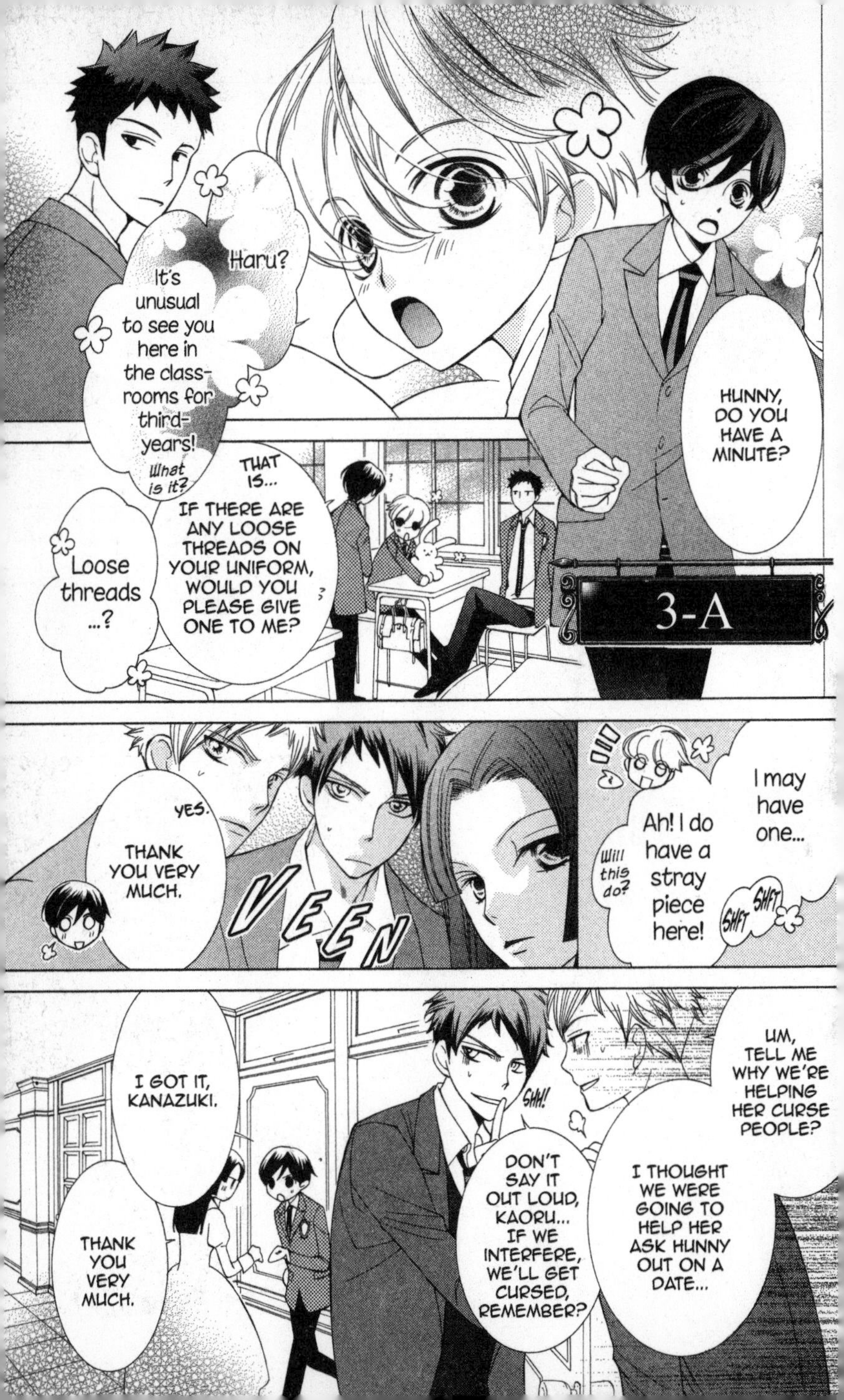
HUNNY, DO YOU HAVE A MINUTE?
Haru?
It's unusual to see you here in the class-rooms for third-years!
What is it?
THAT IS... IF THERE ARE ANY LOOSE THREADS ON YOUR UNIFORM, WOULD YOU PLEASE GIVE ONE TO ME?
Loose threads ...?
3-A
I may have one...
SHFT SHFT
Ah! I do have a stray piece here!
Will this do?
VEEN
YES.
THANK YOU VERY MUCH.
UM, TELL ME WHY WE'RE HELPING HER CURSE PEOPLE?
I THOUGHT WE WERE GOING TO HELP HER ASK HUNNY OUT ON A DATE...
SHH!
DON'T SAY IT OUT LOUD, KAORU... IF WE INTERFERE, WE'LL GET CURSED, REMEMBER?
I GOT IT, KANAZUKI.
THANK YOU VERY MUCH.

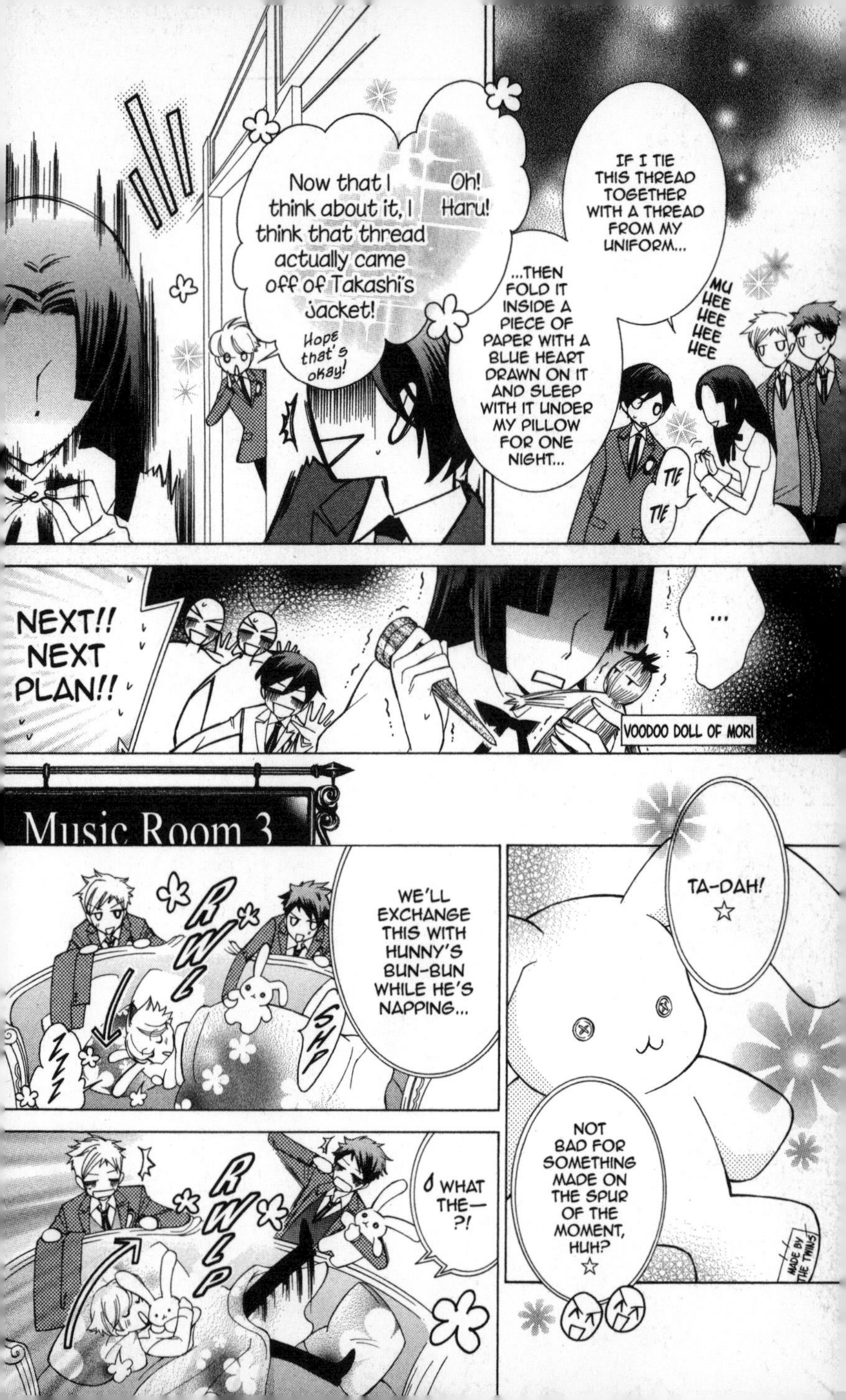

IF I TIE THIS THREAD TOGETHER WITH A THREAD FROM MY UNIFORM...
...THEN FOLD IT INSIDE A PIECE OF PAPER WITH A BLUE HEART DRAWN ON IT AND SLEEP WITH IT UNDER MY PILLOW FOR ONE NIGHT...
MU HEE HEE HEE HEE
TIE TIE
Oh! Haru!
Now that I think about it, I think that thread actually came off of Takashi's jacket!
Hope that's okay!
...
VOODOO DOLL OF MORI
NEXT!! NEXT PLAN!!
Music Room 3
TA-DAH! ☆
NOT BAD FOR SOMETHING MADE ON THE SPUR OF THE MOMENT, HUH? ☆
MADE BY THE TWINS
WE'LL EXCHANGE THIS WITH HUNNY'S BUN-BUN WHILE HE'S NAPPING...
SHP
RWIP
ZZZ
WHAT THE—?!
RWIP

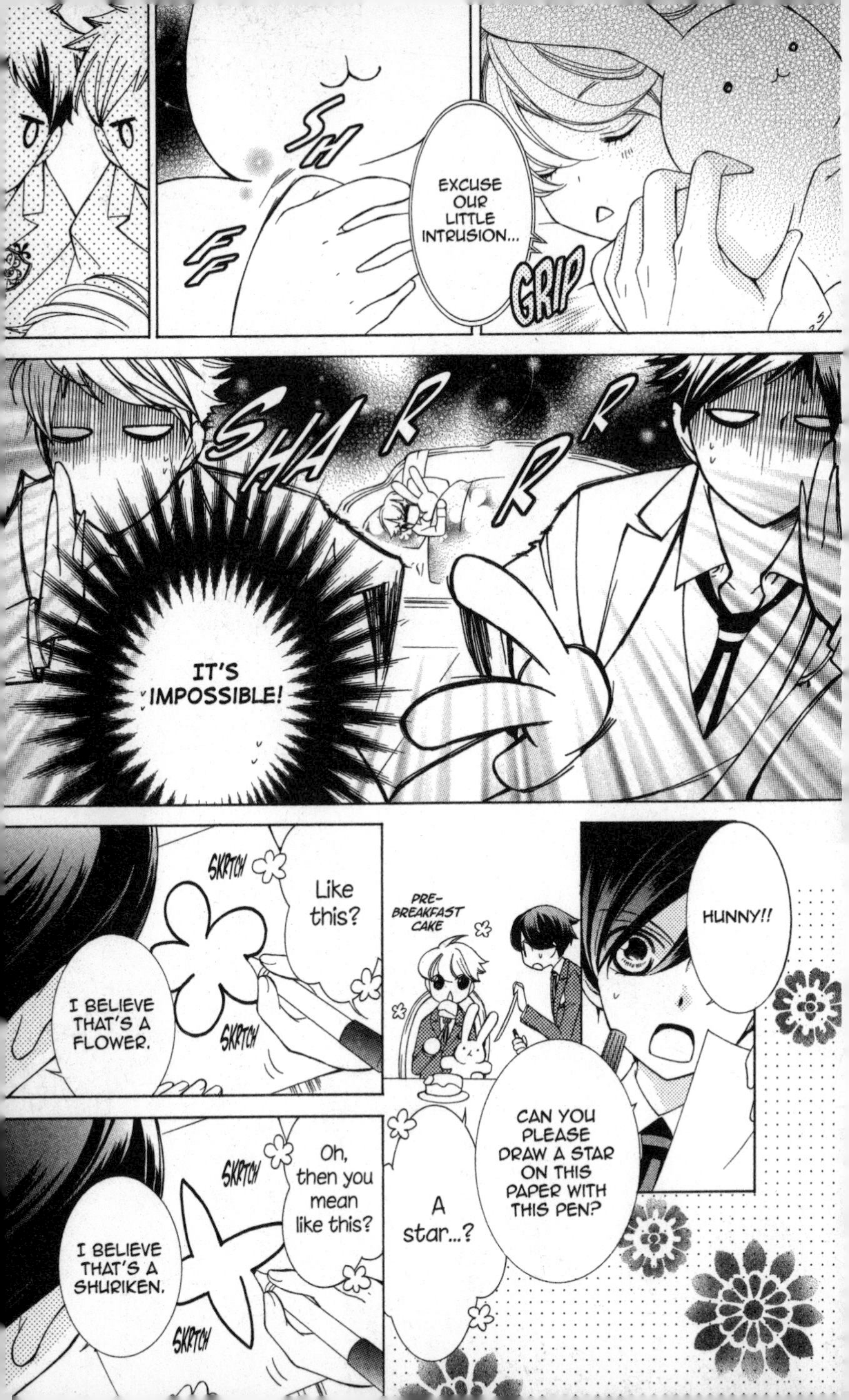
EXCUSE OUR LITTLE INTRUSION...
GRIP
SHFF
SHARRRR
IT'S IMPOSSIBLE!
HUNNY!!
PRE-BREAKFAST CAKE
CAN YOU PLEASE DRAW A STAR ON THIS PAPER WITH THIS PEN?
A star...?
Like this?
SKRTCH
SKRTCH
I BELIEVE THAT'S A FLOWER.
Oh, then you mean like this?
SKRTCH
SKRTCH
I BELIEVE THAT'S A SHURIKEN.

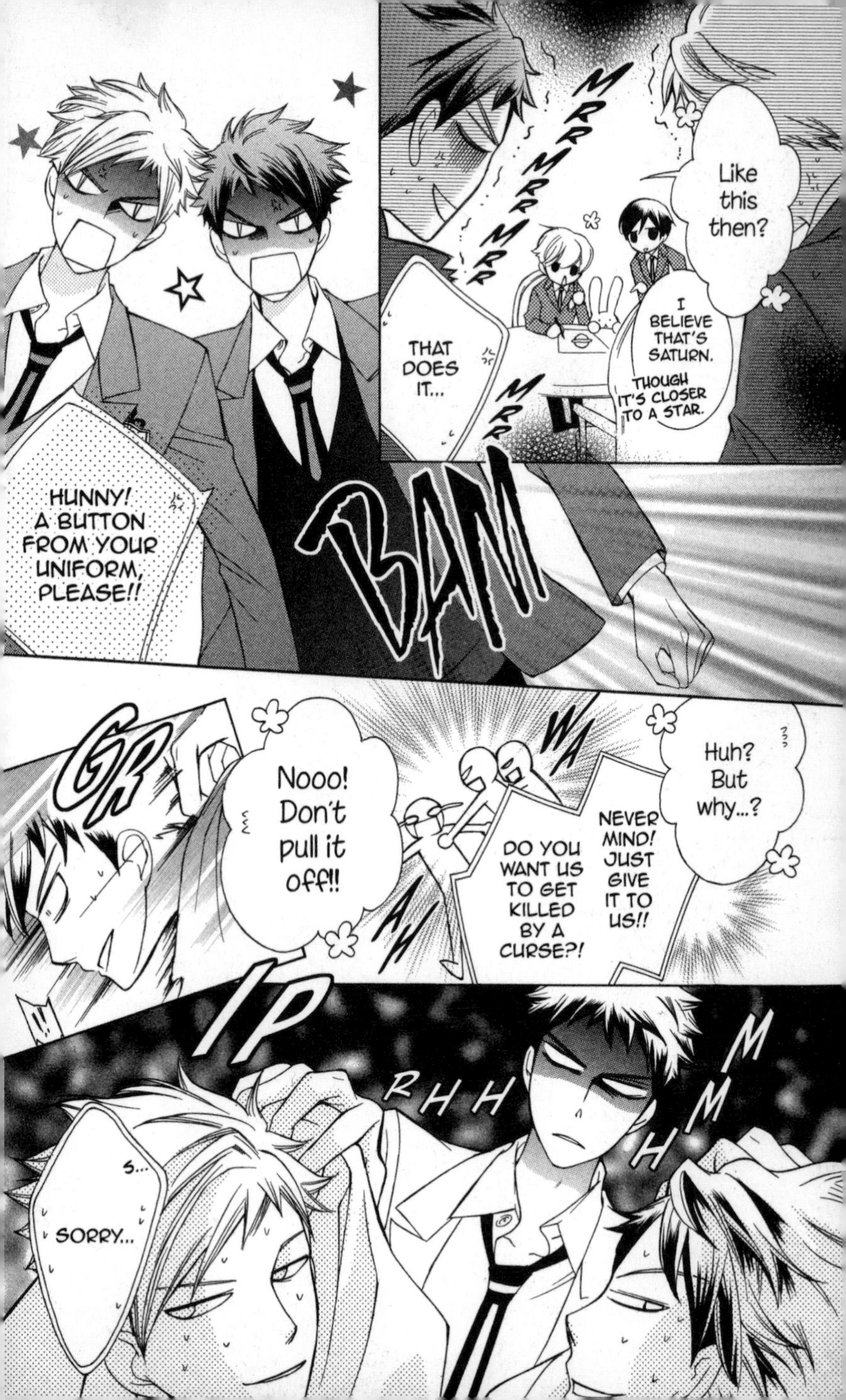
Like this then?
I BELIEVE THAT'S SATURN.
THOUGH IT'S CLOSER TO A STAR.
MRRMRRMRRMRR
THAT DOES IT...
MRR
HUNNY! A BUTTON FROM YOUR UNIFORM, PLEASE!!
BAM
Huh? But why...?
NEVER MIND! JUST GIVE IT TO US!!
DO YOU WANT US TO GET KILLED BY A CURSE?!
WA
AH
Nooo! Don't pull it off!!
GR
MMMH
RHH
IP
S... SORRY...

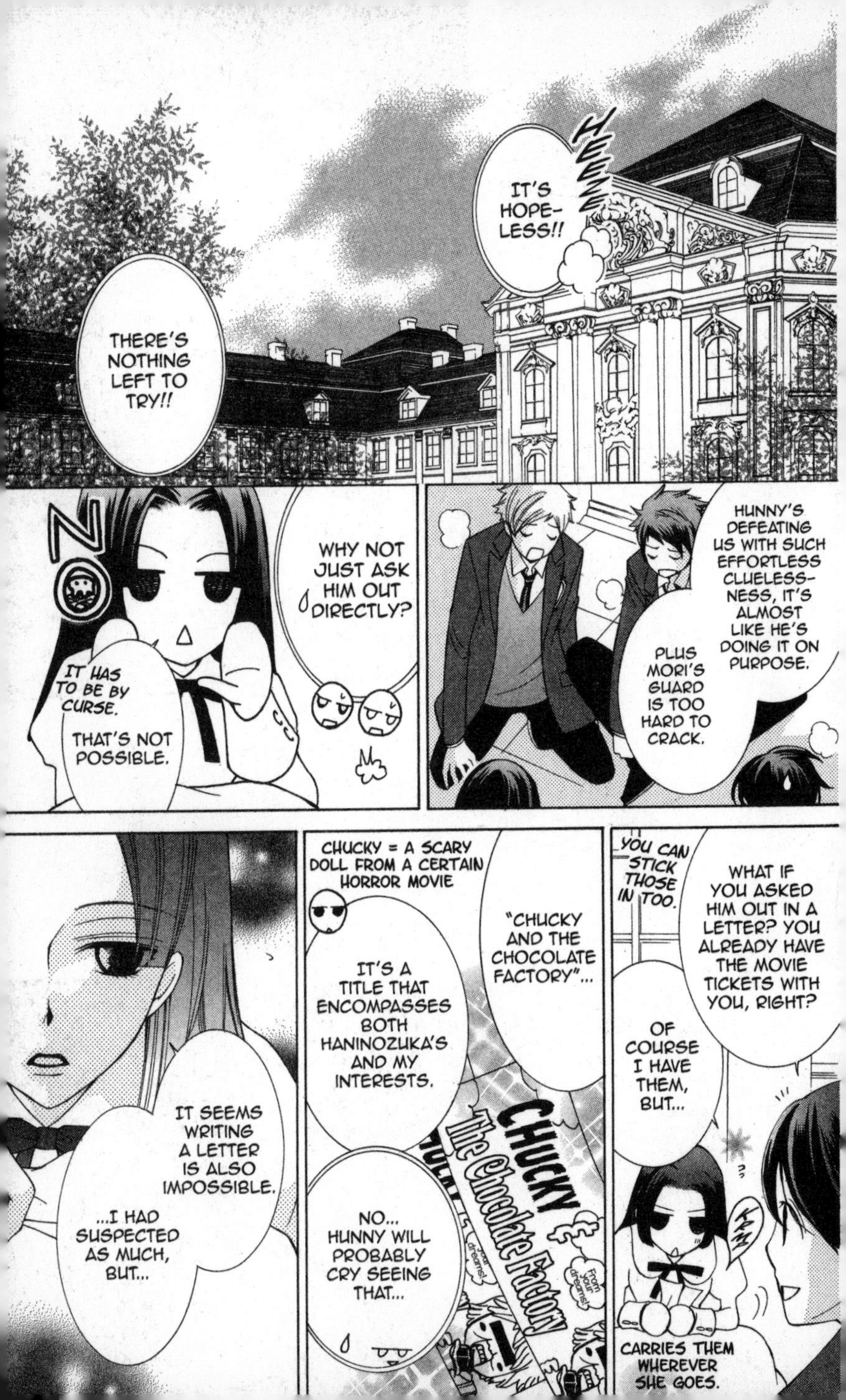
IT'S HOPE-LESS!!
THERE'S NOTHING LEFT TO TRY!!
HUNNY'S DEFEATING US WITH SUCH EFFORTLESS CLUELESS-NESS, IT'S ALMOST LIKE HE'S DOING IT ON PURPOSE.
PLUS MORI'S GUARD IS TOO HARD TO CRACK.
WHY NOT JUST ASK HIM OUT DIRECTLY?
NO
IT HAS TO BE BY CURSE.
THAT'S NOT POSSIBLE.
YOU CAN STICK THOSE IN TOO.
WHAT IF YOU ASKED HIM OUT IN A LETTER? YOU ALREADY HAVE THE MOVIE TICKETS WITH YOU, RIGHT?
OF COURSE I HAVE THEM, BUT...
CARRIES THEM WHEREVER SHE GOES.
"CHUCKY AND THE CHOCOLATE FACTORY"...
CHUCKY = A SCARY DOLL FROM A CERTAIN HORROR MOVIE
IT'S A TITLE THAT ENCOMPASSES BOTH HANINOZUKA'S AND MY INTERESTS.
NO... HUNNY WILL PROBABLY CRY SEEING THAT...
CHUCKY The Chocolate Factory
From your dreams!
IT SEEMS WRITING A LETTER IS ALSO IMPOSSIBLE.
...I HAD SUSPECTED AS MUCH, BUT...

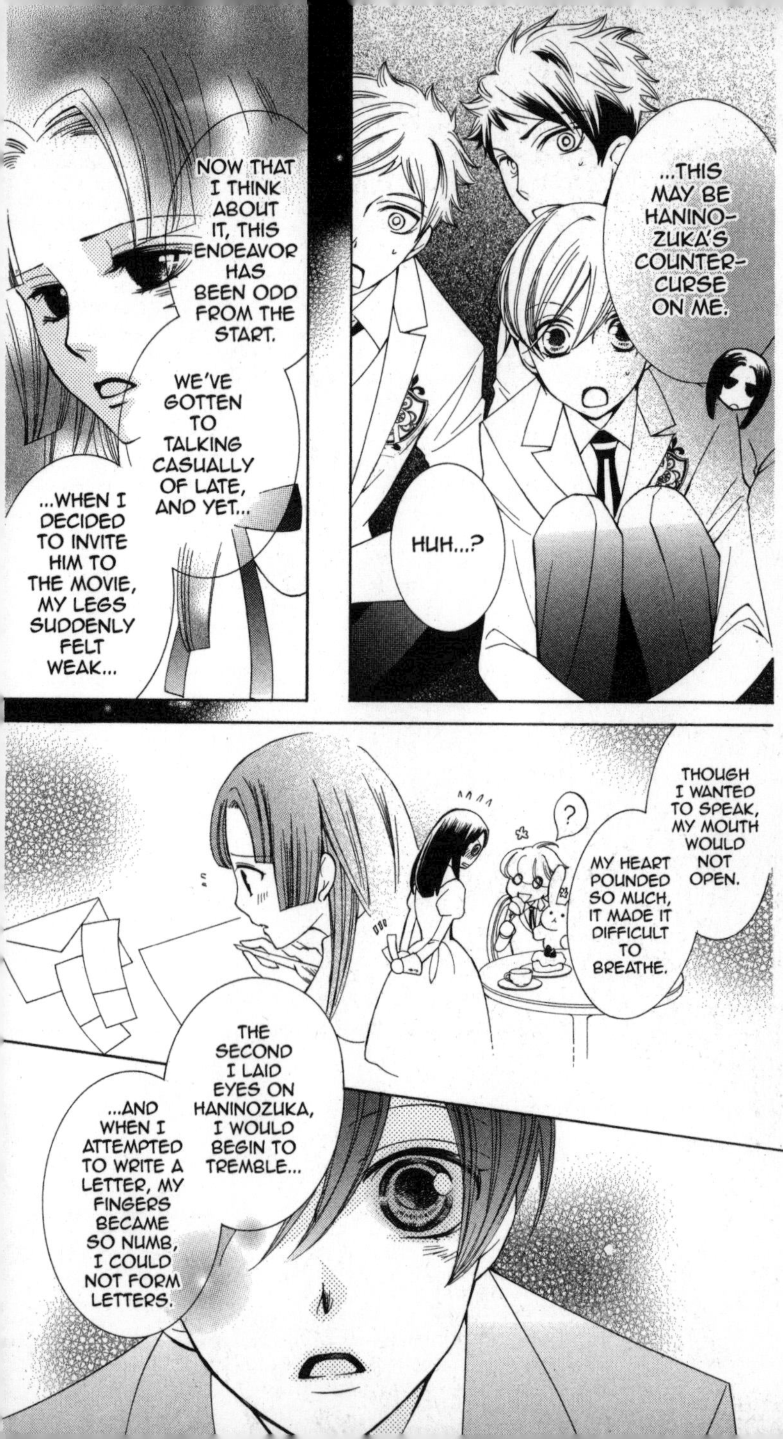
...THIS MAY BE HANINOZUKA'S COUNTER-CURSE ON ME.
HUH...?
NOW THAT I THINK ABOUT IT, THIS ENDEAVOR HAS BEEN ODD FROM THE START.
WE'VE GOTTEN TO TALKING CASUALLY OF LATE, AND YET...
...WHEN I DECIDED TO INVITE HIM TO THE MOVIE, MY LEGS SUDDENLY FELT WEAK...
THOUGH I WANTED TO SPEAK, MY MOUTH WOULD NOT OPEN.
MY HEART POUNDED SO MUCH, IT MADE IT DIFFICULT TO BREATHE.
?
THE SECOND I LAID EYES ON HANINOZUKA, I WOULD BEGIN TO TREMBLE...
...AND WHEN I ATTEMPTED TO WRITE A LETTER, MY FINGERS BECAME SO NUMB, I COULD NOT FORM LETTERS.

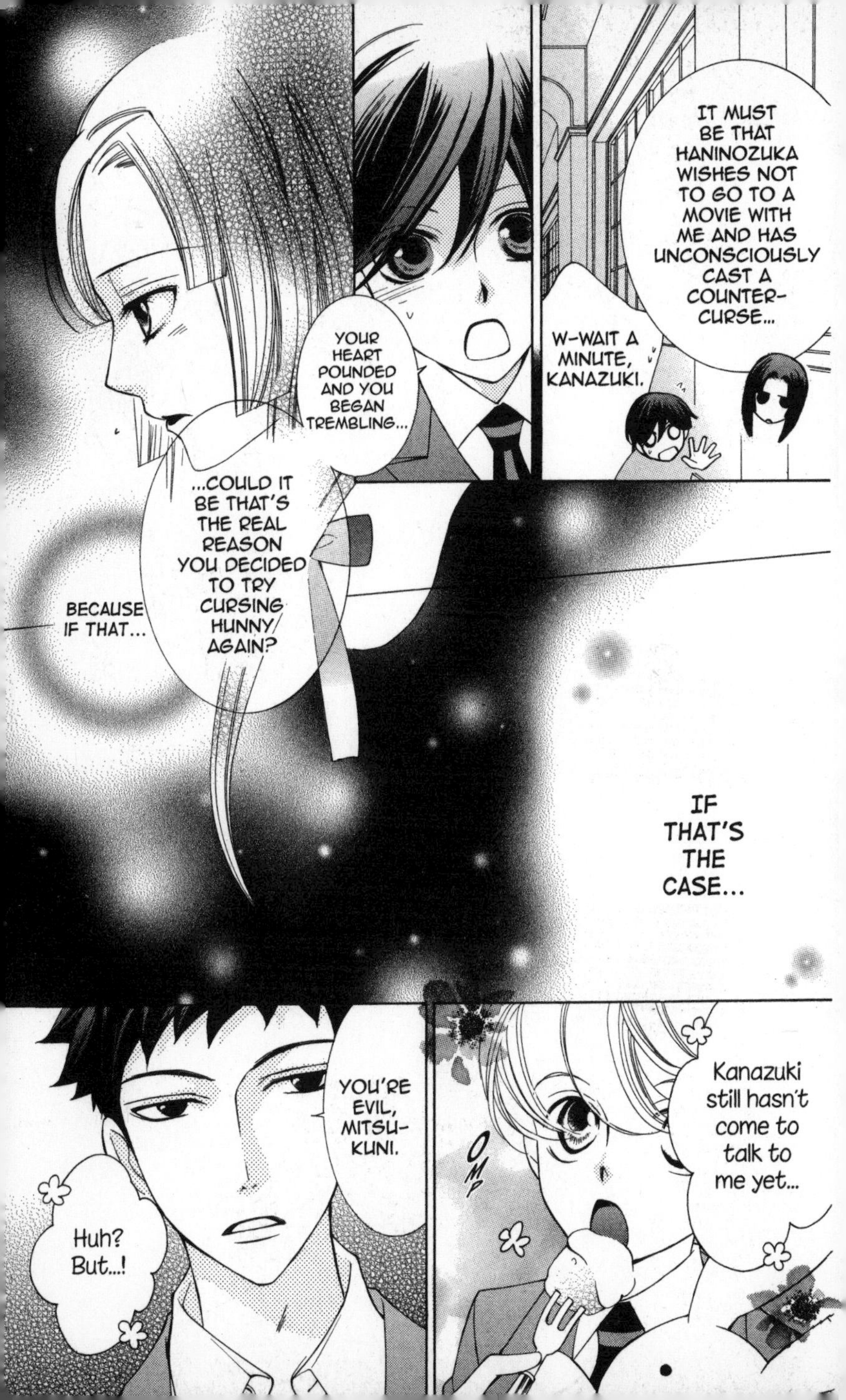
IT MUST BE THAT HANINOZUKA WISHES NOT TO GO TO A MOVIE WITH ME AND HAS UNCONSCIOUSLY CAST A COUNTER-CURSE...
W-WAIT A MINUTE, KANAZUKI.
YOUR HEART POUNDED AND YOU BEGAN TREMBLING...
...COULD IT BE THAT'S THE REAL REASON YOU DECIDED TO TRY CURSING HUNNY AGAIN?
BECAUSE IF THAT...
IF THAT'S THE CASE...
Kanazuki still hasn't come to talk to me yet...
OMP
YOU'RE EVIL, MITSU-KUNI.
Huh? But...!

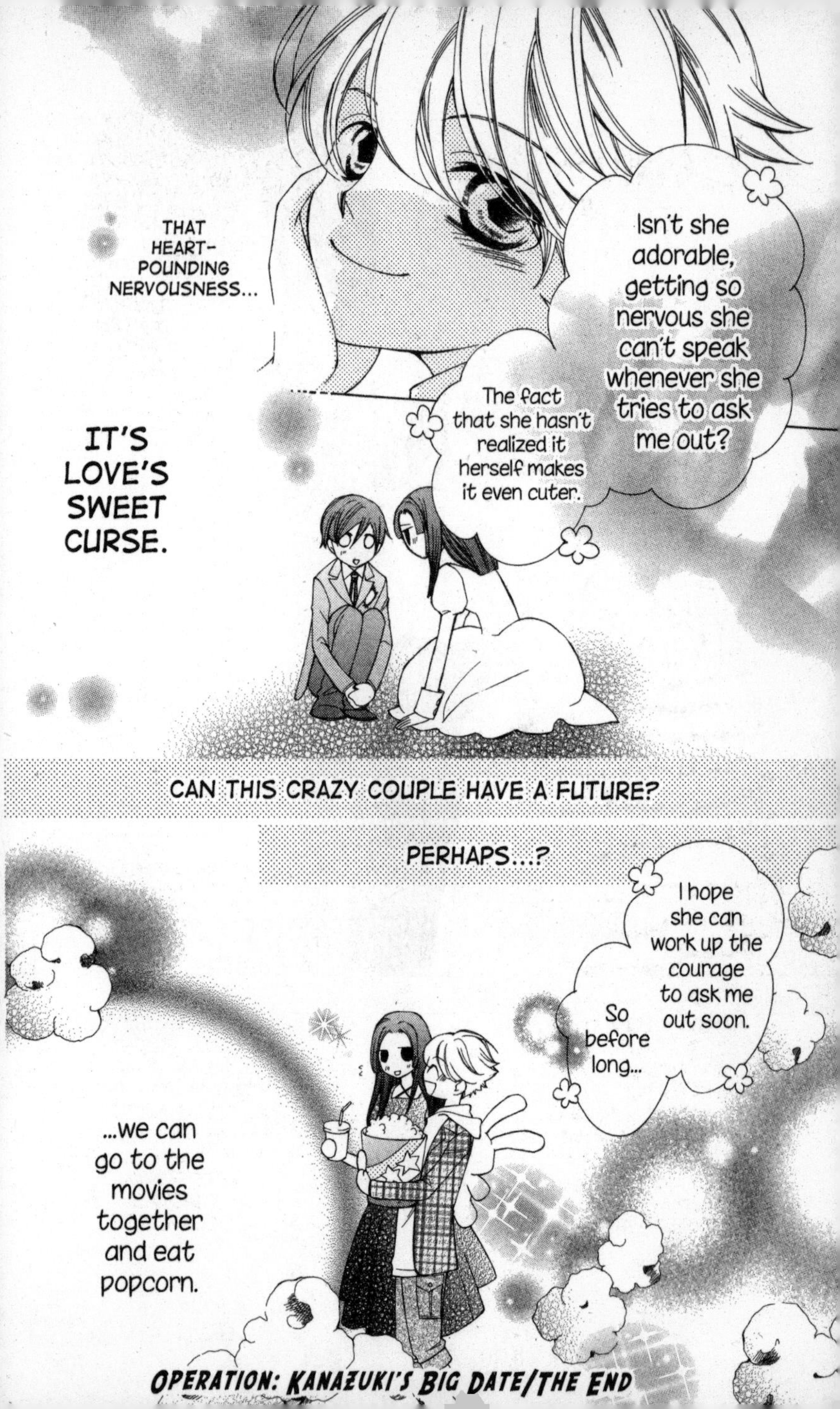
Isn't she adorable, getting so nervous she can't speak whenever she tries to ask me out?
THAT HEART-POUNDING NERVOUSNESS...
The fact that she hasn't realized it herself makes it even cuter.
IT'S LOVE'S SWEET CURSE.
CAN THIS CRAZY COUPLE HAVE A FUTURE?
PERHAPS...?
I hope she can work up the courage to ask me out soon.
So before long...
...we can go to the movies together and eat popcorn.
OPERATION: KANAZUKI'S BIG DATE/THE END

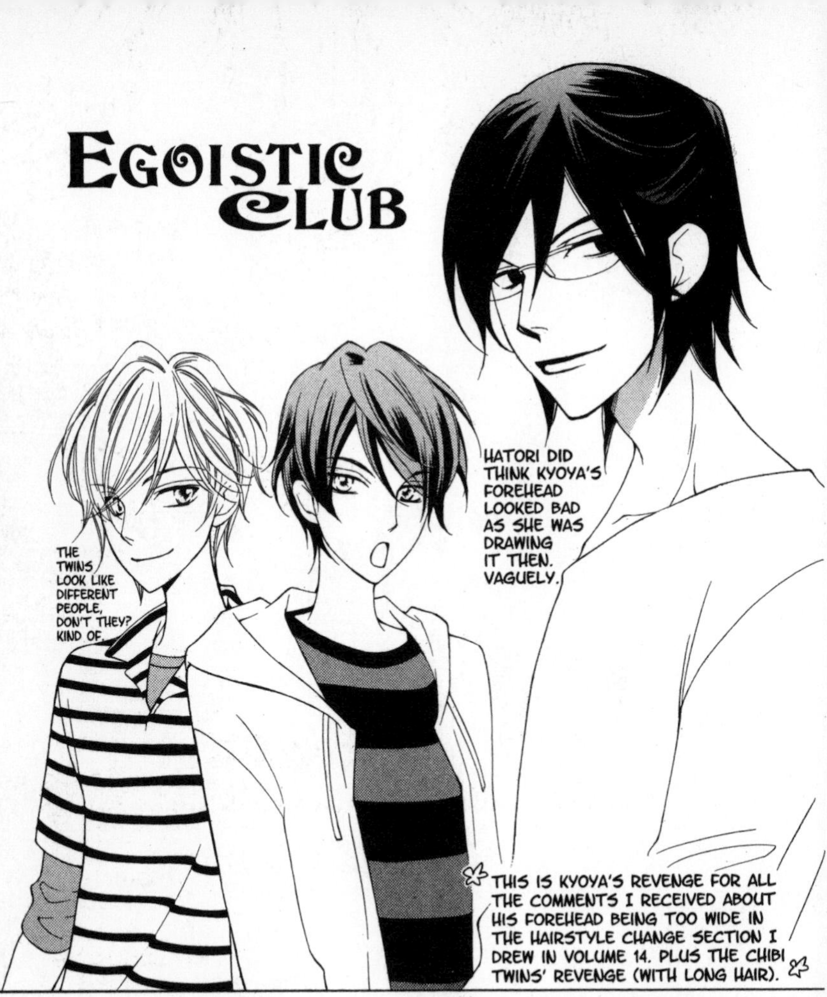
EGOISTIC CLUB
HATORI DID THINK KYOYA'S FOREHEAD LOOKED BAD AS SHE WAS DRAWING IT THEN. VAGUELY.
THE TWINS LOOK LIKE DIFFERENT PEOPLE, DON'T THEY? KIND OF.
THIS IS KYOYA'S REVENGE FOR ALL THE COMMENTS I RECEIVED ABOUT HIS FOREHEAD BEING TOO WIDE IN THE HAIRSTYLE CHANGE SECTION I DREW IN VOLUME 14. PLUS THE CHIBI TWINS' REVENGE (WITH LONG HAIR).

WOW, VOLUME 15--THAT'S INCREDIBLE, HUH? DOUBLE IT AND THAT'S 30... NOT THAT I'M IMPLYING I WANT TO DRAW UP TO THAT MANY VOLUMES. "15"... OH, WHAT DOES IT MATTER?! SORRY!!

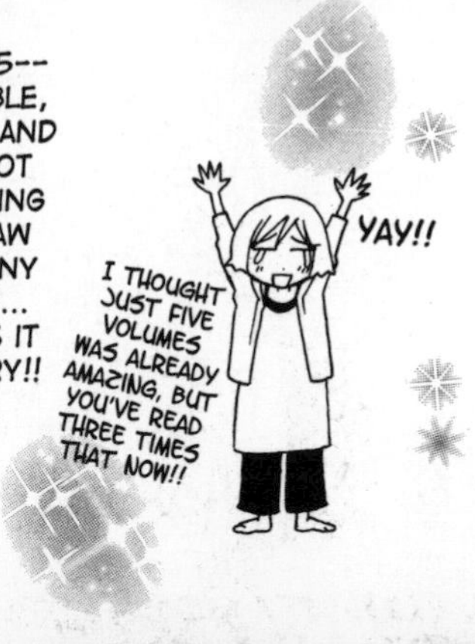
YAY!!
I THOUGHT JUST FIVE VOLUMES WAS ALREADY AMAZING, BUT YOU'VE READ THREE TIMES THAT NOW!!

LADIES AND GENTLEMEN, GOOD WORK READING UP TO THIS POINT!! THANK YOU SO MUCH FOR PERSEVERING THROUGH VOLUME 15!

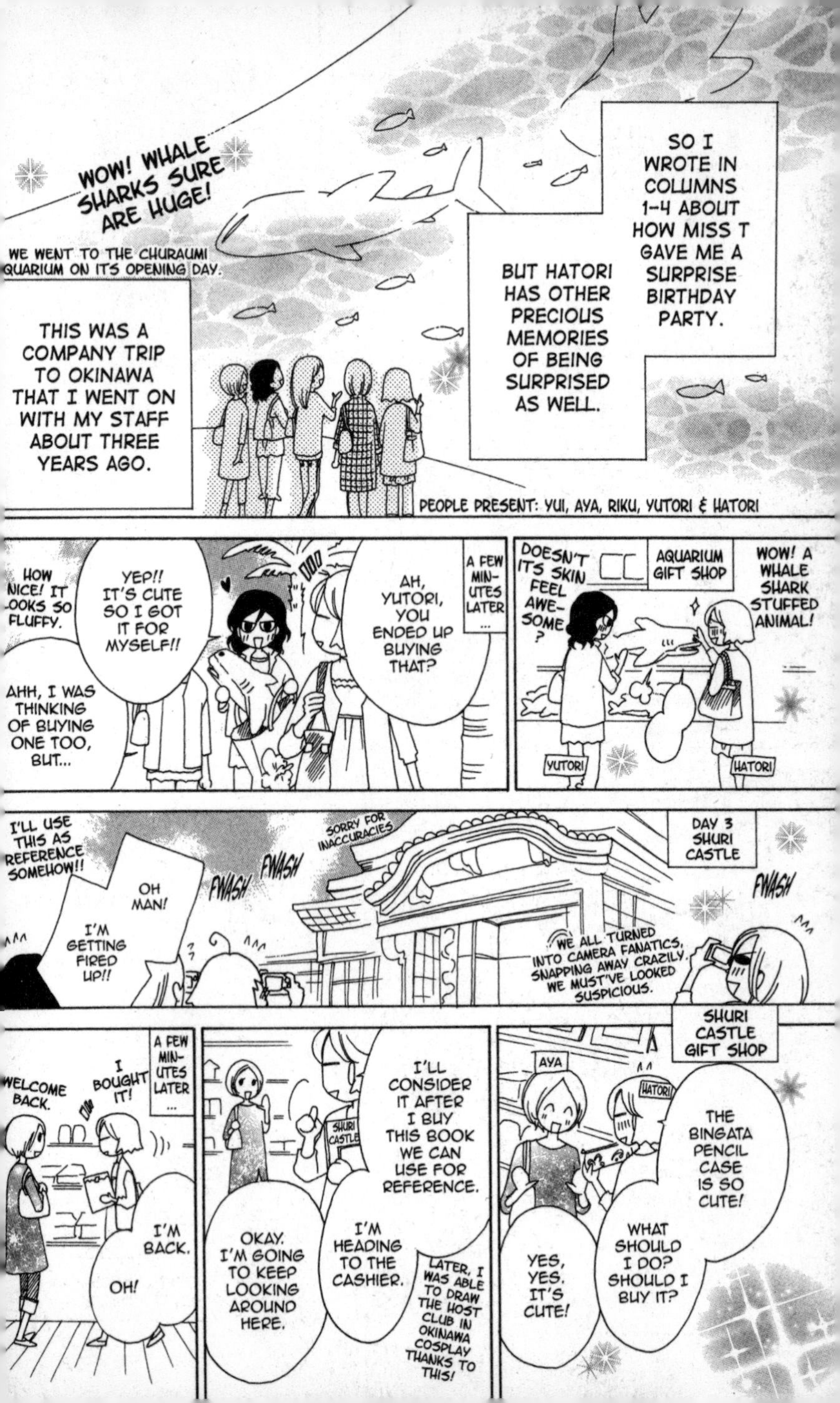

SO I WROTE IN COLUMNS 1-4 ABOUT HOW MISS T GAVE ME A SURPRISE BIRTHDAY PARTY.
BUT HATORI HAS OTHER PRECIOUS MEMORIES OF BEING SURPRISED AS WELL.
WOW! WHALE SHARKS SURE ARE HUGE!
WE WENT TO THE CHURAUMI QUARIUM ON ITS OPENING DAY.
THIS WAS A COMPANY TRIP TO OKINAWA THAT I WENT ON WITH MY STAFF ABOUT THREE YEARS AGO.
PEOPLE PRESENT: YUI, AYA, RIKU, YUTORI & HATORI
AQUARIUM GIFT SHOP
WOW! A WHALE SHARK STUFFED ANIMAL!
DOESN'T ITS SKIN FEEL AWESOME?
HATORI
YUTORI
A FEW MINUTES LATER...
AH, YUTORI, YOU ENDED UP BUYING THAT?
YEP!! IT'S CUTE SO I GOT IT FOR MYSELF!!
HOW NICE! IT LOOKS SO FLUFFY.
AHH, I WAS THINKING OF BUYING ONE TOO, BUT...
DAY 3 SHURI CASTLE
FWASH
WE ALL TURNED INTO CAMERA FANATICS, SNAPPING AWAY CRAZILY. WE MUST'VE LOOKED SUSPICIOUS.
SORRY FOR INACCURACIES
FWASH
FWASH
I'LL USE THIS AS REFERENCE SOMEHOW!!
OH MAN!
I'M GETTING FIRED UP!!
SHURI CASTLE GIFT SHOP
AYA
HATORI
THE BINGATA PENCIL CASE IS SO CUTE!
WHAT SHOULD I DO? SHOULD I BUY IT?
YES, YES. IT'S CUTE!
I'LL CONSIDER IT AFTER I BUY THIS BOOK WE CAN USE FOR REFERENCE.
SHURI CASTLE
I'M HEADING TO THE CASHIER.
OKAY. I'M GOING TO KEEP LOOKING AROUND HERE.
LATER, I WAS ABLE TO DRAW THE HOST CLUB IN OKINAWA COSPLAY THANKS TO THIS!
A FEW MINUTES LATER...
I BOUGHT IT!
WELCOME BACK.
I'M BACK.
OH!

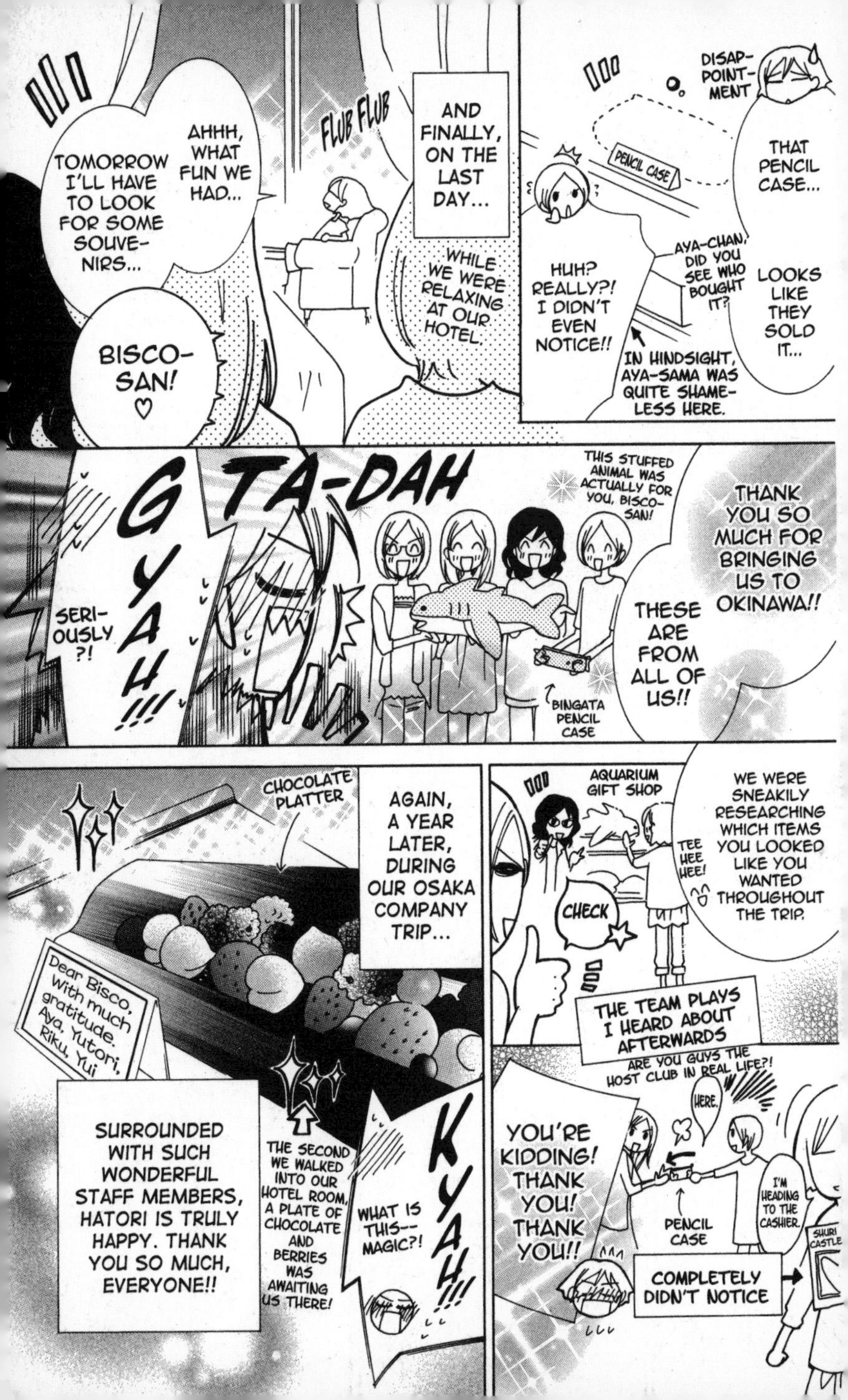
DISAP-POINT-MENT
THAT PENCIL CASE...
LOOKS LIKE THEY SOLD IT...
PENCIL CASE
AYA-CHAN, DID YOU SEE WHO BOUGHT IT?
HUH? REALLY?! I DIDN'T EVEN NOTICE!!
IN HINDSIGHT, AYA-SAMA WAS QUITE SHAME-LESS HERE.
AND FINALLY, ON THE LAST DAY...
WHILE WE WERE RELAXING AT OUR HOTEL,
FLUB FLUB
AHHH, WHAT FUN WE HAD...
TOMORROW I'LL HAVE TO LOOK FOR SOME SOUVE-NIRS...
BISCO-SAN! ♡
THANK YOU SO MUCH FOR BRINGING US TO OKINAWA!!
THESE ARE FROM ALL OF US!!
THIS STUFFED ANIMAL WAS ACTUALLY FOR YOU, BISCO-SAN!
BINGATA PENCIL CASE
TA-DAH
GYAH!!!
SERI-OUSLY?!
WE WERE SNEAKILY RESEARCHING WHICH ITEMS YOU LOOKED LIKE YOU WANTED THROUGHOUT THE TRIP.
TEE HEE HEE!
AQUARIUM GIFT SHOP
CHECK
THE TEAM PLAYS I HEARD ABOUT AFTERWARDS
ARE YOU GUYS THE HOST CLUB IN REAL LIFE?!
I'M HEADING TO THE CASHIER.
SHURI CASTLE
HERE.
YOU'RE KIDDING! THANK YOU! THANK YOU!!
PENCIL CASE
COMPLETELY DIDN'T NOTICE
AGAIN, A YEAR LATER, DURING OUR OSAKA COMPANY TRIP...
CHOCOLATE PLATTER
KYAH!!!
WHAT IS THIS-- MAGIC?!
THE SECOND WE WALKED INTO OUR HOTEL ROOM, A PLATE OF CHOCOLATE AND BERRIES WAS AWAITING US THERE!
Dear Bisco, With much gratitude. Aya, Yutori, Riku, Yui
SURROUNDED WITH SUCH WONDERFUL STAFF MEMBERS, HATORI IS TRULY HAPPY. THANK YOU SO MUCH, EVERYONE!!

AT THE SAME TIME VOLUME 15 IS GOING ON SALE (SEPTEMBER 2009), A FAN BOOK AND THE SECOND HOST CLUB NOVEL ARE BEING RELEASED TOO. PLEASE DO GO CHECK THOSE OUT! ♥♥ PLUS, IN ISSUE 11 OF LALA MAGAZINE (ALSO COMING OUT IN SEPTEMBER), A DRAMA CD WILL BE INCLUDED, SO PLEASE LISTEN TO THAT!!

I KEEP THINKING I OUGHT TO START A BLOG WHERE I CAN MAKE THESE KINDS OF ANNOUNCEMENTS. ❀

FLIRTATIOUS(?) DRAWING

THE HIGHLY REQUESTED CHIBI MORI AND HUNNY PICTURE! (AROUND AGE 10)

EVEN AT THIS AGE HE HAD HIS HAREM OF CUTE, SMALL CREATURES.

THERE'S NO CHARACTER WHO HAS AGED SO LITTLE FROM HIS YOUNGER DAYS AS HUNNY... HE'S TOO UNCHANGED.

Special Thanks!!

2009. Sep.
Bisco HT

❀ MISS T-SAMA AND EVERYONE AT THE COMPILATION OFFICE
❀ EVERYONE INVOLVED IN THE PRODUCTION OF THIS BOOK
❀ ALL OF MY STAFF: YUI NATSUKI, RIKU, AYA AOMURA, YUTORI HIZAKURA, SHIZURU ONDA, UMEKO, AND HATORI'S MOM
❀ ALL MY EXTRA HELPERS: NATSUMI SATOU-SAMA, YOUKO SANO-SAMA, AND SHIGEYOSHI KOUKI-SAMA

AND THANKS TO ALL OF YOU WHO READ THIS BOOK! THANK YOU SO VERY MUCH! ♥♥

EGOISTIC CLUB/THE END

EDITOR'S NOTES

EPISODE 67
Page 6: For more about the "Uki Memo," check out volume 1, episode 3.

Page 16: *Umeboshi* is a pickled plum.

EPISODE 68
Page 57: *Glass Mask* is a long-running shojo manga by Suzue Miuchi that was adapted into a play. The people at dinner are talking about characters from the manga.

Page 63: The Kansai region (where Kobe is located) is famous for its comedians.

EPISODE 71
Page 153: Masami Tsuda is the mangaka of *His and Her Circumstances*, and Tomio Umezawa is a famous Japanese actor and singer.

Author Bio

Bisco Hatori made her manga debut with *Isshun kan no Romance* (A Moment of Romance) in *LaLa DX* magazine. The comedy *Ouran High School Host Club* is her breakout hit. When she's stuck thinking up characters' names, she gets inspired by loud, upbeat music (her radio is set to NACK5 FM). She enjoys reading all kinds of manga, but she's especially fond of the sci-fi drama *Please Save My Earth* and *Slam Dunk*, a basketball classic.

OURAN HIGH SCHOOL HOST CLUB
Vol. 15
Shojo Beat Edition

STORY AND ART BY BISCO HATORI

Translation/Su Mon Han
Touch-up Art & Lettering/Gia Cam Luc
Graphic Design/Amy Martin
Editor/Nancy Thistlethwaite

Published by VIZ Media, LLC
P.O. Box 77010
San Francisco, CA 94107

10 9 8 7 6 5 4 3 2 1
First printing, December 2010

www.viz.com   www.shojobeat.com

Don't Hide What's *Inside*

OTOMEN
by AYA KANNO

Despite his tough jock exterior, Asuka Masamune harbors a secret love for sewing, shojo manga, and all things girly. But when he finds himself drawn to his domestically inept classmate Ryo, his carefully crafted persona is put to the test. Can Asuka ever show his true self to anyone, much less to the girl he's falling for?

Find out in the *Otomen* manga—buy yours today!

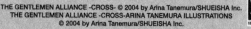

WELCOME to Imperial Academy: a private school where trying to become SUPERIOR can make you feel INFERIOR!

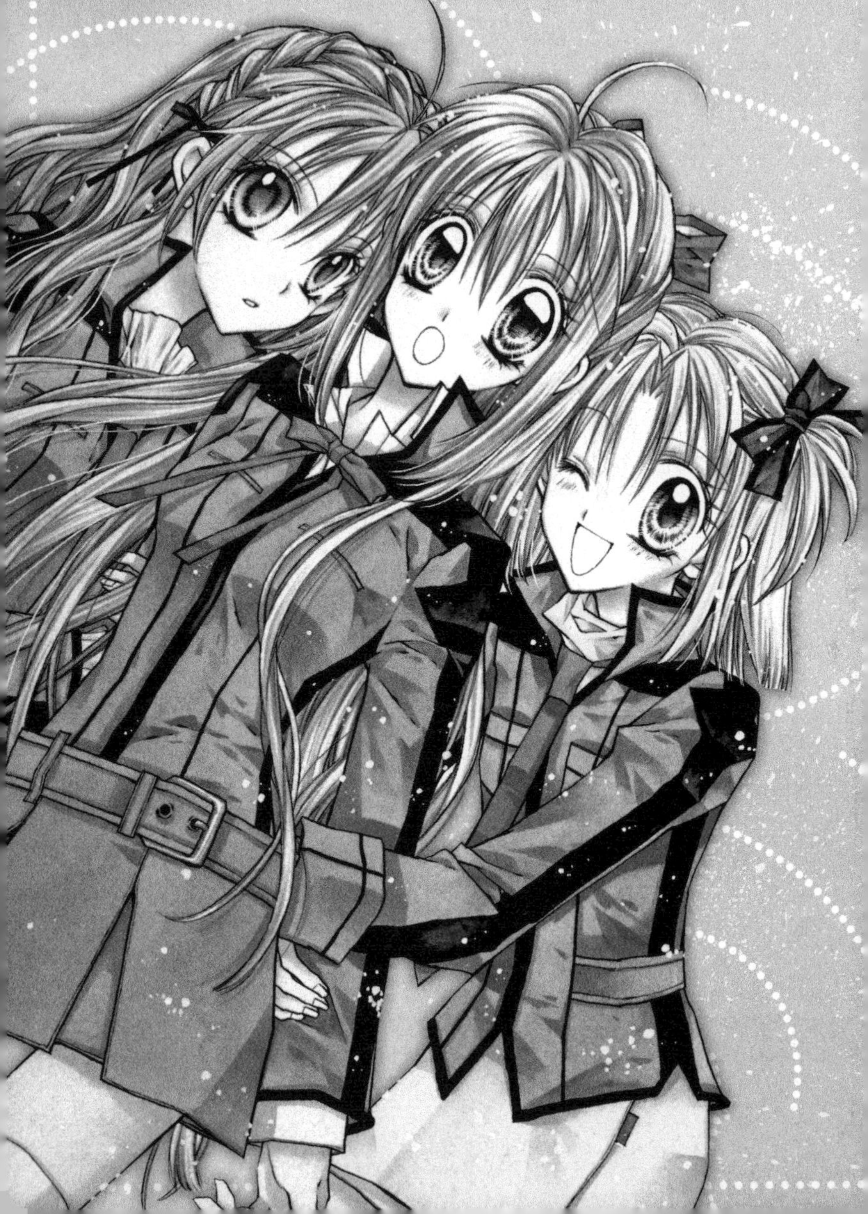